A Cultural History of Dress and Fashion
General Editor: Susan Vincent

Volume 1
A Cultural History of Dress and Fashion in Antiquity
Edited by Mary Harlow

Volume 2
A Cultural History of Dress and Fashion in the Medieval Age
Edited by Sarah-Grace Heller

Volume 3
A Cultural History of Dress and Fashion in the Renaissance
Edited by Elizabeth Currie

Volume 4
A Cultural History of Dress and Fashion in the Age of Enlightenment
Edited by Peter McNeil

Volume 5
A Cultural History of Dress and Fashion in the Age of Empire
Edited by Denise Amy Baxter

Volume 6
A Cultural History of Dress and Fashion in the Modern Age
Edited by Alexandra Palmer

A CULTURAL HISTORY OF DRESS AND FASHION

VOLUME 4

A CULTURAL HISTORY OF DRESS AND FASHION

IN THE AGE OF ENLIGHTENMENT

Edited by Peter McNeil

Bloomsbury Academic
An imprint of Bloomsbury Publishing Plc

B L O O M S B U R Y

LONDON · OXFORD · NEW YORK · NEW DELHI · SYDNEY

Bloomsbury Academic

An imprint of Bloomsbury Publishing Plc

50 Bedford Square   1385 Broadway
London   New York
WC1B 3DP   NY 10018
UK   USA

www.bloomsbury.com

BLOOMSBURY and the Diana logo are trademarks of Bloomsbury Publishing Plc

First published 2017

British Library Cataloguing-in-Publication Data
A catalogue record for this book is available from the British Library.

ISBN: HB: 978-0-8578-5761-3
        HB set: 978-1-4725-5749-0

Library of Congress Cataloging-in-Publication Data
A catalog record for this book is available from the Library of Congress.

Cover design: Sharon Mah
Cover image by Frances Alleyne. Courtesy of Richard Green Gallery, London.

Typeset by RefineCatch Limited, Bungay, Suffolk
Printed and bound in Great Britain

CONTENTS

LIST OF ILLUSTRATIONS

INTRODUCTION

CHAPTER 1

CHAPTER 4

CHAPTER 7

CHAPTER 8

CHAPTER 9

Introduction

PETER McNEIL

Fashion: custom, usage, manner of dressing, of adjusting oneself, in a word, everything that serves the "parure" and of luxury; therefore fashion can be considered politically and philosophically.

—D. de Jaucourt, *Encyclopédie*, 1765.

Fashion may be considered in general as the custom of the great.
It is the dress, the furniture, the language, the manners of the great world.
Which constitute what is called the Fashion in each of these articles,
And which the rest of mankind are in such haste to adopt,
After their example.

—A. Alison, *Of the Nature of the Emotions of Sublimity and Beauty*, 1790.

Aileen Ribeiro, in her magisterial publication *The Art of Dress*, cited two authors, one eighteenth-century French and one British, to demonstrate that considering fashion and dress to be a part of cultural, philosophical or even scientific change was considered plausible at the very time the fashions were made and consumed.[1] Contained in these short quotations are many of the ideas that would color future theoretical speculation by the likes of late nineteenth- and twentieth-century writers such as Thorstein Veblen and even Pierre Bourdieu: that fashion is something that stretches to encompass much more than sartorial fashions, that fashion is hastily copied, and that it also serves to identify and situate individuals and societies. In the expression "adjusting oneself" there is even contained the suggestion of the embodiment which has come to provide new impetus in writing about fashion in recent years. I will take these three themes to structure my overview of dress during the Enlightenment: the fairly elastic definition of "fashion" that pertained during the long eighteenth century, the uptake, diffusion or indeed, rejection, of fashions by individuals and groups, including rural élites, and the relationship of dress and the body to Richard Sennett's famous formulation of interlinked "flesh and stone," that is, the linking of dress, body and the built environment in the rapidly transforming towns and cities of eighteenth-century West Europe.

LOOKING AT FASHION: PRIORITIZING THE EIGHTEENTH CENTURY

The relatively large survival rates of the dress of the élites compared with that of demotic dress creates various distortions in studying the field of fashion history.[2] Indeed, the majority of images to be found in this volume represent well-to-do people. There were various ways in which the collection and study of dress proceeded in the past, influenced by personal tastes and preferences, ranging from the views of the aesthete collector, to the archeologist or ethnologist, the antiquarian, the stylist (photographer Cecil Beaton, for example, in the 1970s), or the connoisseur (Diana Vreeland).

Nineteenth-century essayists thought fashion to be central to *zeitgeist*. Charles Baudelaire's mid-nineteenth-century opinion regarding the significance of fashion as extracting an essential "jus" concerning past and present is well known. Hippolyte Taine used a similar approach in arguing why fashion mattered: "I go up to Estampes [the print collection of the Bibliothèque National] and I looked at the sixteenth century masters . . . A fold of clothing is a trace of passion like an epithet. I endeavoured to rediscover and to experience those of the sixteenth century."[3] Taine, visiting the famous connoisseurs of firstly the French rococo and later Chinese art, the Goncourts brothers, in 1863, examined their eighteenth-century engravings:

> Nothing teaches history better. It seems that one comes straight from living in the century. The fineness, the gaiety, the taste of pleasure, these three gifts beget the rest. Nothing as delicious as these toilettes, these "levers" [risings in the morning] of pretty naked women with the large embroidered curtained beds. These pretty gilded and turned furnishings . . . It's the cuisine of pleasure. It's the genuine France.[4]

This delicious and erotic aspect of eighteenth-century costume, as well as its temporal distance from the late nineteenth century [it was then barely "antique" or one hundred years old], made it popular when it began to be collected. The late nineteenth century witnessed a veritable explosion of interest in the "eighteenth-century woman."[5] In 1877, the Museum of Fine Arts, Boston, was given its first costume for the collection, an eighteenth-century dress, cataloged under the technical textile categories of "brocade, weaving, embroidery, etc," which was the case with many of the other burgeoning public collections of the time, established among other things to create encyclopedic and educational holdings of world cultures, improve taste, and provide models for better manufactures. Examples include the Victoria and Albert Museum, London (established 1852), the Museum of Applied Arts and Sciences, Sydney (established 1879, where the director, a botanist, selected antique laces from a London dealer that referred mainly to botanical specimens that interested him)[6], the National Gallery of Victoria, Melbourne (the first textiles collected in 1895 were Indian block prints; fashion arrived around 1948)[7], and the Royal Ontario Museum, Canada (established 1912, where the founding archeologist director, Charles T. Currelly, collected broadly within categories such as "Islamic art," which included textile culture). The majority of the garments collected at such institutions, with the exception of non-Western dress, were the clothes of the upper classes or élites, in part because they were made of splendid or intricate materials that delighted and challenged viewers and makers to emulate their aesthetics and skills. Many more women's than men's clothes were collected, although eighteenth-century men's silk suits and embroidered waistcoats were numerous in museum collections, probably because they looked so very different from the dark nineteenth-century suit. Others had personal connotations, with many old labels (some apocryphal) claiming that they were wedding suits. Suits for presentation at court also rank as high purported survivals.

In 1963, the Museum of Fine Arts, Boston, exhibited an overview of its dress collections; it had established its costume department after the Second World War. Significantly, the show was all about women, rather than men. Entitled "She Walks in Splendour: Great Costumes 1550–1950. An Exhibition of Costumes, Costume Accessories and Illustration from the Museum's Permanent Collection" (October 3–December 1,

1963), formal concerns rather than social ones were used to justify the collecting practice in a slightly apologetic preface by Perry Townshend Rathbone: "There is some constant quality, some inherent merit in the designer's handling of line, shape and color that transcends superficial considerations of fashion and lends the favored raiment the esthetic validity of a good painting or sculpture."[8] The *Introduction* by Adolph S. Cavallo, Curator of Textiles, discussed the suspicions with which "costume" was viewed by the Art History of his day. Although a great deal has changed since the 1960s, as late as 1984, Philippe de Montebello, Director of the Metropolitan Museum of Art, posed the claim that a dress could not possibly be as significant as a good piece of Sèvres: "Costume belongs among the applied arts . . . and even then it doesn't rank as high as porcelain—and it's certainly not so important as textiles . . . If anyone claims that costume is anything more than a minor applied art, I should have some serious doubts about his broader intellectual framework."[9]

The focus on the splendidly colored clothing of women and men that survives in many collections and looks down on us in beautiful portraits is also a little misleading. Our imagination about the past is very much colored by what we can "see." Sometimes the facts, compiled by hard working historians, particularly in France but also in Germany, Sweden, and Denmark, yield surprising results, and this enterprise of interlinked historical, art historical, political, and economic research is creating much new knowledge and information regarding the transmission of fashion and regional specificity within eighteenth-century dress.[10]

Not all eighteenth-century dress was as extravagant and beautiful as costume dramas and the highlights of museum collections might suggest. The great historian of everyday French life, Daniel Roche, argues that "the excessive expenditure of the intimate court circle has been exaggerated by moralists and preachers," and that one quarter of the nobles spent little more on their clothes than a prosperous shopkeeper or merchant.[11] In terms of colors, the wardrobes of eighteenth-century female nobility were brighter than those of men, even though others such as the historian François Boucher argued that the splendor of men exceeded that of women at that time.[12] Roche's research into French noble inventories reveals that dark colors made up more than one third of the wardrobe of men; fewer such clothes survive in collections today. In 1789, 42 percent of colors in the (mainly) Paris inventories of men were somber and low key, of these 25 percent were black.[13] Wearing bright shades would have been an expensive but also impractical consideration for many men. It puts the efforts of a figure such as the English macaroni into a different relief. Dark colors were a part of fashionable dress in Paris, too, by the last third of the eighteenth century. A penniless Mozart wrote to his father, "you can go anywhere in black dress" because "it is country dress and full-dress at the same time."[14] In England, more somber tones were worn as early as the 1730s. This reflected both the ascendancy of a puritan middle class that valued sobriety and thrift, but liked lots of material culture such as linen and bed sheets, as well as the attachment of the aristocracy to their landed estates where plain broadcloth was more suitable for outdoors than useless patterned silk. Yet dark colored or black suits surviving in museum collections are quite rare. It has been argued that they were worn until they wore out, or passed on to the servants, but it may well be that they were simply considered too uninteresting to save by the nineteenth-century mindset. High fashions were popular as a part of actors' wardrobes and fancy dress boxes, and hence many are in poor or altered condition, and rarely shown in museum collections due to their damaged states. Nobody really knows with regard to a very wide pattern as to why clothes from the past have survived, unless they are royal survivals, or relics, or a part of an indexing system such as the samples kept at the Foundling Hospital to identify children, or trade samples.[15] However, the authors assembled here demonstrate that an array of social, cultural, political, economic, technical, and biographical data can be arrayed to create a mosaic view of the dress fashions and clothing worn by the people of western Europe in the long eighteenth century.

BOOK OF MATERIALS

Although there is a vigorous debate regarding the date of commencement of fashion studies, amateur attempts at systematically recording the appearance and motives of the dress of the past were certainly pursued as early as the eighteenth century. It was in this century that amateur historians and dilettantes of many persuasions began to prepare and compile their thoughts on the history of "costume," as it was then called. That famous English wit, diarist, and antiquarian, Horace Walpole, imagined he might write such a project. Walpole's extensive and well-documented library contained works such as Jean Baptiste Thiers' study of wigging, *Histoire des Perruques* (Paris 1690).[16] Walpole's "Book of Materials," unpublished, now protected in the delightful surroundings of the Lewis Walpole Library (Farmington, Connecticut), as well as providing many details about country house visiting, also contained his notes for a vast uncompleted work on English customs and costume.[17] Walpole also contemplated writing an account of the streets of London based on Germain-François Poullain de Saint-Foix's similar book for Paris, *Essais historiques sur Paris* (1776). Horace Walpole was fascinated by the inter-linked relationship of fashion, customs (often used as a synonym for "costume"), the personalities, members of the nobility and peerage, and eccentrics of his day. For example, he wrote a parody of the first three *Letters of Lord Chesterfield to his son*, which concerned the ways in which a young man should prepare for the *mondaine* society of Paris on the Grand Tour.[18] Walpole's trenchant wit had much to say regarding Chesterfield's views of manners, urbanity, and his son. In his own copy, he made 300 marginal notations. When Chesterfield writes in Letter LXXI (October 9, 1746):

> Dress is of the same nature; you must dress: therefore attend to it; not in order to rival or to excel a fop in it, but in order to avoid singularity, and consequently ridicule. Take great care always to be dressed like the reasonable people of your own age, in the place where you are; whose dress is never spoken of one way or another, as either too negligent if too much studied.

Walpole notes at this point: "Ch. [Charles] Knew that his son was ill bred & rough and so, in spite of all his father's pains, he remained."[19] When the father notes of his son, "Your figure is a good one," Walpole replies, "short and clumsy."[20]

Walpole's interest in fashionable clothes was not simply a matter of antiquarian tastes or a fascination with high society assemblies and masquerades. His outlook was akin to that of an aesthete observer of the following century. Walpole would also have been very aware of the long held classical precepts regarding dress: "You, then, must respect your clothes," had written Alberti during the Renaissance. "Color makes it possible to attract people's attention just as a magnet attracts iron filings," said Arisoto.[21] Clothes had to be appropriate within this formula, but not necessarily beautiful: Giovanni Della Casa's *Galateo: The Rules of Polite Behaviour* (Venice, 1558, much reprinted) and the Humanist Baldesare di Castiglione's *The Courtier* (1528) demanded "clean well cut and appropriate" dress.[22] Young men could be "vivacious and elegant" but gaudy clothes were the province of "mercenaries, itinerant musicians and homosexuals."[23] Walpole was also very concerned with rank and alert to those who aped or followed fashions. This was a typical eighteenth century concern: Adam Smith's *Theory of Moral Sentiments* (1759) said of fashion and people of high rank: "as soon as they drop it, it loses all of the grace which it had appeared to possess before."[24]

Clothing is always bound up with the household, moral and political economy. It is also bound up with our psyche, however we define that, and our sense of aesthetics. Walpole had a keen sense of beauty and the everyday, as well as the wonders of the applied arts and painting. Clothing did not spring from the same source as the high arts of painting and sculpture, but in the past many artisans with access to artistic models and precepts were involved in its making. The historian Johan Huizinga, in his famous work *The Autumn of the Middle Ages* (1921), after discussing "the art of weaving," that is tapestries, has this to say of clothing: "Clothing, too, belongs undeniably to art, but it is part of its very purpose that allure and ostentation predominate over beauty itself. Moreover, personal vanity pulls the art of clothing into the sphere of passion and sensuousness where the qualities that comprise the essence of high art, balance and harmony, come second."[25] Ann Hollander, the late twentieth-century literary, dress, and art historian, had this to say on the matter in 1971: "The Human figure is the only element in the whole range of artistic subject matter which may, and indeed must, be taken personally . . . the clothed figure commands the same immediacy in all its variations upon the dialectic of drapery and anatomy [as the nude]."[26]

PINNING UP

One of the most important developments in the transmission of fashion in the eighteenth century was the rise of print culture and reading publics. Drawings were transformed into the medium of print, and print then had further potential for innumerable transformations. The street-selling of prints was a significant part of urban life. They were sometimes strung from twine by "pinners up," on walls and railings, with an admixture of ballads, broadsheets, almanacs, chapbooks, and satirical prints. There are images of this system being used in France, Germany, and Italy. Sometimes old type was used, battered and a century out of date.[27] At the time of the Revolution the visitor to London, D'Archenholz, noted:

> I beg leave to mention the BALLADS [sic], among the singularities to be met with in this nation. These, it is true, are also common in France, but not sold publicly as in London. It is usually females who are employed in this avocation. They wander about the most populous streets of the capital, stop now and then and draw a crowd around them, to whom they sing their songs, which they sometimes accompany with music. In these, witty expressions and humorous sallies are often contained; and one is sometimes sorry to see such talents as the writers must undoubtedly possess, employed in celebrating the trifling occurences of the days. . . These ballads, being printed on coarse paper, are sometimes sold for a farthing, and sometimes for halfpenny a piece. The populace purchase them with the utmost eagerness and consider them to be as so any delicious morsel.[28]

The fine genre or "fancy" painting now in the Tate Gallery by Henry Walton, *A Girl Buying a Ballad* (exhibited 1778), is a study in contrast between a finely-dressed young female urbanite and a sad, old man holding his hat up in the attitude of a beggar (Figure 0.1).

FIGURE 0.1: *A Girl Buying a Ballad*, Henry Walton (1746–1813), exhibited 1778, oil on canvas. Tate Gallery.

That he is a man, and not a woman, selling prints in the street underscores his degradation. The contrast with the printed scenes of finely-dressed soldiers above him would suggest that a point is being made about the injustice of men who return from service, as well as the depressing views held at the time about the progress of the Revolutionary War with America (from 1775). He might also be a reference to the blinded general Belisarius. Walton had studied under the painter Johan Zoffany, an elegant craftsman in paint who was in fact "macaroni" (ultra fashionable) in his youth when he arrived in London from Switzerland.[29] Carington Bowles reissued the painting as a print entitled *The Pretty Maid Buying a Love Song*, which as has been noted, "emphasises the potential eroticism of the exchange of glances between the ballad seller and the young woman."[30] In the print, the eyes of the ballad seller are upcast, not downcast, and such an erotic exchange is not present in the painting; rather the latter seems to concern privilege and gender, as well as contemporary affairs and a rather melancholy view of the urban street. The young girl's clean, striped cotton or silk dress, access to money through the slit in her skirt where her pocket is located, clean apron, and beribboned summer hat, are all characteristics in strong contrast to the shabby brown suit of the seller and his lack of material possessions. His waistcoat buttons are missing and this garment is held together with tapes, an attempt at dignity, neat and clean. This also becomes, in Roche's terms, a feminizing act, as the "button is a mark of masculine power, for women and children fasten their garments with pins and laces" in this period.[31] The shoes of the old man are scuffed and dirty and most significantly, he wears trousers rather than knee breeches. He seems to wear a wig that has not been dressed but is in disarray. The handkerchief around his neck, possibly Indian, might be an indication that he is a former sailor: Beverly Lemire has argued that "these accessories were a ubiquitous part of plebian dress" and much traded among eighteenth-century seamen, and his buckled shoes are also characteristic of sailors, as well as his round hat.[32] The broom next to him suggests he can also act as a street sweeper for a passing clientele, a debased occupation that was often associated with child labor. The young woman exhibits a type of freshness that Matthew Craske notes became a trait of English taste: during the eighteenth century the "English became associated with a stylish naturalness in demeanour, dress and landscape."[33] The work also exhibits the qualities of a new form of art "created for new publics vis-à-vis invention of new forms which appealed to passions, feeling, sympathy or sentiment," that removed the requirement for élite learning for viewers.[34]

A new category of periodical that appeared regularly and addressed both women and men appeared in France in the mid-1760s and later became known as the "fashion magazine." Such publications were not the type of thing likely to be strung up by a ballad seller in the street, but were often subscribed to by well-to-do cosmopolitans such as the Banks household in London. In the 1780s, either Sophia or Joseph Banks, but probably Sophia, took the new French fashion periodicals *Cabinet des Modes*, *Journal de la Mode*, *Costumes Parisiens à Paris*, and *Gallery of Fashion*.[35]

Such publications sometimes included information with names and addresses of the suppliers, from milliners to *marchandes de modes*, or even the new fashion identities of the day, such as Monsieur Léonard, hairdresser to Marie-Antoinette, Queen of France (Figure 0.2). They illustrated the new "happy families" as Carol Duncan has put it, and images of motherhood and new garments for children that developed in tandem with new theories of childhood development and education (Figure 0.3).[36] The carefully rendered images illustrated the revolutionary new "small clothes" or nether garments for well-to-do little boys, such as the trousers and sailor suit that appears on the cover of this very volume within the Fector family. Such juvenile garments as the "matelot simple et les manches retroussés" also illustrated here (Figure 0.4) derive from the clothes of working men and sailors: as John Greene and Elizabeth McCrum have argued in their research on Irish "small clothes," the "converging development of the dress . . . of the poor, military

o o   222.

Le Clerc del.   *Dupin Sculp.*

Coëffure d'une Dame de qualité coëffée par M Leonard Coëffeur de la Reine

A Paris chez Esnauts et Rapilly, rue St Jacques a la ville de Coutances . A . P . D . R .

FIGURE 0.2: Pierre-Thomas LeClerc; engraved by Nicolas Dupin. *Gallerie des Modes et Costumes Français,* published by Esnauts et Rapilly. *38e Cahier des Costumes Français, 9e Suite des Coieffures à la mode en 1781.* oo.222 "Coiffure d'une dame de qualité coëffee par M. Leonard Coëffeur de le Reine," 1781. Photo: © 2017. Museum of Fine Arts, Boston.

Les Enfans de Mgr. Le Comté d'Artois sçavoir Monseigneur le Duc d'Angoulême Fils ainé Monseigneur le Duc de Berri et Mademoiselle accompagnés des Gouvernantes dont une tient dans ses bras le Duc de Berri le plus jeune des trois.

FIGURE 0.3: Pierre-Thomas LeClerc; engraved by Nicolas Dupin. *Gallerie des Modes et Costumes Français*, published by Esnauts et Rapilly. *36e Cahier des Costumes Français, 28e Suite d'Habillemens à la mode en 1781.* 1er Cahier pour le 3e Volume "Les Enfans de Mgr. Le Comte d'Artois . . .," 1781. Photo: © 2017. Museum of Fine Arts, Boston.

FIGURE 0.4: Pierre-Thomas LeClerc; engraved by Nicolas Dupin. *Gallerie des Modes et Costumes Français*, published by Esnauts et Rapilly. *32e. Cahier de Costumes Français, 25e Suite d'Habillemens à la mode en 1780.* hh.190 "La petit Fille vue de face est vétue d'un foureau de tafetas garni de gaze . . .," 1780. Photo: © 2017. Museum of Fine Arts, Boston.

and naval personnel and of children with the fashionable was revolutionary, literally so in France."[37]

Perhaps the most elegant late-eighteenth-century journals for the quality of its drawing, scale, balance, and coloring of its illustrations is the periodical *Gallerie des Modes*, whose correct title is *Gallerie des Modes et Costumes français dessinés d'après nature, gravés par les plus celebres artistes en ce genre, et colorés avec le plus grand soin par Madame Le Beau*. The magazine was published in Paris by "les Srs Esnauts et Rapilly," in the "rue St Jacques, à la ville de Coutances, avec privilege du roi" from 1778 to 1787. It is unusual to name the colorist-director for a publication of this date, and this might explain the great care taken with different impressions of this publication. As color is central to fashion knowledge, this is not surprising.

Plate (*planche*) no. 161 in the twenty-seventh series (*cahier*) "*de costumes français— 21e suite d'habillemens [sic] à la mode en 1779*" is the engraving "*Vêtement dit à la créole*" ("clothing said to be in the Creole manner"; Figure 0.5). The draughtsman (*dessinateur*) was Sebastien Le Clerc and the Engraver (*graveur*) was Patas. The plate was listed in Colas' comprehensive *Bibliographie Générale du Costume et de la Mode* of 1933, an essential tool for the fashion historian, as the changing nature, designers and publishers of the eighteenth-century magazines can be scanned in an instant.[38]

The fashionable—a woman of early-middle age—holding her very long cane and fan is beautifully balanced across the blank field of the page, her feet on a little island of grass and country earth. The convention of situating a fashionable woman or man on the suggestion of ground, street or floor, without disruptive background detail, both reinforces the point of the print—fashion information—and also creates an "otherworldly" or rather theatrical space for the consumption of such fashion images.[39]

The plate is an indication of the cosmopolitanism of eighteenth-century fashion, weaving the French-American and also possibly the South American colonies into a European fashion narrative. We are informed by the copywriter that this is the type of dress worn by French women in America, a muslin gown with a belt and ribbon in the manner of a *robe à la Lévite*, a dress that featured a loosely tied sash (Figure 0.6).

The woman dressed "*à la créole*" wears a *caraco*, a short jacket with, in this case, short sleeves. Her enormous trimmed hat is styled "*à la Grenade*" and features flowers, feathers, ribbons, and a flag. Although many viewers today claim that such garments might be preposterous, or invention, the research of Johannes Pietsch proves that dresses of the types seen and named in such fashion magazines survive in museum and private collections, and that they are not fanciful.[40] Hats are much more rare survivals and the evidence for their accuracy would require an assessment of inventory and other sources, which tend to be generalized and not sufficiently precise for people of the middling sort.

The original rendering of "Vêtement dit à la creole" (Swiss private collection) includes a lightly striped white dress and a caraco in a shade of orange. When the prints were subsequently colored, a variety of transformations occurred; versions of the prints differ widely in terms of detail and effect. The example in the Swiss collection has strong contrasting colors and deploys a shade of rose pink as the contrast to white and blue striped muslin. The Museum of Fine Arts, Boston, example has blue stripes that are much paler, the ribbons in the hat are pale blue rather than rose, ostrich feathers are yellow not green, the flowers are more exuberant, and a flag with a red cross is inserted in the hat. The latter underscores the topical reference to the Battle of Grenada (July 6, 1779) in which the French won a victory over the British in the West Indies.[41] The sash is also blue rather than rose in the MFA version. The Boston example adds a rose petticoat and

FIGURE 0.5: Pierre-Thomas LeClerc; engraved by Nicolas Dupin. *Gallerie des Modes et Costumes Français*, published by Esnauts et Rapilly. *27e Cahier de Costumes Français, 21e Suite d'Habillemens à la mode en 1779.* cc.161 "Vêtement dit à la Créole . . .," 1779. Photo: © 2017. Museum of Fine Arts, Boston.

Robe à la Lévite, a deux plis par derriere, toute droite, arrêtée à la taille avec une écharpe dont les bouts se terminent par des glands. Coëffure; un chapeau de paille garni de gaze en pouf et orné de fleurs.

A Paris chez Esnauts et Rapilly, rue S.t Jacques, à la Ville de Coutances. A.P.D.R.

FIGURE 0.6: Pierre-Thomas LeClerc; engraved by Nicolas Dupin. *Gallerie des Modes et Costumes Français,* published by Esnauts et Rapilly. *21e Cahier des Costumes Français, 15e Suite d'Habillemens à la mode en 1779.* V.124 "Robe à la Lévite, a deux plis par derriere . . .," 1779. Photo: © 2017. Museum of Fine Arts, Boston.

different colored lower trimmings. LeClerc provided much more detailed botanical information of the flowers that garnish the woman's hat. They resemble the fuschia, a hanging plant very popular by Victorian times, introduced from San Domingo (modern day Haiti) in the late seventeenth century by Frenchman Charles Plumier (who named them after the German botanist Leonhart Fuchs). For some reason, the colorists simplified the flowers; perhaps they had not seen one, as they are difficult to grow. The flower reinforces the connection to foreign climes and new fashions; as Kimberly Chrisman-Campbell notes, there was a fashion for linen to be bleached in San Domingo and the chemise à la reine is possibly influenced from clothing worn there.[42] There is of course a debate about exactly when prints are colored and they can be "touched up" later, but these colorings appear to be of the date. It is significant that as no color apart from muslin (assumed to be white) is specified in the text, the colorists have used artistic licence. It is possible that variations were welcomed at the coloring workshop as an exercise of taste. They are certainly very common in surviving prints of this type.

Such detail is not a matter of being pedantic; fashion was transformed in the eighteenth century through the exercise of "taste" and individual discrimination. As Matthew Craske notes in his excellent survey of art in eighteenth-century Europe, "it was no accident that the cultural preoccupation with taste emerged in tandem with that for clothing and manners . . . [a] cultural fascination with sartorial display and the moral connotations of clothing which grew as fashionable garments became available to a broader spectrum of society and ceased to be reliable signs of social distinction."[43] All manner of choices and judgments were made about clothing and for the first time, details were often provided in fashion plates as to who retailed the items depicted in the images. A place was found for the new woman reader who was often addressed by and through the concept of fashion. Prints such as this might have been consumed individually or in imaginative groupings about which much more is yet to be uncovered.

Such prints also had afterlives in the nineteenth and also the twentieth centuries as playful *collages* and within extra-illustrated books and later "scrapbooks." To modernist artists of the first half of the twentieth century, the strange effects of decontextualized and old-fashioned imagery was a spur to creative re-combinations. In the 1930s, British *Vogue* advocated that its readers visit London book and print shops and cut up eighteenth-century prints, journals, and books to pursue the "fashionable" revival of scrap-books promoted by the likes of photographer and stylist Cecil Beaton. A great many prints and fashion information must have gone by the "way side" as a result of this practice; such materials were not considered rare or precious at that date. Eighteenth-century material culture was often little respected. A major Thomas Patch painted caricature was found turned into a folding screen and for sale in the window of a London antiques shop in the post-war period.[44] In the work of Beaton we see a type of interwar cannibalisation of fashion: a "fashionista" consumes fashion itself in order to generate the new. This was the female intelligence of the eighteenth century now transmitted in truncated form by the new male stylists and ensembliers of the twentieth century.

DRESSING THE PART

Dress of the past was always multifarious and complex in ways that illustrated histories of styles sometimes obscure, as they must always present a picture of the general taste of the day. People in the past did not always wear what we thought they should be wearing. Men wore backless shoes, like slippers, for their private retreats. They clearly did not always go about in their high-heeled buckled shoes or riding boots. Thomas Jefferson wrote to London for a pair of leather slippers for walking in his garden.⁴⁵ He must have wished to be comfortable and also close to nature. Although few men wore all-cotton clothing in eighteenth-century Europe (their shirts were nearly always linen and it was mainly their banyans or informal wrappers that were of printed cotton), there were exceptions. In southern France, the famous manufacturer Wetter was depicted in a wall-mural by Joseph Gabriel Rossetti entitled *The studio of the brush-painter women (pinceauteuses) in the factory of the Wetter Brothers of Orange* (1764) pointedly wearing his own printed cotton creation in the place of what would normally be a silk-brocaded three-piece suit.

Improvization with clothing was always possible. In 1712, while describing the acquisition of a new snuff box, Swift wrote that "the Duchess of Hamilton has made me Pockets for like a woman's with a Belt and Buckle, for you know I wear no waistcoat in Summer, & there are severall divisions, and one on purpose for my box, oh ho."⁴⁶ People were unlikely also to be wearing completely new sets of clothing from top to bottom, unless they were particularly rich, and even then, people often remade their clothing such as jackets, waistcoats, overcoats, and dresses. As Ann Hollander remarked, even those who claim to be disinterested in fashion still face fashion through that very act of knowing defiance: "Fashion in dress is always fluid and shifting both in time and space, so that at any given moment many people are dressing differently from one another; but in a later period, all those differences will have noticeably altered according to a new set of conventions which will have developed from the previous ones."⁴⁷

Expenditure on fashion was a part of the cadence of the year in the long eighteenth century, and often consisted of modest but meaningful necessities such as hairdressing and other purchases; for others, little luxuries were more common. The Lewis Walpole Library holds a "Ladies daily companion" for the year 1789 in which a well-connected lady describes some of her expenditure and social life. On some days she had no company, on other days she "drank tea; with friends and sometimes had dinners." She generally made the point whether she had stayed home or had company, and enjoyed on occasion walking in St. James's Park and going to Christie's, visiting the famous cross-dresser Mlle D'Eon and "went to Wedgwoods." In April, she reported that "Papa dined with Sir Joseph Banks." Many of her expenditures were on accessories and for her hair. In February, she bought some hair curlers for 6d, two yards of pink "riband" at 5d a yard, a yard and a half of black gauze at 3s, and a "striped satin sash" at 6s 6d. In July, she needed more hair rollers at 1s, lavender water at 1s 2d and a "court plaister" (a black patch for the face) at 6d. In October, she bought some ribbon for 1s, gloves for 3s and "ribone" at 1s 6d. In November, it was gloves at 1s 2d and more ribbons at 2s 1d. She bought a new hat at "Davies's the Hatter in Bond St." mid-year. She noted a new pencil and memorandum book for the year and then "bought ribond for shoe ties" for 5d. Even though her expenditure and horizon of travel was modest (she went to Stonehenge and Salisbury during the year), her pocket book also contained an account of the "new fashions at Paris" including details of a head-dress "a puff of plain gauze, from which hangs a long veil behind, tied round with a chocolate-color ribbon, forming a handsome knot on the left side . . . but whether they bear any affinity to the Indian fashions, of which the Robe is said to be a copy, we are at a loss to know."⁴⁸

From a more elevated social rank is an unpublished account book held in a French private collection. It records the expenditure of a young man of title living near Avignon in the period c. 1750–80. Single, he regularly went in his coach to Marseilles and

Aix-en-Provence to purchase contraband tobacco, as well as tea, sugar, and "orange blossom" water. He drank a great deal of coffee including some from America: "coffee expressed modernity and the triumph of trade," notes Roche of the period.[49] The young minor aristocrat regularly bought faience dishes, crystal, and other such dining wares that were uncommon in the countryside except among the very rich.[50] The most regular account was for the management of his hair. He often paid his wigmaker for a year's hairdressing past and hence. Wig-bags must have worn out or become soiled, as they were regular purchases about once a year, as well as a pair of shoes and one or two pairs of silk stockings on average once a year. Every now again he acquired a very expensive accessory such as a Malacca cane with gold handle, a gold cord for the cane, or had his gold shoe buckle reset with a "stone." He rented a domino and mask for *mardi gras*. Materials such as silver were exchanged in turn for the making up of a new accessory such as buckles with old for new. His laundry was extensive, including having thirty-four shirts washed at the one time. Many of his clothes (jackets, etc) were repaired or relined, and textile purchases were costed first (including gold braid paid for by weight) and then extra fees (much lower) for the making up by the tailor added. The place of manufacture of most of the goods and the names of the tradesmen involved was noted, which is significant, as it reveals that consumers had a high awareness of the origins of their goods. Relationships with suppliers must have been intimate but also concerned the cost of materials and record-keeping, as a great many such entries were made. Some purchases such as stockings came from pedlars. A set of books to read was bought about once a year, comedies and histories generally. In 1775, a taffeta parasol was purchased. Fine hand mirrors, a silver shaving basin or soup plate in the Paris taste, a "very expensive" taffeta-covered screen and a great many coffee pots suggested the house had an air of luxury, and the general impression accords very much with the conclusions of Daniel Roche concerning those lucky enough to benefit from the consumer revolution of France.

The mirror is significant. Their use led to satiric complaints from the English that "Noone who is not a Frenchman could bear to see men comb publicly in the streets, or the women carrying little mirrors in their hands (as is often the practice of both)."[51] Of such reflective devices, Hollander notes, "the image reflected in a mirror is a visionary self-portrait which has been generated in the imagination beforehand, and which may be created and re-created at will. The materials of which it is composed are visual facts, but the total image is a fiction."[52] Looking good and keeping up with fashion every season (as well as recycling one's old clothes), eating from a new range of dishes and condiment sets, having more comfortable furnishings, reading a little for pleasure and studying maps and compendia were central to a new mental outlook for those with means:

> through different consumptions or different ways of using things, the subjects could construct themselves differently and re-adjust their relationship to the collective . . . The revolution in linen and clothing was of essential importance in the economic, social and moral debate, because it overturned the values of the Christian and stationary economy, initiating people into the economy of circulation, personal change and individualism.[53]

For north Germany and the Low Countries in this period, historians benefit from the research project of the historian Dagmar Freist (Carl von Ossietzky-Universität Oldenburg) and her team who have worked on the rural élites of the Friesian marshes.[54] Such work is important for the way it modulates the matter of "English exceptionalism" and the eighteenth-century consumer revolution, as noted in a long critical review by Craig

Clunas concerning "consumption and the rise of the west."[55] It is also helps us shift beyond the standard Anglo-French comparative models that dominate the study of eighteenth-century dress in the English speaking world. Freist's research collective examines not the super rich or even the middling sort, but rather rural élites in a particular part of northern Europe and their different approaches to their self-presentation and self-fashioning. Her general argument is that estate society became more differentiated with the impact of new rising social groups. The performance of field specific social practices, according to Freist, was not an imitation of, for example, the nobility, but an "overwriting" of the script of the élite by rising social groups. They acclaimed the position of a social élite by performing the expected social and cultural practices, and in the process they created themselves as a specific and recognizable group rather than imitating what was already there. The region that formed the focus of the study is the Frisian Marshes, an area in which wheat and livestock generated wealth in the seventeenth and eighteenth centuries. As Gerd Steinwascher noted of the area, "the German Northwest is a very exciting area for examination. Spiritual and secular state formations, mixed denominational, Catholic and Lutheran religious conditions are encountered as well as the manor and free peasants or sovereign tenant farmers." The term "*hausleute*" in north-west Germany does not denote a peasant, but rather a figure who is somewhere economically and socially between a farmer and a trader. From the thirteenth century onwards, they were allowed to own and sell land in this region. Although very few of the *hausleute* went far from their own region, they "were very aware of their dependency on global economic developments." They were, according to Frank Schmekel, "a social group between local rootedness and global involvement." They are therefore extremely interesting in terms of the topics of distinction and consumption of all fashionable goods including dress fashions.

Schmekel cites a contemporary source: "the public predominantly loves the foreign without respect for the quality or the beauty of a thing." Two hatters from Norden in a supplication against Dutch hats were discovered to be importing Dutch hats themselves and pretending that they were of local production. In May 1774, the potter Schmeding complained about the dressmaker Meyer who "dares to deal in all kinds of foreign earthenware." Meyers fights back by stating that the potters have inferior products both technically and aesthetically. Clearly it was quite common to have foreign goods in this marketplace and there was a rising diversity of shopping. High quality was not equivalent to a high price and the prices also dropped as a consequence.

Philippe Jarnoux made important historiographical points regarding rural France. In the 1960s, historians studied the economic and social point of view; material culture seemed to be a function of the economic conditions and not a topic in itself. He noted that the French cultural history tradition of the study of fashion concerns mainly urban life. Peasants of lower Brittany did not speak French and consumed differently than in a center such as Paris or even a large rural town. Ten to twenty percent of them were well off; others very poor. Although the Breton peasants were close to the ports bringing back colonial goods, they chose not to consume most of them. More important to the peasants was the household and the "visualization of furniture" therein—rich peasants amassed quantities of fairly limited types—chairs, beds and wardrobes, for example. Most important were the large marriage chests (armoires) of cherry wood that were carried publicly through the streets and processed into peasant houses. Peasants also liked to acquire a great quantity of certain goods—bedding, shirts, clothing—but not luxury clothing or "rare and specialized furniture." In terms of clothing, the second-hand market was very large and this made those who wore the new and clean clothes more striking.

Rarity and novelty are of little interest but rather accumulation was the preferred model. Exceptions are local priests, who behaved more like urban folk. Many people shopped after Mass as well as at the "Pardons" or religious feasts and pilgrimages.

Brittany also provides a fascinating account of the role of small accessories in shaping fashionable appearances. A pedlar, Hubert Jenniard, had the misfortune to be killed by soldiers in Crozon in 1761. The magistrate investigated the matter and recorded that he had on him the following: eighteen rings, seventy-two knives, four mirrors, sixteen snuffboxes, sixteen scissors, seven ivory needles, forty-two shoe buckles, twelve kerchiefs, sixteen combs, nine flutes, twelve pens, six earpicks, one crystal flask, five brushes, five bells, five crosses, and 170 pairs of buttons.[56] This is a striking list as it demonstrates how important small accessories and instruments of grooming were to fashion at this time and the very large amounts of certain fashion items carried into the countryside by one pedlar. To a Breton peasant, wealth was not a means to start a great deal of consumption. It was instead "a guarantee against social and economical crisis" and secondly used to assert a social position. In Breton society in the eighteenth century, there is little evidence of a consumer revolution. Change is "slow and progressive." The main issue is to be the first in the village, not in the outside world, even when peasants become prominent in Paris, at the time of the Estates General for example. The city was seen as a foreign society, according to Janoux.

Freist summed up in the following ways. Rural élites differ around Europe and they are also differentiated within themselves. The analysis of social distinction should not be limited to the analysis of what people possessed in terms of luxury goods. Social distinction also comprises forms of behavior, habitus, and social practices. Material culture has different roles in social interaction: it can be instrumental in signifying social status, it can be part of a *Habitus*, it can also be a culturally impregnated way of claiming a specific social position within a specific field or social group. Rural élites were linked to supra-regional markets but they did not always engage in global forms of consumption. The engagement with supra-regional markets and access to "global" consumer goods triggered of a process of adaption and "re-modeling" of consumer goods according to local tastes, custom and traditional ideas of social prestige. Rural élites had access to media on politics, science and fashion. They created their own infrastructure for social and cultural events and exchange.[57]

"FLESH AND STONE"

The study of fashion has flourished in recent years, not simply as a result of the efforts of the *Annales* school to restore a dignity to the stuff of everyday life, but also because of the "cultural turn" in the humanities of the 1980s and 1990s, which was closely linked to feminist studies, gay/queer issues, and new histories of race and cultural difference. As Joan W. Scott wrote in her article "Gender: A Useful Category of Historical Analysis" (1986), "Investigations of these issues will yield a history that will provide new perspectives on old questions (about how, for example, political rule is imposed, or what the impact of war on society is), redefine the old questions in new terms (introducing considerations of family and sexuality, for example, in the study of economics or war), make women visible as active participants, and create analytic distance between the seemingly fixed language of the past and our own terminology."[58]

Richard Senett's *Flesh and Stone: The Body and City in Western Civilization* (1996), although not primarily concerned with clothing, is useful for the way it enables connections to be made between changing dress fashions and the changing nature of cities. As a long review of his work by Mark S.R. Jenner points out, Sennett originally wished to create a collaborative work with Michel Foucault. Sennett connects the history of the human body with the history of the built environment, in a panoramic sweep from the Ancient Greeks to contemporary New York. There is considerable focus on the densifying cities of West Europe in the eighteenth century, particularly Paris and London.

It was in Paris that the squares, streets, and quais began to resemble a rational map, rather than the jumbled haphazardness of a medieval city. It was in Paris, we learn, that the first one way street system was developed, which Sennett argues relates to Harvey's new knowledge of the one dimensional flow of blood through the human body. Such streets and shops encouraged a new relationship of city folk to their urbanity and their clothes. As his reviewer notes:

> There was, one should stress, a diverse range of early modern bodies . . . Bodies were not only enmeshed in Foucauldian webs of power, discourse, and signification. Human beings were and are also surrounded by a range of material culture—clothes, houses, tools, food. Such artefacts construct and permit human cultures and are strangely absent from most current approaches to the history of the body.[59]

Urban retailing was transformed in this period, as depicted in the English print of "In Gosnell Street. Antient inconvenience contrasted with modern convenience" (1807) (Figure 0.7).[60]

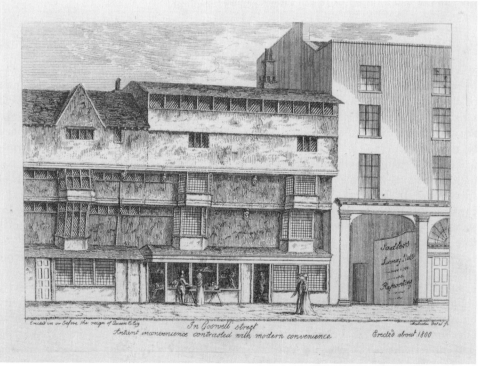

FIGURE 0.7: *In Gosnell Street,* James Peller Malcolm, London: Longman, Hurst, Rees, and Orme, 1808. Courtesy of the Lewis Walpole Library, Yale University.

Shoppers pass by Elizabethan rickety structures in which artisans work in the same space where they sell their wares, with fold down shutters to display the odd chosen ware. This is contrasted with a new "Georgian" building next door with large, regular windows, the suggestion of a ground floor bowed window or entrance, fanlights over the front central door and fine signage for "Sadlers Livery Hall Repository." There is also no sign of work.

THE EXTREME ARTIFICE OF THE EIGHTEENTH CENTURY AND ITS AFTERLIFE

In 1818, Madame de Genlis published her *Dictionnaire critique et raisonné des etiquettes de la cour*. She lamented the loss of the court but not its excessive powder and toilette. She complained that old women should stop thinking that they can ever wear roses, the emblem of freshness and youth.[61] She felt that the *toilette* had been an absurd habit for women, undressing in front of men, and painting oneself at the toilette; and that the excessive use of perfume in men in the past was both effeminate and inexcusable, and that it was absurd that men aged thirty to thirty-five had worn such large "nosegays" or "bouquet": corsages that were later able to be fed to the pigs.[62] Men of the *ancien régime*, she claimed, had taken their fashion from women, the sleeves, the large rings, and earrings, and this Madame de Genlis ("the scribbling trollop" was Walpole's misogynistic name for her) felt to have been a deficit.[63] Elizabeth Vigée-Lebrun, court painter to Marie-Antoinette, had a rather different view of what had happened:

> It is difficult to convey today an idea of the urbanity, the graceful ease, in a word, the affability of manner which made the charm of Parisian society forty years ago. Women reigned then, the Revolution dethroned them.[64]

In the post-Revolutionary period, dress "heightened awareness of the theatrical nature of clothing itself." Wearing the dress of the *ancien régime* became dangerous. Silk and satin, embroidery and patched faces for men fell out of favor. But the streetscape of the city of Paris did not become dull. New groups of men and women who were identified by their clothing and lifestyle sprang up very quickly and were depicted by the print-makers and painters who survived the Revolutionary years. Best known were the *Incroyables and Merveilleuses*, *Directoire*-period types who included a newly rich class of speculators or *agioteurs*. The men replaced knee breeches with tapering trousers, a garment from the wardrobe of seamen, buckled shoes were replaced with boots and even shoe-lacing. Women wore thin muslin dresses with flat shoes, sometimes with lacings (Figure 0.8). Cashmere shawls and extreme hairstyles, sometimes feather cut to recall the action of the guillotine, were fashionable. However, their clothes were of extreme elegance, although very exaggerated, and they did not look cheap or vulgar.

Sandra Gilbert notes that literary figures such as Carlyle wrote in the 1830s "obsessively about the significance of clothing" and that literary modernists of the nineteenth century operated rather differently, dependent on their gender.[65] Male writers tend to oppose false to true clothing, hence the importance of bohemianism. Literary women "and their post-modern heirs ... imagine costumes of the mind with much greater irony and ambiguity, in part because women's clothing is much more closely connected with the pressures and oppressions of gender and in part because women have far more to gain from the identification of costume with self or gender."[66] We will conclude, then with a passage from Virginia Woolf's novel of gender transition, *Orlando* (1928):

> Vain trifles as they seem, clothes have, they say, more important offices than merely to keep us warm. They change our view of the world of the world's view of us . . . Thus, there is much to support the view that it is the clothes that wear us and not we them; we may make them take the mould of arm or breast, but they mould our hearts, our brains, our tongues to their liking.[67]

FIGURE 0.8: Cup and saucer, painted with an *Incroyable* (on the saucer) and a *Merveilleuse* (on the cup). Chrétien Kuhne Etterbeck factory, Brussels, c. 1795. Inv. Ar 02222. Collection Musée Ariana, Ville de Genève. Photo: Nicolas Lieber.

CHAPTER ONE

Textiles

TOVE ENGELHARDT MATHIASSEN

To what extent can we talk about a fabric or dye as being "enlightened"? This intriguing question will be addressed here. From an art historical perspective, the years from 1650 to 1800, the Age of Enlightenment, encompass the baroque, the *régence* (French period of regency style), rococo, and the first neoclassical styles. When applied to fashion and fabrics, these stylistic approaches are different in almost every aspect, be it textile design, the preferred fibers used for dress, or the favored colors. Looking at deeper social and technical processes, during the 150 years in question, manufacturing methods and the lives of people involved in the production of these goods went through massive changes too. Closely related to these social conditions, access to fashionable fabrics and other materials used in garment construction changed conspicuously from 1650 to 1800.

We will start at the end of the period, by considering what is perhaps the most obvious outcome of the Enlightenment when it comes to fashion, the neoclassical *"robe en chemise."* In Denmark the classic and first-known example[1] is the 1787 painting by the famous Danish painter Jens Juel (Figure 1.1).[2]

The story of its creation reveals interesting aspects of the link between morality and fashion towards the end of the eighteenth century. The painting is of Duchess Louise Augusta, half-sister of the later Danish king, Frederik VI. She was called "la petite Struensee," even at court, because she was the result of a love affair between Queen Caroline Mathilde and the king's personal physician, Johan Friedrich Struensee.[3] She was born in 1771, her older half-brother in 1768. In spite of her paternity, Princess Louise Augusta held an elevated position at court and married the duke of Schleswig-Holstein-Sønderborg-Augustenborg in 1786. Her husband wanted his wife to be portrayed in the newly fashionable *"robe en chemise."* This was a thin tubular dress with links to both juvenile and also Creole dressing. People were not used to seeing European women wearing such clothes. The artist Juel was very uneasy about the commission and the highest-ranking court official Johan Bülow was virtuously indignant, for to the contemporary eye this type of dress had very obvious connotations of being akin to underwear. Bülow recorded the awkward prelude in his diary, January 3, 1786:

> Professor Juel, Court Painter, brought to me *Esquisse* for a Portrait of Princess L. Augusta painted as a Greek Nymph, I said that it was not a decent Dress, in which he agreed and wished that he was allowed to make it differently but that he has had express Commands from the Crown Prince and the Prince of Aug. to do it in this Way.[4]

Bülow tried to explain to the crown prince that it was improper to have his sister portrayed in her undergarments. The crown prince objected and got angry when Bülow commented: "You have just Actresses and your Mistress painted like that, but a Princess! and Juel has the

FIGURE 1.1: Duchess Louise Augusta in her *"robe en chemise,"* Jens Juel, 1787. The Museum of National History, Frederiksborg Castle, Denmark.

same Idea as I and so certainly have many others." HRH Frederik broke off the conversation and ordered that Bülow read from the dispatches. The case also brings to mind the famous scandal regarding Queen Marie-Antoinette, who was painted by Elisabeth Vigée-Lebrun in the *chemise à la gaulle* or *chemise à la reine* (Figure 3.16), a fashionable muslin dress so scanty that the work was taken down at the Salon of 1783 and replaced with a new version in which the Queen wore a conventional silk dress with tightly fitted sleeves.

The loose-fitting dress, which pulled over the head, was indeed a daring example of the novel neoclassical garment for women of the late Enlightenment. The gown brought to mind a Greek nymph in thin, transparent fabrics that originally were likely "Coan" silks rather than cottons, but that for the late eighteenth century were either made of fashionable cottons like high-quality muslins as well as light dress silks.[5] In Louise Augusta's case, she also wore a fine, white gauze veil striped with closer-set warp threads along the edges in her coiffure, the same sort of edging to her collar, and had sleeves of very thin fabrics. In theory, such an outfit meant that she was able to dress herself without the help of a lady's maid—a dramatic departure from the demands of earlier dress styles. She could also wear this dress without stays—a very *risqué* choice indeed in the eyes of her contemporaries, and again one that represented the beginnings of a massive shift in fashions and sensibility. Her "enlightened" dress, therefore, allowed her and other fashionable women to be self-reliant and to move without the bodily restraint of stays. Not only could they be independent while dressing, most women would possess the skills needed to sew such clothes themselves—if they so desired—without the help of professional tailors and dressmakers. It was indeed a revolution in fashion.

THE STORY OF FIVE TEXTILES

This chapter proceeds by "unpacking" some of the myriad textile terms familiar to an eighteenth-century consumer, but little known outside expert circles today. Established in 2004, the objective of the Danish research project Textilnet is to make a historical and contemporary digital dictionary or term base available (at www.textilnet.dk) to preserve and communicate the cultural heritage of concepts for dress and textiles. The hand written and typed records of two Danish researchers, Dr. Erna Lorenzen and Ellen Andersen, were the starting point of the project. From 1959 to 1979, Erna Lorenzen was curator of dress and textiles at Den Gamle By, the National Open Air Museum of Urban History and Culture,[6] and from 1936 to 1966, Ellen Andersen held a similar position at the National Museum of Denmark. Every term in the database based on their research is supported by evidence from scientific literature, dictionaries and other such handbooks.[7] When compiled from these sources, the terms for textiles dated before 1807 number around 1,000. It would be impossible in the scope of this volume to publish or describe all of them. Instead, I will discuss five textiles from Textilnet that are significant for, or typical of, the period under study, and complement their discussion with the evidence of material artifacts in the collections of Den Gamle By as well as some comparative material. Doing so will give an impression of the abundance of fabric types available to the "enlightened costumer," and also of the place of textiles within the economy and within networks of trade. Through these five different examples, therefore, we can glimpse the global connections in the dress and fashion of this period, the social conditions that shaped their production and use, and also the key changes in textiles at this time.

It is important to underline that in the eighteenth century, every textile was made of either plant or animal fibers, or, as was quite often the case, of mixed fibers, including also metal threads of different kinds. The fabrics for discussion are, using the names by which they were known in Denmark: *Abat de Macedoine* (a coarse woolen), *Drap d'or* (a luxurious cloth), *flandersk lærred* (flax), *chintz* (printed cotton), and *kastorhår* (felted beaver). Between them they cover the main textile types of the long eighteenth century: woolens, silk, linen, cottons, and prepared fur.

In the textile *Abats* or *Abat de Macedoine*[8] we find embedded the history of slavery and global networks in a condensed form. The term is found in two Danish encyclopedias of merchandise: Juul, dated 1807,[9] and Rawert, dated 1831.[10] Both encyclopedias are examples of the Enlightenment drive to order phenomena in categories, and to systematize and diffuse knowledge. Rawert's definition runs as follows:

> Abat de Macedoine, a sort of coarse, woolen fabric for clothing of poor people; furthermore for wrapping, especially of tobacco. Considerable amounts were earlier sent from Smyrna [now called Izmir] via Marseilles to West India to use for clothing of negroes (p. 2).

In stating that the same coarse fabric was suitable both for the wrapping of tobacco and for the clothing of slaves and poor people, this example makes it abundantly clear that the world of textiles was always integrated with social history. While a technical explanation of the fabric is not available in this example—and neither Florence Montgomery nor Elisabeth Stavenow-Hidemark[11] give a definition or analysis of *Abat de Macedoine*—it nevertheless emerges clearly that this term has a French origin, which is common in Danish eighteenth-century expressions for dress and textiles.[12] Rawert further informs us that *abats* are a sort of coarse fabric from Macedonia, sold in Turkey, Italy, and partially in France; he then gives the information about clothing the slaves in the West Indian colonies. Until they were sold to USA in 1917, Denmark owned the West Indian islands of Saint Croix, Saint John and Saint Thomas, and some uninhabited smaller islands. *Abats* could not be defined as fashionable fabrics in the sense that people of fashion would wear them, but considering the economic system of their production, *abats* show us how the expenses of clothing the cheap labor force were kept as low as possible, and that it was seen as profitable in a global network of trade to weave coarse, low-quality fabrics in southeastern Europe and transport them across the Atlantic Ocean. *Abats* were not alone in being sold in the West Indies. Cheaper cotton goods, as for example Guinea cloths and *chelloes*—rough fabrics that were either striped or checked—also found a market (Figure 1.2).[13]

"Guinea cloths," too, played a somewhat grim role in the global market and consumption of textiles, and in the history of humans as cheap labor in the colonies. Guinea cloths and other types of cotton fabrics were purchased in India and resold in West Africa in exchange for slaves, who were then forced to travel across the Atlantic to work in the plantations in the Americas.[14] In a grim irony, some of these plantations were producing cotton.[15]

While *Abat de Macedoine* was a low-quality woolen fabric, already in the pre-modern period Europe was producing exquisite fabrics made of wool. Fragments of textiles from the northern part of Europe indicate an organized production of woolen cloth as early as the Hallstatt culture in the seventh and sixth century BC. Signs of an organized distribution of woolens to a larger area are also found in Roman times.[16] Before 1200, Flanders specialized in the production of high-quality woolen cloth: wool from England and, from the fourteenth century, from Spain, was imported to be woven, fulled, cut, and dyed in the workshops of the growing merchant towns there and was exported to other European

FIGURE 1.2: The second sample at top right is "chelloes." Letters and documents from Guinea.
Photo: Vibe Maria Martens. Rigsarkivet (The National Archives of Denmark), Copenhagen.

countries.[17] For the Danish consumer in the Middle Ages, woolen cloth from Flanders
was very popular.[18] Woolens and worsteds continued to be produced in the age of the
Enlightenment and were Europe's chief textile contribution to the worldwide trade.
Interestingly, some clothing of the Japanese samurai of the Edo period (1615–1868) used
woolen cloth of European origin.[19] In the eighteenth century, woolen cloth was the
fundamental part of the Englishman's suit, not only practical for horse-riding and hunting,
but increasingly influential in urban contexts across Europe. Woolens were also used for
capes, mantles, women's riding habits, and in fine-quality weights also for winter court
dress, when they were sometimes embroidered (a fine late-seventeenth-century example
is held in the Metropolitan Museum of Art, New York).[20] Den Gamle By holds a colorful
but practical waistcoat for a well-to-do man, c. 1750, of glazed woolen, lined with woolen
twill (Figure 1.3).

At the other end of the social scale from the *Abat de Macedoine* we have *drap d'or*,
literally cloth of gold but defined by Juul in 1807 as a cloth of silk with interwoven gold
or silver threads, or *lahn*. These fabrics

> are woven in many patterns and are the true touch-stone for the artistic weaver in
> which he can develop his totality of taste and art. [. . .] The art to weave these
> fabrics was invented in Venice, Florence and Genoa, and from there it was brought to

FIGURE 1.3: Waistcoat dated 1750s. Glazed woolen cloth embroidered with woolen thread and supported with several layers of fabrics and horsehair. Buttons of *passementerie*. The back part made of linen tabby. Lined with woolen twill and linen. The waistcoat belonged to a wealthy merchant in the second largest city of Denmark, Aarhus. © Den Gamle By. Photo: Frank Pedersen.

France where it, especially in Lyon, has developed to a high level of perfection. (p. 440).

Juul also mentioned the Danish term *gyldenstykke*[21] as equivalent to *drap d'or*. He gives no indication of the costs of luxurious fabrics of these types, but the eighteenth-century consumer would have belonged to the richer part of society.

In the collections of Den Gamle By is a suit consisting of a coat, waistcoat and breeches that is dated c. 1770 and sewn of a *drap d'or* fabric with dots of velvet (Figure 1.4).

The fabric was probably woven in Lyon,[22] the most significant European silk-weaving center in the eighteenth century. Lyon was famed for its varieties of silks, such as those featuring meandering ribbon patterns combined with flowers, feathers, and even simulated fur (Figure 1.5).

In 1961, the *drap'dor* suit was incorporated into Den Gamle By collection in spite of its very fragile state.[23] The ground weave is a cream-colored silk warp with extra wefts of gold thread. The fabric has small dots made by extra warp threads of light green, purple, a yellowish red probably dyed with madder, and cream-colored silk cut like velvet. By the 1960s, the fabric and the luxurious buttons had lost most of their previous beauty and shine. The buttons are made of linen covered with thin gold foil, edged and trimmed with golden details and colored spangles. In all probability the buttons are of French origin, as buttons like these were not produced in Denmark. Unfortunately nothing is known about the suit's first owner but he must have been a man of means, and probably also of a social class legally entitled to wear silk and metal threads: a cloth like *drap d'or* is witness to a society in which wealth could be materialized in clothing, and where—through sumptuary

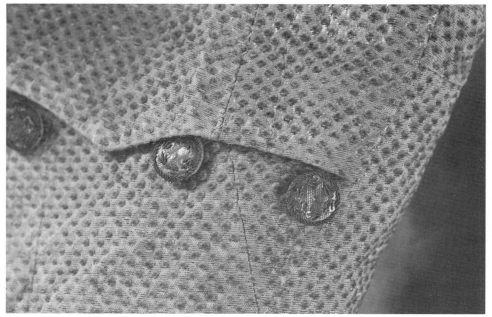

FIGURE 1.4: Detail of man's suit dated c. 1770. The silk and metal tread fabric "*drap d'or*" with dots of silk velvet. Buttons of linen with a cover of gold foil decorated with golden details and colored spangles. The last owners were actors. © Den Gamle By. Photo: Frank Pedersen.

FIGURE 1.5: Detail of silk dress dated 1770–5. Ground weave in striped silk rep and brocaded flower, foliage and lace patterns. Probably from Lyon. The bodice is supported by iron sticks and lined with white linen. The dress belonged to German nobility who moved to Denmark at the end of nineteenth century. © Den Gamle By. Photo: Bodil Brunsgård.

legislation—different social strata had different rights of access to the consumption of goods.[24]

Men also enjoyed wearing accessories that shone. Shoelaces were considered effeminate until the very end of the eighteenth century, and so shoes were fastened with buckles. Buckles might be of silver for the extremely rich, but were also made of silver-plate and other substitute materials. In the 1770s, buckles made from steel were extremely fashionable, as were steel buttons; for women, steel belt-buckles might also be embellished with new materials such as Wedgwood china from England (Figure 1.6).

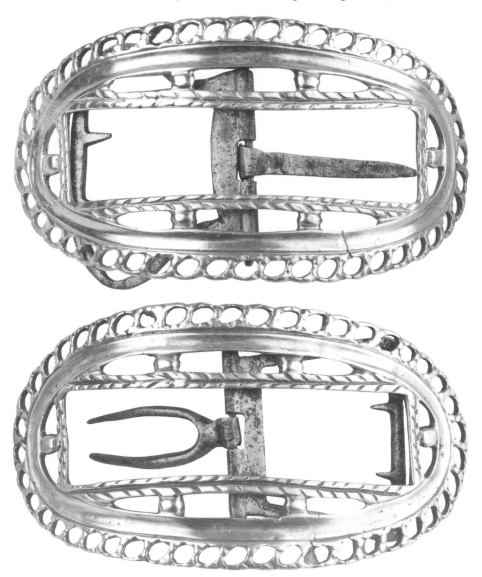

FIGURE 1.6: Male shoe buckles of silver with iron catches, dated late eighteenth century. In rococo garments, silver often constituted closing devices such as buttons and buckles. © Den Gamle By. Photo: Frank Pedersen.

Velvet is attested from the Middle Ages, and its luxury forms a very important part of fashionable fabrics of the Renaissance and the earliest part of the baroque. Velvets combined with silk brocades and white elements made of linen can be seen in portraits of powerful men and women of Europe from the mid-seventeenth century. Italy and later France produced these fabrics. Writing in 1807, Juul concurred, stating that the best qualities of silk velvet came from France and Italy, and that velvet also was produced in the Netherlands, Germany, and England but that these products were not of the same quality. *Drap d'or* is just one example of a luxury fabric produced for the Western elite.

It is interesting, however, to consider modern notions about sustainability and pollution in this context. Some of the fabrics of the Enlightenment—such as *drap d'or* for instance, or the glazed worsteds of Norwich—were extremely impractical. The metal threads of *drap d'or* could be tarnished and could wear the thin silk threads of the fabric. Embedded in this textile was in fact its own decay. As for the glazing of the worsteds, this could be spotted when exposed to rain—which was not very practical either in England or the Nordic countries, considering the climate—and the glazing would eventually disappear during washing.[25] Perhaps a part of the appeal was keeping the fabric fresh and protected from the damp with the use of mantles or capes, as parasols and umbrellas were something of a metropolitan affectation used mainly by the French.

The next fabric we will consider is *Flandersk lærred*,[26] which translates to English as "linen from Flanders." Before cottons became so very fashionable during the eighteenth century, fabrics made of flax—linen—constituted the most easily washable part of clothing. Used for shirts and shifts, flax was also the prime fiber in those finer fabrics, like lace, that so whitely accessorized at the collar and in women's headgear. John Styles has pointed out how the so-called cottons of the eighteenth century could have warp threads made of flax,[27] and the fact is that cottons only conquered flax fabrics gradually. Even at the turn of the nineteenth century, Juul was able to write that *Flandersk lærred* designated linen produced in Flanders and in the-then French regions of the Schelde and Lys, and that the local growing of flax, the preparation of the plants to fibers, the weaving, and the treatment of the woven fabrics in this area had been developed to a very high level of perfection. He goes on to say that the flax mills of the area are called the gold mine of Flanders and rightly so, and he lists all the relevant textile towns. At last he mentions the products—from the finest lawn, cambric, and batiste, to the coarsest linen of tow—and their specialized names, such as *aplomades, prexillas, brabantes crudos, brabantes gantes, brabantillas, florettas,* and *hollandas.*

The fourth fabric to consider is *chintz*,[28] a textile that played a crucial role in the Enlightenment and in the economies of fashion, production and trade (Figure 1.7).

In 1807, Juul defined chintz as an English fabric, writing that it was produced at the mills in Manchester in two types: one with a genuine madder-red ground, another with an artificial, painted red color. Despite the exactness of his description of this fabric, the term "chintz"—like some other textile names—is remarkably slippery, and has changed definition several times. A Danish definition from 1937, for example, goes like this:

> Chintzes are printed tabby qualities that are made shiny, [. . .] with a glazing and hard calandering [. . .] The term chintz is also used for some printed, thin fabrics which are not shiny but have printed Persian patterns (paisley) usually on a red ground. They are available in tabby and twill and are used for quilted duvets.[29]

A quite different definition emerges from the more diachronic explanations in research contexts and in newer Danish handbooks. Here we learn that it derives from *chit*, an

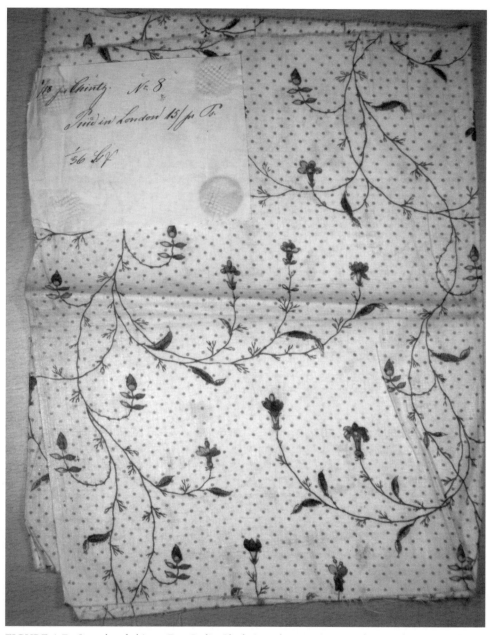

FIGURE 1.7: Sample of chintz. East India Cloth Sample 4064A. Rigsarkivet (The National Archives of Denmark), Copenhagen. Photo: Vibe Maria Martens.

Indian term for printing—although the chintzes of India were produced by a combination of many different techniques besides printing. These techniques, which were mastered in different locations in India, are an important key to understanding how cottons conquered even the luxurious patterned silks and worsteds, whether patterned in the weaving or by surface embroidery. The techniques applied to cottons included various kinds of printing with wooden blocks, painting and penciling, wax-resistant dye processes to keep areas of the patterns white, the use of mordants to bond dyes to the fibers, and of course the knowledge and availability of dyestuffs:

> The differentiation between printing, painting and penciling includes a variety of sub-specialisations. In West India and Gujarat, for instance, chintzes were printed with wooden blocks by using one or more of the various techniques that included "direct printing", "bleach printing" (bleaching the design on an already dyed cloth), "mordant printing" (printing with mordants and then bleaching the unmordanted areas) or "resist printing" (printing a viscous substance, followed by dyeing, followed by the cleansing of the substance). Several Indian sources confirm that the degree of division of labour in calico printing was highly refined and that the process could involve as many as a dozen separate dye transfers to the cloth.[30]

The superiority of the colors and patterns of Indian chintz over anything that could be replicated at that time in Europe is key to understanding its success in the eighteenth century. Not only did they look good, the chintzes were washable to a degree not possible to master in European dye-works and printers' workshops at the time, so they were in high demand both for their exotic beauty and also their durability. As Amelia Peck has pointed out, compared to silks and velvets, chintzes could be purchased at an affordable price, which promoted both their extraordinary success and a democratization of fashion:[31]

> Produced mainly for clothing, these relatively inexpensive cottons were worn by all classes and, indeed, created something of a social revolution, since previously it had been easy to distinguish between the gentry, dressed in patterned silk, and the common folk, in plain wools and [coarse] linens. When everyone could afford and preferred the fashionable, highly decorative patterned cottons, class lines blurred.[32]

In a final ironic demonstration of the global reach and profound influence of textile production and trade, Giorgio Riello has shown how the Western world learned from the techniques of Asia, made its own technical progress and used other structures in commerce and production—including slavery—to become the world's largest producer of cottons. From the end of the eighteenth century for the next 200 years, these cottons were then in fact exported to India.

The last textile story concerns *kastorhår*[33]—in English, beaver wool or beavers' hair—the preferred water-resistant material for the production of high-quality hats. Traded by Native Americans in return for textiles, beads, and consumer goods such as tobacco, beaver fur was the major focus of the trade conducted by the French and later the British in the region of the drainage basin of Hudson Bay that became known later as a part of Canada.[34] *Kastorhår* has been chosen for the way that it underlines the health problems connected with the production of textiles and other elements of garments. Roughly speaking, there were three issues at stake: first the exposure to dust particles and the inhalation of tiny scraps of fibers; second, the exposure to chemicals; and third, harmful working positions including the design of working facilities. In 1807, Juul wrote about *kastorhår* that the soft and fine hair of the beaver is used for hats, stockings and mittens. In 1831 Rawert added that beavers' hair is seldom for sale, as the hatters prefer to cut it off the pelts and sort it themselves.

> The cutting was in many workshops a specialty [. . .] but the process left its mark on the person in another way [apart from the excellent skills]: The dust that the cleaning and the beating of the furs brought about ruined his lungs, and the cutter is remembered as an asthmatic man, who hawking and coughing was bent over his monotonous task.[35]

However, the health issue was even more serious: before the cutter inhaled the dust and dirt from the furs, the pelts had in fact been treated with a toxic mixture of hydrochloric acid, lead, and mercury.[36] As for the third issue of working facilities, the fulling of the felt also severely compromised the hatters' health:

> During working hours the vapor lay thick and dense in the room so the workers could hardly be seen. Draught had to be ensured or the work would be intolerable, but still the man was standing at the fulling mill only clothed in shirt and pants, and in the summertime he even took off his shirt. That rheumatism was hard on most old hatters is obvious.[37]

The fashionable elite of the Enlightenment, then, used hats made out of beavers' hair, but the production of these items exposed the craftsmen to serious health-threatening procedures. In this, *kastorhår* is merely emblematic of a systemic problem in which the production of eighteenth-century textiles was based on the labor of craftsmen, whose health was frequently undermined by the processes that kept them employed. It is a problem that even today we have not solved: the growing and treatment of cotton involves the use of pesticides, textile sizing is potentially harmful, and as the 2013 collapse of a clothing factory in Bangladesh shows, workshops can still be unsafe.

PINS

In our period of fast fashion, it is hard for us to imagine a time when clothing was cherished, nearly always of some value, and not something that we could just "slip into." In theory, clad in her chemise gown, the Danish duchess Louise Augusta would have been able to dress herself, but in the beginning of the period covered by this volume, this would have been an impossibility for fashionable women. The reason was twofold. The stays were closed with laces at the back, and pins were used directly in the garments as fastenings and closures. Fashionable women of the seventeenth and eighteenth centuries consumed metal pins on a scale which is almost unbelievable for us today. In 1632, the Danish Lady Sofie Brahe purchased 12,000 pins for two Thalers[38]—to give an idea of price comparison, that the same year she paid Jacob, an Odense goldsmith, four Thalers for making three rings with rubies.[39] Sofie Brahe acquired pins again three years later in 1635, although we do not know how many as the purchase was recorded in her accounts as a single entry along with two small violins and twelve locks.[40] Again, in 1636 she bought pins, this time entered into her accounts with more obvious products in that they all related to clothing: different kinds of strings and ribbons, black silk and another fabric, and hooks, for a total amount of more than three Thalers.[41] This was her only purchase of hooks in the thirteen years from 1627 to 1640 covered by her accounts. The last time we learn about a purchase of pins is in 1639, when she bought 4,000.[42] Lady Karen Rosenkrantz de Lichtenberg purchased pins no fewer than twenty-six times from 1771 to 1796, and hooks just three times.[43] This underlines that hooks and eyes, which in the nineteenth century were very much used as a means of closing women's garments, were not very common in this earlier period.

In 1647, the Dutch artist Gerard van Honthorst painted the Danish duchess of Schleswig and Holstein, Leonora Christine, in his studio in Utrecht.[44] Leonora Christine, the daughter of the Danish king Christian IV, was at the time part of a European fashion consuming elite. When studying her luxurious garment in this painting it is very obvious that the dress, made of exquisite red silk velvet lined with a brocade of probably silk and metal threads in warm yellow shades, has no shoulder seams or even a sleeve seam. Instead, the sleeves are fastened to the bodice with elegant brooches adorned with large pearls, an extremely popular gemstone of the baroque. In fact, it has been suggested that the very term "baroque" might stem from the Portuguese "*barocco*," which designates the natural and irregular pearls so very fashionable at the time. The dress of Leonora Christine in this painting is an example of how a garment could be fastened with very valuable items. While other examples show the less distinguished, but more commonly used, pins, they feature the same system of detachable sleeves, and garments which are open at the shoulders.

The portrait of Elizabeth Vernon, countess of Southampton, painted by an unknown artist c. 1598, even though it somewhat pre-dates the period of this volume shows in detail the fastening technology that continued to be used through the eighteenth century (Figure 1.8).

The young lady is seen combing her hair. Next to her is a table on which her open jewel box stands—several splendid bracelets, brooches, and strings of pearls spread out on the tablecloth of purple velvet. From the point of view of pins, the most fascinating element in the painting is an item that in Elizabeth Vernon's time was probably seen as utilitarian and totally mundane: behind the luxurious jewels, sitting at the very back of the table, is a gray pincushion with all her pins. The pincushion is not deep (perhaps 2–3 cm) compared to its overall dimensions (perhaps 25 × 12 cm), is rectangular with rounded corners, and is covered with a dense forest of pins. Elizabeth Vernon is depicted as not yet fully clothed. Her embroidered jacket still needs to be fastened, and her ruff (seen hanging to the right)—layers of transparent white linen, probably lawn, edged with rows of needle lace— has yet to be attached. She, or rather her lady's maid, would have had to use pins to fasten the ruff to the stiff, padded collar at the back of her bodice. Elizabeth's collar could have been stiffened with baleen, which was a typical material of the period and which we will deal with shortly.

In the late seventeenth/early eighteenth-century handwritten Danish dictionary by Mathias Moth, the seventeenth-century Danish term for pin—*knappe-nâl*—is explained as follows:

> A pin/the pin/is an oblong, round, thin and sharpened piece of brass, a sixteenth long, with a small knob at the top end, which is used for fastening.[45]

Brass is an alloy of mainly copper and zinc. Needle makers were known in the larger Danish markets towns from the sixteenth century, though it was only in the capital, Copenhagen, that there was a needle makers' guild, established February 3, 1755. From that date it was illegal to import foreign-made needles and pins into Denmark. According to Rawert, who in 1850 published a review of Denmark's industries, this ban was effective until the end of the Napoleonic wars (1815).[46]

FIGURE 1.8: *Elizabeth Vernon, Countess of Southampton*, c. 1600. Portrait of Elizabeth
Wriothesley née Vernon, Countess of Southampton, at her toilette, wearing an embroidered
jacket or waistcoat over a rose-colored corset and a rich petticoat, combing her hair with
a dog at her feet, oil on panel. By kind permission of the Duke of Buccleuch and Queensberry
KBE.

The pins in Elizabeth Vernon's pincushion and the ones that Sofie Brahe and Karen Rosenkrantz purchased were probably made of brass wire, and their production was a skilled and time-consuming process. Nevertheless, these ladies and their fashionable peers used thousands of pins to dress. This consumption has left its mark on language: even as late as the nineteenth century—when the sewing machine was common and garments closed with buttons and hooks—the earlier importance of pins was shown in the term "pin money," the "money that a woman gets (from her husband or father) for the payment of her personal expenses."[47]

BALEEN AND THE SUPPORTED BODY

Another material widely used in the fashions of the Enlightenment was baleen, which functioned as stiffening and support in garments. Baleen is an extraordinary product because it is flexible, strong even when cut into thin strips, and it can be shaped, then heated, after which it keeps its new shape. But the popularity of baleen also led to the intensive hunting and extinction of certain types of whales: DNA-analysis of baleen in existing stays has identified types of whales unknown in the present day.[48] Baleen whales belong to a suborder which still has around ten living species. The much sought-after product of the baleen whales—apart from blubber, which was used for lighting in the capitals of Europe—is found in its mouth. This type of whale has plates of keratin (a kind of protein, also important in human skin, hair, and nails)—the baleen—hanging from the upper part of its mouth, which it uses in filter-feeding.[49] The plates vary in number and size in different species. There are about 260 in the gray whale, and around 960 in the fin whale; in the bowhead whale these plates can be up to 5 meters long.

Baleen was used in women's garments to shape the body and support the fabrics, which for most of the eighteenth century were quite stiff compared to the softer cottons worn at the century's close. Men's clothing was also supported in various ways, baleen being one of them. In the words of Norah Waugh, the doublet of the seventeenth century used several layers and materials to achieve the right shaping of the fashionable male body:

> The outer material of the body of the doublet and the sleeves was always mounted on a very strong linen interlining, which usually had been stiffened with gum or paste (buckram). Sometimes there is an extra strip of this stiffening up the centre fronts, and the collar had usually three layers. The belly-pieces, attached to the interlining, might be of pasteboard or cut from three layers of buckram further stiffened with vertical whalebones.[50]

The baleen (whalebone) thus forms part of a complex combination of solid fabrics (of flax and possibly cotton fibers) and other materials such as gum and paste, to create the right masculine silhouette of the seventeenth century. Gum could be made of natural rubber from the rubber tree, *Hevea brasiliensis*, which was also used for stiffening the pads of linen worn under women's skirts from the 1680s to around 1710. Placed on the wearer's bottom under the skirts, the pad was called "*cul de Paris*" or "*la criarde*" because of the creaking noises it made, a joke about the rear. Gum was also used for another version of "*la criarde*," namely a short petticoat supporting the dress.[51]

In eighteenth-century male garments, coarse linen, horsehair and paper to some extent replaced baleen. While the doublet was no longer in use, fashionable men wore coats instead, whose fullness was likewise supported (see Figure 1.3):

All eighteenth-century coats have the full length of the centre front edge and centre back skirts strengthened with a firm strip of linen, or buckram, about four inches wide. A small piece of firm linen, sometimes backed with paper, is attached to the top of the side pleats and top of back slits. Until c. 1760 the very full coats have the front skirts, from the pockets down, interlined with linen or buckram, which is often covered with a thin layer of teased-out horsehair. The pleats of this coat are also interlined with a thin woolen material or teased-out wool fibres.[52]

Again we see a complex composition of fabrics, now also including animal fibers such as wool and horsehair, and materials such as paper (which at that time was handmade) (Figure 1.9).

Baleen was used in women's garments for a much longer period and well into the nineteenth century. Lady Sofie Brahe, who bought thousands of pins, had no whalebone listed in her accounts, although in 1643 she purchased what was described as "whale fins."[53] It is mentioned in the same entry as paper and ink, and also 9½ *alen* (almost 6 meters) of *kanifas* to the tailor. *Kanifas*[54] was a rather coarse fabric, likely "canvas" in English, which Sofie probably used in the construction of her clothes, along with the "whale fins," being another term for baleen.

Karen Rosenkrantz de Lichtenberg, on the other hand, purchased whalebone six times in the period from 1775 to 1793.[55] On January 19, 1782,[56] for instance, de Lichtenberg paid the tailor Wulmer to alter her *manteau* (*klædning*) of black silk satin with new bodices, sleeves, and what she called *over Puder*, which would be side hoops. In Denmark, the French term *poche* was normally used for these garments made of linen stiffened with baleen.[57] Furthermore, Karen paid for *trille*,[58] a fabric woven with three shafts of flax yarn (and later also cotton), which was probably used for the side hoops. She also bought black silk, black sewing thread, and a very small amount of baleen, namely

FIGURE 1.9: Handmade paper used inside a cover for a rococo fan. © Den Gamle By. Photo: Frank Pedersen.

three *Lod* (46.5 grams), which again probably went into the side hoops. On another occasion, June 22, 1789,[59] the roles were intriguingly reversed when Karen *sold* one kilo of baleen to Iørgen Skrædder. *Skrædder* means tailor in Danish, and in this case it is both the man's name and profession. She might have removed baleen from old garments, in this way turning used and unwanted resources into income. The last interesting entry dates from December 19, 1793,[60] when Karen paid the tailor to make a green and white dress, and a purple dress of woolen cloth. In the same entry she paid him for two *Lod* of baleen, that is 31 grams. By this time, at the end of the eighteenth century, fashions across Europe were simpler in design, and in drawing on neoclassical inspiration, softer fabrics, and more "natural" forms, women's garments were much less shaped and constrained by complex underclothes. The use of baleen to the support garments and bodies was therefore much reduced, as we can see from Karen's modest order at this time.

Costume historian Norah Waugh, in writing about the use of baleen in bodices and stays, came up with the term "the whaleboned body."[61] Baleen was used to shape the skirt into various fashionable forms over the long eighteenth century, from about 1650 to 1790. It was also the perfect material for shaped bodices, by which it controlled waists and torsos for the greater part of the period. When considering the Enlightenment in terms of its dress forms, therefore, we may feel as though there is a serious disjunction. If by "enlightened" one means liberated from suppression in any form, be it political or economic, cognitive or scientific—or even of the body—then stays, but also other garment forms, could be seen as a symbol of the bodily suppression of women and as such definitely not an "enlightened" item. However, as we saw at the beginning of this chapter when looking at Juel's 1787 painting of Duchess Louise Augusta's cutting-edge neoclassical fashion, she probably wore only soft stays, or perhaps no stays at all, under her *robe en chemise*. This was another reason for Johan Bülow's moral scruples, for he was used to women with boned bodies. The period does indeed therefore close with a more "enlightened" dress for women—risqué in its newness and revealing nature when modeled by Louise Augusta, but whose general forms would come to be worn across Europe.

DYES AND COLORS OF THE ENLIGHTENMENT

Glancing through pictorial sources of garments from 1650 to 1800, there is an obvious change from the rather dark colors of the baroque, to the new pastels of the rococo, and at last to the fashionable, white garments of the first neoclassical époque. The very often black or dark shades of yellow or red found in fashionable garments of the baroque was emphasized by contrasting white elements, such as embroidered or laced collars, light-colored gloves, and for women the white accessories in their headgear. The rococo had a more varied palette, and many shades of light colors (Figures 1.10 and 1.11).

Either this lightness derived from the techniques and composition of the weave or, as with surface embroidery, was set on a light-colored ground. In the neoclassical fashions of the late eighteenth century, the palette was again more reduced, but with mainly light colors and white for women, and darker colors for men. The important exceptions were men's fashionable breeches in nankeen,[62] a yellowish cotton fabric, and of course the immaculate white shirt. Until the middle of the nineteenth century and the development of aniline dyes, all dyestuffs were derived from plants or, to a lesser extent, from animals. This does not mean, however, that the dyeing was free of chemicals, for mordants—either

FIGURE 1.10: Detail of skirt dated to the second half of the eighteenth century. Colorful fabrics like this were produced in Norwich and exported all over the Western world. © Den Gamle By. Photo: Bodil Brunsgård.

mineral salts, or metals like copper, zinc and iron—were necessary for the dyestuff to bond to textile fibers.

Recent research has highlighted the extent to which the change in the fashionable color palette mentioned earlier—the larger variety of the rococo—was a direct outcome of Enlightenment thought, achievable only through the new focus on scientific advance, empirical research, and the classification and dissemination of knowledge.[63]

> Although the global search for and cultivation of dyestuffs were first and foremost matters of commerce and profit, they also represented a quest for scientific knowledge, part of the gathering and "ordering" of the natural world that characterize the Age of Enlightenment. [. . .] By the late seventeenth and early eighteenth centuries, the spirit of scientific discovery and the advent of laboratory experimentation in Europe had greatly expanded the understanding of the chemical nature of color.[64]

As well as being emblematic of an Enlightenment expansion of knowledge, dyestuffs illustrate for us the truly global nature of contemporary fashion and its networks of trade that spread throughout the known world. Blue and black colors, for example, stem from different natural dyestuffs. In Europe, the source was woad, which could be grown even as far north as Denmark. In the middle of the sixteenth century, however, indigo began to be imported into Europe. The indigo plant is native to southeast Asia, tropical

FIGURE 1.11: Detail of a quilted and embroidered silk skirt dated between 1760 and 1780. The Chinese inspired embroidery with several shades of the same colors became very popular in the second half of the eighteenth century. © Den Gamle By. Photo: Bodil Brunsgård.

Africa and, as was discovered by Europeans after 1492, to tropical America too[65]—it was grown by the pre-Colombian Maya.[66] Over the course of the eighteenth century, improvements in the dying process contributed to indigo's increasing popularity. Likewise, another source of blue and black dyes was logwood, which is native to Central America[67]and was brought from America to Europe—as was American indigo, which was also sold in the American colonies. The abundance of paintings from the second half of the eighteenth century that depict fashionable rococo men in their blue or black coats of woolen cloth and white wigs, and women with blue dresses or perhaps wearing printed or woven blue motifs, show their sitters adorned with the product of international commerce:

> Early European printed cottons were therefore the result of Asian knowledge, dyes imported from both Asia and the Americas, and plain cotton textiles and design models borrowed from India. The knowledge and material borrowing of Europe from Asia and the Americas produced an overall reinterpretation of the very processes of decoration of a cloth.[68]

Riello has also emphasized the extent to which this technical innovation and mercantile activity was given institutional support and impetus:

> the overall reinterpretation of Asian knowledge was in many cases fostered by state-sponsored bodies such as academies, government bureaux, but also privileges, patents and copyright protection, all areas that historians consider part of the institutional forces influencing economic development in Europe in the eighteenth century.

To conclude: dyestuffs and textiles were truly global. A Japanese surcoat—very similar to the one pictured (Figure 1.12)—could be made of a scarlet woolen cloth, possibly woven in the Netherlands.

Its scarlet color, derived from cochineal (which comes from an American insect[69]), imported from Mexico, was dyed with a tin mordant developed in the first half of the seventeenth century by Dutch and British chemists. The lapels of the garment are seventeenth- or eighteenth-century silk lampas sections with gilt-paper strips, possibly Chinese. The shoulder pieces of the garment date to the 1760s, and were made in Europe of silk brocaded with silk and metal-wrapped thread. A garment such as this is truly global.[70]

The Scottish philosopher David Hume, a proponent of the liberal economy, drew attention to the fact that the prosperity of a nation depended on the well-being of all of its citizens.[71] In 1751, he published these phrases, which I argue is important for the comprehension of the changes pinpointed in this chapter:

> The same age, which produces great philosophers and politicians, renowned generals and poets, usually abounds with skilful weavers, and ship-carpenters. We cannot reasonably expect, that a piece of woollen cloth will be wrought to perfection in a nation, which is ignorant of astronomy, or where ethics are neglected. The spirit of the age affects all the arts; and the minds of men, being once roused from their lethargy, and put into a fermentation, turn themselves on all sides, and carry improvements into every art and science.[72]

Cloth, then, the foundation of fashion, both was made possible by, and responded to, the changing social, political and economic developments that transformed dress over the long eighteenth century.

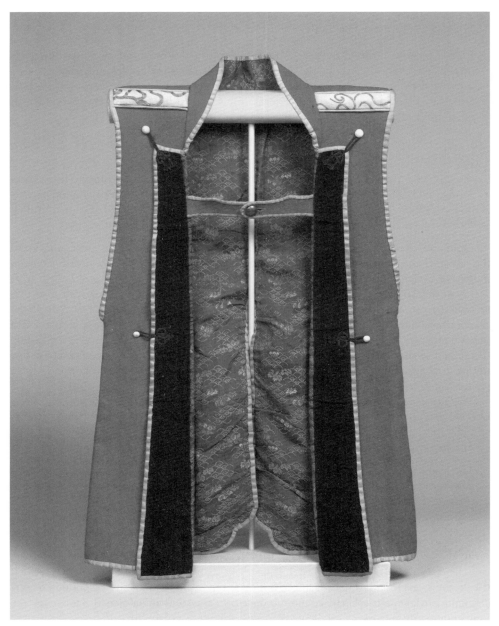

FIGURE 1.12: Japanese surcoat (*Jinbaori*), late eighteenth to ninteenth century. Made from wool, silk, metallic yarns. The Metropolitan Museum of Art, New York.

CHAPTER TWO

Production and Distribution

BEVERLY LEMIRE

European authorities addressed the practice of fashion with startling frequency in the long eighteenth century. On the one hand, secular and religious officials repeatedly demanded that commoners embrace more temperate habits, renouncing excesses of clothing and furnishings—but to no avail.[1] The making, sale, and use of textiles, whether in apparel or furnishings, were deeply political. And while authorities bemoaned the blurring of material boundaries between ranks, they also focused intensively on building their states as suppliers of cloth and crafters of fashions. Political cachet aligned with the production of fashion. The highest officials in Europe plotted for fashion advantage, like Jean Baptiste Colbert, Louis XIV's finance minister. For Colbert, ensuring the dominance of the French silk industry was a primary matter of state.[2] The reasons for his interest are clear, for the production and distribution of cloth and clothing employed a major part of the workforce and the best European fabrics represented the highest technological skills. Protectionist policies abounded during this mercantilist era, aimed at retaining artisans, and artisanal skills, within discrete political spheres, at the same time as foreign trade was promoted with other states. Achieving the right balance of imports and exports, and the approved modes among one's subjects, preoccupied Enlightenment thinkers and Enlightenment governments. The stakes were high. Vast resources were engaged in local manufacturing and retailing, while immense investments were wagered on overseas trade in textiles whether among European states, between Europe and the Ottoman Empire or with Asia.[3] Cloth and clothing were big business, as well as a very personal affair, and fashion animated politics in royal courts and city streets.

The production and distribution of textiles and clothing, from various points across the globe, made fashion increasingly possible for a greater number of middle ranked and plebeian peoples. These broad commercial dynamics were not sustained by high fashion or court fashion exclusively—for, while the wealth of kings and nobles was substantial, the costs of long distance trade demanded a wider market for the loads of textile goods carried by land or sea. Early modern fashions sparked changing patterns of dress and décor, most particularly in urban centers, among a surprisingly broad cohort.[4] European and Asian societies were founded on hierarchies of dress and furnishings, and while both raggedness and scarcity remained commonplace in years of lean harvests, wars or disease, especially among the laboring poor, this was above all a period of material change, even as authorities resisted plebeian innovations. Regardless of official edicts, material options grew in scale and increased in variety, as the street theater of style became evermore dynamic. The European historian Fernand Braudel claimed that the social mixing that took place in early modern European cities helped to "increase tension, accelerate the rhythm of exchange and ceaselessly stir up lives."[5] Cities were growing—most dramatically in parts of northwest Europe, with influences that penetrated deep within the countryside. Production of textiles and clothing increased, along with retail systems to bring these goods to market.[6] The generations living through this era noted startling shifts in the norms of everyday life, touching even the humblest women and men.

The Age of Enlightenment in Europe is associated with philosophical writings about the functions of government, the nature of the individual, and governmental trade policies. These themes animated discussions in Parisian salons among elite *literati*, in London and Amsterdam coffeehouses frequented by commercial folk, as well as in smaller ports and towns across Europe.[7] The subjects of their conversations also included the changing dimensions of material life and the visible alterations in comforts and luxuries within European society.[8] Changes in cloth and clothing were part of this broad transformation. In this chapter I assess the production and distribution of key categories of cloth, plus major elements of clothing and domestic accessories within Europe, goods that signaled innovations in fashion and comfort. The diffusion of Asian silks and later Indian cottons unsettled the existing hierarchy of wool and linen textiles that had so long defined the European cloth trades.[9] New sources of textiles and indigenous fabrics represented opportunities for some producers, bringing exceptional profits to Asian trading companies, encouraging European imitation of Asian exemplars, and enabling shopkeepers and pedlars to sell more and different items to a range of consumers.[10] Fashion drove these innovations as Europe was more closely integrated into global networks of production and distribution.

TEXTILES AND CLOTHING—HOME AND AWAY

Production

China devised the techniques of silk production long before the Enlightenment. Thereafter, the lure of this fabric drew traders from Eurasia and beyond, bringing bales of cloth back along the Silk Road. Envy and ambition drove the diffusion of silk technology to India, Persia, and the Ottoman Empire until it ultimately arrived on the shores of medieval Sicily and thence crossed to Italy. Italian city-states competed for skilled artisans, convinced of the importance of cultivating mulberry trees and silk worms, and learning the technologies of silk spinning and weaving. These became prized additions to the Italian pantheon of trades.[11] Silk was immediately a contentious fabric, sparking repeated admonitions from clergy and city officials, barring its use through sumptuary edicts for all but the elites. The sheen, colors, and infinite textures of this cloth stirred anxieties among the authorities that legislated against visible innovations that visually blurred social boundaries. Silk was proscribed in Renaissance Florence for women's sleeves; silk ribbons could only be worn by middle ranked women if of a certain width. But regulations in towns like Siena relaxed somewhat as the local silk industry began to flourish. Sumptuary regulations were commonly issued and just as commonly defied.

At the same time, the silk industry diversified and its products multiplied.[12] Italian artisans developed enhanced spinning technology, resulting in thread that became renowned for its quality.[13] Italian silk dominated the European markets during the Renaissance era, a source of profits for landowners who planted mulberry trees, for gentlemen who invested in silk manufacturing and for thousands of non-guild (female) spinners and guild (male) weavers who crafted the products in cities and countryside. Merchants marketed all manner of silk cloth, clothing and accessories and the allure of these products swept Europe, representing over a third of all imports to the Low Countries in the late 1500s. An Italian contemporary explained that the silk industry enjoyed "very great privileges in all Italy . . . and deservedly so because it is a craft that exalts the rich and helps the poor; and great skills are needed to ply it."[14] Silk manufacturing remained a staple of Italian industrial life in many regions into the 1700s; yet Italian silk manufacturers faced intractable competitors in Europe who yearned to replicate their success in other locales.[15] Close study of the silk industry opens key questions of fashion in the Enlightenment Age.

The silk industry has been called "the spoilt child of mercantilism": petted and protected, the object of obsessive attention from ministers and kings, esteemed, some might argue, to a greater degree than it deserved.[16] Wherever mulberry trees could be grown, local authorities strived to transplant the silk trade, which rooted in France, Spain, the German territories as well as Italy long before the 1600s. Silk industries were nursed along in other regions with the use of imported silk thread and through stratagems to lure skilled hands to resettle in new locales. City guilds set the standards for manufacturing in most European kingdoms and also competed with each other as each developed local specialisms. They also sought to keep local skills within local bounds. But knowledge spread as people moved, like the French Huguenot and other Protestant refugees who fled France and the Southern Low Countries to relocate in German territories, the Netherlands, and England in the years around 1600. Later, in the 1680s, new waves of religious refugees fled from France, injecting new dynamism into textile industries in their newly adopted homelands. Many parts of Europe developed viable silk sectors that competed stubbornly with more naturally endowed regions.[17]

Silk making was treasured in all areas, generating a range of local goods including a variety of silk and mixed silk fabrics (sometimes combined with wool, linen, and cotton for cheaper and different visual and tactile effects). Silk ribbon and stocking making also burgeoned, as regional product lines, as well as the production of silk thread, braid and thread buttons specialities. In the 1600s, the areas around Cologne became known for their braid, organized outside city guild control by merchants who employed many hundreds of country folk in manufacturing silk and cotton braid.[18] Nondescript garments were elevated by a touch of braid at the wrist or pocket, while a copious application of braid produced a majestic effect. The dark silk velvet suit in Figure 2.1 provides a stunning contrast to the many meters of wide, finely worked braid on the coat and the more modest trim on the breeches.

The gleam of even small silk accessories attracted a growing range of buyers and manufacturers who were astute enough to innovate ever-changing stocks of goods. Others fashioned the most costly and exquisite fabrics for more notable clientele. But European manufacturers did not have a monopoly on the silk sold in European markets.

By the 1660s, the English East India Company (1600) and Dutch East India Company (1602) carried shiploads of textiles back to Europe; these adventurers were joined by the French East India Company (1664), the Danish East India Company (1616, 1670), the Ostend (Austrian) Company (1722), and the Swedish East India Company (1731). Trade with China initially focused on silk goods at the turn of the eighteenth century, while India provided masses of cotton goods, with only small quantities of silk. The arrival of Asian textiles in bulk was a catalyst for new tastes. And in the later seventeenth century these companies competed fiercely with each other, as tons of textiles were unloaded in European ports. Cottons came principally from the Indian subcontinent; while both India and China provided vast quantities of silks and mixed silk fabrics for European and

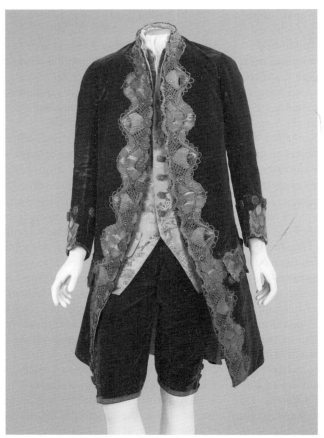

FIGURE 2.1: Italian silk velvet suit, with gold braid, c. 1740–60. The Metropolitan Museum of Art, New York.

colonial markets. Bengali silks became a fashion craze in the 1680s and Chinese silks also secured the devotion of shoppers. In 1681, the English East India Company emphasized the importance of capturing the fashion *zeitgeist*: "Know this for a constant and general rule, that in all flowered silks you change the fashion and flower as much as you can every year, for English ladies and they say the French and other Europeans will give twice as much for a new thing not seen in Europe before, though worse, than they will give for a better silk of the same fashion worn the former year."[19] European super-cargoes, charged with purchasing textiles in Asia, closely attended all news of rivals when based in Canton and struggled to secure the best quality products from local Chinese merchants.[20]

The fabric and accessories of a gown, suit, or *ensemble* were critical determinants of style—the cut of garments followed several basic formats and was not decisive in determining stylishness. Thus the materials making up a garment received the greatest attention and represented the greatest investment. As the varieties and quantities of textiles increased, tensions rose about the circulation of these commodities—every nation manoeuvred to secure advantage over their neighbors. Intermittent protectionist laws were instituted as European nations jousted one with the other. On occasion, governments enacted outright prohibitions of silks from elsewhere in Europe or applied high import duties. From the 1660s, official French policy was to promote French luxury trades and a series of regulations were passed to this end, combined with the tripling of duties on imported silk goods.[21] Intense rivalry prevailed in efforts to defend local industries and support national East India Companies. Importantly, there were also sharp internal conflicts within European countries, as local manufacturers lobbied against imported Asian goods. Guilds and civic bodies fought to establish precedence within their home markets in campaigns that continued into the 1720s. The French government made clear its priorities in the 1680s when they banned the importation of all Asian silks and cottons from their territories, part of their long-run mercantilist strategy to build and protect local manufactures.[22] French officials decided that French textile workers would meet the needs of fashion and utility, with regulated manufactures produced on French soil, employing French workers. Silks and cottons in the Asian style were now being made in Europe by this time, providing an added rationale for this legislation. But smugglers also flourished moving Indian calicoes to French and other buyers, defying legal constraints.[23] However, protectionism remained a lynchpin ideology of this era, mercantilism in action, epitomized by legislative bans enacted throughout Europe from the late seventeenth through the eighteenth centuries. Officials aimed to exclude Asian imports by fiat, beginning a contest between government, retailers and consumers that would persist for over a century until government regulations were finally repealed.[24]

The city of Lyon became the most important beneficiary of French policy. Its entrepreneurs were licensed to make a variety of silk fabrics such as those in the "Genoese style," or in the fashion of Bologna and Naples. An Italian immigrant, Octavio May, who settled in Lyon, discovered the techniques of creating lustrous taffetas, or "lustrings" as they became know in English, a variety that became a Lyonnais staple.[25] The skills required to produce the delicate thread, to design, and weave plain, patterned, brocaded or velvet cloth represented the height of textile technology and would generate continued mechanical innovations through the 1700s. With the political support of the French government, the Lyon silk industry became the byword of quality and fashion, feeding Parisian, French, and foreign markets through a complex cycle of designer/merchant/client interactions. Almost 40 percent of Lyon's population was involved in the silk industry in the 1780s,[26] a trade described by a contemporary as: "the nourishing mother of all the other manufactures . . . that this city of commerce encloses in its bosom. It sustains more than 15,000 workers, occupied solely with its products, and it brings to a hundred thousand merchants, manufacturers and artisans of all kinds, its benefits and bounty."[27]

The business of silk was not simply the provision of high cost luxury goods for the court of Versailles, as Lesley Miller cogently argues. Manufacturers in Lyon were divided almost equally between those who made plain goods, which relied on color and gloss for their appeal, and those who made patterned cloth. Moreover, the latter category was not dominated by magnificent brocaded fabrics alone, for many patterned goods were relatively quickly made, employing a well-used repertoire of visual motifs—stripes, spots, and floral—for everyday fabrics. But even everyday silks had to be à la mode. Large retailers in Paris were instrumental in relaying advice on current styles, with communications sent from Lyon manufacturers to Paris retailers six days a week. With advice from Paris, designers based in Lyon could then invent new patterns, or make minor changes in color or line to existing favorites in the hopes of commercial success. Manufacturers and retailers focused on creating new designs year in and year out, an exercise that built complementary specialist knowledge and employed extensive resources.[28] The Lyonnais silk industry is a case study in the dynamic connections between producers and retailers in the fashion trades, evident in many other sectors of the European textile and clothing industries, with manufacturers depending on timely and routine intelligence of market conditions and fashion trends. These relationships were critical to both sectors, building Lyon's reputation as a unique provider of fabrics in the latest style.[29]

Industrial espionage was also the lifeblood of Enlightenment era fashion industries. Artisans and machinery were secreted from one part of Europe to another throughout this period, in defiance of local regulation, to capture strategic advantage. Competition was endemic in this mercantilist era and entrepreneurs planned and plotted to produce local substitutes for popular foreign-made goods. Ribbons are a seeming trifle, but were a varied and essential decorative addition to many items of dress and furnishings. Figure 2.2 is an elegant confection, a small purse whose charm depended on the wreath of looped green ribbons encircling its borders.

Bows of ribbon also defined the look of shoes and headwear. Their popularity in all social circles explains the many disputes among producers competing hotly with each other.[30] A new piece of technology entered the scene in the later 1600s, called a ribbon frame, which dramatically affected production. This equipment enabled one handler to weave twelve and then twenty-four ribbons at a time, with striking results on the availability and cost of ribbons by the 1670s—threatening the traditional skills of ribbon weaving. Despite protests, the loom was widely employed in the Netherlands, especially in Haarlem and Amsterdam, creating a regional specialty in ribbons that dominated the European market for several generations. Inevitably, this "Dutch loom" or "Dutch engine"

FIGURE 2.2: Woven silk and metal thread purse with silk ribbon trimmings. French c. 1650–1700. © Victoria and Albert Museum, London.

was carried into other likely settings, at the behest of local or national governments and entrepreneurs. Silk ribbon making reached new heights by the eighteenth century and rolls of ribbon piled up high on shop shelves over this period becoming ever-cheaper, ever-present items in pedlars' packs and shopkeepers' stores. Ribbons in novel designs and colors were a constant lure to shoppers and the cry to "Show us some of your newest fashion Ribbonds" was heard in retail establishments across Europe.[31]

Haberdashers, drapers, mercers, general shopkeepers, and pedlars carried accessories like ribbon as a matter of course, items that would be more easily and repeatedly sold than large quantities of fabric. They were the ultimate "fast fashion" item in this period, as a new set of ribbons could quickly change a look with very little investment by the buyer. For all these reasons, manufacturers focused closely on innovations in the making of accessories. Knitted silk stockings were another staple fashion item. The English silk stocking knitting technology was increasingly successful over the 1600s, and the secrets of the trade were closely guarded. But inevitably competitors uncovered the technologies. In 1663, French authorities granted James Fournier a twenty-year monopoly to make knitted silk stocking "in the English style," with striking results. By the 1670s, his distribution through France was impressive and exports to Spain soared. Governments sponsored spies to investigate and extract information potentially useful to the development of their textiles sectors. In the 1750s, the expatriate Englishman John Holker brought back 115 samples of English fabric to his French employers: eight from London, the center of the Spitalfields' silk industry; eight from Norwich and Yorkshire, the centers of the worsted trade of light wool and mix-fiber cloths, and ninety-nine from Lancashire, home of the thriving cotton and cotton/linen industry. Both Norwich and London produced pure and mixed silk fabrics of some interest to French officials, but France's foremost focus was on the burgeoning cotton industry.[32] Authorities railed against the machinations of foreign competitors. Lyonnais silk manufacturers were certain, for example, that the use of sample books by traveling salesmen resulted in the piracy of their designs by foreign competitors, with resulting loss of sales. From the 1760s onwards, they campaigned to end the use of sample books and protect their investment in new designs.[33] Governments made every effort to stem the flight of skilled artisans to other jurisdictions—a migration often prohibited by law—and they denounced the stealthy extraction of technologies by foreign competitors. But "technology transfer" was unstoppable and the diffusion of skills persisted despite all the restrictions imposed by authorities. At the best, innovators who suffered the piracy of their inventions could hope for a time lag in the effective application elsewhere of their new systems of production.[34]

Artisans and entrepreneurs combined the pilfering of techniques with their own experimentation in the hope of producing greater quantities and more original commodities, at lower costs. In 1716, the English Lombe brothers successfully uncovered Italian spinning technology for the production of silk thread for knitted stockings. This knowledge was put to work back in Derby in the East Midlands of England, already the center of silk thread button making. The brothers spent several years building a water-powered mill that incorporated the Italian technology, opening their new spinning mill in 1721, one of the largest of its kind constructed at the tremendous cost of £30,000. The Lombe brothers were convinced that their investment would be profitable as there was such strong demand for silk thread for the stocking knitting industry and the cost of imported Italian thread was high. Their strategy paid off handsomely and presaged the new patterns of industrial production to come. The 300 men and women they employed heralded the growing scale of manufacturing that would redefine relationships of production. Matilda Hemming's rendition of the Derby mill in 1809, seen in Figure 2.3, celebrates the exceptional scale of this factory, contrasting this man-made edifice with the river that powered it.

The drive to produce silk thread—not cotton, linen, or wool—resulted in the first large-scale industrial mill and set the template for the industrial structures to follow later in the century.[35] Silk was a catalyst, hybrid commodity in many ways. At its finest, it was the stuff of royalty and nobility. But light silks, half silks, and accessories of every kind were also an occasional indulgence for many European middle-ranked and common folk, and it was this level of demand that inspired industrial innovation. There were many new indulgences for European consumers at this time. This period saw the wholesale transformation of European textile industries in response to shifting standards of taste, with new categories of light fabrics made of fine spun worsted wool, lighter fustians, and new kinds of linen cloths, plus the dramatic appearance of cottons from India. I focus here on the impact of silk textiles, with their powerful cultural associations of luxury and exclusive consumption. But silks were much more than this. They arose within a complex environment where fabric prices dropped from generation to generation in parts of Europe, an era of invention and experimentation, stimulated by the forces of global trade.[36]

FIGURE 2.3: *Silk mills, Derby*, Matilda Heming, 1809. © The Trustees of the British Museum.

Apart from knitting technologies, clothing manufacture did not undergo significant mechanical interventions until the mid-1800s. However, in Britain, technologies of clothing production did develop dramatically during our period of study. Thomas Parke Hughes defines the social and physical facets of technological systems as blending the force and talents of a range of occupations aimed at designing and controlling a "human-built world."[37] The ready-made clothing sector in the Enlightenment era exemplifies a new technological system—the large-scale manufacture of apparel to provision the military. The model of this development comes from Britain; but there are doubtless other ready-made sectors waiting to be uncovered. Government financed, this industry relied on networks of contractors and sub-contractors who employed tens of thousands of predominantly urban female workers to stitch shirts, waistcoats, trousers, and jackets for the navy and the military. The fabrics used in these garments were sourced from diverse textile industries. These were basic garments, not in themselves fashion items. Yet, these ready-made clothes came to define a community of mariners who amassed an exceptional cultural cachet over the 1700s, becoming "fashionable" plebeian men defined in part by their distinctive clothes. These garments were a striking contrast to tailor-made or seamstress made-to-measure apparel that was then the norm for most men and women. This ready-made trade was revolutionary in the relative uniformity of the garments. In this system, outworkers picked up their bundles of clothing pieces at central workshops where the pieces had been cut to pattern; workers were paid when they returned their completed garments in the time allotted. Tons of baled clothing were stockpiled at naval dockyards in Britain, to be shipped out for the seamen's use or to resupply British naval centers in the Mediterranean, Caribbean, and Indian Ocean.[38] This model of mass production, to set patterns, with distinct sizes, defined the new rational modes of making that arose in this era.

For the other social groups—high, middling, and low—clothing was acquired through a combination of made-to-measure and the re-making of apparel. All social classes resorted to these strategies, as the value of cloth demanded its careful use and reuse, whether a stunning silk brocade or hardwearing wool duffel. Elites were served by the finest tailors, who constructed, repaired, and remade gentlemen's and ladies' apparel; indeed, tailors enjoyed a monopoly of this trade in many parts of Europe. Informally, women also made garments to order or for general sale. But it was not until the later 1600s that this activity was formally approved in some precincts. In France and England, for example, seamstresses insisted on their right to supply women and children with garments and, in France, they were granted guilds approving their craft after 1675. The making of clothing was always a contested trade, with male workers seeking to exclude or minimize the presence of women in this essential occupation.[39] Girls of all ranks were routinely trained to the needle, an essential feminine skill. Poor girls would turn their hands to many types of needlework, often involving the making and mending of clothing. As domestic servants, they were called to make shirts and shifts, basic undergarments increasingly essential for all social ranks. As milliners' employees they stitched similar accessories either ready-made or to order. Others worked in the ready-made clothing trade, as described earlier. Some seamstresses developed reputations as reliable workwomen and built independent businesses in urban or rural communities, moving from house to house, constructing new wardrobe items and repairing old for clients on a seasonal cycle.

The provision of clothing involved a hierarchy of producers, men and women. They might be found in shops on the major streets of capital cities or in less respectable byways, serving distinctive communities of customers. Most villages boasted a local tailor. Genteel provincial residents would not commission jackets from such men, relying on metropolitan craftsmen for the cutting and construction of costly garments. But even genteel men needed breeches re-seated or tears repaired. Rural tailors often did as much repairing as they did making. Yet rural young workingmen ordered new pieces of clothing from village tailors, these customers having less refined tastes than local lords and ladies. In England, even laboring people acquired some new items of clothing, typically in late youth or early adulthood, when interest in self-presentation was at its height.[40] There were innumerable ways through which clothing could be acquired, new and second-hand, of high, middling or low quality. Hierarchies of skill and gender shaped the context in which clothes were made and the value assigned the makers. The Enlightenment era culminated with new scales of production of thread, cloth, and clothing, in ways that defined the burgeoning industrial age.

DISTRIBUTION

Cities provided luxuries, as well as new necessities, hosting specialist and general retailers unmatched by small towns or rural locales. But the influence of cities extended beyond their borders, with commercial penetration throughout the European countryside. This was a notable feature of urbanizing Europe. Access to retailing grew with the size of cities and the multiplication of commercial ventures in and through rural areas. Urban population densities increased in northern Italy, the Rhineland, northwest continental Europe, the south and Midlands of England, and the lowlands of Scotland. Europe's population rose from about 125 million in 1700 to 200 million in 1800, with seventeen cities of over 100,000 and both London and Paris stood at over half a million people in 1700, with London reaching one million in 1800.[41] These large conurbations powered trade, stimulating all aspects of retailing. Jan de Vries notes the diffusion of urban interests throughout the Dutch countryside, with basic retailing in even the smallest town.[42] By the late seventeenth century, there was also a clear hierarchy of retailers at work, from the largest Parisian *marchand mercier* on rue St Honoré, to the general shopkeeper in provincial Cheshire to essential pedlars who traveled to customers by foot across the countryside.[43] The quality of goods they offered varied sharply and pedlars could not carry the range of items stocked in large shops. But there were commonalities in the categories of goods on offer: accessories like ribbons, braid, and buttons; household wares like pillowcases, sheets, and draperies; and wares much in demand like pottery, tobacco, and tobacco pipes. These goods—clothing, domestic wares and ephemeral consumables—reflect distinct categories of consumption where dramatic material changes were underway. There was a routine intersection of retailing with webs of commerce enmeshing large distributors and small. Larger traders regularly employed pedlars, while small shopkeepers bought and sold from wealthier *confrère* and often took goods in exchange from pedlars if the deal was to their liking. At the lowest level of trade, street hawkers took goods on credit from shopkeepers at the start of the day, hoping to sell or barter new or used goods by the day's end, getting a small profit. Second-hand clothing figured as a mainstay in these negotiations. Trading old goods for new was a strategy widely employed at all levels of retailing that stimulated sales.

Over the course of the eighteenth century, the penetration of fashionable items extended well beyond the middle classes in many parts of Europe, as new standards of material behavior evolved. For example, poor men and women in the Netherlands enjoyed access to coffee, tea, sugar, and Indian cottons in marked ways. Proximity to major shipping and smuggling routes, as well as interactions with cities and towns shaped material opportunities.[44] Regional patterns of consumption were also clearly influenced by culture and economy—in England, for example, those leaving probate inventories in Cornwall owned different and fewer goods than those living in the southeast county of Kent, so close to London and major ports. South of Barcelona, in rural Spain, peasants likewise displayed distinct material habits "regardless of income," with selective, increased acquisition of products. Material changes occurred slowly, argues Belén Moreno, with the most notable changes in material goods evident among the peasantry living close to towns or cities.[45] Most notably, there were broad investments in both domestic fittings and in apparel. These new priorities offered opportunities for a variety of retailers and in some instances encouraged the development of distinct trades. Both were shaped by fashion and culture. Major consumer changes often appeared first in household goods, like soft furnishings, and arose next in clothing. Attention to one sector illuminates the other.

The structures of early modern homes altered over time, particularly in northwest Europe. Sleeping quarters became more specialized spaces and beds received greater investment. Between 1690 and 1719, feather beds were found in over 60 percent of probate inventories from Kent, a relatively wealthy English county, while in poorer Cornwall only 28 percent of inventories listed these high-quality types of beds. Quantities of linen sheets also varied markedly at this time with 86 percent of Kentish households noting the purchase and use of sheets, while only 15 percent of Cornish households followed suit.[46] Clearly, the opportunities for retailers in Kent were much more robust than in Cornwall. Locality mattered. But changes percolated through all areas of Europe, even as local populations prioritized their options. In the Enlightenment era, Catalan peasantry invested increasing amounts of money in household textiles in preference to spending on their clothing—bedspreads, tablecloths, towels, and sheets were acquired in lavish amounts, speaking to the distinct ways in which the home expressed status or celebrated lineage. Some Catalan peasant inventories listed over forty sheets, acquired from shops or pedlars, reflecting a conscious fashioning of the domestic. Even the poorest Catalan peasant owned more sheets than shirts; while the middling and wealthy peasants owned more than two and three times the number of sheets than shirts.[47] The material concerns of this rural community were clear and it is vital to recognize the consuming priorities of discrete communities.

Figure 2.4, offers an artistic representation of a deathbed scene in a modest British dwelling c. 1800. All the material elements depicted here are worth careful attention. White linens are evident everywhere, from bedding to head-coverings. Check curtains frame the window. Order and comfort are exemplified in the everyday textiles maintained by these women, whether family or servants. This artist deploys the furnishings, as well as the clothing, as cultural products, epitomizing the expected material standards of even modest British families.

New sensibilities proliferated through the long eighteenth century. In this respect, the use of textiles in the production of meanings in domestic environments is surely as significant as the crafting of personal appearance.[48] Upholsterers initially appeared in European capitals like Paris, Amsterdam, and London, where they consulted with clients preoccupied with the design and construction of items like beds and bedding.[49] The numbers in this trade grew in conjunction with cultural and material importance of home embellishment, with upholsterers becoming a feature even of smaller towns.[50] Women found a niche in the furniture trade, employing their knowledge of textiles, trim, and décor, skills often acquired in the making of apparel. Specialist trades in cabinet-making

FIGURE 2.4: *Cottage interior, deathbed scene*, William Johnstone White, c. 1804–10, pen and ink and watercolor. © The Trustees of the British Museum.

and upholstery expanded to feed an increasing appetite for goods that might be opulent, tasteful, or merely comfortable, as social ambition and resources allowed.[51] Figure 2.5 is a trade card of George Miller, a Southampton upholsterer, appraiser, and auctioneer, his card showcasing the delights of fashionable settings, the bedroom being very much a semi-private space.

Silk furnishings were particularly sumptuous additions to domestic life that would lend a dazzling reflective lustre by daylight or by candlelight. The wealthy employed tens of meters of silk fabric in *sets* of objects, to demonstrate rank and status (real or aspirational).[52] But even wealthy families acquired goods in prosaic ways, through the second-hand circulation of items bought at auctions or through second-hand dealers, as suggested in George Miller's trade card. A wealthy Glasgow merchant who died in 1755 owned copious amounts of bed linen at the time of his death, many embroidered with initials, none of which matched those of his family members. These were likely acquired at household auction similar to the one that dispersed his housewares to other buyers. At least fifty-five people attended another auction of a Glasgow merchant in 1786, with

FIGURE 2.5: *George Miller, upholsterer, appraiser, and auctioneer,* engraved by Morrison and Clark, Moorfields, London. Courtesy of the Lewis Walpole Library, Yale University.

almost half the attendees buying small lots of second-hand linen.[53] Retailers of various kinds were essential to supply the items needed for magnificent, fashionable, or simply comfortable homes. The Catalan example, noted earlier, also prompts us to recognize the breadth of interest in remodeling domestic spaces and the range of manufacturers and retailers involved in provisioning Europe's diverse householders.

There is not necessarily a firm divide between textiles employed for the home and those used for clothing. Indeed, the check curtains portrayed in Figure 2.4 might well be used in aprons, men's shirts, or other garments that became markers of status and occupation. This fabric was one of the linen and cotton/linen fabrics made throughout Europe in ever-wider quantities. There were many general and specialist shopkeepers who sold goods and fabrics for both purposes. Linen, linen/cotton, and cotton textiles were sold ever more widely over this period, to dress the home and the body. The preeminent purpose of these fabrics was to exhibit cleanness and whiteness in household and body linens. Habits of hygiene changed during our period, initially among the elites, with increasing emphasis placed on techniques of laundering to ensure continuing whiteness. Clothing was the most visible, mobile, interactive system signaling mastery of new cultural standards and, understandably, received the most attention among commentators and retailers. A panoply of trades were involved in this social "invention of linen,"[54] beginning with those spinning the linen thread, weaving the fine or mid-weight cloth, bleaching of the fabrics, selling the bolts at linen markets, followed by the dissemination of these textiles through retail networks. Once launched along the retail chain, there were other sets of hands employed to make the shirt, hem the handkerchief, or embellish the linen cap covering a woman's head. The purchase and use of these goods were shaped by new cultural priorities as each generation learned the "regulatory system for instinctual acts, [where] clothes constantly served to express and enunciate the norms."[55] Once the garment or accessory was acquired there were also recurring interventions to wash, blue, or starch the linens, skilled intercessions inside or outside the household, to help materialize the ideal. Whiteness was not easily maintained.

Clothing was worn within discrete cultural contexts and fitted within systems of politeness, deference, and compliance. Urban residents in particular required appropriate instruction in the use of apparel, plus the supporting services to achieve sartorial standards for social, working, and religious lives. Differences in knowledge as well as differences in the quality of garments marked social divides. Domestic servants, shopkeepers, their assistants and apprentices, and specialist tradeswomen needed familiarity with the evolving norms of hygiene among the nobility and middle ranks. Mrs. Grosvenor was celebrated for her laundering skills and the client she served, being "Laundry Woman to the [British] Queen." The print produced in the second half of the eighteenth century, Figure 2.6, shows some of the tools of her trade; but it also demonstrates her participation in these processes as her apparel is spotless.

Order is expressed in her dress and her occupation. Instructional books provided guidance and were important ancillary factors shaping the distribution and use of apparel. Instruction also circulated through training and the power of influential figures within communities. There was a growing cohesion in the priorities, as outlined by this 1740 French guide. "Propriety being a certain fitness of the clothes to the person . . . it is necessary to fit our clothes to our form, our condition and our age . . . for if your clothes are clean, and especially if your linen is white, there is no need to be richly dressed: you will feel your best, even in poverty."[56] The trade of laundering figures centrally in the functioning of apparel and household linens and the application of soap, bluing, and starch should be considered as important in the material dynamics of the Enlightenment Age as the selling of commodities. Only through routine repeated laundering was the purpose of linens achieved. Great and middle ranked urban households directed their servants to the task, aware that there was a differentiation in skill required in the washing and care of sheets, fine linens, or fragile lace-trimmed caps. Sending great bundles of linen to be washed at a family estate was a feature of elite life. Laundry was also dispatched from thousands of small apartments or one-room lodgings. Along with specialist textile shops of all description, large European cities were filled with laundries where anonymous legions of women worked to remake dirty into clean. Linen was even sent from the colonies to be washed in Paris. Figure 2.7 is an early nineteenth-century jigsaw puzzle, German made, presenting the interior of a respectable laundry where women and children labored in the endless pursuit of whiteness.

FIGURE 2.6: *Mrs. Grosvenor, Laundry Woman to the Queen*, anonymous three quarter portrait, c. 1750–1800. © The Trustees of the British Museum.

This children's game confirms moral and aesthetic lessons that by this date were internalized through much of European society.

Daniel Roche calculates that approximately 250,000 shirts needed laundering every day in Paris later in the eighteenth century, as the numbers of garments per person increased and the social compulsion for cleanliness took hold. Naturally, linens proliferated among the wealthy during this period; but Roche also traced the growing numbers of linen and cotton items purchased by shopkeepers, artisans, and the wage earning classes, with a notable switch to cheaper cotton fabrics in their apparel over the 1700s.[57] The clothing pawned with George Fettes, in York in the late 1770s, likewise shows the arrival of cotton clothing and the significance of both cotton and linen apparel among the working poor and lower middle ranked clients.[58] This larger population now employed a wider range of clothing, with their own sartorial standards. The behavior of John Sauley Eyres suggests the changing sensibilities even among the laboring classes. One morning in the spring of 1746, Eyres was finishing up a night of work with his grandfather on the River Thames, where they worked for the East India Company shifting cargo from ship to shore. Eyres was on his way home "for some clean Linnen" when he was press ganged into the British navy.[59] The naming of this priority survives by chance, but encourages us

FIGURE 2.7: Jigsaw puzzle, "Die Wasch und Büglstube" (The washing and ironing room), anonymous, early nineteenth century. © The Trustees of the British Museum.

to think of the many who valued not only shirts, but also clean shirts, as a foundation of everyday manly comfort and display.

WRAP-UP

I end this chapter with the most vivid and culturally fluid accessory of the Enlightenment Age, the handkerchief. Handkerchiefs were ubiquitous, framing gestural displays with a wave, an extended hand, in the taking of snuff. Snuff taking marked aesthetic refinement, with scripted motions, etiquette and accoutrements signaling a privileged standing. The delicate pinch of snuff, followed by the deft use of a white handkerchief (or temporarily white handkerchief) was part of the theater of consumption, differentiating gentleman from plebeian. A polite sneeze climaxed the performance; the soiled once-white handkerchief was soon replaced with another equally white, the whole cycle of snuffing, sneezing, and handkerchief an illustration of elite resources that combined the cultural value of snuff and symbolic importance of white linen handkerchiefs to social ends. European linen came in many varieties and the finest was used to construct cambric or batiste handkerchiefs, edged in lace or embroidered for effect. These accessories served rhetorical and functional purposes, profiting many. Their manufacture was a source of profit for linen makers from the Rhineland to the Low Countries, from northern France to the lowlands of Scotland and beyond. Milliners produced fanciful confections to satisfy discerning customers. The creation of handkerchiefs employed the needle of gentlewomen or their servants, to serve as gifts for many purposes. Handkerchiefs figured as plot devises in a plethora of literary and theatrical texts, so assured were writers of readers' intimate knowledge of these objects and their fluid meanings. The qualities of the handkerchiefs attested to character of the hero or heroine.[60]

This era also saw the proliferation of new-style handkerchiefs carried in vast cargoes from India: printed, painted, checked, or striped (Figure 2.8).

Patterned India cotton handkerchiefs became emblematic of long-distance mariners, the spoils of their private trade, and a sign of their cosmopolitan lives. Handkerchiefs circulated as ubiquitous smugglers' wares, readily sold at taverns or docksides, a bright and colorful addition to men's or women's attire. The fictional Molly Milton, oyster

MOLLY MILTON, the PRETTY OYSTER WOMAN.

FIGURE 2.8: *Molly Milton, the Pretty Oyster Woman*, published by Carington Bowles, 1788, after Robert Dighton. © The Trustees of the British Museum.

woman, framed her notable charms with a brightly patterned handkerchief, with a white cloth at hand to mop up after customers. She is clearly a denizen of the port community, admired by men of several ethnicities, her evident sexuality heightened by her choice of attire. Women like Molly, living in ports, had access to the gleanings from maritime men, among whom handkerchiefs were a favorite. These accessories also served as carrying devises, holding precious contents for those who would feel the cost of their loss. The patterned handkerchief, stuffed with a person's worldly goods, became symbolic of plebeian material culture, the handkerchief an essential tool and a favored addition to many forms of dress by men and women. The resale of handkerchiefs stolen by enterprising pickpockets shocked visitors to less salubrious areas of London about 1800, a sort of business that flourished in many cities and ports, and served a less squeamish clientele, as the demand for handkerchiefs was boundless. Handkerchiefs are a fitting wrap-up to this chapter. They illustrate the dynamics of European textile production, the impact of international commerce and the ways and means by which new-style textiles and clothing were acquired by women and men of many ranks and interests. The systems of making, trade and use defined the age.

CHAPTER THREE

The Body

ISABELLE PARESYS

In the engraving entitled *The Modern Venus, or a Lady of the Present Fashion in the State of Nature* (1786) we see the depiction of a pair of vastly outsized female buttocks and breasts. According to the subtitle of the print, "This is the Form, if we believe the Fair/Of which our Ladies are, or wish they were" (Figure 3.1).

The printmaker was satirizing the fashionable puffed-out and puffed-up silhouette of Western Europe in the mid-1780s: however, the dressed female body was reaching the end of a race towards an artificially inflated silhouette that had begun in the Renaissance, a tendency also apparent in the exaggerations of male fashion, such as the high hair of the macaroni and high heels of male courtiers. Despite the satirical nature of this print, however, it underlines very well how much the fashionable garment reshaped the natural body. From the late Middle Ages, dress built an artificial and sometimes spectacular look that created a substitute for the natural physical outline. Once clothed, the body of cloth turned out to be even more flexible than the body of flesh. This fashionable body was always cultural: it revealed the relationship that Western peoples had with their physicality. But it also drew the "social being" into the world: dress is the envelope that enables the human body to be seen on the social stage and that defines its identity (age, gender, job, religion) and also the sense of its belonging to a given hierarchy, from the prince to the field worker. Clothes also adorned the body, protected it from cold and heat, and safeguarded—or exhibited—its intimacies.

Surviving in part now in private or public collections, old clothes are relics of the bodies that wore them but that have long since vanished, for the relationship of dress to the body is always intimate. Most of these garments are elegant items that belonged to the well to do, because everyday clothing and also the garments of the lower orders were so well worn and reused that they were literally turned to rags. Nevertheless, these extant clothes are a conservatory of the techniques of hand stitching and of the inventiveness regarding the underwear and underpinnings that reshaped the human anatomy. They often retain patches of human fluids (sweat, for example), the lines of the wear made by the friction of gestures, or the pleats of bodily movement. They may also give us an idea of their wearer's size. For example, the eighteenth-century bodices and stays in the collection of the Colonial Williamsburg Foundation (USA) have waistlines ranging from 21½ inches to 34 inches, with an average of slightly over 25 inches.[1] It must be noted, however, that these are the surviving examples—they are not proofs of the generality or the norm. All of these silent but eloquent testimonies give an emotional presence to the body that once dwelled in these garments that survive from the past.

This chapter will attempt to redraw this cultural history of body and clothing, presenting an overview of what was significant in the relationship between the body and

FIGURE 3.1: *A Modern Venus, or a Lady of the Present Fashion,* unknown artist, after Miss Hoare of Bath (possibly Mary Hoare, 1744–1820), engraving, 1786. The New York Public Library.

dress between 1650–1800 and what took place to create a new and more modern culture of dressing. While the emphasis is on French examples, this is justified in this case because France was a leader of fashion at the time and its rapidly changing sartorial styles, sustained by a vigorous textile industry and state support, were diffused over much of the Western world. The essay first explains how fashionable clothes, as extensions of the body, re-shaped it, sometimes in extravagant ways. Then it examines the mechanics of underwear that sustained these metamorphoses of the body, and how fashion was a matter of bodily deportment within society. Finally, it addresses how the fashioned body became an important matter of health in the eighteenth century and how the fashionable silhouette evolved towards more ease and liberty.

RE-SHAPING THE PHYSICAL BODY

How did the fashionable silhouette evolve from the 1660s? This is not the place to enumerate the various styles and the names of the garments that appeared and disappeared.

Many books of costume and fashion history present this in detail. Let us rather consider the major principles of the re-shaping of the body by the fashionable garment that pushed the dressed figure to extreme limits. These principles were unchanged from the Renaissance, and are distinguished by the increase of volumes in the clothing and its tight fit. Both come together in particular ways to shape the outline of the dressed body over the course of the long eighteenth century.

The increase of the volume of clothes is certainly the most noticeable characteristic of the long period that runs from the late Middle Ages through to the end of the nineteenth century, over the course of time becoming gendered as a particularly female practice. The spectacular extension of the female hips by the adoption of a very wide petticoat created the basic distinction between female and male appearance. The further basis of this distinction was of course the visibility of the legs; men had begun to show their legs for the first time on a regular basis in early fourteenth-century Burgundy. Just as divided lower garments (breeches, then later trousers following the French Revolution) became the sign of male dressing, so the hoop petticoat of the "fair sex" became an icon of fashion in the Age of Enlightenment. Later, the three-piece suit became so for men. From the 1620s to the end of the seventeenth century, fashionable women's gowns had given up the Renaissance "farthingale" and moved towards a more natural line, with simple pleated skirts and a narrow-waisted bust. The exception were the ladies of the Spanish and Portuguese courts, who in the 1660s still wore an impressive half-round and elongated farthingale called the *guardinfante*. English and French courtiers were not overly happy with these "monstrous machines" and thought that they made women ugly, even the bodies of their new queens, Catherine of Braganza and Marie-Thérèse d'Autriche.[2] Around 1670, the fashionable French-waisted and open-front *manteau* (mantua) spread the volumes of its tails towards the buttocks, and was elongated by a massive train when worn at court. The sack-back gown or *robe volante*, born from an informal *négligé* as the mantua was at first, was to dethrone it in the beginning of the eighteenth century. Unfitted at both front and back, this loose flowing dress had a bell shape because of a hooped petticoat underneath. Becoming an open robe by the 1730s, and more tailored, this *robe à la française* dominated European formal female dress of this century, with its famous *paniers* distributing the volume of the skirt over the hips on each side like butterfly wings. However, a tight-fitting gown deriving from the mantua was developed in England and became known as the *robe à l'anglaise*, being very fashionable until late in the century, and worn over a hip pad that distributed the excess skirt material to the back.[3] Such a dress was widely worn in France and England but could never be considered full court dress.

Men's garments also had a propensity to inflate the body. The French *galant homme* (fop) of the 1660s wore under his short, bolero-like "doublet," a set of loose "petticoat breeches" (*la rhingrave*), trimmed with many ribbons. This fashion was perceived as too effeminate and immodest in some countries, as in the anti-French England of Charles II, where men generally preferred to wear a simpler outfit. The three-piece suit was taken up there by the king himself from 1666, and would become widely adopted in Europe.[4] Its long vest-waistcoat was worn over narrower breeches and under a coat whose French name was *le justaucorps*, meaning that this outfit was better shaped to the natural body. Indeed, the French *élégants*, who later adopted this coat, preferred a tighter-fitting item (Figure 3.2).

Male fashion, however, soon reintroduced volume into its repertoire: firstly, a full pleated and flaring skirt under the tightly fitted body of the coat, which made a sort of small "*panier*" on the hips, before being given up in the second half of the eighteenth century for a more fitted look. Later in the century, padding was sometimes introduced,

FIGURE 3.2: *Seconde chambre des Appartements*, 1694, Antoine Trouvain. Playing cards in the second room of the apartments of Louis XIV, among the guests, Maria Anna of Bourbon-Conti, Grand Dauphin Louis, Julius Henry III of Bourbon-Conde, Anna of Bavaria and Louis Joseph de Bourbon-Vendom. Photo: Getty Images DEA/G. DAGLI ORTI.

and the new fashionable waistcoat that was slightly plump signified health and prosperity. On a woman, the volume of textiles covered her legs and modesty, transforming the lower part of her body into a base that showed to advantage its higher part, particularly the breasts, *décolletage*, and neck. Male clothes, on the other hand, were shorter, and visually increased the length of the legs.

At the same time, both men and women were engaged in a search for a vertical extension of the fashionable body. They used complicated hairstyles and high heels that became vertiginous and spectacular. Fashion set a new model for those who could afford not to engage in any manual activity. Paintings, prints, and museum collections testify to the craze for high-heeled shoes, which reached their maximum size in the eighteenth century (although the platforms or *pianelle* of the Renaissance had been higher still). In the 1740s, in France, it was not uncommon for a man to wear shoes with heels two inches high; by the 1780s, heels were so high that ladies of fashion sometimes had to use walking sticks.[5] While the effect of high heels was to stretch the body downwards and forwards, some extraordinary hairstyles spread it upwards. Men had adopted long hair in the seventeenth century, wearing a wig when the fashion was for thick curly hair. Some commentators claimed this was an allusion to the fine hair of the youthful Louis XIV, although this cannot be proven. Late in the seventeenth century, the French court brought into fashion new heavy-bottomed wigs, and also the habit of powdering them. The periwig became bulkier above the forehead, where it divided into two points from the 1690s. This male silhouette matched well that of women, who in the 1680s had adopted the so-called *fontanges*, a scaffold of curls over the forehead surmounted by several "fences" or stiff, upright rows of costly lace, building the hair up into a tower (see Figure 3.2). From the late 1760s, towering coiffures for both sexes reappeared, including the "sugar loaf" wigs of the English maraconi, the wide hair with large ostrich feathers worn by women in the mid-1770s, or ballooning caps or "poufs" for women in the 1780s. All of these complicated hairstyles were objects of a wild graphic satire, as with other clothing extravagances.[6]

Extensions of the hip were not only the expression of a visual performance of dress, they also had the aim of contrasting with a torso that was itself adjusted by clothing. Indeed, the torso was perhaps the main part of the body where the western dress code worked to shape the natural anatomy. With the insertion of whalebone within the bodice or with boned stays as underwear, clothes could themselves exert pressure. This pressure became a real constraint on the female body, pushing it away from its natural lines so that the quest for a slender waist, a curvilinear torso, and a high bosom were the aesthetic ideals until the end of the eighteenth century. This enthusiasm for the corset was not reserved solely for the idle social elite: well-dressed servants, farmers, artisans, and tradespeople came to share these styles.[7] Nor were tight-fitting garments the sole preserve of female fashions. From the middle of the century, when the waistcoat shortened and the baggy breeches were given up for a slimmer male silhouette, some of the silk culottes fit so tightly over the male anatomy that it was said that one could easily read there the intentions of a wearer towards an attractive woman. The Comte d'Artois's fashionable English-style chamois leather breeches were so tight that four lackeys were needed to help him put them on, and it was claimed that some men were lowered into their riding breeches.[8]

At the end of the eighteenth century, there was a move towards a more natural look. The body began touching the margins of dress, with a slimmer *silhouette*, a French word in fact, which appeared at the very same time as the homonymous medium for drawing portraits.[9] The trend began in the latter third of the century, with the search for a more comfortable and lighter garment for both men and women. Numerous factors were at work. The spread in Europe of the new lighter silk and cotton fabrics (even for those in the middling and lower orders)[10] that were less stiff than the luxurious fabrics previously worn by the rich, or the heavy hemp and serge clothes worn by rural folk in the countryside, was one major influence. The impact on the European elites of the English fashions that were more informal in character than the French also hastened the search for a more natural body. This was further heightened by the vogue for Greek Antiquity and its draperies, which started mid-century in the areas of architecture and furniture design, but became more pronounced in dress fashions from 1770. A garment that was particularly symbolic of this tendency was the "chemise" gown, a new type of simple dress with a high waist that was influenced by neo-classical design. During the French Revolution (1789–99), this enthusiasm for Antiquity encountered the ideals of liberty, republicanism and democracy, which brought ramifications in dress. A revolutionary law of October 29, 1793, for example, allowed every citizen to wear the clothes he or she wanted, regardless of their social standing, except to adopt the clothes of the other sex.[11] Although the dress of this period adopted a relative simplicity, and was indicative of a slow move towards the autonomy of the female body, we should not forget the mechanics of the underwear that had previously controlled the female silhouette.

THE MECHANICS OF UNDERWEAR

Many ingenious techniques of extension or constraint of the dressed body were mobilized to build the fashionable looks of the eighteenth century. Associated with the cutting and sewing of cloth—in Western dress practices, the more that clothes were adjusted to the body, the more elaborate became the cutting techniques—and the effects of fabric and ornament, a whole mechanics of underwear contributed to the making of the visual performance of fashionable dress, a performance that was also a bodily one. Let us explore this through three emblematic types of undergarment: the shift or shirt (terms used interchangeably here), the corset, and the petticoat.

The long shift that descended to the knees was the item of clothing that enjoyed the closest contact with the body (Figure 3.3). This was so intimate that in eighteenth-century France, wearing a shirt was conceptually similar to being stripped naked (the term in French is *nu en chemise*—naked in the chemise).[12] The white muslin *robe-chemise* of the late eighteenth century was thus linked to a sense of nudity, explaining its very common appearance in the erotic paintings and print culture of the period. From the Renaissance,

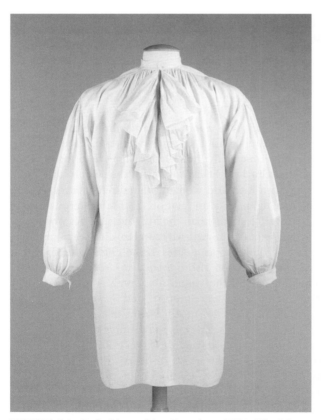 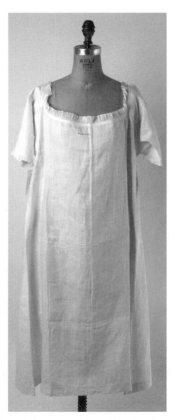

FIGURE 3.3: Left: Linen shirt, French, c. 1780. The Metropolitan Museum of Art, New York. Right: Chemise (linen and cotton), American, c. 1780. The Metropolitan Museum of Art, New York.

body linen had become increasingly visible, emerging mainly in the collar and at the wrists. If the ruff had disappeared, from the 1650s linen and lace variants of male neckwear, such as large cravats for example, substituted for its "orthopaedic offices." Precious lace and the overflowing of underwear also became accessories of finery in the feminine wardrobe, seen at low-cut necks, cuffs, or forearms. For both men and women, linen highlighted the relationship between clothing and flesh, and demarcated the limits of both. Made of fine linen or cotton batistes, this underwear had to be as white as possible. This meant that the cleanliness of the body was directly related to the change of shirt that often took the place of washing with water.[13] As Georges Vigarello so famously put it, "The Enlightenment was linen." He emphasized that it was the management of the body wiped with cloth, sometimes scented, and the regular changing of the shift, that announced one was "proper" (propre being the French for "clean"). It was therefore important to own several shifts (and stockings) to enable a change every day. The underwear of the elite was of the finest fabrics, softer than that worn by those of more modest means. The lower orders wore heavy and rough shifts woven of hemp, though from the seventeenth century these were owned in increasing numbers.[14] It is for these reasons—linen's intertwined significations of propriety, cleanliness, civility, and status—that in eighteenth-century Canada, the way the Amerindians wore and adopted European shirts frightened European travelers. The former wore worn dirty shirts, slopped with vermilion colors, that were even threadbare, these being signs of appropriation and valorisation within native cultural systems. To Europeans, this was perceived as a sign of savagery and proved the very necessity to civilize them.[15]

The basic function of the shift was to protect the naked body from the clothes worn on top. For a woman, it also protected her skin from the pressure exerted by the whalebones (baleen, from the mouth of baleen whales) that were inserted into the bodice of her dress, or by the boned stays worn as underwear (Figure 3.4). The stays were either laced at the back, or at the front with a stomacher pinned under or over the lacing. Hand-stitched and demonstrating more and more elaborate techniques—as the patterns of the famous Diderot and d'Alembert Encyclopedia (1767) or Garsault's Art du tailleur/Art of tailoring (1769) indicate—the century of "Reason" also went to work upon the materiality and the inventive production of clothing.[16] Stays were adapted by the stay-maker to the client's body, and to different uses and varying degrees of comfort. Pregnancy, for example, might require a different level of constraint, as might riding or breast-feeding; court dress required a very stiff corset. We can fairly assume that when sold on the second-hand market—so important a source of dress for everyday people—the already worn corsets would have lost some of their stiffness. Stiff corsets could, however, be reinforced by the introduction of an elaborate fan of boning, further aided by a busk. This was a single strip of wood, horn, metal or whalebone, inserted into a sleeve at the front of the stays to keep the torso straight. Often given as a love gift, busks could be carved and painted, and ornamented by a personal message that the woman kept intimately close (Figure 3.5).

In the mid-seventeenth century, the shoulder straps of the stays were positioned off the shoulders for a fashionably low neckline, echoed by the bodice worn on top. This style encouraged an upright posture and forced the chest forwards. One century later, stay-makers had developed sophisticated skills of boning, stitching the bones into directional channels that could press the torso into a fashionable cone shape, boosting the breasts and throwing the shoulders behind. From around 1828, the invention of metal eyelets to reinforce the lacing holes allowed women to be even more tightly laced.[17]

FIGURE 3.4: Red stays, side hoop, and linen shift, English. Hoop, 1778; shift, 1730–60; stays 1770–90. © Victoria and Albert Museum, London.

Although the light and white muslin female silhouette of the very late years of the eighteenth century seem to do without corsets, the reality was probably different. Certainly, at least some women needed a kind of bodice or early form of *brassière*, or softly boned stays to smooth their flesh and push up their breasts to achieve a fluid and slender look.

If the painters of the Age of Enlightenment praised a naked plump female form, the fashioned body disregarded the natural curvatures to define an outline modeled in two conical halves. The scale of the bottom cone emphasized the visual effect of a slim waist, one of the criteria of beauty. The upper, inverted cone was placed above an ever-widening volume of skirt that from the beginning of the eighteenth century increasingly outgrew the legs and hips beneath it. This was a fashion with economic repercussions: it thwarted the fall in the price of materials by multiplying the quantities of fabric that were used.[18] At the English court in the 1740s, the narrow oblong hoop petticoat could be six feet across at its widest point (Figure. 3.6).

FIGURE 3.5: Stay busk made from wood, eighteenth century. The Metropolitan Museum of Art, New York.

Enlarged *paniers* like this were the rule in the European courts, and the gowns worn on top required up to twenty-five meters of luxurious fabrics. In England, immured in sartorial traditions, court dress held on to the hoop and mantua until 1820, even as they became ludicrously old-fashioned elsewhere.[19] In their heyday, however, various types of hoop petticoats coexisted and several types of support were used to bolster the skirts. The largest, in the eighteenth century, were very like the Spanish farthingale of the Renaissance, with an underskirt reinforced with graduated wicker, willow, or whalebone hoops. From the mid-century, shorter *paniers* appeared. Some of them had the shape of two whalebone bags tied one either side of the waist (pocket hoops). Others were built with a system of metal hoops held together by strips of fabric, articulated with hinges that allowed the large skirt to be pulled upwards when entering a doorway or sitting down in a wing chair or in a coach (Figure 3.7).[20] In the 1780s a stuffed bum roll, called a *cul* (bottom) in French, meant the volume of the skirt moved towards the back. These were reminiscent of the horse-hair bottoms from the end of the seventeenth century, required for gowns with trains

FIGURE 3.6: Court dress, c. 1750, British. The Metropolitan Museum of Art, New York.

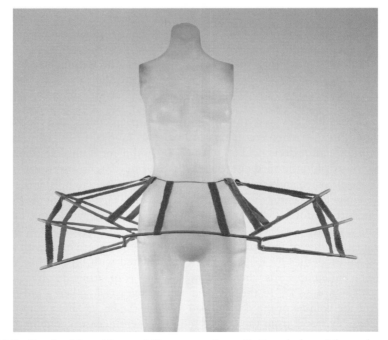

FIGURE 3.7: *Panniers*/hinged hoops (silk, cane, and metal), French, late eighteenth century. The Metropolitan Museum of Art, New York.

FIGURE 3.8: Pair of pockets, England, 1700–25. © Victoria and Albert Museum, London.

Pairs of tie-on and detachable pockets, rather like bags, were worn under the skirt and accessed through slits in the overdress (Figure 3.8). Women placed their various small artifacts (scissors, handkerchiefs, coins, letters, miniature portraits) that were key to their experience of interiority and privacy. As women did not usually wear any drawers (legged underwear) and as a consequence of their position close to the body, pockets also suggested an intimacy.[21] However, under the light fabrics draping the body dressed by the new neo-classical fashion, these tie-on pockets would disturb the required sculptural effect, so small *reticules*, or purses, that were carried in the hands began to replace them. The reticule could become a little work of art: some of mesh, others cloth, some elaborately worked, and others even shaped like pineapples, or—influenced by the contemporary fad for Chinoiserie—little pagodas (Figure 3.9). Square sack-like "handbags" do appear before this date, made of brocaded silks for the rich, but they seem to have been much less common.

The female body was certainly more controlled and constrained by the mechanics of underwear than was the male, but men also had plenty of tricks to shape their form. In the first half of the eighteenth century, the fashionable male coat had pleated skirts stiffened with an interlining made of woven horsehair and buckram (stiffened linen or cotton) (Figure 3.10). A small cushion of hair could be placed at the point where the folds fell. Padding and quilting at the upper part of the coat could also amplify the importance of the man's stomach or chest, depending on the focus of changing fashions. In the 1740s, for instance, the male stomach achieved prominence—literally—and the stylish belly was convex and rounded. In the 1770–80s, the focus shifted to a flat stomach

FIGURE 3.9: Reticule (silk, cotton, and metal), British, first quarter of the nineteenth century. The Metropolitan Museum of Art, New York.

but instead emphasized the chest. Some men of the late eighteenth century were even laced into stays; many military uniforms of the early nineteenth century provide a proof of this practice.[22] When intended to correct bodily shortcomings—supplying by art what nature had withheld—padding had to be discreet. In the case of insufficiently sturdy legs, for instance, the calves—sheathed in silk stockings—were sometimes plumped out with wool.[23]

Such mechanics of underwear were the delight of satirists, who produced pamphlets and wild graphic satire within the context of an expanding press that flourished in the eighteenth century. There was particularly intense activity in England and France, but the Low Countries too were important centers of printing and graphic satire, as were the

FIGURE 3.10: Detail of coat, showing pleated skirts stiffened with an interlining of woven horsehair and buckram, and a layer of unspun wool, probably French, 1740–49. © Victoria and Albert Museum, London.

German states and principalities.[24] The satirists were quick to denounce distortions of the body engendered by the fashions that some considered extravagant. The hoop petticoat, corsets, big hair, and perukes, and hats and caps were favorite targets, and their performances were denounced as ridiculous by the caricatures that generally made use of a combination of words and image to make the hidden supporting structures of fashion a laughing matter.[25] Such satires did not simply represent fashions but participated in the creation of new fashionable currents, interest and obsessions.

A MATTER OF BODILY DEPORTMENT

Supported by these mechanics of underwear that enforced a specific deportment, fashionable garments created real constraints and could bring the body to the edge of imbalance. To be dressed in such a way was a performance for the wearer. It was a real physical effort, if we take into account the weight of the clothes and hairstyles, their bulk or their bodily discomfort. Princes' and courtiers' bodies were certainly the most constrained; their life-style involved performance at court, and the magnificence inherent in their social position was articulated through the most elaborate of fashions and the most luxurious of fabrics. For example, court dress was extremely heavy at the end of Louis XIV's reign. In 1697, the silver cloth wedding dress of the twelve-year-old duchess of Burgundy—the bride of Louis' grandson—was so heavy than two gentlemen had to help her to wear it.[26] At this time the long trains were so cumbersome that ladies had to have it carried by lackeys. The Roi Soleil himself, even in old age, maintained the same standards. During the reception of the Persian ambassador at Versailles in 1715, he wore the most beautiful diamonds from the crown sewn onto his dark suit, which made him bend under its weight.[27] The largest of wigs could be so heavy that they caused discomfort in the nape of the neck, migraines, dizziness and even, when coupled with a lack of hygiene, pruritus. This was a source of great interest to the new type of doctor who emerged in this period, who sometimes wrote popular treatises on the topic of dress fashions and health, as will be seen later.

The generation who experienced the metamorphosis of women's fashions in the mid-1790s could testify to the inconvenience of the dress forms of the *ancien régime*, such as the "stays" or corset that resembled a hard shell and hampered movements, hardly allowing the wearer to raise her arms.[28] Mme de la Tour du Pin wrote in her memoirs:

> The women's suit had to transform the dance into a sort of torture. Narrow heels, three inches high, which put the foot in the position where we are on tiptoe in order to reach a book on the highest board of a bookcase; one heavy and stiff whalebone petticoat, stretching right and left; a one-foot high hairstyle topped by a cap named Pouffe, on which feathers, flowers, diamonds stood some on the others, a pound of powder and pomade that the slightest movement brought down on shoulders: such a scaffolding made to dance with pleasure a misery.[29]

She also complained of the dimensions of the huge skirts that necessitated that the wearer, entering a room or a coach, make a sideways movement through a door or alternatively squash her petticoat upwards. However, the consequences of such spatial negotiations were for her less funny than for the women mocked in satirical engravings.[30] In 1787, she several times struck her *panier* in doorways when running in the Palace of Versailles, which, she believed, provoked a miscarriage.[31] The very high heels that gave the impression of "walking on some sort of stilts"[32] didn't help when trying to keep balance (Figure 3.11). In a letter of 1721, the princess Palatine remembered that she had a fit of the giggles when she heard her sister-in-law, Louis XIV's wife, Maria Theresa of Austria, saying "Ah! I fell!" every time she stumbled over because of her very high heels. And the queen often fell.[33] These constraints on the body and its enforced imbalances appeared, to women writing their memoirs in older age from the perspective of more comfortable fashions at the beginning of the nineteenth century, to have been a torture. But the bodies of their youth had been trained to these discomforts and educated to avoid awkward gestures. To be fashionable was beyond price, even a physical one. Furthermore, these fashions often managed and contained the social control exerted on the body, particularly on the bodies of women.

This fashionable body had its own deportment, characterized by an upright posture and an elegance in walking that made a farmer who met some creatures wearing hoops

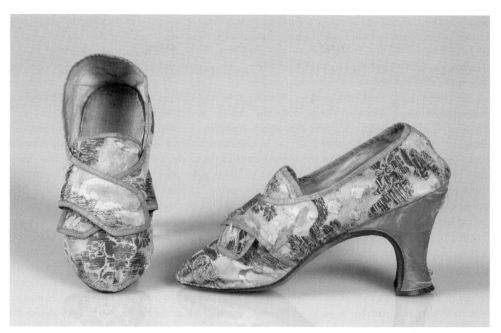

FIGURE 3.11: Woman's shoes, 1760–75, probably French, silk, metallic. The Metropolitan Museum of Art, New York.

and high heels around 1710, say that they seemed "to lean on the earth only disparagingly," with a "languishing gait" never seen on rustics. By comparison the poor peasants seemed to him "as a sort of cattle with human faces."[34] This clearly expresses the social distance that the rich Western elite displayed with their clothing and bodies. We know that from the Renaissance, the elite paid close attention to their clothes and bodily deportment as signs of social distinction. Posture and gestures were educated from childhood with methods that constantly taught the discipline of the body and developed a "semiology of rectitude."[35] Clothes and their accessories were staunch allies in this control of physical expression. Their constraints or volumes helped to obtain the entitled—even haughty— posture expected, even if it meant not being able to get dressed alone as garments became more complicated to wear. In a way, dressing joined the logic of verticality that haunted the conception of the child's body at that time. Thought of as a mouldable wax, the baby had to wear a wrap (swaddling) to keep its limbs straight and well formed. Both boys and girls wore the same unisex dress until four or five years old, before graduating into the garment of their own sex.[36] This moulding and orthopedic understanding of garments continued in the corset, worn from earliest childhood even by boys.[37] For example, Louis XIV's heir had a very strict education and was regularly beaten by his irascible tutor. One day in 1671—when he was aged ten—his body was more bruised than usual, but his life had been saved by the corset he wore to "keep the trunk straight," for it protected him from the violent punches.[38] As for fencing, riding, and dancing, the body had to be trained in, and to conform to, its fashionable display. For this reason, ladies, when first presented to the king and queen at Versailles, had to practice before their début. Etiquette required that a complicated series of reverences was performed when advancing and retiring in the royal presence, all to be achieved wearing a huge petticoat and very hard stays. "It's necessary to remember the lessons we took in walking backwards, in kicking out the train, in not upsetting our mules and falling, which would be the depths of the insolence and distress," remembered the baroness of Oberkirch.[39] (Such a performance and training lasted up until 1939 at the British court, with trains and ostrich feather fans being required to be worn by the women presented.)

Although the details of women's clothing changed during the Age of Enlightenment, this should not lead us to forget that the female system of dress had in essence not evolved since the Renaissance: it was still formed by a décolleté dress with a wide skirt and a shaping bodice. Neither had the social control over her body changed—a body that was, after all, more constrained by its clothes than was the male anatomy. The corset clearly marked out the territories of public and private. Its upright posture carried symbolic meanings about female virtue and chastity, as well as bodily self-discipline. An uncorseted woman was considered morally lax.[40] In commentaries about the hoop petticoat we see articulated further arguments for the supervision of the female body. According to the sartorial truisms of moralists and satirists, the hoop proceeded from female vanity, the result of her weakness of mind; it was created to allow secret pregnancies to go unnoticed; its extreme size depleted family fortunes; and finally, it was both sexually restrictive and attractive. As a protective and defensive shell, the hoop petticoat precluded physical contact with men and bared access to the sexual organs.[41] But it also permitted a public view of women's legs—a fashionable first—which could be considered as near-nudity and a moral outrage: "Since women wore no underpants, the sight of the nude leg undoubtedly carried rather intense associations with undefended nudity higher up."[42]

FASHION AND DRESS AS A MATTER OF HEALTH

In 1759, Nolivos de Saint-Cyr wrote that, by comparison with previous centuries, "our clothes, our hair and shoes are more shaped to our bodies than they ever were."[43] However, other authors of the Enlightenment would doubtless have disagreed, for they were denouncing the dress of their time as a danger to the body and to health. In the *Encyclopédie*, Diderot and Jaucourt analyzed the physical damage caused by clothing transformations.[44] In *L'Émile ou De l'éducation* (1762), so popular and influential among the cultured and well-to-do, Rousseau advocated a more natural approach to the clothing of children and women. From the 1760s, clothes had also become a major subject of interest for physicians, particularly in France.[45] Prompted by worries about human degeneration or children's physical education, this remedial discourse generally appeared in books of medicine, but specific studies on dress and health increased after the 1770–80s, at least in France. Let us now examine one of the recurrent themes that expressed the medical fear about the decline of the human species.

There were many criticisms of the swaddling and corseting of children, practices undertaken to help their pliant bodies grow straight and sure because, as traditional Galenic medicine explained, the young were very sensitive to the excess of humours that could move their bones and cause deformities. After 1750, physicians advocated a freer body and a more restrained use of stays and bodices for children, or at least the adoption of softer corsets. The moulding capacity of clothing came to be accused of disrupting growth and impeding movement.[46] Fashions for the children of the elite were certainly influenced by this medical discourse. Girls' dress became lighter, white muslin gowns with a lighter bodice that anticipated the chemise dress. The boys' "skeleton suit" appeared in the 1770s, a comfortable loose-fitting pair of trousers (worn for many years by sailors and peasants) and a shortened jacket (Figure 3.12).

Dressing children like miniature adults was no longer on the agenda in fashionable Europe. Now children had a specific garment, whose benefits the Duke of Croÿ recognized in 1773 in reference to his own grandsons: the *matelot* (seaman) suit—as this boys' suit was called in France—was "convenient" and allowed the wearer "to take strenuous exercise, to undertake enormous efforts and achieve suppleness, and this new way of education was greatly superior in strengthening the body."[47] Three years earlier, the Austrian empress Maria Theresa would not allow her daughter Marie-Antoinette, just married to the French Dauphin, to dispense with her stays—she was concerned that the fifteen-year-old princess wear them daily while her body was "shaping up." However, she proposed to send Marie-Antoinette softer corsets from Vienna because "those of Paris are too strong."[48] Dressing children with easier-fitting garments seems to have been the custom from a rather earlier date in England, where from the 1760s foreign visitors admired the distinctive national informality.[49]

It is significant that new thinking was emerging in the second part of the eighteenth century, which was based on the idea of bodily fibers whose contractions were the driving force of the body and whose weakness caused its illness. The idea of an active body, shaped from within by dynamic forces, was gaining ground over the understanding of the body as passive, and moulded by static forces.[50] In response, physicians recommended an overall lightening of clothing so the cold could exercise its vitalizing effect. For example,

FIGURE 3.12: *Susannah, Philip Lake, and Maria Godsal: The Godsal Children,* John Hoppner, 1789. The Huntington Library, San Marino, California.

the pudding around a child's head, worn to protect it in case of fall, came to be regarded as useless, because exposing the head to the action of the air was thought both to toughen it and provide thick hair. The lightening of clothing allowed for physical activities such as walking, which was highly recommended for health and for its invigorating effects by the Swiss doctor Theodore Tronchin, famous throughout Europe. The Duke of Croÿ's grandsons were thus brought up to take long walks in winter. For women, Tronchin advised short gowns without *paniers*, as being suitable for walking outdoors and which, for obvious reasons, were nicknamed *tronchines*. Other physicians talked about shoes that were more suitable to the natural shape of the foot, more appropriate for walking.

All of this did not mean that humoral medicine was abandoned when considering dress and health. The changing of personal linen continued to be seen as vital for hygiene and health, and for the expulsion of bodily excretions and the overabundance of humors. But physicians turned against all garments that acted as ligatures, and that made harmful barriers to the body's humoral flow. Published in the *Gazette de santé* in July 1775, a letter written by a doctor called Dufour, who was concerned by the headaches, dizzy glares and vertigo of a man of twenty, clearly expressed current medical opinion: Dufour blamed these ailments on the man's tight and constrictive clothing, such as "the fashionable very high collars"[51] According to medical writings, therefore, it was necessary to loosen the collar from high ties and necklaces; to move away from the dependence of the breasts on stays and belts; to free the wrists from close cuffs, the legs from garters, the feet from protruding metal buckles, the armpits from close arm holes, the lower belly from a tight jacket, and the testicles from narrow breeches. In short, the entire fashioned body was scanned and remediated by physicians.

Not only was the health of the individual thought to be at risk from certain forms of dress, the survival of the human race that was at stake in the issue of "clothing health." Some titles were very explicit, as in Jacques Bonnaud's *The degrading of the human species by the use of the whalebone stays* (1770).[52] Corset controversies raged throughout the century and Bonnaud's aim was to make accessible to a broad audience the specialist writings of the medical opponents of the corset and of child swaddling. He also referred to Rousseau's educational thinking that advocated the ease of garments in the manner of Greek Antiquity. Bonnaud wrote an apocalyptic inventory of the damages of tight-lacing on women's bodies (painful digestion, headaches, faintness, hot flushes, suffocation, difficult deliveries, miscarriages), and on the bodies of children (fetal developmental malformations). However, the damage wrought by constrictive clothing was felt to be even more profound, in fact causing a decrease in the population. Not only did the constraint of the stays on the mother's womb make for a declining birth rate, so too did pressure on the male reproductive organs. The physician Clairian wanted to free men from the pressure of the fitted and fashionable "culotte," so that abundant semen could be preserved. He dreamed of men wearing kilts, because people without underwear "have more well-developed reproductive organs."[53] Likewise, according to Bonnaud and others like him, women needed to have their breasts free under their clothing in order to nurse their babies. The corset was accused of preventing the free flow and good quality of a mother's milk. At the time, breastfeeding was promoted among elite women as a more natural practice than wet-nursing, and better for healthy children (Figure 3.13). The attacks made on corsets in the promotion of breastfeeding were, however, not necessarily without ideological freighting of their own, and were "often linked to ideological campaigns in favor of motherhood, reflecting fears that if women broke away from their domestic sphere, the entire social order would be threatened."[54] In one sense they sought

FIGURE 3.13: *Mère allaitant son enfant*, Jean-Laurent Mosnier. Mâcon, Musée des Beaux-Arts. © Photo: Josse/Scala, Florence.

to free women from constraint, in another sense they represented a further case of the social control of the women's bodies.

AN APPEARANCE OF EASE AND FREEDOM

In the Age of Enlightenment, the idea of Nature, advocated by philosophers like Rousseau, certainly had a significant impact on the search for a simpler way of dressing that was more comfortable and offered greater freedom of movement. In *L'Émile* (1762), Rousseau advocated a neo-classical ideal of dressing that would marry natural proportions, comfort, and ease of activity, a position often echoed in medical discourse, as we have seen.[55] Bonnaud wrote that renouncing corsets was a "law dictated by Nature," clearly observable in that no animals wore such garments. Furthermore, "low people and rural people among us; among strangers, the Chinese, Japanese, Americans & Africans raise their children without stays, & these are tall and well shaped"—whereas there are "hunchbacked and deformed bodies" in Europe.[56] The dress philosophy of the Enlightenment had furthermore a moral underpinning, based on the opposition between "being" and "appearances," between nature and artifice. It opposed "natural clothes" to "artificial attire," an argument ultimately derived from the notion of deceptive appearances that had been constantly repeated since Christian Antiquity. Rousseau particularly campaigned for an "abundance of only necessary items," without, however, seeking to change the articulation of traditional social identities.[57] The philosophers pleaded for a reformation but not for a revolution of dressing.

It is important to note, however, that the dress of the *ancien régime* was not always uniformly complex and constrictive. Even in such a codified court as the French one, on everyday occasions the *gens de qualité* could wear loose dress and concentrate on comfort—when being "backstage" from public life. These informal garments were shown in the first fashion prints at the end of the seventeenth century. Although an elegant woman still wore her stays, on top was a negligée or a *robe de chambre*, a loose and flowing dressing gown made of rich materials that was more comfortable than a formal garment. Likewise, men also used dressing gowns throughout the eighteenth century for informal and undress comfort, a practice memorialized in Diderot's famous essay, *Regrets on Parting with My Old Dressing Gown* (1768).[58] Some of these gowns were influenced by Eastern design: kimono shapes, Chinese decorative motifs, or Indian fabrics (Figure 3.14).

FIGURE 3.14: *Portrait of an Unknown Man*, Carle Van Loo, c. 1730–40, oil on canvas. Château de Versailles. Photo: Fine Art Images/Heritage Images/Getty Images.

The adoption of simpler fashions like these was not only motivated by a quest for comfort. The desire of a particular class of individuals to distinguish themselves from the formality and stiffness of mainstream French fashion spread throughout sectors of the European elite. This lay behind the adoption of the three-piece suit in England in 1666, and even in France saw some young gentlemen affect an unkempt look, with an open coat and an untucked shirt worn without a waistcoat.[59]

The search for greater ease and simplicity in dressing appeared earlier in England, and a sense of studied informality can be seen in aristocratic English portraiture from the 1750s onward. This look deeply influenced both French and wider European fashion in the last decades of the eighteenth century. English society was less centered on the court than in absolutist France and enjoyed a higher social mobility. Often living on his lands (rather than in the city or at court), the English aristocrat managed his domains and loved outdoor pursuits, very often choosing to be depicted by painters amid his country estates. The portrait of *Sir Brooke Boothby* by Joseph Wright of Derby (1781) shows him wearing a sober brown cloth suit with a frock coat and a plain linen shirt. He eschews ostentatious lace and instead sports a cravat, a long muslin scarf knotted at the front (Figure 3.15). Lying somewhat uneasily in a wooded glade, he holds in his hand a book by Rousseau, who so famously advocated the supposed simplicity of country life.[60] This informal style, based on a pared-down and sober elegance, privileged comfort and simplicity: a convenient frock for riding (*redingote* in French from "riding-coat"), a round hat, useful boots, plain linen, all better adapted to the movements of daily wear than to codified performances of wealth and protocol. After the Glorious Revolution of 1688, this loose look was associated with an English male national identity and with his political liberty. In 1752, for Arthur Murphy traveling in France, this contrast with the formality and stiffness of French fashion was emblematic. English dress was "an emblem of our Constitution, for it lays a man under no uneasy restraint, but leaves it in his power to do as he pleased."[61] It was for this reason that, with their extravagant attire, fops at the end of the seventeenth century and macaronis in

FIGURE 3.15: *Sir Brooke Boothby*, Joseph Wright of Derby, 1781, oil paint on canvas. London, Tate Britain Gallery.

FIGURE 3.16: *Marie-Antoinette*, Elisabeth-Louise Vigée Le Brun, after 1783, oil on canvas. Timken Collection, National Gallery of Art, Washington.

the 1760 to 1770s were jeered at in print and graphic satire, their complicated look assimilated to the feminine, to the French, and to the social upstart.[62] At the same time, on the Continent, Anglomania (*Anglomanie*) successfully disseminated simpler attire.

During the three last decades of the eighteenth century, female dress was also seduced by a more moderate and lighter style, first with the *robe anglaise* and then the *polonaise*. Both of these gowns were worn with lighter underwear (very small hoops or hip pads) and shorter skirts. As discussed earlier, however, it was the chemise dress—a white muslin dress whose soft fullness was drawn in with a sash at the waist—that took the definitive move towards the natural body. Rejecting padding and a complicated cut, this style was popularized when adopted in the 1780s by the French queen Marie-Antoinette (Figure 3.16).[63]

CONCLUSION

The relationship between the body and dress evolved fundamentally during the Age of Enlightenment. The fashioned body really was a body in performance on the social stage.

Dress reshaped the physical body into a social and cultural body characterized by variation in the volume of the clothes or hair, and by constraints imposed by the mechanics of underwear. Such a dress system worked to articulate an elite ideal of bodily control and of social distinction. However, the criticism of this fashionable body increased. In the eighteenth century, dress became a matter of health concern, and the body was reconceptualized as needing to be protected from damaging fashions that could harm its reproductive or nutritive organs, and impede its movements. Henceforth, the trend was to a more natural body and simpler fashions, further encouraged by a contemporary neo-classical aesthetic and the growing trade and manufacture of light-weight fabrics.

The high-waisted dress of white light muslin perfectly embodied the movement in the Age of Enlightenment away from the old sartorial regime and its carapace-clothing towards a new autonomy of the body (Figure 3.17). However, by no means was this universal. For example, in a part of the counter-revolutionary Vendée, the peasant women still wore stays of rough canvas that formed, as a royalist countess recounted, "a kind of shell difficult to hole; so the Blue soldiers (republicans) complained about the difficulty of

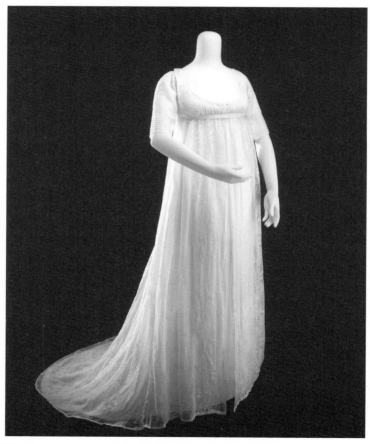

FIGURE 3.17: Muslin gown, made in England from Indian fabric, c. 1800. © Victoria and Albert Museum, London.

killing these women."[64] Such was the slow and unequal democratization of the new fashions and fabrics at the eve of the nineteenth century. Ironically enough, this was to be a century that would soon re-establish clothing forms emblematic of the old sartorial regime, in the shape of the *cuirasse* corset, the crinoline and the bustle, some of the most incredible examples of the manipulation of the human body.

CHAPTER FOUR

Belief

DAGMAR FREIST

> Your *Habit* is your modesty best expressed: your disposition best discovered. The
> Habit of the mind is discerned by the state or posture of the body; the condition or
> quality of the body by the *Habit*.[1]

This quote captures the widespread belief in early modern and Enlightenment Europe that
outward appearance and social practices were a legible guide to a person's inner self and
social status. It also conveys the double meaning of *habit* as dress *and* a set of practices based
on the shared beliefs of appropriate behavior in a given time and space. It is echoed in the
French expression *à la mode*[2] and the German term *Mode*, meaning not only the "prevalent
mode of social behaviour" based on a common understanding of the world, but also "a
variable type of dress, and the specific arrangement of any type of adornment of the body."[3]

The above definition of habit as the embodiment of a disposition, a mind, a posture,
and a condition or quality, goes to the heart of the phenomenon of dress and belief: it
implies that an implicit knowledge of styles, tastes, demeanor, and social norms is
anchored in the body and in daily practices of individuals and social groups.[4] A person's
habit was further charged with beliefs about rank, gender, modesty, religion, and honor
that were reproduced through the performance of a set of corresponding social practices
and displayed upon the body. It was intelligible, without being explicit, to those who
shared the underlying cultural codes and a general understanding of the world. Dress in
this wider sense as habit was a vital component of self-regulation and of legal means for
the control of social order and conduct. However, because of its significance as a social
marker, the choice of dress could also pronounce status claims, and it could diffuse the
social order and gender hierarchies, as well as disimulate one's inner self.

Modern cultural theorists and sociologists have been powerfully attracted by the idea
that the organization, reproduction, and transformation of social life is based on
"embodied, materially interwoven practices centrally organized around shared practical
understandings," rather than on rational choice and individual action.[5] "Embodied" in
this context means that forms of human action are entwined with the fabric and character
of the human body. The fashioning of bodies—skills, activities, gestures, surface
presentations and physical structures—is embedded within specific contexts of social
practices and beliefs, and it is constitutive of social order. Accordingly, the meanings of
dress are arbitrary, relational, and culturally constituted in social practices at a given time
and space and related to a set of shared beliefs and cultural codes. The material properties
of cut, color, and fabric of dress are "inalienable, inherent qualities, and they affect the
meanings that cultures then ascribe to clothes."[6] Thus velvet and silk as such were not
reprehensible, and they adorned the dress of social elites. However, worn by a pastor's

wife, they could acquire a meaning of sinfulness.[7] The social rank and role of the wearer alter a garment's meaning, a phenomenon which conveys the multiple meanings of particular clothes and accessories within different social ranks.

In the highly visualized society of Enlightenment Europe, a person's habit in its double meaning of dress and practices was the key to understanding the fabric of social relations. At the same time, it was the most contested issue during a period when traditional sartorial markers of social hierarchy and beliefs were being superseded by new ideas and practices of how to dress. The familiar grammar of how to read society was increasingly lost with the rise of luxury consumption, the new-found fashionability of non-elites, and the capacity of clothes to dissimulate social status.

If we want to understand the meaning of dress and belief in Enlightenment Europe, we must place it in the wider social and cultural context of appearances, dispositions, beliefs, and social practices. The analysis of dress and belief therefore concerns more than studying the correlation between religious or secular beliefs and the cut, fabric, and color of a dress—such as the plain and sober dress of Quakers as a "testimony of simplicity,"[8] the reservation of silk, satin, and damask for the nobility as a sign of social distinction, or its usage by social inferiors to mark subversion.

This chapter begins with a discussion of changing attitudes to dress, self-fashioning,[9] and social hierarchy in Enlightenment Europe, the period of time roughly from 1650 to 1780. It will look at the debate regarding vice and luxury, and the underlying belief that extravagant and expensive clothes were co-actors in immoral social practices. Some choices of clothing— cut, color, and fabric—were read by social critics as the display of a disposition that suggested sexual promiscuity and prodigality. Dissimulation and falsehood, too, were among the key concerns of social critics in the face of a growing obsession with self-fashioning. Contemporaries were worried about the extent to which the choice of dress could subvert the fine line between inner intentions and outer appearance and practices. The choice of clothes could disguise one's true intentions, so went the argument, and render one's real self and gender invisible to the human eye. Both men and women sported items of clothing that were said to suit the other sex, and the heated debate about effeminacy of male dress and masculinity of female dress, which quickened in England in the early seventeenth century, was taken up again repeatedly in eigtheenth-century Europe. Inauthenticity and artifice was another issue of the debate on dress and belief; fashion was viewed as a social mask and contemporaries worried that artificial beauty affected the senses.

This chapter then discusses religious belief, dress, and the body, and looks at various dress practices of both the clergy and lay believers. It will be asked on what grounds moralists upheld the complicity of apparel and the inward moral state of a person—which was central in early modern (protestant) religious thought—in the light of consumerism. While religious arguments against fashion and luxury merged with the growing debate on civil virtues, radical religious groups created dress codes and practices as an exhibition of godliness. However, these practices were challenged by changing social and religious mores and a reshaping of the display of religious identities under the impact of consumption and the new ideas of the enlightenment.

SELF-FASHIONING AND SOCIAL HIERARCHY

Since the medieval age, sumptuary legislation had created an elaborate hierarchy of fabrics, colors, and cuts for each social rank, and social moralists believed that people's moral and personal worth should be judged by appearance and practice, in other words, by their habit. Rank, in turn, determined the life style and consumption pattern to which a person was entitled. There was a socially-constructed complicity of dress, social order, and practices, and people believed that dress protected and asserted the social hierarchy and public morality. These convictions came to be challenged from the end of the seventeenth century, with the transformation from a stratified society of rank into a functionally differentiated consumer society.[10] The erosion of the society of orders, in which status was assigned by birth, was replaced by a more fluid social structure, in which individuals could assert social distinction through the display of social capital,[11] which was anchored in the growing importance of education, taste, politeness, respectability, and wealth. Furthermore, the rise of commercial luxury affected men and women from all social ranks, and people able to buy luxury goods[12] started to emulate social superiors in numerous ways, and began to create their own material self-expressions inspired by what was defined as fashionable in their own milieu.[13]

One of the earliest works in England to criticize the ostentatious display of apparel and its moral shortcomings was Philip Stubbe's famous *Anatomie of abuses* (1583), in which he outlined the particular fashions of the day as well as their attendant sins. His concerns were replicated in sermons[14] and pamphlets, they were fiercely discussed among Puritans and English separatists, and sparked off a clothes controversy for several decades.[15] Sermons, pamphlets, and correspondence of the late sixteenth and early seventeenth century provide amazing details of social practices and choices of dress by non-elites, and the meanings ascribed to fashionable details of cut, color, and fabric by the observing elite social critics.[16] At issue were the questions of modesty against pride in apparel and social practices, and the very feasibility, in a commercial society, of upholding the traditional social order of rank, the hierarchy of appearances and the compliance of being and habit.[17]

As early as the seventeenth century habit, mode, and fashion were couched in economic terms and the language of desire,[18] and traders were expected to provide dresses in new patterns, colors, and cuts with each new season:

> Now this for a constant and generell Rule, that in all flowered Silks you change ye fashion and flower as much as you can every year, for English ladies and they say ye French and other Europeans will give twice as much for a new thing not seen in Europe before, though worse, they will give for a better silk for [of] the same fashion worn ye former years.[19]

Furthermore, with the changing nature of clothing fabrics in the long eighteenth century, the rise of linen and cotton, and the import into Europe of printed Indian calico with exotic floral patterns, new clothing styles were introduced among all social ranks.[20] The choice of clothes, fabrics, colors, and accessoires reinforced, but also differentiated the hierarchies of society through the "overwriting" of elite social practices by rising social groups.[21] The habit of the nobility was no longer imitated by those aspiring to a higher social status. Instead, the rising middle classes, who in themselves were highly differentiated, struggled to redefine social distinction in their own terms through the display of wealth, education, polite manners, simplicity as a statement of political authenticity, and the symbolic capital of taste. "Inherent in these activities were forces reflecting both a new perception of the individual's place in society and new relations within society as a whole."[22] Disputes over dress and manners not only divided social ranks but also turned into generational conflicts about the propriety of dress and social practices as represented in the famous print "Welladay! Is this my son Tom!" which represents a young man in the extravagant macaroni fashion in England around 1770 (Figure 4.1).

FIGURE 4.1: "Welladay! Is This my Son Tom!", A Collection of Drolleries, 1770–97, fol. 75
C697 770. Courtesy of the Lewis Walpole Library, Yale University.

AMBIGUITY OF DRESS AND THE CIVILIZING
INFLUENCE OF FASHION

Those social critics who wrote in favor of luxury consumption pointed to the civilizing
influence of commerce and its impact on taste and polite behavior. The civilizing influence
was apparent, for instance, in the obsession with cleanliness and the display of white linen
at collars, ruffs, cuffs, and caps. The whiteness of linen contributed to the attainment of a
more distinctive status among all social ranks across Europe[23] and it signaled the wearer's
"commitment to concepts of cleanliness (and) their membership in a common community
of respectable citizenry."[24] The first half of the eighteenth century saw the rise of the
culture of respectability and propriety, and the emphasis on "thinking and acting
appropriately."[25]

Its critics, however, argued that the stress on performance and propriety "led to artifice, insincereity and dishonesty, not least in matters of dress."[26] Creative and extravagant uses of clothes became the "very expressions of the contrasted being of the age, signs of instability and artifice."[27] Appearances were "deeply troubling"[28] for a society that was trying to hold on to the compliance of habit and status, as appearances did not represent being but seeming, and people were unsure how to act and how to read social performances and new dress codes.

The different concepts of taste and fashion, and the ambiguity of dress were regularly discussed in the pages of periodicals such as the English *Tatler*, *Spectator*, and *Gentleman's Magazine*, the German *Journal des Luxus und der Moden*, and the French *Cabinet des Modes*, with the majority of authors acclaiming the superior moral authority of gentle birth and propagating the traditional social order.[29] At the same time, these journals facilitated the exchange of the most recent fashions, accessories, and lifestyles at an even faster pace across Europe and into the colonies, and novelty gradually surpassed antiquity as social markers. Contemporaries compared society to a theater where people took on different roles but lacked the skill to read the underlying social script. One of the most favored pastimes of the period was the masquerade, assemblies at which many participants dressed in disguise or in enveloping cloaks.[30]

These flourishing sartorial extravagances were opposed by an alternative code of manners from the mid-eighteenth century, which demanded that habit, social status, and the inner self should accord, and emphasized authenticity, sensibility, sincerity of emotions, and honesty. Over the course of the eighteenth century, change in fashion as a social marker was a change from "a crude to a subtle method of expressing social superiority,"[31] exclusiveness and belonging. Fashion journals played a crucial role in this emergence of taste and aesthetics.

PROGRESSIVE CONSUMPTIONISM AND NEW VIRTUES

Under the influence of these changes, and with the spread of new ideas and beliefs fostered by an increase in literacy and public opinion, the discourse on dress and belief turned into a multi-vocal chorus of voices based on religious, on medical, on moral and aesthetic, on gender, on rank, and on national arguments.

Consumption was a contested act. Traditionally it was cast negatively, and classical philosophical and religious arguments saw it as a problem of expenditure and ruin, vice, and the blurring of social distinction, a position that continued to be articulated throughout the long eighteenth century. However, beginning with the generation of mercantilists active in the late seventeenth century, consumption also began to be seen as the key to national prosperity. As the eighteenth century advanced, and ideas of taste and refinement spread, so consumption was increasingly viewed as a social good rather than a moral or social challenge. Notwithstanding, several religious groups—such as Quakers, the Mennonites, Puritans, and orthodox Jews—adopted a contrary position, creating a specific dress code as a marker of their religious identity and godliness.

From a religious point of view, one's outward behavior and appearance revealed one's inward moral state, and theologians "attempted to define the new and amended norms of an ascetic and devout appearance."[32] For the reformed church and its flock, which was drawn in large part from the prospering middle classes, the changing fashions presented not so much a problem of the toppling of hierarchies, but a moral problem: "the use of wealth in a system of social inequality" and the transformation of luxury into charity.[33]

LUXURY, DISIMULATION, AND ARTIFICE

The increasing public appearance of women in sites such as the theater, in coffee houses, in parks, markets, and shops, and the display of their bodies in the most recent fashion was highly criticized by contemporaries for the inherent danger of unrestrained vice, luxury, and insubordination. Women's preferences in England for the newly-imported Indian fabrics of printed linens and calicos, which were said to threaten both the national economy and female virtue, turned women's bodies into a battlefield between traditional woolen dress and the new colorful fabrics. Wool, contemporaries believed, would "guide all other Habits of the Body."[34] The discourse against luxury and vice was highly gendered, and women were considered to be enslaved to luxury and sexual indulgence. Similar dress practices and behavior in men was characterized as effeminate.

There was also a fear of dissimulation and falsehood "under saintly show," arising from a belief that a woman's real moral conduct was not legible in her fashionable dress and manners, that she was inherently false.[35] Poems, plays, and satirical pamphlets from the late seventeenth century mocked women as a mass of artifice that disguised them from top to toe.[36] In an attempt to define behavioral and bodily signs that could testify to a woman's authenticity, conduct was rejected as unreliable; contemporaries believed that a woman could wear a mask of modesty to hide her real self, just as she could don a black velvet mask at the theater to cover her face. Conduct books compared women to female actresses who deceived through role play, and admonished them to "Be indeed what you desire to be thought."[37]

ARTIFICE AND MANHOOD

Similarly, artifice in male fashion, interpreted as effeminacy, was attacked in woodcuts and social satires as a debased and imperfect version of manhood. In the seventeenth century, the targets were tight-fitting doublets, large colored ruffs or reticella lace collars, earrings, perfumed and powdered false hair, the love-lock, and richly embroidered and pattened breeches that looked like a stiffened skirt. The choice of these clothes, the fabrics and patterns from which they were made, and the time and money-consuming self-fashioning, all evoked an effeminate habitus that contemporaries defined as "womanish; soft to an unmanly degree; voluptuous; tender; luxurious."[38]

In the second half of the seventeenth century, the stiff and upright male silhouette was superseded by French casual elegance, emphasized by long hair, unbuttoned short doublets and extremely wide open-ended "petticoat breeches" (Figure 4.2).

In the eyes of contemporaries, the "fop" strove to "imitate women in their aparell, viz. long periwigs, patches in their faces, painting, short wide breeches like petticoats, muffs, and their clothes highly scented, bedecked with ribbons of all colours."[39]

From the 1760s, the macaroni provoked another moral onslaught against fashionable male dress practices. Graphic and painted caricatures portrayed him in small slipper-like shoes, silk stockings, and tightly-cut suits, small hats, and fine waistcoats.[40] Most significant, however, was his elaborate and luxurious hairstyle: an enormous wig, "combining a tall front with a fat queue or 'club' of hair behind" (Figure 4.1). It was this "feature that epitomized the macaroni's extravagant artifice."[41] Caricaturists presented these fashionable young men with wigs turned back to front, "so that the tail hangs down over the face like a floppy penis."[42] In contrast, the erect wig suggested potency and sexual indulgence. Because of its extreme size and extravagance, and the latent sexual meanings traditionally

FIGURE 4.2: A man dressed in *rhingrave* or beribboned petticoat breeches, with a short unbuttoned doublet. This print belongs to a series of costume prints, from *Figures à la mode*, dedicated to Mr. Le Duc de Bourgogne, edited by Etienne Jeaurat, Paris, c. 1685, printmaker, Sébastien Leclerc. Rijskmuseum, Amsterdam.

associated with hair, the macaroni wig seemed to subvert traditional meanings of masculinity and ally instead with feminity and homosexuality. The figure of the macaroni was a catalyst for disputes over the social and moral bounds of male fashion, embodying the dangers of inauthenticity and effeminacy that excess seemed to entail.[43]

The social construction of effeminacy in public discourses on male fashion formed a striking contrast to the eighteenth-century perception of manliness that was articulated via a religious rhetoric.[44] This latter "embraced moral or cultural as well as physical facets of being a man" and was anchored in the belief that "reputation and honour may have been the measure of all things, but they did not rest on behaviour and appearance alone. They depend upon the solid inner qualities which were always implicit in 'manliness', such as courage, resolution, and tenacity."[45]

DEGENERATION, AUTHENTICITY, AND CIVIL VIRTUES

Whereas religious arguments against artificial beauty continued throughout the seventeenth and eighteenth centuries, enlightened philosophers also entered the debate, "arguing for a complete rejection of all forms of artifice by men and women alike."[46] Under the impact of the new science of physiognomy, which claimed to discover a person's character in the reading of facial traits, the call for a return to natural beauty became prominent. The lavish use of cosmetics and scents were criticized as vile masks that attempted to hide a corrupt physiognomy, and increasingly ridiculed for being both artificial and vulgar.

A new tone was introduced into disputes over cosmetics when doctors placed themselves as the purveyors of beauty advice at the center of the growing debate on fashion and artifice. Based on their professional authority, doctors advised men and women to keep their faces clean through a series of practices and succesfully evoked the dangers of cosmetics.[47] From about the mid-eighteenth century, the debate on artificial beauty in Europe dovetailed with medical literature on the senses, and in sources as varied as recipe books and household manuals spread the belief that contemporary material culture and fashion conspired to weaken the body.[48]

This rethoric of corporal degeneration provoked the call both for an organic renewal and for civic virtues, in an increasingly national discourse on character, conduct, and dress. In France, the Marquis de Mirabeau, known for his work on political economy, described in vivid colors how excessive consumption enervated the human body:

> A man whose hair is done up with two hundred curlers is hardly prepared the next day, when his musk-scented head comes out of a case in which it has been preserved like Italian flowers, to wager fifteen days of provisions on the tennis court; instead he stretches out on a lounge chair and reads a pamphlet. Hence, he has no more strength.[49]

Mirabeau shared the belief of his time that "mad spending and the pursuit of refined pleasures overloaded the senses and caused a variety of nervous disorders—anxiety, lethargy, ennui, colic, fainting, and convulsions—which he lumped under the rubric 'vapors'."[50] To overcome these acute signs of degeneration, some authors suggested the creation and introduction of a national dress and came up with the most amazing schemes. Whereas in Sweden, a competition was launched for the creation of a national dress under the auspices of Gustav III,[51] in Germany, ideas were aired in the leading fashion journals of the time of how a national dress could be successfully introduced into society and what it should look like to highlight national civil virtues.[52] All in all, there was a debate between classical notions of dress and fashion as corruption, degeneration and impoverishment, and a new discourse that de-moralized dress and fashion in the process of naturalizing commerce.[53]

RELIGIOUS BELIEF AND CLERICAL DRESS

Clerical dress in Catholic Europe at the eve of the Reformation was criticized for its splendor and extravagance, and associated with a luxurious life style and the episcopal emulation of wordly rulers. In contrast, the new dress codes introduced by Lutheran and Calvinist reformers emphasized simplicity and decency in apparel as a testimony of a modest and godly life. The distinctive black, loose-fitting and wide-sleeved cassocks with white starched preaching bands worn by protestant ministers were related to their role as spiritual teachers and to their "position as examples of moral propriety and agents of discipline within their communities."[54]

There were also confessional differences in the meaning ascribed to vestments (liturgical dresses) such as the surplice and the square cap for Catholic clergy as vestures of holiness imbued with magical power, or the protestant cassock and academic gown as a sign of learning and discipline. In Catholicism, a variety of vestments served different liturgical roles during mass and functioned as ancient markers of sacred bodies,[55] as well as separating the priest from the laity. By contrast, in Protestantism emphasis was put on godliness rather than on sacrality, and vestments were viewed critically as remnants of Catholic superstition. Nevertheless, it was considered important among the early reformers that pastors should wear distinctive liturgical clothing during service to emphasize the dignity and solemnity of occasion and to reflect their authority. Both royal and episcopal authorities established the standards of clergy dress across protestant Europe.

Restrictions were also placed on the everyday dress of Protestant clergy, including their wives and children. They were instructed to wear simple dress, avoid bright colors and unnecessary decorations on their clothes or bodies. The idealized protestant vicarage as a sanctuary of morality and decency was expected to uphold standards of public and private morality, and to set an example in appearances and practices for the whole congregation. Lutheran and Calvinist ministers were instructed to dress in dark cloaks, which lacked any ostentatious decorum but still represented their distinctive high social status as a representative of learning, of moral integrity, and of God's calling. Furthermore, the cut of their dress was to hide their body and be sober in color, in order to supress any erotic fantasies.

RELIGION, THE BODY, AND THE SEDUCTIVE POWER OF DRESS

Christian attitudes to dress were closely connected to attitudes towards the naked body. In contrast to classical philosophy, which celebrated the aesthetics of nudity, Christian belief regarded the body "as shameful, indicative of suffering, humiliation and, because of Eve, of betrayal."[56] With the Reformation and the enhancement of marriage as the Christian ideal lifestyle, sexuality was approved in marriage and the body seen as natural and morally neutral. However, the weakness of the flesh remained as a constant source of lust and immorality, especially incriminating women outside marriage,[57] and it had to be overcome by prayer, discipline, moderation, and chastity. The fashioning of the body was interpreted as a sign of a wearer's weakness and the source of a beholder's sexual fantasy. Protestant clergy in early modern Europe shared the view that "the greatest provocations of lust come from our apparrell"[58]—thus theologians created catalogs of fashion items and cross-listed each in regard to its offensiveness according to the Bible and the rules of modesty and natural gender divisions.

Generally speaking then, moralists in the seventeenth century agreed that "beauty implied sexual voracity in women" and that extravagant apparel was a snare laid out for men.[59] Criticism directed against male fashion, however, focused on its effeminacy and artificiality and differentiated between tasteless gallants or fops in search of vice and entertainment, and the man of taste and good manners, recognizable in his more restrained elegance and sober appearance.

Although the fascination with extravagant fashion even increased in the eighteenth century, religious moral strictures against dressing that had so characterized the seventeenth century were less prominent in the public discourse on dress, belief, and conduct. Furthermore, the civilizing influence of good taste in dress and the emphasis on good manners, politeness, and propriety with the rise of the middle classes almost outvoted notions of sinfulness in extreme dress. Such arguments were considered rather ridiculous by the end of the eighteenth century. However, religious sentiments against extravagant dress and its connotations of pride, sin, prodigality, and sexual promiscuity entered secular disputes over clothes in novels, journals, and pamphlets, and were alluded to by defenders of the traditional estate society.

DRESS PRACTICES AND RADICAL
PROTESTANT BELIEF

In late seventeenth- and eighteenth-century Europe and in the colonies, religious arguments survived more explicitly in the beliefs and culture of radical Protestant groups, such as the Quakers, Mennonites, Pietists, Moravians, and the Methodists. The moral criticism of extravagant apparel and spending voiced by these religious groups conflated with their strong emphasis on charity, compassion, and pedagogical initiatives, and their belief that modest appearance and conduct would mark them as the children of God and quicken the Second Coming. Through their apparel and social practices they were eager to document God's work in their individual and collective lives. In spite of differences, they were united in their concept of communitas, the formation of strong networks, their emphasis on inward edification, and their critical attitude towards religious doctrine and orthodoxy. Contemporaries noted that these religious groups had set themselves off from the rest of society with their speech, dress and behavior,[60] and they started to figure prominently in novels, clearly visible as Quakers or Methodists by their habit.[61]

The Quaker Habit

The distinctive plain and dark-colored apparel of Quakers with their specific hat wear for men and bonnet for women soon became known as "Quaker dress," and was connected to a specific habit including speech and demeanor. In her memoirs, Elizabeth Fry reflected on the impact of the apparel she had adopted when becoming a Quaker:

> I used to think and do now how little dress matters. But I find it almost impossible to keep to the principles of Friends without altering my dress and speech . . . They appear to me a sort of protector to the principles of Christianity in the present state of the world.[62]

That a change to Quaker apparel, speech, and conduct had a strong impact on self- and group-identity—and that it at times transgressed generally shared beliefs and codes of conduct—becomes evident in Jospeh John Gurney's account of personal experience. He describes his preparations for a dinner he was to attend for the first time in his "Friend's attire and with my hat on."[63] Gurney was accustomed to the polite manners and conventions of his time, which included hat honor—the removal of one's hat with a slight bow when greeting a lady or a superior. For Quakers, however, the refusal to remove the hat had become a fundamental symbol of freedom and equality under God. Gurney described how he dreaded the moment he had to enter the drawing room and shake hands with the mistress of the house without removing his hat. He repeated this behavior with the bishop and commented on the result: "I found myself a decided Quaker, was perfectly understood to have assumed that character, and to dinner parties, except in the family circle, I was asked no more."[64] In his 1806 study of Quakerism, Thomas Clarkson described the uniqueness of their dress:

> They stand distinguished by means of it from all other religious bodies . . . Both sexes are also particular in the choice of the colour of their clothes. All gay colours such as red, blue, green, and yellow, are exploded. Dressing in this manner, a Quaker is known by his apparel through the whole kingdom. This is not the case with any other individuals of the island, except the clergy . . .[65]

Habitus, Religious Belief, and Self-formation

Methodists, too, were careful in chosing their apparel in order to avoid "'a bold immodest look' which can be created by 'the profusion of ribbands, gauze or linen about your heads'."[66] In a sermon on dress, John Wesley, one of the key figures of the Methodist movement in England, drew a direct comparison to Quaker dress, which he described as plain but costly, and admonished his audience to opt for plain and cheap clothing instead:

> I conjure you all who have any regard for me, show me before I go hence, that I have not laboured, even in this respect, in vain, for near half a century. Let me see, before I die, a Methodist congregation, full as plain dressed as a Quaker congregation. Only be more consistent with yourselves. Let your dress be cheap as well as plain; otherwise you do but trifle with God, and me, and your own souls. I pray, let there be no costly silks among you, how grave soever they may be. Let there be no Quaker-linen, — proverbially so called, for their exquisite fineness; no Brussels lace, no elephantine hats or bonnets, — those scandals of female modesty. Be all of a piece, dressed from head to foot as persons professing godliness; professing to do every thing, small and great, with the single view of pleasing God.[67]

Similarly, Mennonites, Moravians, and Pietists were known by contemporaries for their simple and plain dress, both as a sign of group identity and as a renunciation of worldy pleasures in favor of a spritual life.[68]

Clothes as signifiers of religious beliefs and self-formation were also vital in missions across the world. Moravians, for instance, sent paintings and portraits presenting co-religionists in their respective dress codes in order to create uniformity of religious dress practices around the world.[69] So far, research on European congregational settlements overseas has concentrated on the impact of networks and newsletters as the basis of virtual religious communities and their identity, or has analyzed missionary reports for their ethnographic richness. The role of fashion and of everyday social practices for a sense of belonging in missions has been widely ignored.[70] The increasing interest in the globalization of trade and fashion in the seventeenth and eighteenth centuries tends to focus on its impact on Europe, and its relevance for the transformation of European society. As modern elites built up a new set of self-defining social practices in the eighteenth century, overseas imports such as tea, coffee, sugar, tobacco, and cotton came to play central roles in the performance of respectable identity.[71]

However, there is ample evidence in private correspondence that the most recent fashion was also of vital importance to European settlers around the world. In the second half of the eighteenth century, Manon Émerigon, who had married into the wealthy trading family Ruste de Rezeville, had her own fashion shop in French Martinique, which she ran with two other women. Her letters not only give evidence of the organization of her import and export fashion business, but list in great detail which fabrics, colors, and cuts were wanted in the Caribbean.[72] When France intervened in the American Revolutionary War in 1778, M. Buger, who was based at the French Fort Royal in the Caribbean, only briefly commented on the outbreak of war. However, he asked his correspondent, M. Louis Bertrand in Bourdeaux, if his shipping company was able to send a whole range of luxury goods and fabrics in the most fashionable colors. He added a shopping list: "Florance" (probably the taffeta "Gros-de-Florence");[73] gauze made of different thread with dots, stripes or in one color; crème-colored gauze and demy plain gauze; gauze made of decorative thread; black silk gloves for ladies; black embroidered ribbon, that is fine, no. 9, the same in white and pink; "these are the goods I would like you to send me to the value of 10.000 livres."[74] Private people, too, asked for the most recent fashions and fashion journals to be sent to them, and offered in return to send whatever might be of interest back to Europe. The late eighteenth-century wife of a plantation owner in Paramaribo, Surinam, asked for a bonnet decorated with lace, and with a ribbon exactly like the sample sent with her letter. She even gave the name and address of the fashion shop in Amsterdam where she wanted the items to be bought, and further desired a copy of a fashion almanac[75] (Figure 4.3).

Furthermore, far from necessarily bringing with it a sense of being a fashion "provincial," life in colonial settings seems to have provided an air of fashion liberty to ordinary Europeans, whose choice of dress and social practices subverted any sense of rank, dress, and habitus. For example, living in a colony such as the French Antilles

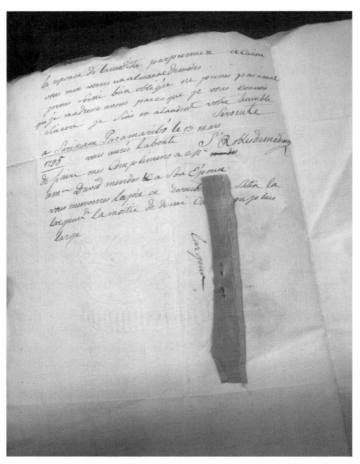

FIGURE 4.3: Letter sent by the wife of a plantation owner (name not legible) in Paramaribo to her brother in Amsterdam, asking for fashion journals and a variety of fashion articles, including a "Bonnet Cornette," decorated with lace and a ribbon just like the included; dated March 13, 1795. High Court of Admirality (HCA) 30/374. © Crown copyright images reproduced courtesy of The National Archives, UK. Photo: Annika Raapke.

permitted more playful experimentation with fashions, with more appropriation of aristocratic motifs and allusions than might have been permitted back in Europe.[76] The French missionary Jean-Baptiste du Terte described the arrival of newcomers as a kind of rebirth and self-fashioning. In their dress, these "French urban poor assume the power of travesty and the freedom to reinvent themselves," showing "the social significance of dress in a society situated entirely outside the bounds of traditional mechanisms for determining and policing class boundaries."[77]

The desire of migrants to dress themselves in European fashion was also shared by religious groups. However, for them it was important to display their beliefs upon their bodies. When the Moravians as the first large protestant missionary movement founded the Surinam mission in 1735, they soon after established a tailor's shop. We also know from private letters that dress, fashion, and artifacts as markers of religious—and of European—identity played a vital role in the new world,[78] especially in contrast to the "nakedness of negroes." The Moravians in Surinam ordered gray, dark blue, and dark green fabrics from their brethren in Germany, to tailor, wear, and sell their specific plain and dark-colored religious garments locally.[79] One of the brethren also ordered "blue scarfes" from Neutiedendorf in the duchy of Sachsen-Gotha-Altenburg in Germany, on "behalf of our negroes," who, so he explained to his correspondent, had seen the beautiful dark-blue scarves that had recently been sent from Europe and had asked for the same.[80]

The extent to which these imported European fashions blended with local dress and created new trends that might have influenced fashion and taste both outside Europe and *within* the European market, is an open question. Studies so far seem to suggest that the foreign was either imported into Europe as the exotic, that the indigenuous people imitated Europeans, or that fabrics and cuts were adapted to the taste of the European market.[81]

SUBVERSION OF PLAIN APPAREL

In spite of the strong emphasis, the protagonists of these religious groups put on plain apparel, modest conduct, and unity of religious dress, the believers were far from united in thought and demeanor, and not as conformist as their elders would have liked them to be. In the early eighteenth century in the Dutch Republic, criticism was voiced against wealthy Dutch Mennonites. In 1713, a poem by the popular poet and playwright Pieter Langendijk, lamented the corrupt manners of many Dutch Mennonites, their pompous splendor, vanity, and spiritual impoverishment.[82] A similar note was struck by Mennonite pastors in their own sermons:

> I have watched with a broken heart, and with grief and misery I still notice daily that in general the *Doopsgezinden* [Mennonites] increase the ostentation of their houses, household goods, weddings, feasts and clothes; that they follow on the heels of those who serve the world and imitate them in their jauntiness of manners, so that one can see little or no difference between them and the others (with the exception of those who are good). This especially does not suit them, for while it is adornment for the Christian to conform to the humility of Jesus, this other ostentation and excessiveness conflict with the confession and foundation of their religion.[83]

Many Dutch Mennonites had profited from the economic growth of the Dutch Republic through their widespread religious and economic networks, and their participation in international trade, especially the textile trade, ship-building, whale and herring fishing, the growing banking and insurance systems in Amsterdam, and speculation in commodities.[84] They had been able to gather substantial wealth, which was kept within their families thanks to inner-marriages.[85] Wealthy Mennonites in Amsterdam, who belonged to a liberal branch of the Mennonites, the Waterlanders, had their portraits painted by Rembrandt and many other artists, which present them in plain black clothes with the well-known white collars, head coverings, and without jewelry.[86] One of the most well-known paintings in this style was that of the wealthy Mennonite cloth merchant, ship owner, and preacher Cornelius Anslo, and his wife, which dates from 1641 (Figure 4.4).

The paintings were clearly meant to express Mennonite religious identity and the compliance of habit and conduct: plain, modest, pious. About one hundred years later, the style of self-representation had changed dramatically.[87] Mennonite portraits in the eighteenth century follow the general fashion of the time rather than aim to mirror religious codes of conduct and apparel. In a portrait from 1763, the Mennonite physician Dr. Simon Stinstra from the small town of Harlingen in the northwest of the Dutch Republic is shown wearing a fashionable "Indian red" silk jacket and a powdered wig (Figure 4.5).

FIGURE 4.4: *The Mennonite Preacher Anslo and his Wife*, signed by Rembrandt, 1641. Gemäldegalerie der Staatlichen Museen zu Berlin. Photo: Fine Art Images/Heritage Images/ Getty Images.

FIGURE 4.5: Portrait of Dr. Simon Stinstra (1735–82), deacon of the United Mennonite Congregation of Harlingen, signed by Tibout Regters, 1763, oil on canvas. Amsterdams Historisch Museum, Amsterdam.

In a companion portrait, his wife Anna Braam is portrayed in a blue dress decorated with fine white lace (Figure 4.6). She wears a lace cap on her head, and around her throat a necklace of red coral with a central silver adornment. There is more jewelry on her hands and wrists.[88]

Similar departures from plain and austere apparel as an expression of a modest and godly lifestyle happened in other parts of Western Europe, and in reaction, provoked contemporaries to condemn the Godly as hypocrites. In early eighteenth-century Prussia, where "material and career incentives were clearly linked with Pietism, insincere Pietism became common."[89] Not practicing what they preached, these "disingenuous" Pietists were criticized for feigning an ascetic lifestyle. They were parodied in cartoons and plays, and Luise Gottsched's characters "Herr Scheinfromm" and "Frau Glaubeleichthin" were easily recognizable by contemporaries.[90] However, a feature of German Pietism was that a number of highly-educated noble women joined the Pietist movement, and their apparel had to strike the right balance between the social distinction of the nobility, and the image

FIGURE 4.6: Portrait of Anna Braam (1738–77), deaconess of the United Mennonite Congregation of Harlingen, signed by Tibout Regters, 1763, oil on canvas. Amsterdams Historisch Museum, Amsterdam.

of a pious woman. Portraits like that of Henriette Catharina von Gersdorff represent her in moderate dress of the early eighteenth century—made, however, of costly materials such as velvet and lace—surrounded with religious artifacts as a testimony of her piety.[91]

FASHION, HABITUS, AND LACK OF DEVOTION

Criticism also came from within these religious groups when some members broke away from the idealized unity of habit and belief, and started to engage with contemporary fashion. Fellow religionists criticized them for their lack of sincerity and devotion, and in some religious groups severe frictions surfaced. This can be observed, for example, among Jewish communities in Western Europe, when under the influence of the Haskala (the Jewish Enlightenment) and the demands for emancipation and the granting of civil rights, many Jewish men and women adopted non-religious dress practices. They also demanded secular education to complement religious teaching, and argued in favor of the native

FIGURE 4.7: Portrait of Madame Kaulla, court Jew and wealthy trader; original by Johann
Baptist Seele, copy C. Berger, c. 1805. Photo: H. Zwietasch; Landesmuseum Württemberg,
Stuttgart.

mother tongue rather than Hebrew.[92] Wealthy Jewish merchants, especially in port cities,
and the so-called court Jews, who already dressed according to the fashion of their times,
have been defined as the seventeenth-century forerunners of these changes,[93] which were
then widely adopted by a new generation of Jewish men and women in the eighteenth
century (Figure 4.7).

Jewish critics of these developments formed the so-called Jewish Orthodoxy and
heavily attacked the Haskala for its threat to Jewish identity. The friction cannot be more
visible than in the self-representation of Jews in modish or artistic dress, as opposed to the
dark and austere habit of religious orthodoxy. A fine example is the rococo-style portrait
of the Jewish intellectual Henriette Herz (who had opened one of the first famous literary
salons in Berlin)[94] as the Greek Godess Hebe (Figure 4.8).

Henriette is shown with loose uncovered hair and bare shoulders, holding a chalice
with wine. Both posing for such a portrait and its iconography was revolutionary for
many Jews, and traditional fellow religionists accused her of indecency, sexual promiscuity,
indulgence in alcohol and idolatry.

FIGURE 4.8: Portrait of Henriette Herz (1762–1847) as the Greek goddess Hebe, signed Anna Dorothea Therbusch, dated 1778. Staatliche Museen zu Berlin, Nationalgalerie. © bpk–Bildagentur für Kunst, Kultur und Geschichte/Nationalgalerie, SMB.

FASHIONING CIVIC VIRTURE

Under the impact of the Enlightenment the redefinition of religious identity and self-fashioning gathered momentum. There was a growing public engagement among some members of religious minorities, especially among successful merchant dynasties of religious diasporas. This engagement was characterized by classical learning, involvement in works of charity, an interest in the fine arts and fashion, and the public display of connoisseurship and taste coupled with wealth. All this contributed to a change in habitus. This did not necessarily imply a lack of religious devotion, but a change in the outward appearance of religious identities, dress, and belief.

With the rise of civic society, the extravagant dress practices of the long eighteenth century and its attendant public discourses on the vices of indulgent self-fashioning were counterbalanced with a more sober, yet elegant, presentation. At first sight, appearances were not standardized, however, there was a "proliferation of secondary significations which culminated in the refinement of tact and habits."[95] In their choice of clothes, cut, fabrics, and colors, men and women opted for "natural" beauty and demeanor as a marker of a new social class that dissociated itself from the aristocracy as well as from the laboring poor. Appearances changed dramatically within the European Enlightenment. Habit as the embodiment of a disposition, a mind, a posture, and a condition or quality was carefully fashioned to comply with the new morals of civic society: decency, modesty, and an economy of manners visible in the transformation of social practices and beliefs of the time.

CHAPTER FIVE

Gender and Sexuality

DOMINIC JANES

Fashion in the Age of the Enlightenment was shaped not only by legal and commercial pressures, but also by changing ideas about embodiment, gender, and sexual pleasure. Moreover, changes in dress can be seen both as reflecting such wider changes in society and as having made a contribution in their own right to patterns of cultural change. In early modern Europe, aristocrats and a proportion of wealthier townspeople and artisans dressed in accordance with changing styles at court. However, by the end of the eighteenth century, fashion was being embraced by the burgeoning middle ranks of society and was coming to be strongly shaped by their spending power. Social competition spurred on the demand for new modes and those in the industry of production and distribution of clothing and accessories had every incentive to encourage the purchase of new clothes to replace those that were not worn out but were simply out of style.[1] Unwanted items were then sold locally, remade or else handed over to servants, who sometimes expected cloth and clothing as a perquisite. The desirability of the garment in question, as in the case of the erotic allure of a dress, was widely equated with its degree of finery in materials and construction, and also its adherence to current styles. Many female prostitutes, for instance, attempted to dress themselves as much like fine ladies as they could, a practice that appears to have been copied by some of their male, cross-dressing "molly" counterparts both in European cities and in their equivalents across the Atlantic such as Philadelphia.[2]

The European center of fashion was Paris, but status-conscious inhabitants of other countries often relied on local reproductions of French styles. This was because of the import tariffs that were levied by states such as England and Prussia which were periodically at war with France. Moreover, those countries in particular saw a sustained moral critique of French patterns of consumption which had the effect of promoting the development of plainer styles. This was particularly the case in relation to men's fashion which sometimes referenced the dress of the country gentry or of the army. In their turn, the British sporting styles, which were convenient to wear on horseback, were adopted and adapted by the French. In addition to this new wider European fashion in clothing, many regions of Europe and the wider transatlantic world continued to maintain their own local traditions of dress, in which the mechanisms of fashionable change operated to a greater or lesser extent depending on degrees of prosperity and the extent to which local regimes persisted in maintaining forms of sumptuary legislation.[3]

Fashion in the course of the eighteenth century was increasingly associated with women; however, many of those who controlled the fashion industry or commented upon its products were men. Enlightenment, notoriously, did not result in anything like equality for women. This sometimes resulted in dismissals of the realm of fashion as being something that was essentially frivolous because it was feminine, and feminine because it was frivolous.[4] On the other hand it was increasingly retorted, in later eighteenth-century periodicals, that it was only natural, and indeed rational, for women to want to please their menfolk.[5] Such debates notwithstanding, fashionable styles for men evolved almost as quickly as did those for women and this generated much of the critical heat that appeared during this period concerning the rationality or morality of styles of dress. This chapter explores these wider developments while presenting a case study of the allegedly effeminate, fashion-conscious man. It also focuses on stylistic relations between Britain and France which produced some of the most dynamic and sustained controversies over dress, gender, and sexual preference during this period.

The broad pattern during the Age of the Enlightenment was for men's and women's dress to become increasingly distinct. Brightly-colored fabrics, and the use of materials such as lace were employed by both sexes in the late seventeenth century, but mostly by women a century later. What underlay this was a momentous shift in the relations between biological sex and the performance of gender. The work of the cultural historian Thomas Laqueur has played an important in role in aiding our comprehension of these changes. In the early modern period, men and women were thought of as being different in degree, with the latter being seen as a similar, albeit (physically and mentally) lesser, version of the former.[6] While still retaining theories of female inferiority, scientific opinion changed such that by the middle of the eighteenth century women were seen as distinctly different in *kind* from men.[7] This shift in opinion has been seen by social historians as having originated in a change in the conceptualization of the household from a unit of production in which men and women essentially shared the work, to one in which a female domestic sphere was imagined as distinctively separate from male public life.[8] Men and women were increasingly seen as different both mentally and physically, such that the latter were understood as being essentially fragile, vulnerable, emotional, nervous, and passionate. A side effect of this process was that it became increasingly obvious that some women and men neither fitted these evolving stereotypes nor the new fashions which made novel attempts to assert a clear sense of gender distinction.

Randolph Trumbach has argued that it was in this context that we can understand the eclipse of early modern understandings of gender indeterminacy. These were rooted in the classical figure of the hermaphrodite, a being who possessed a blend of male and female anatomy. In its place, he argues, there arose the figure of the effeminate sodomite who was genitally masculine but physically and mentally weak.[9] Fashions which failed to preserve a sufficient difference from those worn by women could thus threaten to transform the body of the normative male into that of the loathed sodomite, a man who had deviant sex such as with another man. Status in fashionable society, and this was particularly true of Britain after the Glorious Revolution of 1688 and of France after the French Revolution of 1789, was increasingly defined by displays of gendered taste rather than simply of spending power related to rank.

The sexually desirable female form of the period tended to emphasize the hips through the use of various forms of stays, corseting, paniers, and hoops. The aim of the latter was to give volume to skirts and their tendency was to increase in size over time. Thus, in Britain, the hooped petticoat appeared around 1710 and then proceeded to enlarge dramatically to a peak around 1750, at which point fashionable women began to find it difficult to get through the doors of their own dress shops. Such voluminous dresses used up ever greater quantities of material and, as such, acted as an obvious site of conspicuous consumption.[10] The broadening of the woman's profile also implied lush fertility and while substantial skirts appeared to keep lusting men at arm's length they did have a tendency to become upset and thus afford sudden glimpses of leg. The dangers (or opportunities) in this respect were even greater in Britain than they were in the France of Jean-Honoré Fragonard's *The Swing* ("La balancoire") (Figure 5.1) since women of the island race did not wear underwear (since drawers were regarded by the gender-conscious British as being distinctively masculine).[11] All that notwithstanding, it can also be argued

FIGURE 5.1: *The Swing*, Jean-Honoré Fragonard, 1767. © By kind permission of the Trustees of the Wallace Collection, London.

that the larger female garments of the period also acted to emphasize the physical presence of their wearers and can be read not simply as encumbrances but also as tools for visible self-assertion.

The use of strips of whalebone (baleen or *baleine*) with lacing at the front, back, or both sides of a separate garment had begun in the mid-sixteenth century, and it formed an essential element in French women's fashions for most of the following two centuries. Propriety demanded that stays be worn but medical opinion was, however, frequently hostile to tight lacing, notably in German-speaking areas of Europe. Reports of the dangers of stays spread from the 1740s onwards and even developed legal force in Austria with the intervention of Emperor Joseph II in the 1780s.[12] He was particularly concerned with the health of children who were typically dressed by the aristocracy in miniature versions of adult styles.[13] That these concerns had specifically sexual connotations is clear from considering the attitudes of the author of *Emile, ou de l'éducation* (1762) which was to have a remarkable impact on fashionable attitudes to child rearing. Jean-Jaques Rousseau (1712–78) is one of the founder figures of Romanticism and of the cult of the (supposedly) natural life. In 1751 he had fallen ill and, in a secularized version of Christian renunciation, vowed to lay aside worldly pomp if he were to recover.[14] Not only did he reject elaborate dress in favor of plainness, but he advocated that others should do the same. But his enthusiasm from the liberation of the youthful female body from the bondage of tight constraint was precisely founded on his strong awareness of the sexual forwardness that this style implied.[15] After all, the fact that mothers and daughters were dressed in the same way meant that there was no clear difference between the dress of sexually experienced women and virgins.[16]

Eighteenth-century fashions for women were, generally speaking, meant to be sexually alluring even though women were also required to aspire to virtue as an essential female quality. Flirtation, if not seduction, was the order of the day and its most sophisticated and intense expression was probably to be found in salon society in Paris where many of the women were far from the empty-headed male fantasies painted by the likes of Jean-Honoré Fragonard for various of his male patrons (Figure 5.1).[17] Nevertheless masquerades were quite as popular among the London bourgeoisie as they were among the more libidinous elements of *ancien régime* France. Under the cover of the masquerade, identities could be swapped and sexual indiscretions committed.[18] By the mid-eighteenth century, London had grown to such an extent that fashionable public gardens such as those in Vauxhall on the south bank of the Thames were places where various social ranks could, to a degree, mingle promiscuously. Fashions developed in fancy dress such as for the wearing of elements of "oriental" costume such as loose, Turkish trousers by women. These evoked erotic fantasies of the Turkish harem or even forms of gender transgression.[19] Similarly the taste for *chinoiserie* in silks, employed both for dress fabrics and for hanging on domestic walls, offered the pleasures of sensual ornament.[20] Yet it is important to emphasize that the parties at which young ladies cross-dressed as soldiers and footman as Persian kings relied for their effect on the entrenchment of norms of gender and sexual performance.[21] Yet this evolving society, for all its concerns over sex and gender, was on the whole productive of a vast expansion of fashion as an expression of erotic desire. It was in this period that, perhaps for the first time, substantial numbers of people were able to buy clothes, the main point of which was to look attractive, rather than to keep their wearers warm and respectable.

GENDER AND SEXUALITY BETWEEN FRANCE
AND GREAT BRITAIN

The fact that ostentation was a key element in the display of power in *ancien régime* France does not mean that it was innocent of elements of travesty. Indeed, it can be argued that it was the very strength of the legitimating role of rank in that aristocratic society that allowed play with aspects of gender identity to be seen as a matter of triviality and amusement. That certain aspects of life at the court of Versailles were self-consciously mannered exhibitions of excess rather than simply expressions of power through conspicuous consumption is implied by the behavior of Philippe de France (1640–1701), the brother of Louis XIV (1638–1715) who, on occasion, dressed in public as a woman and required his attendants on such occasions to do the same.[22] Thus, when the king hosted staged ceremonial battles on the "fields" outside the palace, the attendance of his brother in women's clothing expressed aristocratic entitlement and self-confidence. That notwithstanding, it has been argued that the verb "to camp" owes it origins to those self-same fields ("*champs*") of fakery and knowing transgression.

"Monsieur" married twice and fathered seven children (Figure 5.2). It is possible that he may have been what in later ages would come to be referred to as a "bisexual"

FIGURE 5.2: *Philippe de France with His Daughter Marie Louise*, School of Pierre Mignard, c. 1670, oil paint, Château de Versailles, MV 2161. Photo: © RMN-Grand Palais (Château de Versailles),

but it is important to emphasize that his appearance and behavior need to be judged in relation to the attitudes of his time. By twenty-first century standards, even the male fashions of the French court were colorful and flamboyant, but the message they gave was one of access to wealth and power, and not of effeminate weakness. However, the eighteenth century marked an important period of transition towards increasingly sharp distinctions in the fashions thought appropriate for men and women in terms of color, cut, and materials. The broad pattern was for spending on clothing to rise steadily during this period, with steeper rises for the rich than for the poor and for women rather than men.[23] Nevertheless, society remained strongly patriarchal and the dominant discourses of the time on fashion in general continued to be shaped primarily by men even as the role of women as consumers grew steadily in importance. A key aspect of the period was a desire for novelty.[24] Older and cheaper modes were passed down through the social ranks.[25] At the same time, and particularly in Britain, there were tendencies for men's fashions to rise up the social spectrum, notably in relation to sports and country clothing where the aristocracy took up styles previously sported by the gentry.[26]

A key aspect of this latter tendency was that it promoted the wearing by men of simpler and darker clothing, a powerful trend that John Flügel conceptualized as the "great masculine renunciation."[27] In the seventeenth century, however, black was worn quite widely around Europe and had a variety of local connotations. In parts of Italy and in Spain, the wearing of dark colors appears to have been derived from the status of Catholic piety at court whereas in the Netherlands black clothing was widely adopted by Protestants as a mark of commercial sobriety.[28] It is true that the French aristocracy had a tendency to employ lighter shades and that men, in that country, took to brighter colors in the course of the eighteenth century. But even in France, black was much worn at the beginning of the century.[29] In England, dark clothing was sometimes associated with Puritans but it is, perhaps, better to emphasize that such people advocated "plain style" in speech and deportment as well as dress.[30] Fine black cloth evoked social status simply because it was relatively expensive.[31] Black was a difficult color to dye successfully and fine gradations were carefully judged. What is revealing, however, is that the tendency for plainness outlasted Cromwell and his Commonwealth.[32] Evidence for the origins of the men's three-piece-suit have often been traced to the entry made by Samuel Pepys in his diary on October 7, 1666 in which it was recorded that Charles II had declared that he would abandon doublet and hose, and appear in a vest (the precursor of the waistcoat, worn together with coat and breeches), a style which may ultimately have had Persian antecedents.[33] The resultant costume was first made fashionable by royal patronage but was subsequently to become widely associated with manly virtue. Men of a range of political persuasions came to embrace a fashion for what was taken to be a relative degree of sobriety in dress: "guarding the boundaries of the aristocratic polity meant donning the image of noble simplicity, presenting the landed gentleman as true-born Englishman and the moral backbone of the nation."[34]

Bourgeois and aristocratic elements mingled in varying proportions in the various parts of Europe. Even after events such as the Glorious Revolution of 1688 that pushed the balance of power in Britain towards mercantile as opposed to landed interests, the upper ranks of society continued to be dominated by those who had inherited their wealth and status. Moreover, success among the rich and prominent in society continued to depend heavily upon the management of personal connections. It was, in fact, the persistence of aristocratic forms in the context of weakened aristocratic power that meant that dress and deportment became, if anything, even more important as elements of the advocacy of the self. It was the activities of this group of people, sufficiently exclusive that they would come to be referred to as "Society" (with a capital S), that sustained the growth of the "season" in London. This was when "provincials" and the landed gentry flocked to the capital to meet each other, to shop, and to see and be seen. One of the major differences between the life of the "beau monde" in London, and its equivalent in Paris, was that the latter was dominated to a much greater extent by court protocol, although this lessened after 1700 when more and more nobles moved to live in Paris among traders, financiers, and the like. British politics can be dissected into the operations of "Tories" and "Whigs" who placed more or less stress on the operations of the Houses of Commons and Lords respectively. However, many of those in the Commons were the younger sons of peers and it was not until the 1880s that new money was clearly to become dominant in the junior chamber.

This did not mean that the upper ranks of society were socially static in the old regime. The seventeenth century had seen the creation of baronets, for instance, and this was repeated under Queen Anne. Those who were jockeying for favors from the powerful could employ fashion as a way of calling attention to themselves while projecting a self-image of success. Elite clothing, in such circumstances, was not just concerned with personal pleasure because it was of career importance. This applied just as much to a man seeking a sinecure or a rich wife, as to a woman seeking an attractive or wealthy husband. Those who had a title, power, style, and deportment were admired and imitated. These processes, at least to some degree, descended the social spectrum. Such practices, in combination with the steady importation of new styles from France, and egged on by merchants eager for new business, drove an increasingly rapid cycle of consumption. In both Britain and France, increasing prosperity led to a steadily rising scale of expenditure on fashion through the course of the eighteenth century, particularly on the part of women. Because the boundaries of the "beau monde" were ill-defined, it was possible for people to enter it or pretend that they had done so.[35] The aim of such pretence might extend to the possibilities of life outside such elite circles, for while those in the upper ranks knew each other, people of lower station had to judge by appearances. Therefore, to be able to pass as a lady or a gentleman greatly expanded the potential for obtaining credit from tradespeople.[36]

It has been argued that "an overriding emphasis on cultural qualifications offered considerable opportunities to certain cohorts within the beau monde, arguably most significantly to women who were able to establish themselves as leaders of fashion in their own right."[37] Why, then, did many men, when compared to women, apparently take a step back from the establishment of the self through fashionable ostentation in dress? One answer has been provided by those who regard the Age of Enlightenment as witnessing a radical reorganization of the gendering of men. Thomas King has argued that such changes were pioneered in Britain. He argues that across Europe, and with varying degrees of speed and intensity, an older model of courtly manhood dependent upon the patronage of social superiors was gradually replaced by a new ideal of the autonomous head of the patriarchal household. In this schema, participation in civic life was no longer to be at the whim of a social elite but was, at least in theory, to be determined by personal virtue.[38] Such novel ideas of manliness were reinforced by the denigration of those men who continued to seek the patronage of the elite as being effeminate toadies. In the process, sexual normativity became firmly bolted to the performance of duties as father and husband, and practices of vying for favor at court became associated not merely with effeminacy but with associations of aristocratic arrogance and sodomitical favoritism.[39] In the process new modes of respectability required that men perform sobriety and reject flamboyance and theatricality. This helps to explain why it was that panics over male effeminacy and sodomy were so much more frequent and prominent in Britain than they were in France, where rank more clearly trumped gender as a mark of status before 1789.[40]

One important result of these changes was that interest in fashion became increasingly regarded as being a preoccupation characteristic of women and of effeminate men. This also meant that French men were increasingly read in Britain as effeminate. Such notions fed into the development of discourse and cultural practices that aimed to secure masculinity as being the peculiar characteristic of particular nations. Something similar happened in Spain where the fashion for "*majismo*" saw the social elites copying forms of lower-class dress and demonising those emerging from Paris as being those of the "*petimetre*."[41] The "*petit-maître*" ("little master") was read in Britain as being an effete social upstart who attempted to rise to prominence in society through copying French modes. Under a wide variety of names such as fops, fribbles, and beaux, the prominence of such figures in satire is eloquent testimony to the prevalence of concern about male effeminacy understood in relation not merely to femininity and androgyny, but also to both mental and physical weakness, reckless expenditure, and unpatriotic enthusiasm for foreign culture and mores.[42] However prevalent they were in real life, such characters were a mainstay of contemporary theatrical comedy as in Sir Novelty Fashion's appearance in Colley Cibber's *Love's Last Shift* (1696). These stereotypes inverted the older model of the man of mode as the possessor of social power and implied that he was now a trespasser on female prerogatives. It is no accident that also at this time male milliners, and others working in the fashion industry, were increasingly stereotyped as effeminate.[43] Furthermore, they were periodically associated with outright gender travesty and sodomy. Thus in 1703, Thomas Baker's play *Tunbridge-Walks* included a cross-dressing character called Maiden, who had worked in fashion.[44] And in the first of William Hogarth's *Rake's Progress* series it is also no accident that the tailor is shown kneeling before Tom Rakewell's crotch intent on (measuring) his thigh.[45]

It is important to stress that connections between effeminacy and sodomy were in development during the eighteenth century.[46] Previously, sodomitical desire was associated most often with libertinism and perverse lust as an aspect of masculine excess. It is notable for instance that in John Vanburgh's *The Relapse; or, Virtue in Danger* (1696) it is not Lord Foppington who is a sodomite but another character called Coupler.[47] The shift in the public mood can be judged, however, by a newspaper comment on this play from 1764 in which it was argued for its bowdlerisation on the grounds that Coupler's "proposals to young Foppington would be, if that part were acted [today], sufficient to congeal the blood in the veins of a modern audience."[48] Tobias Smollett, in his picaresque novel *The Adventures of Roderick Random* (1748), depicted examples of the two forms of male behavior that fell under particular suspicion of sodomitical desire, that of the unscrupulous and disgusting rake (Strutwell), and of the scented effeminate (Whiffle). While Strutwell was wont to take active sexual advantage of men in the pursuit of wealth, it was Whiffle who signaled the presence of innately feminine tastes, implicitly including sexual tastes, through his dress and deportment.

> Whiffle, for that was his name, took possession of the ship, surrounded with a crowd of attendants, all of whom, in their different degrees, seemed to be of their patron's

disposition; and the air was so impregnated with perfumes, that one may venture to affirm the clime of Arabia Foelix was not half so sweet-scented.[49]

He and his companions are singled out as a certain type of man who behaves in a feminine way and who associates with others of similar tastes. The implication is that Strutwells would take the active part in sex while Whiffles would take the passive. In the light of Randolph Trumbach's work, it can be argued that what was being depicted here derived respectively from an older, libertine model of male behavior in which evil men might consort with both whores and boys, and a newer model involving dangerously passive effeminate men (sometimes referred to as "mollies," who, like women, sought penetration by men, and in search of this made themselves up to look as young and feminine as possible).[50] Thus it was spotted in *Faustina,* a satirical poem of 1726, that in the "Sodomite's Club," some "doat on Men, and some on Boys."[51]

It is important to stress, however, that sodomy was simply one of a series of valences which might visit the stereotype of the ridiculous man of fashion. As Susan Staves wrote in her important article, "A few kind words for the fop," it was often the case that "the so-called effeminacy of these old fops was an early if imperfect attempt at the refinement, civility, and sensitivity most of us would now say are desirable masculine virtues."[52] The figure of the fop was meant, above all, to flatter those men in the audience who felt that they had achieved a polite and cultured balance between the lurid excesses of the rake, on the one hand, and the pathetic vaporings of the fop on the other.[53] This careful balancing act depended on the cultivation of taste and a discerning approach to fashionable culture. It required, if anything, ever greater care in the selection of clothes, so as to avoid mockery for being either under- or over-dressed.[54] Thus, although a fop was not the same thing as a sodomite, the function of the phobic stereotype was to entrench standards of sexual normativity and, arguably to originate aspects of what would come to be known as the (homosexual) closet.[55]

Something of a crisis of male self-representation was to erupt in the 1760s and 1770s in the form of the "macaroni" craze for male sartorial excess which was to end shortly after a series of sodomitical scandals. In David Garrick's *The Male-Coquette* (1757), a woman cross-dresses as the foppish Marchese di Macaroni.[56] The reference here is to the notion that Italian aristocrats, like their French counterparts, were allegedly luxurious and effeminate. There was a further reference behind the name of this character, which was to the supposed cultural dangers of the Grand Tour (of France and Italy). The author and politician Horace Walpole referred in a letter of February 6, 1764 to gambling at "the Maccaroni [sic] Club" which, he said, was composed of "all the travelled young men who wear long curls and spying-glasses."[57] While the aims of the Grand Tour were lofty ones of educational improvement, satire suggested that the results in practice were rather less impressive.[58] There was, in fact, a distinctly libertine air to the phenomenon in so far as young men were often expected to have their first sexual experiences in the course of their travels in lands where the climate supposedly predisposed the population to libidiny.[59] While there is no evidence that there was a formally constituted "club" for macaronis, the well-known, one might say infamous, Society of Dilettanti, became a focus for rakish excess, including play acting at private parties as randy Roman Catholic priests.[60] Catholicism was widely received in Protestant Britain as being associated with public pomp and private turpitude.[61] It also participated in the construction of sodomy as being a continental vice that was widespread among the (unmarried) Catholic clergy.[62] Georges Rousseau has argued that the rumors of vice in Italy underpinned that region's attractions for men who, and in this he includes Walpole, were sexually attracted to other men.[63] But does that suggest that the macaronis that he identified in 1764 were similarly inclined and that their flamboyant use of fashion is evidence of sexual tastes and identities?

One thing we do know a good deal about is what macaronis were alleged to look like. This is because they became the center of a satirical craze for macaroni prints. These are by no means uniform but they do have a tendency to return to a set of stereotypical characteristics which centered on the puny but over-dressed man. A precursor of this type can be seen from the pen of Walpole himself in the form of his drawing of Clotworthy Skeffington, the second Earl of Massereene (1743–1805), whom Walpole had met in Paris in the winter of 1765–6 and who was an extravagant man of fashion who remained unmarried until 1789 (Figure 5.3).[64] His style can be compared

FIGURE 5.3: *Clotworthy Skeffington, 2nd Earl of Massereene*, Horace Walpole, c. 1765–6, drawing. Courtesy of the Lewis Walpole Library, Yale University.

with, for instance *Lord - - - [Villiers] or the nosegay macaroni* (c. 1773) which was in Walpole's collection of prints (Figure 5.4).

In "Macaroni dresses for 1740 and 1776" (c. 1776) (note, however, that the term "macaroni" was not in use in 1740) the key difference is that the figure has become thinner, the stance more upright, and the cut considerably tighter. In *How d'Ye Like Me*

FIGURE 5.4: *Lord - - - [George Villiers] or the Nosegay Macaroni*, published in *The Macaroni and Theatrical Magazine*, February 1773, p. 193, etching. Courtesy of the Lewis Walpole Library, Yale University.

(Figure 5.5), brought out by the London publisher Carington Bowles in November 1772, the macaroni appears as an effeminate and androgynous simpleton, fashionably dressed, standing in an elaborate French-styled interior, who seems to be caught in the act of flirting with the purchaser (and that would often be a male purchaser) of the print.[65] The classical discourse of the hermaphrodite was referenced by depicting this simpering figure with but a vestigial sword and with a prominent vulva-like crease where his penis ought to be.[66]

HOW D'YE LIKE ME.

FIGURE 5.5: *How d'Ye Like Me*, published by Carington Bowles, 1772, hand-colored mezzotint. © The Trustees of the British Museum.

The moment at which macaroni style, or at least satirical depictions of macaroni style, became enmeshed in issues surrounding sexuality as well as gender was the summer of 1772 when Captain Robert Jones was found guilty, although subsequently pardoned, for committing sodomy with a thirteen-year-old boy. He was well-known in the world of London society having been involved, among other things, with popularizing fireworks and skating as fashionable diversions. Various reports in the popular press not only attacked Jones but, by implication, the social circles in which he moved. Thus a letter to *The Public Ledger* on August 5, 1772 contented that Jones was "too much engaged in every scene of idle Dissipation and wanton Extravagence"; it condemned "this MILITARY MACCARONI," and continued, "therefore, ye Beaux, ye sweet-scented, simpering he-she things, deign to learn wisdom from the death of a Brother."[67] Three days later, *The Morning Chronicle and London Advertiser* reported that an "effeminate prigg of a Macaroni" was set on by a mob when he said he was glad that Jones had been "respited."[68] Meanwhile in Islington, a fashionable northern suburb of the city, a huge crowd gathered, "proposed hanging a Sodomite in effigy," and was only prevented by a magistrate who read out the Riot Act.[69] It was reported that Jones was about to take himself into exile in Florence, and that he had letters of credit and recommendation "to many people of fashion there."[70] Peter McNeil has argued that associations between macaroni fashions and sodomitical tastes were confirmed rather than created by these events: "by the 1760s when the macaroni emerged, such attention to fashion was read as evidence of a *lack of interest* [emphasis original] in women, or as potentially unattractive to women."[71] It seems clear that supposedly excessive forms of fashion, notably those that rejected more sober British forms of male attire, could be condemned by reference to sexual tastes by the 1770s. Moreover, though this is much harder to determine, such fashions may have been used to indicate sexual preferences. Macaroni and (what might be termed) proto-homosexual subcultures are likely to have overlapped.[72]

Just as there was no such thing as a clearly formed homosexual identity in the eighteenth century there was also no use of a term directly analogous to "heterosexual." Nevertheless, it can be argued that the events of this time can also be read as part of wider process of identifying fashions with normative sexual as well as gender identities. To give just one example, on July 30, 1773 a group of young men who leered at a certain Mrs. Hartley as if she were a prostitute when she was out walking in Vauxhall Gardens, on the banks of the Thames, were denounced by her friend and companion, Henry Bate, as effeminate macaronis: "the dress, hat and feather, — miniature picture, pendant at his snow-white bosom, and a variety of other appendages to this *man of fashion*, were naturally seized upon by me."[73] The crowd joined in Bate's laughter and Mrs Hartley's honor was vindicated. But the key point is that the fashionable dress worn by these aggressively rakish men was used as evidence that they were pathetic, narcissistic effeminates. In this scene, ostentatious male dress was reconfigured from being positively evocative of male empowerment (including libidinous entitlement) and now appeared as the evidence of social and sexual failure.

One way to look at this situation is to say that fashion was becoming increasingly enmeshed in a culture in which there was not only increasing awareness of sexual preference as an aspect of identity but which increasingly looked to polite regulation of male desires. Thus when one looks at two survivals of suits from around 1765 owned by John Chute, a member of Walpole's (allegedly) sodomitical social circle, what one sees is not great ostentation in style of material but great care in construction, notably in relation to *internal* tailoring.[74] What this might tell us is that fashion could be employed in the second half of the eighteenth century subtly to encode a variety of aspects of messages, including, potentially, those concerned with aspects of sexual identity. The connection between male effeminacy and same-sex desire needs to be considered, of course, in relation to the evolving nature of notions of sex and gender in the eighteenth century.[75] During this period significant changes occurred in relation to attitudes towards those who did not fit normative expectations of men and women. The classical concept of the hermaphrodite, a being possessing both male and female sexual attributes, came to be fused with the medieval figure of the sodomite, one who transgressed sexually against God's laws. The result was to create the perception of a sort of person in whom physical and moral aberration was joined. Nineteenth-century sexology was to label such people as "homosexuals." However, the development of what was to become the homosexual subject was hindered by the fact that sodomy was associated with fearful violence against the moral order and effeminacy with pathetic weakness. This meant that there was no single, clear system of classification in the eighteenth century of types of people by sexual preference.

While the sin of sodomy was well known and duly criminalized, there was no such equivalent transgression in the case of sexual acts between two women. This was partly because of the sexist and phallocentric nature of the law. Women who were powerfully emotional towards one another were, typically, read as (excessively) sentimental rather than as sexually deviant. However, the adoption by women of men's clothing was a matter for public notice and, it has to be said, a considerable degree of consternation. Some lesbians in the twentieth century have lived with a same-sex partner in a way that appeared to mimic heterosexual marriage in so far as one partner adopted the dress and mores of a husband and the other of a wife. It is, therefore, tempting to read a household such as that of Mary Hamilton, alias George, who married her partner when disguised as a man, as being a lesbian one. While it is impossible to know exactly what currents of desire were involved it is revealing to examine male responses to such circumstances as, for instance, were displayed in Henry Fielding's *The Female Husband* (1746). What is perhaps most striking is his sense of fascination with the figure of a masculine, "Amazonian" woman.[76] Moreover, such beings received a significantly better press than did the effeminate male as can be seen from the case of the Chevalier d'Eon (1728–1810) who was a man who cross-dressed as a woman but was widely understood in his own lifetime to have been a woman who cross-dressed as a man.

As has been seen in the case of Philippe de France, occasional cross-dressing was a feature of court life at Paris. In the service of the king of France, d'Eon had attended masquerade balls at the court of Catherine the Great between 1756 and 1757, where men were required to dress as women and vice versa.[77] However, it was only after he fled into British exile in the following decade that he is recorded as having appeared in women's clothes in daily life. The fact that he was able to do so implies that he did not face immediate hostility for doing so even thought he was noted for his muscular physique and was not able to "pass" as a woman with ease. However, he did face some hostility because of his nationality and the mounting panic over sodomy and effeminacy made his position rather more difficult.[78] Thus his friendship with the politician John Wilkes became something of a liability when the latter began further to stir up the anti-sodomitical climate by attacking the king's pardon for Captain Jones so as to draw attention from gossip that linked him with d'Eon as part of a alleged sodomitical cabal.[79] By 1776–7, d'Eon was being accused of consorting with mollies (sodomites associated for cross-dressing) or even of being a molly himself (Figure 5.6).[80]

Lnd. Mag. *Sep.* 1777.

MADEMOISELLE de BEAUMONT, or the
CHEVALIER D'EON.
Female Minister Plenipo. Capt. of Dragoons &c.&c.

FIGURE 5.6: *Mademoiselle de Beaumont, or the Chevalier d'Eon,* published in *The London Magazine* 46 (1777), p. 443, engraving. Courtesy of the Lewis Walpole Library, Yale University.

However, d'Eon was never generally shunned by high society, despite the slurs that were flying about in the press. On his return to France he was refused a return to the army and was required to remain in women's attire. It seems that he was most widely understood to be a fascinating case of a woman whose masculine nature made her unattractive to men which was why she remained unmarried. Because masculinity was widely seen (by many women as well as men) as a superior state it was not considered reprehensible for a woman to aspire to a degree of masculinity. Disputes over d'Eon's status continue today, with opinions that range from those that label him a male transvestite to others that argue that his behavior was rooted in a feminist critique of male norms.[81]

Radical and revisionist stances towards gender reform rose in importance after the outbreak of the French Revolution but they never attained a position of great influence. Nevertheless, they drew on developing currents of thought that advanced what were presented as more "natural" styles of behavior and dress for both men and women. The rise of notions of male politeness and the development of the cult of sensibility were currents that to some degree counteracted the trend sharply to distinguish male and female natures. However, the degree to which politeness ruled male behavior in the second half of the eighteenth century is much disputed.[82] Furthermore, male fashions at the end of the eighteenth century were to be fired by a return to expressions of more overt virility in the context of the militarization of Europe that developed as the French Revolution ended and the Napoleonic Wars began. In 1789, servants' liveries and a variety of other indicators of social distinction were abolished in France.[83] Revolutionary virtue was expressed through short-lived crazes for red, white, and blue clothing or, and perhaps ironically, for an increased enthusiasm for the plainer English modes on the part of leaders such as Marat.[84] Even outside the areas subsequently conquered by Napoleon, aristocrats had to work increasingly hard to combat the decline of social deference and concomitant accusations of parasitism. The American Revolution had, of course, inspired similar developments in the newly established United States. Calls for national uniforms, however, generally fell on deaf ears and the fashion industry survived into a new age in which styles were shaped more by the taste for Romanticism and the choices of the bourgeoisie rather than of aristocratic attendees at royal courts or the advocates of moral reform.

CONCLUSION

The eighteenth century has sometimes been referred to as "the century of sex."[85] And it is no coincidence that it was during the eighteenth century that the concept of fetishism first appeared.[86] The origins of the notion of the fetish lay in European encounters with Africans who, the former thought, had a tendency to value certain objects disproportionately. In the course of the nineteenth century, Karl Marx was to theorize that such mystification was a key element not so much of "primitive" societies as of the operation of contemporary capital. His concept of "commodity fetishism" was then joined by that of "sexual fetishism" which aimed to explain why particular objects, particularly garments, were sometimes regarded as being charged with a particular degree of eroticism. Sigmund Freud, for example, argued that men had a tendency erotically to identify with objects that they understood as "completing" the body of a woman (modeled on that of their mother) viewed as incomplete because it lacked a penis.[87]

Whichever theory of fetishism one may wish to employ, it is quite clear that links between sexual desirability and commodity culture had grown increasingly strong in the course of the age of the Enlightenment. Ironically enough, black Africans often appear in paintings of the time as fetishized, exotic possessions.[88] Fashionable clothing should be seen in relation to the bodies it was designed to contain and the architectural or landscape contexts those bodies inhabited. Thus, if sexually fetishized material culture was often strongly associated with the eroticization by men of women, the female dressing room became the place of femininity and eroticism par excellence. Dressing rooms and closets appear in house designs from the middle of the seventeenth century.[89] Depending on the women concerned, such spaces evoked various combinations of lasciviousness and moral virtue, but in both cases the identity of the occupant was powerfully constructed through her choice of garments.[90] In the dressing room, "objects were like extensions of the body, part of a wardrobe that, correctly worn, could turn the activities of elite existence into dances of artful persuasion."[91] The degree to which clothing accentuated, concealed, or displayed the female body fed the development of an erotic imagination that moved from the contemplation of Classical nudes to the imagined delights of naked women.[92] In a British satirical print from 1786, a dress literally stands in for a woman (Figure 5.7). With

FIGURE 5.7: *The Bum-Bailiff Outwitted; or the Convenience of Fashion*, S.W. Fores, 1786, at the Caracature Warehouse, Piccadilly, hand-colored etching. Courtesy of the Lewis Walpole Library, Yale University.

its accentuation of breast and "bum," this formidable construction saves a lady from the attentions of "The Bum Bailiff" between whose legs she is able to crawl away unnoticed.

In the case of women, social competition had a tendency to drive the scale of ostentatious consumption such that items such as skirts and wigs had a tendency to grow in size and use up ever greater quantities of expensive materials. The visible effect of this was, in essence, to increase the overall size of a woman's dressed form in a society that also valued the slender waist. The resulting contrast between giant skirt and narrow waist was undoubtedly spectacular but became increasingly impractical as satirists and caricaturists were quick to highlight. It was to take the extreme forms of "citizen chic" disseminated in the course of the French Revolution to bring about a temporary deflation of the fashionable female outline into those more "natural" forms advocated by founders of Romantic thought such as Rousseau. Competition in masculine dress came, over time, to focus more on precise detailing rather than in scale of consumption, but such gender distinction as this established failed to solve the problem of effeminacy because it simply led to fears that not only sobriety but masculinity itself was simply a fashion to be put on and discarded.[93] When the Chevalier d'Eon was shown with men's clothes on one side and women's on the other the implicit message was that gender fashioning was an artificial construction (Figure 5.6). Fears that sexual tastes might, therefore, be just as well concealed as displayed by fashionable dress were one of the legacies of the eighteenth century that we have inherited in the world in which we live today.

CHAPTER SIX

Status

MIKKEL VENBORG PEDERSEN

THE EUROPEAN ENLIGHTENMENT

The period in Europe from approximately 1650 to 1800 has been looked at in many ways and carries many different names. One of the most influential and important is that of the Enlightenment. Enlightened thought resonated widely in the eighteenth century, embedding qualities that lead to our world, and providing a way to come to terms with the many societal, cultural, political, and economic changes of the time. Enlightenment ideas informed the debate among the learned, and eventually the unlearned, to gain another tone of color in the Romantic movement in the late eighteenth and well into the nineteenth centuries. The Romantic movement was in its own time perceived as a counter-movement to the Enlightenment; however, it inherited and carried with it much of what had gone before, not least in recognizing the value of each single person *qua* being an individual. This had deep implications for both cultural habits and societal understanding.

The Enlightenment did not arrive suddenly and entirely formed. It was scientifically and philosophically bounded by British natural philosopher Sir Isaac Newton's (1643–1727) *Philosophiae Naturalis Principia Mathematica*, published in 1683, and German philosopher Immanuel Kant's (1724–1804) publications on pure reason in the 1780s. Newton's mathematical treatise launched a profound debate among natural scientists and philosophers, and it deeply informed the early Enlightenment. The Newtonian laws of physics did not only constitute the field until the beginning of the twentieth century, but implicit within them was a revolution of thought. With these laws, the biblically-founded Christian principles of the world were studied and eventually questioned, and as a result instead of relying on an active, directly intervening, and ordering God, humanity began to see itself as responsible for how society could be organized and nature dealt with for humanity's benefit.[1]

This humanistic insight was perhaps made most clear by Immanuel Kant, whose philosophy at one and the same time summed up enlightened thought and in a narrow sense ended the epoch. Kant maintained that the individual should follow the guidance of sound thought embedded within the enlightened individual: Reason. From Newton to Kant, therefore, runs the line that sought, and advocated, insight and intellectual endeavor free from the intervention of (divine) authority. It is easily forgotten that in the context of the absolute monarchies of early modern Europe—monarchies that rested on a conception of society as a fixed and natural hierarchy which expressed God's order—the Enlightenment offered a revolutionary way of thinking. It should not be overlooked that the period encompasses both the beheading of the English-Scottish king, Charles I, in 1649, and the French king, Louis XVI, in 1793.

Europe's political system was reordered with the 1648 Peace of Westphalia that ended the Thirty Years War, and was once again shattered in 1789 with the French Revolution and its following turmoil. It was during the seventeenth and eighteenth centuries, too, that the European colonial endeavor really gained speed. A quadrangle of international trade and colonialism, eventually a (central and west) European increase in wealth, the stirring industrial revolution, and a consumer revolution[2] meant the import of a long list of foreign goods. These not only provided new products and experiences, but also shattered the idea of a stable and fixed world.[3] While most of these goods had been encountered before as very rare and exclusive things, they now poured into Europe at such a pace and in such quantities, that what used to be a luxury became widespread.[4] From the Far East came tea, porcelain, silk, cotton fabric and calicoes, fine shawls, saltpetre for gun powder, and spices and dyes, to name just a few. Africa provided wood, ivory, gold, silver, precious stones and, of course, large numbers of slaves to be transported to the Americas, from where through their drudging toil came sugar, coffee, cacao, rum, and cotton in huge quantities. Cotton truly became widespread as a commodity, both for practical reasons and for its fashionable lure.[5] Of key importance for understandings of dress, it was also during the eighteenth century that a civilization of manners clearly emerged (after beginnings in the Renaissance) in the upper and middle stations of society, providing a cultural form for, and conceptualization of, the new goods and ideas.[6]

Informed by enlightenment thought, the feeling of change, the spread of wealth (however slow it was, the epoch witnessed the rise of a hitherto unknown proletariat too), and the new goods and habits from abroad (soon followed both by European replicas and new commodities inspired by the colonies), this was a time of discussion. These new impulses affected, among other things, the old concept of status as connected to fixed social orders or ranks, and began to craft a new reality. As we will see, the Enlightenment can be understood as a transitional period between the old order—characterized by display, sumptuary legislation, and codified social ranking—and the new concept of civility and the individual, which emphasized personal restraint, control, and novel notions of taste.

In this chapter, we shall first consider the concept of status and its connection with sumptuary law, before discussing mercantilism and the realities of commodity ownership. From here we will turn to the understanding and articulation of status—through the notion of honor—mostly by the rising middle classes. Thereafter, we shall take a small tour into a few examples from those who had apparently little (or no) status at all, and how this manifested itself in dress.

STATUS AND SUMPTUARY LAW

Relative social standing, the demonstration of it, and the cultural, social, juridical, and perhaps economic recognition of it was in the past immensely important to a degree that we today—as children of Enlightenment—often find it difficult to understand. The word "status" derives from Latin, a state (or circum*stance*), meaning *to stand*—and a status symbol is the outer sign informing (or stating!) or crafting the presence of a certain social standing. Obviously, this was the case for the societal elite. In *The Court Society*, sociologist and historian Norbert Elias put it simply that a duke must act like a duke, and hence fulfil his societal and cultural obligations, or soon he will almost no longer be a duke.[7] He must demonstrate—or state and restate—his status to have it recognized and, furthermore, to defend it. This is an ever ongoing process which involves most aspects of life,[8] including dress, personal attire, and manners.

Often, the keen interest in keeping up public rank led to the invention of all sorts of ceremonies, rituals, and ways to handle everyday situations, so social recognition was both demanded and demonstrated.[9] It is in this light that King Christian V of Denmark's (1646–99) table of rank of 1671 can be understood. Tables of rank were known in most European principalities. Their main message is a codification of Norbert Elias's observation that social status and rank goes intimately together with outer appearances, and that a challenge to them is a challenge to personal honor, to the group's social standing, and to societal order. The Danish-Norwegian table of rank from 1671 and its later expansions were perhaps the most detailed and thorough in all of continental Europe outside Russia.

King Christian V's table of rank and its successors also contained several regulations on what luxury goods could be used and worn by which rank. The purpose was to assure that status and appearance followed one another. In this they articulated a very old idea, repeatedly expressed in sumptuary laws. Such legislation is a package notion for the control of the consumption of luxury goods—very frequently dress and textiles—in order to maintain the status and ranks of society, which themselves rested on the estates inherited from the Middle Ages. *Bellatores* (the clergy) were the first estate; *defensores* (the nobility) formed the second. *Labores* (peasantry and craftsmen) established the third estate, which through early modernity had to be expanded to fit reality to include the rising middling sort: tradesmen, professionals, and other burghers (sometimes referred to as a fourth estate). Whether it was in connection to three or four estates or the neatly formed tables of ranks, sumptuary laws sought to create a connection between societal status and consumption. Already in Ancient Egypt and Classical Greece, such mechanisms were known, and famous too is Julius Caesar's *Lex Julia* in Rome. In medieval and in early modern Europe, many different rulers and polities also passed similar edicts that sought to control consumption.[10] How long these remained in place varied considerably: in England they were repealed as early as 1604, in Denmark the last sumptuary laws were passed as late as 1848.

A look at Denmark's energetic pursuit of the sumptuary project is informative. The most important measures of this sort are King Kristoffer III's (1416–48) Town Law from 1443, and King Christian III's (1503–59) Recess of 1558, the latter heavily informed by the Lutheran movement. The Recess was part of the new ordering of the Danish-Norwegian realm following the Reformation of 1536, and tellingly, the fines for offences against its provisions had to be paid to the local hospital or alms house, as the Catholic institutions for taking care of the poor had now vanished—a feature seen throughout sixteenth-century Protestant Europe. These offences were mostly connected with the buying of foreign luxuries such as gold and silver strings, lace and exquisite silk, velvets and brocade textiles for personal or servants' dressing, for caparisons (horse trappings), and for furnishing homes. These early attempts by King Christian III were continued by his successor King Frederik II (1534–1588). The next king, Christian IV (1577–1648), issued consumption laws in 1617, and they were a direct forerunner to the detailed rulings of King Christian V, mentioned earlier, that were supported by his 1671 table of rank—an attempt to order society in a precise way embedded in absolutist thought.[11] After Christian V's death in 1699, the ordinances came thick and fast until the introduction of democracy in 1849.[12]

Sumptuary laws were connected to the fact that luxury in general formed a problem in early modernity, both morally and economically.[13] The legislation thus specified that only people above a certain rank or in possession of a certain income were allowed to wear rich fabrics, fine furs, embroidery, jewels and much more besides—indeed, many of the commodities that were being increasingly imported from the rising colonial empires.[14] It follows that the sumptuary laws of the seventeenth and eighteenth centuries were thorough and detailed. For example, the Danish ordinance of April 16 1736 prohibited the wearing of "Jewels as well as Gold and Silver", in order "to impede the rampant Sumptuousness in Dress, whereby a Part from other Damages much Money leaves the Country."[15]

This level of expenditure did not concern Duke Friedrich Carl I of Schleswig-Holstein-Sønderborg-Plön (1706–61), nor need it have, as he was of (distant) royal descent and thus of the highest rank (in Denmark a duke is not a nobleman, but a prince). In this painting by J.H. Tischbein from 1759, Duke Friedrich Carl is depicted with his family on the terrace of Plön Castle in Holstein (Figure 6.1).

Given his descent and position, the duke had elevated claims to honor and needed to demonstrate both wealth and rank simultaneously. This goal is secured in the painting of the duke and his family through a setting on the palace terrace, through the consumption of a drink from the colonies served by a black servant, and through the rich and fashionable dress of the subjects. On his fashionable red coat, the duke boasts the insignia of the highest Danish Order, the Elephant. The sumptuary law's prohibited "Jewells as well as Gold and Silver" are present in abundance, both as proper jewelry embellishing the young princesses' hair, and as silver braids or "galloon" on their skirts and on the duke's waistcoat. Both he and his companions are dressed in silk and wear wigs, whereas the servant, probably coming from the Danish West Indies, is in exotic clothing typical of the

FIGURE 6.1: *Duke Friedrich Carl I of Schleswig-Holstein-Sønderborg-Plön (1706–1761) with his family on the terrace of Plön Castle in Holstein*, J.H. Tischbein, 1759. The Museum of National History, Frederiksborg Castle, Denmark.

period, with a Turkish turban. The exotic is underlined by the inclusion of the orange tree in the corner of the terrace and the use of the parasol, inspired by the Far East. The effects of the light dress silks suspended across the wicker paniers of the women's gowns and the way in which they rise up when seated can be clearly seen in this carefully crafted painting.

Seen from the point of view of sumptuary law, the depiction of the Fenger family (Figure 6.2) provided greater reason for social and moral concern. Copenhagen merchant and wholesale dealer Peter Fenger (1719–74) with his wife Else Brock (1737–1811) and children was painted by U.F. Beenfeldt in 1769 (ten years after the painting of the ducal family in Plön), and many statements or claims about Fenger's status in society can be read within this portrait.

Not only is Fenger painted with his family, a pertinent fact in itself, but the family portrait also displays many forbidden things: silk, velvet, embroidery, jewels, and wigs are abundant, and the family demonstrates the highest fashions of the mid-eighteenth-century elite. The faux-painted background with its trellis and Classical buildings suggests sources from the Classical world, and could easily lead an unfamiliar party to believe that Fenger possessed gardens and landed estates, which he did not. Instead, the merchant Fenger was a self-made man, who in 1752 established a successful trading company in Copenhagen. He took part in domestic, European, and colonial trade, and from 1770 he also owned a soap factory—an important commodity in keeping the clothes of the period clean. Fenger

FIGURE 6.2: *Det fengerske Familiebillede (The Fenger Family)*, National Museum of Denmark, Modern Collections.

was a member of the merchant's guild in Copenhagen, and he therefore exemplifies the new type of elite rising in the Enlightenment, at first threatening, later mixing with the old elite, such as the nobility. Society was under the threat of change; sumptuary laws sought to prevent or, at least, delay this process, but as this painting demonstrates, the rules were frequently disregarded.

Both paintings also have a further tale to tell. If we look more closely into the actual attire of the depicted persons, standing and sitting in their most formal clothes, the use of wigs is striking. Wigs were one of the best of all tokens to lift one's social standing, and apart from the peasantry and those below that group, no man of respectability before the 1770s wore his own hair; to wear natural hair became fashionable in the 1790s following the French Revolution. Hence, both adults and children are depicted with their wigs. By 1710, the (male) wig was so firmly established in European dress that in Denmark it became open for taxation. Its importance was hence firmly underlined, and so closely was it linked to its wearer that it might follow him into his grave; likewise, people who had had their portraits done earlier ordered wigs to be added to the once-cherished canvases that did not depict artificial hair.[16] It is noticeable, too, that this was an era before children had their own category of clothing; that was an invention of the Romantic period and was not seen among the upper elite of Denmark until the 1770s. For a rising burgher such as Fenger, this would not do. He had to rely on the old, trusted mechanisms of stating social rank, which meant using elite signs and tokens. Thus he is dressed in brown velvet, his wife in fashionable blue silk with flowers, lace, and bows—a sort of modest replica of the ducal gowns and attire seen in the Plön family portrait.

Apart from these general ideas embedded in sumptuary legislation, the rules stated in the 1736 sumptuary law and its many repetitions over the following years are multitudinous, and can be paraphrased as follows. In the two years from 1736, no subject is allowed to use silver and gold in his or her dress, or embroidered or colored silk fabric, if it does not come from China and was not imported to Denmark-Norway on board His Majesty's ships (the reformed Royal Chartered Danish Asiatic Company was founded in 1732). In the two years before the full ban, people may wear these garments, though not on royal birthdays. Immediately from the day of the ordinance, no tradesman or others may buy from abroad braids of silver and gold, fabric, strings and bands, palatines and the like, or embroidered or embellished silk fabrics. None is allowed to use gold or silver braiding or embroidery on liveries, hat strings, furniture and upholstery, wagons and harnesses, horse cloths and/or other dressing and ornamentation, with the exception of military personnel, who are exempt. Everybody may use what they already possess for the next two years, but in the case of furniture they must register with the nearest authority. All lace not of domestic production is banned, with the exception of that which is already owned, which may be worn.

The ordinance continues with accessories. In its fifth paragraph, all use of diamonds, pearls, or other jewels is banned. And then, in paragraph six, the clearest connection to rank appears when it states that people who "are not within Rank" may wear "light and striped Silk Fabrics," such as taffeta, though this is *not* allowed for craftsmen and small shopkeepers or anyone below. The same goes for servants, if not given them by their masters, though they may wear what they possess for two years. In cases where the law is broken, the king's mercy is lost and the offending items confiscated. In addition, the guilty party has to pay a fine of 300 Thaler (if in the first and second rank), or 200 Thaler. For those not of rank, the fine is 50 Thaler. (As a measure of value at the time, in 1736 a good milking cow cost approximately 10 Thaler.) If the fine was not paid, the law stipulated imprisonment.

It is obvious that there is a tension between laws of this sort, hierarchically limiting the ownership and wear of dress according to status and wealth, and the ever-growing abundance of fashionable commodities that were increasingly within the financial reach of a growing middle class. We saw this in the portrait of the Fenger family. However, the increasing consumption of fashionable goods on the part of the non-elite did not just involve dress and attire. In the "silhouette" (a new fashionable form of representation of figures in outline) showing the shoemaker Franz Carl Heckel and his wife at their tea table in Sønderborg Town, in the Duchy of Schleswig (just north of the present-day Danish–German border) in 1770, the couple is not only enjoying the exotic pleasure of drinking tea; he is smoking a long-pipe, and the children are romantically befitting new fashions by standing on each side of their parents with a bouquet of wild flowers (the girl) and a little bird (the boy) (Figure 6.3).

Different from the painting of the Fenger family, the two children are wearing clothes specific for their age, a very modern practice in this family of the middling sort and perhaps in reality only used on this occasion when being models for the silhouettist. The parents' clothes are not seen easily in any detail, though judging from the profile they appear also to be more comfortable than formal attire would have it. She is clearly in a cotton gown of a soft English pattern, what the French would call either a *robe d'anglaise* or a *robe de chemise*; he is wearing bourgeois clothes (perhaps even English half-boots) and what was originally a Prussian-inspired, pig-tail on his wig, called by the French a "queue."

FIGURE 6.3: "Silhouette," showing the shoemaker Franz Carl Heckel and family taking tea in Sønderborg Town, Duchy of Schleswig c. 1770. National Museum of Denmark, Modern Collections.

It was not only shoemakers, wholesale dealers, and dukes who cared for their status. The civil servant who was very present within Danish Absolutism was the pastor of the parish. These men were often the only person in a village who could read and write with any proficiency, and they performed all sorts of tasks for the government, as well as serving their flock as Christian "herdsmen." It was these people, too, who from the pulpit announced the sumptuary laws and royal ordinances on dress and attire. They wore themselves an ornate dress, codified in the 1630s, consisting of a black woolen cassock, an otherwise old-fashioned white linen ruff, and a black cap on the head. Higher-ranking clergy carried felt hats with brims and had their cassocks made of fine cloth—for instance, the court preacher owned a floral velvet and another silk cassock. In 1683, this fine dressing had come so far that a table of rank for the clergy itself had to be issued, according to which only the bishop of Zealand and the king's personal confessor could wear velvet, with others of the highest ranking allowed silk with velvet trimming. Another change had taken place, too, which becomes clear in the reprimand received by the student Søren Thiim in 1657, told off for the "detestable Habit in the Pulpit to show himself . . . in cruel foreign Hair"[17]—that is, with wearing a wig. As mentioned earlier, the wig became one of the most visible signs for people trying to climb the social ladder.

The rise of the wig is evident in the painting of *Pastor Schmedes and his family* from the mid-eighteenth century (Figure 6.4). It shows both father and son wearing the by-now slightly old-fashioned full-bottomed wig.

The pastor himself wears over his black cassock the Netherlands-inspired soft collar instead of his formal ruff, a collar which stayed in use well into the nineteenth century (although not for services). In contrast, the son's dress follows high fashion, with a gray waistcoat and coat, and an elegant shirt almost hidden by the exquisite cravat. The three

FIGURE 6.4: *Praestefamilien Schmedes (The pastor Schmedes family)*, Danish, mid-eighteenth century. © Den Gamle By.

dresses of the girls and their mother also feature three versions of mid-eighteenth-century fashion. The dress of the girl in the middle is of a yellow color with a white stomacher of the same almost transparent fabric as her lace-embellished apron. The older girl is in a red dress with an embroidered stomacher; the mother's dress is more old-fashioned and without a stomacher. These differences in the sitters' clothing and wigs warns us that fashion is seldom followed in full and complete ways. A pastor was apparently more at ease with the old-fashioned wig than a newer, smaller one. His son is more stylish.

In tandem with this material novelty and abundance came, as we saw above, Enlightenment ideas about the place of the individual, the importance of Reason, and the location of person's worth within his or her character rather than as an external function of his or her rank. These were ideas conducive to a meritocracy, and challenged the traditional societal structures that placed a monarch at the pinnacle, the aristocracy beneath, and all other ranks in gradations below that. In the eighteenth century, a bright peasant lad could settle into trade, and if successful end up burgomaster of a provincial town; with diligence and luck, he could even rise to become a member of the landowning gentry.[18] Women of course could rise through a "good" marriage, although the rank-obsessed Danish society was most keen to ensure that the unification of families did not turn out to be *mésalliances*. Therefore, the trusted mechanism of marrying "up," the theme of so many novels and dreams of the eighteenth-century lower middle classes, prevailed only to a small extent in eighteenth-century Danish life.

The repetition of sumptuary laws—a widespread feature of this kind of legislation—whereby they were reissued again and again, speaks to this growing social mobility and expanding commodity ownership. Basically, more honored in the breach than the observance, such laws seem to have had little, or limited, effect. This is supported by studies of the actual consumption of luxury, based both on contemporary inventories and an analysis of import customs lists.[19] Quite simply, the good people of eighteenth-century Denmark had in their homes and cupboards, chests and drawers, all the garments, fabrics, and accessories that had been banned from 1736 onwards, and the merchants involved in international trade could obtain everything the heart desired.[20] This has also been shown to have been the case in other European countries.[21]

There is, however, an important caveat for Denmark, where as we have seen sumptuary legislation lasted much longer than in many other polities. In museums and private collections, many women's dresses that follow the patterns of the first thirty to forty years of the nineteenth century are in fact made of fabric from the late eighteenth century. Whether these dresses were hidden away and kept because of sumptuary laws or just because of changes in fashion is difficult to know. Alternatively, or in addition, it could be that this represents reuse of a valuable material resource, for the hooped skirts of the earlier period used large quantities of fabric, which may have been cut down for the new, slimmer styles at the century's turn.[22]

SUMPTUARY LAW AND MERCANTILISM

It is clear that a major concern in the sumptuary laws was the establishment of a fixed relationship between social standing and attire. However, there was another concern as well: the economy. This can be seen, for example, in the provisions of the 1783 ordinance for restricting "Sumptuousness in Denmark, Norway and the Duchies."[23] The argument in its preamble is that sumptuousness is morally wrong on a personal basis and on a mercantile level too, leading to poverty for individual families and collectively for the state. Both the economic concerns voiced by this ordinance, and the rise of the European colonial empires that enabled the importation at a hitherto unseen scale of all those items of fashion and pleasure, are embedded within the same system of thought: mercantilism.

This theory and practice dominated European trade politics of the seventeenth and eighteenth centuries, although the word "mercantilism" was only coined later. Mercantilist principles prescribed that raw materials should be acquired as cheaply as possible, preferably at the place of production, and then be processed domestically—thus leading to a growth in national wealth measured by the amount of precious metal in the state treasury.[24] This meant two things. First, the use of gold and silver in dress was seen as directly reducing the value of the coin of the realm. Second, buying foreign-made items was thought to drain wealth out of the coffers of the consuming nation, only to pour directly into the purses and pockets of the country that produced and sold the goods. The obvious response was legislation to both limit consumption of luxury foreign goods and to promote consumption of domestically-produced wares. Protectionist legislation like this was therefore common throughout Europe. Such a position is seen clearly articulated in the law of 1736 discussed earlier. This sought, among other things, "to impede the rampant Sumptuousness in Dress, whereby . . . much Money leaves the Country."[25] It stipulated that embroidered or colored silks could only be purchased if imported on the king's ships—the profits in this case in part going into the royal coffers, in part to the share-holders of the nobility and wealthy merchants—and banned all lace unless it was of domestic production.

In Denmark, the ebbing away in the nineteenth century of the eternally reissued sumptuary ordinances is, therefore, not only indicative of changed social hierarchies and organization, but also a token that mercantilist thought was being replaced by liberalist principles. The overhaul of the customs system in the Danish-Norwegian realm in 1797 introduced (national) free trade, and in 1855 most commercial and trade monopolies in Denmark were rescinded, forming the basis of a modern, liberal economy. Sumptuary laws had had their day, both for moral, cultural, political, and economic reasons.[26]

HONOR AND CIVILITY

We need now to turn to the growing bourgeoisie, to explore how status concerns were articulated—and social standing materially displayed and produced—among this group (see Figures 6.2 and 6.3). The best way of describing the code of middle-class civility is as "an aspiration to honor." In Danish, it is to follow an *Honnet Ambition*, and the phrase can be found in both French and German too (as in the doings/aspirations of an *honnête homme* and to follow *eine honette Ambition*). As the eighteenth century progressed, the Enlightenment idea of honor became increasingly hitched not to outward rank, but to inner qualities. Denis Diderot (1713–84) and Jean Le Rond d'Alembert's (1717–83) *Encyclopédie* clearly defines *honneur* (honor) as having to do with self-esteem and the feeling of having the respect of others as a consequence of being guided by principles of virtue in whatever one does. The honorable gentleman is thus connected to merits and deeds of a virtuous kind; the entry *honnête* (honorable) is sided with the moral.[27] In the German *Allgemeine deutsche Real-Encyclopädie für die gebildeten Stände* (1796), *Ehre* (honor) is defined as the recognition of personal values and deeds, as opposed to *Rang* (rank), as the way the precedence of one person over another is demonstrated, often in tables of rank issued by the local sovereign.[28]

Both as a social mechanism and as a personal feeling, the expression of honor was important—and in public this meant having the right manners and the right clothes. These combined to make a successful presentation. As the following illustrates, having the one without the other was not enough. Thus, in eighteenth-century Denmark, a man of merely moderate means—certainly without formal rank or title—might aspire to wear a rapier or small sword. This ancient symbol of the nobility had been adopted by those down the social order, borrowing from a formerly elite sartorial vocabulary. When Jacob Gude, later the director of Copenhagen's Alms House, entered university in 1769, his father gave him not only new clothes but also a silver rapier. The day after, as Gude remembered, he went to the university dressed in his new outfit. However, as the rapier was long and Gude himself short, he stumbled into other people. Every time he clumsily turned to assure himself that he had indeed been noticed, he revealed at the same time that he had borne the rapier only for a short while and that it was, in fact, a borrowed symbol of honor.[29]

A rapier, therefore, did not do it alone; it had to be carried well. In general, one had to move with dignity and grace (two other of these versatile words so important in early modernity). Dance and fencing teachers published one book after another on the right conduct, covering most of life's affairs. In his 1742 translation of German Gottfried Tauber's dance book, for example, Copenhagen dance teacher Heinrich Hieronymi gave directions in how to walk, stand, and greet persons of social standing—what he calls "honorable people." First you look politely on the honorable person with your head turned a bit to the side. Then you make a slight bow with the feet separated, and a slender falling gesture of the arms. To the side of the honorable person you now lift your heel a little, and with both knees bowed lead this first-mentioned foot to the other foot's heel, place it there, and draw it gently towards you with toe on ground so it ends about one step's length from the back shoe's buckle. In this position you bow your head further, then the rest of the body. If the honorable person is of high standing you look down; if you are equal, you look him or her in the eyes. The whole greeting ends with the resumption of an upright body position, with the arms to the side.[30] Rules for handling the hat were just as codified, not to mention how to kiss or, for females, use a fan.

Such performances, in the words of the day, set a claim to honor. They were understood as the outward forms of inward qualities—the public expression of private merit. The place of clothing was clearly of vital importance in such presentations. Not only did the fashionability of garments and accessories play its part—their modishness, fabric, cut, cleanliness—but also their graceful manipulation was a vital part of this display. Social standing, in the eighteenth century, was ineluctably linked to this bodily performance.

STATUS AND DRESS IN POPULAR CULTURE

The snuff box illustrated here (Figure 6.5) was made by a skilled artisan for an elite customer. The taking of snuff was a highly fashionable pastime among the elites and here a visual joke might have been at work.

The snuff box, from the third part of the eighteenth century, rather than showing a mondaine or urbane scene as would have been customary, displays on its lid the four "estates" of society. The nobleman wears red silk and the insignia of the highest Danish order, the star and blue ribbon of the Elephant. The burgher wears fine, grayish-blue silk fabric and boasts a silver ferrule on his cane. The pastor is in his ornate clerical dress, as it came to be codified in Denmark from the last third of the seventeenth century. The peasant, with his back to us, wears his homespun woolen coat, and in addition is the only

FIGURE 6.5: Snuff box painted with the four "estates" of society, c. 1760, National Museum of Denmark, Modern Collections.

one wearing his "natural hair." He makes do with a stool instead of a chair. The wigs of the three other men are different from each other, ranging from the more flamboyant one worn by the aristocrat, to the pastor's official ornate coiffure, and the burgher's well-combed wig with curls. The wigs themselves are telling tokens of how society was ordered and what sort of behavior was culturally permitted for each social station.

However, the small picture on this snuff box lid also reminds us that the connection between status and dress did not concern only the elite. Among people of popular culture in town and countryside, burghers and peasants alike, there were status concerns to be nursed too, although differently from the elite. In many studies of fashion and dress, this relationship has been obscured, as costume historians and students of dress have, for various reasons, tended to devote most of their attention to more fashionable clothes, which are visually splendid and often represented in the visual arts.[31] Clothes have a far wider context, however,[32] and the repeatedly claimed gulf between the garments of ordinary people often seen as standing outside fashion, and the attire of the elites following fashion, hides the fact that the poorer sort were also affected by changing trends.[33] This could be through being exposed to elite fashion as servants—for example, when chamber maids and valets inherited clothes, shoes and ribbons—or it could be while following popular culture's codes of dress and conduct, with its selective incorporation of certain traits of high fashion.[34]

One example will serve to illustrate fashionable consumption among the ordinary folk. In 1787 in Lundager, a village on the Danish Island of Funen, a young couple arrived to work a tenant farm on the Brahesborg estate, the seat of the counts of Bille-Brahe. Young Rasmus and Anne owned agricultural tools and animals, wooden furniture, and traditional clay pots and serving bowls. However, they also possessed an abundance of bed linen, not only featuring homemade types but also novelties such as broad stripes in indigo blue and chenille red.[35] In their daily dress, Rasmus and Anne probably looked typical of men and women in the lower orders, though the particular sources are silent on this point. Rasmus may have had a shirt of (coarse) linen, breeches, and a waistcoat without sleeves in homespun or striped linsey-woolsey, a knitted cap with a tassel, and wooden clogs on his feet. Anne would have been dressed in a shift and stays, skirts—the top one in a nice linsey-woolsey—and a scarf. She, too, would trudge along in Funian clogs. However, in her bonnet there could be silk ribbons, lace could peep out from underneath, and very often silver and golden thread would be embroidered into the bonnet in delightful patterns, if the general picture of Funian peasant dress applies.[36] Rasmus and Anne—and countless others like them—indicate that concerns with appearance and status, the appeal of the modern, and aspirations to the honorable were not limited to the urban and the elite. Indeed, this was very far from the case. Such concerns were a mechanism guiding most people's existence in the long eighteenth century, albeit its concrete manifestations differed according to a consumer's context and cultural horizons.

Around the year 1800, Elias Meyer painted a scene of peasants in the meadows on the estate of Løvenborg Manor, in the northwest of the Danish island Zealand (Figure 6.6).

FIGURE 6.6: *Peasants at the Meadows on the Estate of Løvenborg in Zealand*, Elias Meyer, c. 1800, National Museum of Denmark, Modern Collections.

Very few paintings of eighteenth-century peasants exist and usually they depict scenes of work. This is also the case here, on this summer's day when haymaking is performed, although a young lad has found his chance to step aside with a young woman from the village while their dog looks on.

Clearly Romantic in its style, the painting does, however, show a dressing of the couple that is fairly close to reality in this part of Zealand at the time[37] (an interest in peasant culture was part of the Romantic movement), and, with a little imagination, we might even see them as Anne and Rasmus from the village of Lundager. Dressed for haymaking, the peasants in the meadow and the young couple are without their jackets and wear light, linen clothes; the girl wears an apron, probably made of a light wool. Due to the work, they are wearing light bonnets and hats with broad brims. Such a scene evokes the arguments of the 1980s that raged in British art history as to whether the fashionably dressed farm girls as depicted in scenes of haymaking by Thomas Gainsborough could really have engaged with such fine fashions, or if these were fantasies by the artist that obscured the true nature of work. The general conclusion is that farm workers may well have engaged with fashion, but perhaps not on an everyday basis.[38]

THE HOMELESS—BUT CLOTHED

However, not everyone lived in a house, in a town, in a village, or on an estate. Some, perhaps as many as ten percent of the population, lived in the streets and as travelers, much feared by the rest of the population. They dressed much as other common folk did, though perhaps were more ragged than most, not all having shoes and certainly not that eighteenth-century status signifier, the wig. Travelers, like gypsies, presented decidedly exotic features, such as large earrings, head scarves and, for the women, skirts in bright colors embellished with flounces—though given their traveling life-style and occasional mistreatment by settled people, it was not unusual for this to be combined with an appearance of shabbiness.[39]

Others, like the people of the night, were even more on the margins. In a time before electric lights, the darkness of the night for most people carried anxiety and fear. Towns were fortified and literally locked up. Fire, thieves, and night prowlers threatened decent townspeople, and their worst fears were embodied by the people of the night: "dishonest" people, culturally and legally speaking, like the town executioner, gypsies, and vagrants. Witches' foul rituals happened at midnight. The towns' garbage disposal was taken care of by "night men," revealing their stigma in their name. Just like witches, they did "dishonest" work at ungodly hours. In the villages, one was only too close to supernatural creatures, such as elves and werewolves.[40]

Throughout the Middle Ages in most of Europe, these people on the edges of society carried special signs in their clothing. Town executioners, for example, would often wear bright colors; sometimes their wives had to carry the same head gear as was prescribed for the town's prostitutes. The poor had a different sign, which was codified, as can be seen on this surviving figure of sandstone from the façade of the hospital (almshouse) in Bursø, on the Danish island of Lolland (Figure 6.7).

This particular almshouse was erected in 1703 and the figure is likely to be of the same date. The beggar woman is seen in the dress usual for her social class; the fabric would have been a type of homespun wool and the color likely dark brown, gray, or perhaps blackish. The cross on her left side is a beggar's mark referring to her being authorized as a beggar by the local authorities, that is, the local manor or estate, and the parish pastor.

FIGURE 6.7: Figurine of a beggar woman removed from Bursø Almshouse on the Danish island of Lolland, c. 1703, sandstone. National Museum of Denmark, Middle Ages and Renaissance.

Through her begging income, she could provide some revenue to the hospital; otherwise she was referred to the parish funds and the estate's mercy. However, in early modernity, these traditions began to disappear, and during the eighteenth century they seem to have withered away. It seems that just as in the world of the Enlightenment, sumptuary laws were seen as more and more old-fashioned and unsustainable, so too, the communication of stigma through clear signs in dress became untenable.

CONCLUSION

Nearly all of the examples in this chapter derive from the Danish Realm, in early modernity consisting of the kingdoms of Denmark and Norway, the duchies Schleswig and Holstein, and in the North Atlantic, Iceland, the Faroe Isles, and Greenland. Trading stations in China, colonial strongholds in India—both Tranquebar in Tamil and Frederiksnagore (Serampore) in Bengal—forts on the African Gold Coast (part of present-day Ghana), and colonies in the West Indies on the isles St. Thomas, St. John, and

St. Croix (present-day US Virgin Islands) completed the picture of a middle-size Scandinavian-European principality like so many others on the continent north of the Alps and west of the great Russian plains. However, the relationship between status and dress as discussed earlier unfolded in a similar manner across Enlightenment Europe and, to some degree in its colonies, and much of what has been identified here would in principle go for Europe north of the Alps and for southern and eastern Europe as well (though to a lesser degree in southeast Europe under Ottoman influence and rule).

Early modern Europe was keenly interested in the question of appearances reflecting social status in a society where relative social standing, the demonstration of this placement, and cultural, social, juridical, and ultimately economic recognition of this status was immensely important. Status derives from Latin meaning to stand—and a status symbol is an outer sign informing or pretending a certain social standing. Obviously, this was the case for the highest levels of society; however, the stating of status was not just a concern for them. Also the upcoming bourgeoisie of the long eighteenth century was occupied with status recognition, or, in their own words, aspiring to honor. Peasants had status concerns to nurse as well, though this is too often forgotten. We met bed linen embellished with stripes in indigo blue and chenille red, and saw silk and cotton in their garments. In housing and dwellings, tokens such as the use of free space and ornamented furniture would also be examples of social status for this part of the population,[41] as it was for the elite in their manor houses and castles.

Early modern interest in status led to all sorts of ceremonies, rituals, and codified systems that fixed (or tried to fix) social standing and appearance. Tables of rank and sumptuary laws were among the most frequent of these means by which the absolute monarchies of Europe sought to tie appearance to status. However, in spite of the meticulous work and effort put into them they were never a real success other than in expressing a societal philosophy. At the waning of early modernity, this philosophy altered under the influence of the Enlightenment. No longer the preserve of the titled, for the rising bourgeoisie status began to be reinscribed as dependent on inner qualities expressed through particular behaviors. So deep was the interest this generated, that honor and its performance were considered as suitable entries in the encyclopaedias that were beginning to appear at this time. Clearly, the mechanism that linked dress, appearances, and societal status did not disappear when the format of sumptuary laws and tables of rank gave place to democratic ideas of virtue on merit. Rather, it was expressed differently, through fashionability—hitched to all those new commodities and ideas that were appearing—combined with restraint and personal decorum. Similarly, in popular culture, status and social standing were likewise understood and performed in particular ways, through the complex interactions of certain commodities, aspirations and behaviors, in which fashion played a particularly significant role.

CHAPTER SEVEN

Ethnicity

BARBARA LASIC

Writing in 1680, the *Mercure Galant* noted that "one now only wears Indiennes; but these Indiennes are so well done that nothing adorns one better." A century later, discussing contemporary fashions, the *Magasin des Modes Nouvelles* remarked that "no one could deny that our French ladies influence the fashions of nearly every other kingdom; that said, we must admit that these are nearly all restitutions for, in less than two years, haven't they borrowed their own fashions from Poland, England, Turkey and China?"[1]

These two quotations from some of the most influential and widely read French periodicals of their time testify to fashion's ongoing dialog with exoticism and otherness. French fashions in the early modern period cannot be understood outside of the global commercial networks of exchanges between Europe and the rest of the world. Europe's reliance on imported luxury goods, ranging from porcelain, lacquer, or coffee, has been the subject of extensive scholarly scrutiny. As Maxine Berg has shown, "in the eighteenth century a global trade in luxuries and manufactured consumer goods provided not just the labour and the materials that went into making of new goods, but the designs, fashions, and sophisticated marketing that shaped the product development of the period. Consumer products, if not consumption more broadly, were forged then in a global economy."[2]

The seventeenth-century development of powerful mercantile interests in the East and the dynamism and success of Eurasian trade brought to Europe a wealth of rare and precious goods. The English East India Company played a pivotal role in the dissemination and importation of luxury goods to Europe. Founded in 1600 to trade with the Indian subcontinent, it is considered to be the main agent in the diffusion of luxury goods from the East. It was followed two years later by the establishment of a Dutch chartered company, the Vereenigde Oostindische Compagnie and, in 1614, by the Danish East India Company. Its French counterpart, the Compagnie Française des Indes Orientales, established in 1664, also imported large quantities of precious goods, including spices, porcelain, and textiles. Contracted by Jean-Baptiste Colbert to write a pamphlet intended to attract shareholders for the company, the academician François Charpentier conveyed in no uncertain terms the status of these imported goods as essential luxuries, noting that "importing all these things has now become an indispensable necessity."[3]

The establishment of a number of chartered companies and trading posts in India and China therefore facilitated the importation of large quantities of Indian textiles in Europe. Indian printed cottons had been exported from the Coromandel Coast for centuries before the arrival of European traders and the first known records documenting the trade of textiles date to the fifth century AD. By the end of the seventeenth century, however, they accounted for 70 percent of the East India Company's entire export trade.[4]

Cotton became "the most important commodity traded by the chartered companies between Asia and Europe."[5] While muslin and white cottons constituted a significant part of such imports, they were not as popular and sought after as the vibrant chintzes known as *Indiennes*. As Beverly Lemire and Giorgio Riello have argued, those chintzes were "one of the most revolutionary commodities to appear in western markets" and "one of the most important Asian imports into Europe."[6]

Hand-painted or block-printed and usually characterized by vibrantly colored sprigged and meandering repetitive floral patterns, imported textiles were quick to enchant Europeans.[7] Their exquisite designs were widely employed in the domestic interior as wall or bed hangings, usually in small or intimate rooms. Chintzes also became used for clothing almost immediately. From dresses to waistcoats, petticoats, jackets to linings of straw hats (Figure 7.1), chintzes were ubiquitous, prompting the influential Parisian periodical and taste maker the *Mercure Galant* to remark in 1681 that "all the garments that are currently being done are made of Indiennes."[8]

The appeal of chintzes could be explained in practical terms: pleasant to wear, they had the great advantage of being washable.[9] The physical comfort they might have provided should not, however, detract us from their aesthetic appeal. The fastness of their colors and their rich and varied designs significantly contributed to their desirability. Printing processes enabled the creation of a broad range of patterns and motifs, thereby making chintzes fully suited to the vagaries of fashion.[10]

FIGURE 7.1: Plaited straw hat, English or Dutch, c. 1700. © Victoria and Albert Museum, London.

Chintzes were generally adapted to European tastes. For instance, while Indian consumers preferred pale flowers on darker grounds, Europeans favored flowers on a pale or white background.[11] Merchants never lost sight of the importance of pleasing their European clients. As Olivier Raveux has argued, "the English East India Company played a major role in this development. It decided on a new policy for acquiring textiles when, as early as 1643, its London directors asked their agents to send fabrics with motifs more in line with the tastes of British consumers."[12] Contemporary French fashions could also influence the design of those chintzes and, for instance, Jean Berain's popular grotesques traveled East in printed form and found their way on to an early eighteenth-century printed wall hanging made in the Coromandel Coast, although the patterns' rarity would suggest that it did not find much favor in Europe.[13] The chintzes based on finely drawn European silk patterns were more popular.

Embroidered and hand-painted silks were also widely exported. They constituted one of China's main categories of export goods. The establishment in the seventeenth century of a successful European silk industry underpinned by economically profitable manufacturing centers in Venice, Lyon, and Tours arguably diminished the impact and necessity of such Chinese imports. In fact, as Lesley Miller has rightly shown, by the end of the eighteenth century, France was the one exporting its silks "as far as the Ottoman Empire, the Levant and the Antilles."[14] Nevertheless, Chinese silks offered a suitable alternative to its European counterparts and their desirability was sustained throughout the eighteenth century, as demonstrated by Madame de Pompadour's portrait by Hubert Drouais executed in 1763 where she was depicted wearing a painted flowered Chinese silk *robe à la Française* (Figure 7.2).[15] Rather than being an extension of the traditional Chinese art of painting on silk, the motifs seen on the dress would, however, suggest a skillful adaptation to the popularity of floral motifs founds on Indian chintzes.[16]

The popularity of exotic printed and painted cottons was such that alternative products started being made in France in the 1660s.[17] As a result, by the mid-seventeenth century, the term *Indienne* was used interchangeably to describe both authentic, colorfast Asian textiles and their French imitations. Perceived as a threat to the French silk and wool textile industries, those colorful printed cottons became bound by a strict legislation. In 1686, the importation of silks and chintzes was banned and so was the creation of their imitations, the painted *Indiennes*. The royal ordinance justified its decision by referring to the "millions that had left the Kingdom [. . .] the diminution of the silk, wool, linen manufactures long-established in France [. . .] and the desertion of workers who found themselves out of work and had to leave the Kingdom."[18] Implicit in this statement is the idea of a "brain-drain" that would severely hinder France's ambition to remain the leader in the production of luxury goods. Eventually this extreme protectionism spread to neighboring countries and was also implemented in Spain (1713) and England (1721 for a total ban).[19]

Originally given until December 31, 1687 to get rid of their stocks, merchants and shopkeepers were granted an extension until December 31, 1688 to sell their existing stocks of *toiles*. They were also expected to destroy all their printing blocks. Those disobeying orders were severely reprimanded and were subjected to hefty fines. Some exceptions were nevertheless granted and, for instance, on January 22, 1695, the Compagnie des Indes was allowed to bring back on its ships 150,000 livres worth of painted *toiles* for a duration of three years, but only to be sold abroad.[20]

A series of legal loopholes meant that the cities and regions unchallenged by the central government such as Marseilles, Rouen, Nantes, and the Arsenal in Paris were allowed to

FIGURE 7.2: *Madame de Pompadour at her Tambour Frame*, François-Hubert Drouais, 1763–4. Photo: DEA PICTURE LIBRARY/Getty Images.

continue producing *Indiennes*.[21] Despite these free enclaves, smuggling was rife. Unsurprisingly, the disobeying of orders was carried out in the highest spheres of French society and it was widely remarked that the use of painted *toiles* by the wealthy and the well-born was tolerated: "one does not stop a Duchess in her carriage, or the wife of a tax collector. And even if we succeeded in preventing them from wearing painted dresses outside, we could never prevent them from wearing them at home and for using such fabrics to furnish their apartments in the countryside and in the city."[22] Baron Grimm petulantly remarked that Madame de Pompadour, the king's mistress herself, openly flaunted the ban and furnished her interiors at Bellevue with smuggled fabrics.[23] The blatant use of *Indiennes* in the highest spheres of society, the clandestine factories, and widespread smuggling all contributed to the eventual lifting the ban on September 5, 1759.[24]

Indian chintzes and Chinese silks were firmly established in Western European dress and domestic interiors by the early eighteenth century, but their widespread consumption should not just be envisaged as a reflection of material fashions. The appeal of flowery *Indiennes* intersected with Europeans' general fascination with florilegia and exotic plants. This interest found its manifestation in the numerous exotic gardens such as those at the Tuileries Palace or later at Versailles, Het Loo, and Hampton Court. Illustrated flower books published at the time, such as Crispijn van de Passe's influential *Hortus*

Floridus (1614) and Nicolas de Poilly's *Livre de Plusieurs Paniers de Fleurs* (c. 1680), also ensured that this interest for exotic plants transcended the botanical realm and found a wide expression in the fine and decorative arts, ranging from Jean-Baptiste Monnoyer's colorful canvases to Jan van Mekeren's virtuoso marquetry panels (Figure 7.3).

Importantly, external events also boosted the appeal of exotic fashions. The first Siamese embassy visiting Versailles in 1680 brought to the public eye painted *toiles* with flowers that greatly contributed to spreading the taste for those textiles. The second Siamese delegation of 1686–7 produced, on the other hand, a "Siamese Frenzy" fully documented in the Mercure Galant and prompted a vogue for Siamese dress, as exemplified by Nicolas Arnoult's plate showing a young woman wearing a striped garb in so-called 'Siamese' fabric (Figure 7.4).[25]

The widespread demand and presence of oriental and exotic textiles for dress and domestic furnishings also needs to be seen within the wider context of French polite culture and the growing popularity of orientalist fiction. Victor Hugo's statement that "the reign of Louis XIV was hellenistic and now we are orientalist" is therefore indeed misconstrued.[26] The commercial, intellectual, and political exchanges between France and the East were numerous and it would be misleading to view French intellectual life as an insular entity untouched by these exchanges. France's engagement with the Orient was not just physical and material. Recent studies have demonstrated the importance of Oriental learning within the late seventeenth-century Republic of Letters. It is well known

FIGURE 7.3: *Bouquet of Chamomile, Roses, Orange Blossom and Carnations Tied with a Blue Ribbon,* Jean-Baptiste Monnoyer, 1690s. Photo: Fine Art Images/Heritage Images/Getty Images.

FIGURE 7.4: Nicolas Arnoult, "*Femme de qualité, en habit d'esté, détoffe Siamoise*," from the *Recueil des modes de la cour de France*, 1687. Image courtesy of Los Angeles County Museum of Art.

that, under the impetus of Colbert's ambitious collecting policies, the Bibliothèque du Roi greatly expanded its collections of Oriental texts, thereby laying the foundations for French Oriental scholarship during the following century.[27] A few years later, in 1697, Barthelemy d'Herbelot's *Bibliothèque Orientale* was a systematized attempt at ordering and disseminating knowledge about the Orient which marked the culmination of the intellectual enquiry stemming from France's relationship with the Orient.[28] The vast body of knowledge covered by the *Bibliothèque Orientale* is a testament to the importance of the documentation assembled and created by Orientalist scholars in seventeenth-century France.[29] As early as 1641, Mademoiselle de Scudéry published the novel *Ibrahim ou l'Illustre Bassa* set in a fictional Orient. Antoine Gallant's French translation of the *Thousand and One Nights* in 1704 was arguably the most popular Orientalist novel. It firmly cemented the presence of the Orient into the realm of fantasy and entertainment and Gallant's seductive translations of these Arabian tales captured popular imagination.

Indiennes and their European replicas were not just subjected to European tailoring, they could be used on items whose forms were inspired by foreign clothes. With the waning of the baroque style and the advent of the rococo, the banyan became a staple of

the fashionable urban male's wardrobe.[30] From the Gujerati word *vāniyo*, signifying man
of a trading caste, later employed to refer to either Hindu merchants from the province
of Gujarat or traders employed by European businesses in Bengal, the term came to define
the type of garb that was thought to be worn by those men.[31] As shown in Figure 7.5 the
shape of the actual Europeanized garment was based in fact on the Japanese kimonos that
were first imported to the West by the Dutch East India Company at the beginning of the
seventeenth century.

Usually made of silk or chintz, banyans could be worn wrapped round the body like a
kimono. They were sometimes fastened at the waist with a belt, but some models
resembling a coat secured with buttons also existed. Indoor garments, they were usually
worn at home to receive guests informally such as, for instance, during the all-important
ritual of the *toilette*. Here the luxurious gown would have served as a complement to the
range of precious objects and accessories required for the occasion that would have been
prominently displayed on the toilette table.

Banyans reached a peak of popularity in the eighteenth century but they were already
very much en vogue in the previous century. Molière's play *The Bourgeois Gentilhomme*,
written and first performed in 1670, a sharp satire mocking the social pretensions of the
vain and parvenu main character Monsieur Jourdain, gives evidence of the gown's
sartorial prestige. Keen to transcend his modest middle-class station, the protagonist

FIGURE 7.5: *Banyan, Indian for the Western market*, 1700–50. Image courtesy of Los Angeles
County Museum of Art.

proudly refers to his wearing an *Indienne*: "I had this Indienne done. My tailor tells me that cultured people wear them in the morning."[32] The taste for banyans eventually filtered down social ranks and modest middle class households could afford a share of the exotic, albeit on printed or painted on cheaper, low-quality cotton fabrics such as Smyrnan boucassins. Wealthy clients on the other hand could comfortably assert their privileged social position by claiming the luxury end of the market and enjoying the smooth quality of Persian cottons and calankars.[33]

Banyans were produced and consumed in a range of fabrics and colors and could boast colorful brocades or subdued monochrome silks. As Lemire remarked, when employed in portraiture, banyans came to symbolize successful and erudite masculinity.[34] In 1726, J.S. Chardin's irreverent depiction of an antiquarian monkey nonchalantly surveying his collection of medals dressed in a bright orange silk banyan evidently ridicules the pretension of these connoisseurial pursuits and the type of dress they required. While somewhat subdued in color and devoid of any floral pattern, the silk dressing gown worn by Diderot in Van Loo's portrait of 1767 testifies to the ongoing validity of this association.[35]

The question remains: to what extent were these dressing gowns actually perceived as exotic? The popularity of the banyan was reflected by its inclusion in a number of contemporary fashion plates. In France, the market for such images was dominated by a small number of publishers and print sellers, of which the Bonnart family who specialized in the production and diffusion of fashion plates and almanachs. Cheaply produced and widely disseminated, those prints followed a simple and effective format consisting of showing mostly single figures in relatively sparse though suitably fashionable and elegant surroundings. A plate by Bonnart published c. 1676 shows a man dressed with a "*Robe de Chambre*" or dressing gown "*à l'armenien*," the accompanying text explicitly praising the gown's comfort and fashionable status (Figure 7.6).

The gown's name, however, had little to do with actual Armenian fashions and was more likely inflected by the fact that Armenian merchants negotiated and controlled a large part of the painted and printed chintzes intended for European markets; chintzes which were in turn used as fabrics for dressing gowns.[36] The Armenian appellation was not, however, systematically sustained and a fashion plate from the *Galerie des Modes* published in 1780 referred to the sleeves of a similar gown being "*en Pagode*," thereby shifting the garment's geographical origins further east.[37] Introduced and employed regularly in the early part of the eighteenth century, by the 1780s, the term "*en pagoda*" was effectively used ubiquitously for anything that flared.[38]

The philosopher Jean-Jacques Rousseau was arguably the most famous eighteenth-century consumer of so-called Armenian gowns. While this cemented the garb's inclusion in the erudite realm, legitimizing its identity as the thinking man's uniform, Rousseau's taste was partly justified by prosaic reasons. Plagued by painful and debilitating urinary problems, the gown's loose cut alleviated some of his physical discomfort and allowed for the easy administration of medical treatments. Rousseau made it his main outfit while staying at Motiers-Travers in 1762 and Taraval and the painters Ramsay and Liotard famously immortalized him wearing it. Rousseau's correspondence bears numerous mentions of his engagement with the choice of fabrics which appears to be dictated by practical considerations: "I would wish for the background not to be white and easily stained, with a small pattern that does not climb [. . .] I also prefer quality to good taste."[39] Rousseau was, however, not impervious to aesthetic concerns and, in another letter to his seamstress Madame de Luze, adopting a coquettish tone, he commented on the garb's

Homme en Robe de Chambre
Cette robe d'Armenien,   Et l'on ne scauroit trouuer rien
Est vn des-habillé commode;   De plus grane et plus à la mode.
Chez. h. Bonnart, rue S.t Iacque;   auec priuilege du Roy

FIGURE 7.6: Nicolas Bonnart, *"Homme en Robe de Chambre"* from the *Recueil des modes de la cour de France*, 1676. Image courtesy of Los Angeles County Museum of Art.

pleasing effect: "I will look like a pleasing man from Téflis or Erivan in my beautiful lilac caftan and I think that shall suit me very well."[40] Importantly, given that Rousseau were to make such gowns his main item of clothing, he was keen for them to be perceived formal enough to be worn outside in public, particularly in church. And with that in mind, he requested his gowns to be enhanced with suitable silk trimmings.[41] That said, medical imperatives only partly informed Rousseau's sartorial choices: the gowns intersected with his critique of European civilization. For him fashion "corrupted virtue and masked vice" and his attire was thus also intended as an ostensible statement of his progressive ideas (although his recurrent engagement with the gown's detailing would also belie his complete resistance to the world of fashions).[42] Rousseau's insistence on wearing embellished and enhanced exemplars also highlights a crucial aspect of their use, namely as largely private, in-door garments. As Madeleine Delpierre rightly noted, Oriental or exotic dress was indeed mostly first worn informally at home.[43] For instance, Madame de Pompadour owned several pairs of wide-fitted Oriental trousers gathered at the ankles, or *sirwals*, which she enjoyed wearing at home, only commissioning Carle Van Loo to immortalize her wearing them as part of an elaborately staged and fictionalized exotic setting for one of the over-doors of her Chateau of Bellevue, discussed later.

In addition to being largely worn at home, exotic fashions could be experienced vicariously and the examination of the links between fashion and ethnicity needs to be located within the wider context of the production and consumption of luxury goods. The largely private nature of everyday exotic dress fully echoed the use of exotic furnishings in the domestic sphere. The advent of the rococo style heralded a vogue for exotic ornaments, many of which incorporated pictorial representation of foreign attire as part of their decorative schemes. By the 1740s, they were nothing short of ubiquitous. China and Japan were arguably the primary sources of inspiration but, in parallel to this visual and material consumption of the Orient, the middle decades of the eighteenth century witnessed the emergence of a fashion for all things Turkish which was going to last well until the neo-classical period, as exemplified by the creation of numerous *boudoirs turcs*.

This taste for Turkish ornament needs to be envisaged within a broader cultural framework. The publication of Antoine Galland's *Thousand and One Nights* in several volumes between 1704 and 1717, and the 1721 visit of Turkish ambassadors to Paris, had widely contributed to the popularization of an idealized Middle-Eastern culture. Permeating all aspects of French art, *Turqueries* were very much in demand, as evidenced by the publication of Le Hay's *Recueil de Cent Estampes Representant Differentes Nations du Levant* (1714). Far from being systematically based on direct Oriental or Middle Eastern models, these *Chinoiseries* and *Turqueries* were the products of designers' fertile imaginations and happily mixed real and imagined exotic features. Aesthetic effect was the primary goal and scientific or archeological accuracy was of negligible importance.

From ceramics to furniture, these types of ornament permeated all aspects of material culture and royal workshops and minor craftsmen alike responded with equal enthusiasm to the public demand for this European commodification and standardization of the exotic. Antoine Watteau's painted Oriental figures at the Château de la Muette, executed between 1708 and 1715, were thought to be one of the first large scale inclusion of *Chinoiseries* in a domestic decorative scheme.[44] No longer extant, they are known to us via a series of engravings executed by Michel Aubert and published in 1731. They show a range of European and Oriental figures in exotic garb carefully inserted in the structure of a decorative grotesque.[45] The artist François Boucher, who rose to the position of *Peintre du Roi* in 1765, is often considered as the rococo's presiding genius and one of the most prolific exponents of *chinoiseries* in the new *Goût Pittoresque*. He produced a plethora of designs that were widely applied to the decorative arts. As Perrin Stein noted, he relied on earlier printed sources, successfully adapting them to contemporary rococo aesthetics. Reproduced on the exquisite reserves of pieces of Sèvres porcelain and on large scale luxurious tapestries, Boucher's designs could include complex figurative scenes depicting a range of characters dressed in exotic costume, such as those he produced in 1742 for the *Tenture Chinoise* tapestry woven at Beauvais.

Nicolas Lancret's depiction of a turbaned man in Turkish garb in the painted arabesques of the paneling of the salon of the Hotel de Boullongne in Paris, probably executed in 1728–9, marks the initial appearance of Ottoman figures in fashionable interiors. Almost twenty years later, Christophe Huet's larger and more complex picnic scene showing a group of men and women in Turkish dress enjoying a collation after the hunt testifies to the enduring popularity of painted exotic themes in domestic interiors. Ottoman subject matters were often represented in ceramics. Outside of France, Delft was producing flower holders in the shape of blue and white turbanned busts as early as 1700, while the Meissen porcelain factory started producing painted porcelain figures dressed "*à la turque*" in 1725. Some years later, it produced the figure of the Turc Amoureux, directly copied from the eponymous print by Georg Friedrich Schmidt of Nicolas Lancret's painting of a Turkish musician (Figure 7.7).

While the representation of exotic figures allowed for the representation of costumes, these were not accurate scientific reproductions of real Oriental garments and were often hybrid fantasies mixing imagined foreign dress with elements of contemporary ornament. An example is the case of Ambroise-Nicolas Cousinet's gilded silver figure of a dancing Turkish lady whose dress terminating in lambrequins owed arguably more to contemporary luxury domestic furnishings than to dress. This is not to say that all depictions were entirely fictional and a number of figures were copied from prints published as part of proto-ethnographic volumes intended as visual conspectuses of foreign fashions. Meissen's porcelain sultan of 1741, modeled by Johann Joachim Kändler, was inspired by a figure in Charles de Ferriol's *Recueil de Cent Estampes*, and Chelsea's "Levantine woman" owed much to the plate of a *Greek Lady in her Apartment* from the same volume. Ferriol's *Recueil* was arguably one of the most influential printed source available to eighteenth-century artists. The plates derive from paintings executed between 1707 and 1708 by the

FIGURE 7.7: Le Turc Amoureux, Meissen porcelain factory, 1744. © Victoria and Albert Museum, London.

artist Jean-Baptiste Vanmour, who had traveled to Constantinople with the French Ambassador Charles de Ferriol in 1699. The latter had commissioned him to immortalize the inhabitants of the city, and the paintings were subsequently engraved under the aegis of Jacques le Hay in 1714.

Turqueries and *Chinoiseries* were not restricted to single compositional figures and could be included in larger, more elaborate scenes featuring indoor or outdoor festivities and entertainments. In 1737, Charles André Van Loo, Boucher's contemporary, produced two paintings depicting the unfamiliar and luxurious worlds of sultans and sultanas. His *Grand Turk Giving a Concert*, shown with its pendant *Grand Turk having his Mistress Painted at the Salon* of the same year, effectively contradicted contemporary literary representations of harems as sites of female subjection to masculine authority and privileged instead the representation of the "unparalleled power" of a single woman.[46] Located in an unidentified classicizing space framed by imposing columns and furnished with unmistakably western furniture, Van Loo's painting crystallized the significance of clothes as potent mediators and signifiers of cultural identity. As the only visible indicator of otherness, they served to mark the Ottoman identity of the protagonists who were otherwise depicted with clear European features. While Van Loo's turbans, robes, and furs might have been informed by the study of prints depicting foreign costumes, the artist nevertheless gave free rein to his imagination by including a man wearing a tunic with slashed sleeves characteristic of the rein of Henry IV. Evidently here, temporal and geographical displacement were not perceived as antinomic, but rather as mutually reinforcing strategies. Widely disseminated in printed form, Van Loo's Turkish paintings arguably contributed to familiarizing the French public with exotic dress.

Although largely worn at home up until the second half of the eighteenth century, Oriental dress and accessories could be worn in public when used as props in carefully staged Oriental fictions, some of which employed to serve explicit mercantile interests. The Café Procope in Paris, founded in 1686, one of the city's first public institutions to serve coffee, fully capitalized on the beverage's exotic appeal and employed a team of waiters in Oriental costume—wrongly described as Armenian—to serve its customers. Here, amid a luxurious profusion of marble, gilding, and porcelain, urban armchair tourists could indulge in their Oriental fantasies and be served by affable waiters in exotic work clothes.[47] A driver for commerce, dress in this instance was part of an exotic performance employed to enhance the sense of displacement and wonder experienced by customers.

The world of the theater and the stage were also crucial mediators in the dissemination of exotic fashions. Plays evoking far-away shores and distant customs were indeed recurrent themes in early modern French literature. Moliere's Turkish Interlude in his *Bourgeois Gentilhomme* of 1670, said to have been inspired by the recent visit of the haughty Turkish envoy Suleiman Agha Muteferrika, is one of the earliest inclusion of Ottoman fashions on the French stage. Enlivened by the music of Jean-Baptiste Lully, it boasted extravagant costumes designed by Henri Gissey, draughtsman in the *Chambre et du Cabinet du Roi* in the department of the *Menus Plaisirs* that was responsible for the management of all court festivities. Gissey enlisted the help of Laurent d'Arvieux, who had gained first hand knowledge of Ottoman dress during his travels to the Levant. A surviving watercolor of Lully's character in the role of the mufti suggests some attempts to approximate contemporary Ottoman fashions, although magnificence was evidently the desired effect.[48] A number of plays and ballets sustained the public's interest in the Orient throughout the eighteenth century. Voltaire's call for religious tolerance articulated in his tragedy *Zaïre* (first performed in 1732) was set in Jerusalem at the times of the Crusades. This temporal and geographical displacement was underpinned by a host of costumes "*à la turque*," as evidenced by Hubert François Gravelot's illustrations. More than forty years after the play's first performance, the French actor Henri-Louis Cain (known as Lekain), was immortalized by Simon-Bernard Lenoir as the character of Zaïre's Orosmane (one of his most popular roles) wearing a yellow brocade robe worn under an ermine-trimmed coat and a bejeweled turban on his head. Although, according to the painter Louise-Elisabeth Vigée le Brun, the accoutrement made him "look hideous," it testifies to the ongoing popularity of Turkish costumes on stage and to the public's continued wish to experience some form of coherence between plot and props.[49]

Sartorial verisimilitude reached new heights with Charles Simon Favart's popular play *Soliman II ou les Trois Sultanes*, produced for the first time in 1761. Showing a profusion of lavish exotic costumes that contributed to bolstering the credibility of the play's Turkish setting, it also broke new ground and was said to have included real Turkish costumes made in Constantinople. Praising his wife's visionary outlook (she played the lead female character), Favart noted that she had initiated this change and "dared to sacrifice the agreeableness of the figure to the veracity of characters."[50] As noted in Favart's memoirs, this movement towards a more truthful approach to costumes appears to have been subsequently adopted by other performers. Referring to his wife's sultana "decent and voluptuous" costume, it was not unanimously approved of, suggesting some sort of conflict between the public's desire for credible sets, and its attachment to traditional costumes that might help them identify with the characters on stage.[51]

The public wearing of dress inspired by foreign fashions was not solely the prerogative of actors and stage performers. In addition to plays, royal festivities were also an occasion to wear exotic dress publicly. The spectacular carrousel held in the courtyard of the Tuileries Palace in June 1662 to celebrate the birth of the dauphin featured a lavishly choreographed spectacle performed by 1299 participants on horseback dressed to represent the various nations of the world. This elaborate display was aimed at symbolizing France's domination over the rest of the globe. Participation in carrousels was a prerogative of high rank and that of 1662 was headed by the king himself representing the Sun, and dressed as a Roman emperor leading an army of Roman soldiers. The four other *quadrilles*, representing America, Persia, India, and Turkey, all wore costumes corresponding to their respective countries. Designed by Henri Gissey, they were inspired by sixteenth-century prints and illustrated books of world costume such as François Desprez's *Recueil de la diversité des habits qui sont en présent en usage tant es pays d'Europe, Asie, Affrique*, Melchior Lorck's *Turkish Book* or Abraham de Bruyn's *Omnium Poene Gentium Imagines* first published in 1562, 1575, and 1577 respectively.[52]

Recorded by Charles Perrault in his *Course de testes et de bagues faites par le Roy et par les princes et seigneurs de la Cour en l'année M.DC.LXII*, Gissey's exotic costumes were illustrated by Israel Silvestre and were the subject of extensive descriptions. They were, however, only approximate renderings of real foreign and historic dress. The Prince de Condé, appointed as leader of the Turkish army, was sporting a silver turban adorned with diamonds and turquoises in the shape of a crescent and surmounted by eminently non-Turkish white, blue, and black ostrich feathers. His costume was equally lavish with a crimson and silver vest terminating in lambrequins studded with diamonds and turquoises, and a string of silver crescents attached to the sleeves.[53] The mock Turkish army under the yoke of his temporary military leadership was dressed in matching costumes also adorned with crescents, the unequivocal symbol of the Ottoman Empire.[54]

Masquerades were the other obvious ideal occasion for the adoption of exotic fashions. For instance the masked ball of 1745 held in Versailles to celebrate the marriage of the dauphin saw the deployment of a number of exotic costumes. The engraver Cochin's well-known visual record clearly shows two Chinese characters standing by the yew trees and a number of turbaned men on the right-hand side of the Galerie des Glaces.

The popularity of exotic fancy dress was fully reflected in contemporary portraiture. Rosalba Carriera's pastel portrait of a lady identified as Felicita Sartori wearing a bejeweled turban and what appears to be a silk *kurdi* over an *entari*, a type of waistcoat, is, fittingly, also holding a mask, thereby conveying in no uncertain terms the outfit's fancy and ephemeral nature. Jean-Étienne Liotard employed a similar trope for his portrait of Empress Maria-Theresa: dressed in a red caftan and ermine *kurdi* (no doubt also intended to emphasize her imperial status), she is delicately holding a carnival mask in her right hand. Although the costume was inspired by a pastel that Liotard had executed earlier in Constantinople, it was, however, only an approximation of real Turkish dress, as its tight bodice gave its tailoring a distinctively European character.[55] Liotard's portrait should not just be read as a record of courtly entertainments. As Michel Yonan has argued, the painting articulated Maria-Theresa's imperial power and effectively deconstructed and decomplexified the Islamic East into "something simple, superficial and unthreatening."[56]

Although the fashion for painted Turkish masquerades was sustained throughout the eighteenth century (as can be seen in Jean-Baptiste Greuze's portrait of 1790 depicting a lady in an elaborate approximation of ottoman costume, complete with pearl-clad turban, fur-trimmed kurdi and silk sash), it would be wrong to assume that all *turqueries* portraits were necessarily envisaged as ostensible evocations of festive masquerades (Figure 7.8).

A number of portraits also encompassed real sitters in real Ottoman dress as a number of Western travelers commissioned such likenesses as souvenirs of their passage in the Levant. Usually painted by European artists or by native painters trained in the execution of studio copies, these portraits fully embodied the formal compositional characteristics found in western painting. The painters Jean-Baptiste Vanmour and Jean-Étienne Liotard counted as the most respected of these European artists. The former stayed in Constantinople until his death in 1737 and became known for his depictions of foreign envoys and his pictorial records of ambassadorial diplomatic receptions. His portrait of Lady Mary Wortley Montagu, the wife of the British ambassador to Constantinople, wearing an ermine-trimmed *kurdi* over a gold caftan, one corner of which is tucked in her girdle so as to reveal the smock underneath, shows her adoption of the type of dress favored by Turkish women.[57] Montagu's influence should not be underestimated and both her portraits and letters describing Ottoman dress and customs were widely circulated in printed form, significantly bolstering the popularity of *Turqueries* fashions in Britain.[58]

The pictorial composition of Jean-Marc Nattier's portrait of *Marie-Anne de Bourbon as a Sultana* and the pose of the sitter firmly positioned the Orientalist portrait within an established genealogy of formal portraiture. A reflection of contemporary fashions, the inclusion of an Ottoman setting evoked by the depiction of black servants and a richly colored Turkish carpet (albeit in a blatant Classicizing setting) is also here employed as a justification to Mademoiselle de Clermont's state of undress. Evidently here, the admittedly scantily dressed "Sultane au Bain" was considered a suitable substitute for the traditional bathing Venus or Diana.

A few years later, in the declining years of the rococo, Carle Van Loo fictionalized otherness with more than just imaginary characters. His works encompassed the realm of portraiture, as exemplified by his depiction of *Madame de Pompadour as a Sultana* for her

FIGURE 7.8: *Lady in Turkish Costume*, Jean-Baptiste Greuze, 1790. Image courtesy of Los Angeles County Museum of Art.

Château de Bellevue (1752). Seated on luxurious floor cushions and framed by heavy draperies, she is shown consuming exotic eastern substances: coffee and tobacco. Her dress is unapologetically non-European and the turban, *salwar*, *kaftan*, and *kurdi* all evoke a mysterious East. Although Pompadour was said to own a number of *salwars* that she wore at home, there are no records of her embracing fuller Ottoman fashions. What we see here is the portrait enabling the sitter to wear, albeit vicariously, a type of garb that would not be acceptable outside of the transient realm of the masquerade. Commissioned as part of a series of over-doors for a *"chambre à la turque,"* the painting has been the subject of extensive scholarly scrutiny.[59] It was shown at the Salon of 1753 and enshrined the royal mistress's exalted position while simultaneously asserting her obedience to the king and her superiority over other women at court. Van Loo's geographical and cultural displacement was thus both a response to contemporary artistic fashions and a carefully crafted piece of personal propaganda.

As evidenced by Louise Elizabeth Vigée Le Brun's elegant society paintings, the inclusion of exotic garments in portraiture was sustained throughout the eighteenth

FIGURE 7.9: *Madame D'Aguesseau de Fresnes*, Louise-Elisabeth Vigée Le Brun, 1789. Image courtesy of the National Gallery of Art, Washington.

century. Her portrait of *Madame d'Aguesseau de Fresnes* embodies no fewer than three foreign influences (Figure 7.9).

Her turban recalls Turkish fashions, her flowing white and gold gown alludes to the costumes of Ancient Greece and Rome, and her red velvet robe, or *redingote*, and the prominent Wedgwood cameo at her sash is a clear reference to contemporary English taste.[60] The boundaries between masquerade and fashionable dress had by then become more permeable, and, while Van Loo and Nattier had used stage costumes as props for their artistic creations, the costume depicted by Vigée Le Brun and her peers reflected contemporary fashions. Indeed, the last three decades of the eighteenth century witnessed a surge in the creation and consumption of a range exotic garments intended for everyday wear, prompting the *Cabinet des Modes* to write in 1786 that "French women, particularly those in the capital which is the centre of taste, know how to imitate and to appropriate the costumes of all nations. After the dresses à la Française and à la Polonaise, we have seen a succession of Levites, dresses à l'Anglaise and à la Turque. A pretty woman wearing the latter at the theatre or in a salon would win triumphs more certain and more agreeable than a Georgian or Circassian woman in a harem of Constantinople. Even a Sultana would be jealous of her elegance, her grace and of the hommages which she receives."[61]

As discussed by Kimberly Chrisman-Cambell, up until the 1770s, female fashions had been largely dominated by two types of dresses: the *robe à la française* with a loose pleated piece of fabric falling from the shoulders in the back (also called *plis à la Watteau*), and the *robe à l'anglaise* with a fitted bodice. So as to respond to fashion's imperatives, those two types of dresses were updated with appropriate trimmings, fabrics, and accessories. However, the 1770s saw the proliferation of dresses boasting different types of construction such as the *Polonaise*, the *Lévite*, the *Circassienne*, the *robe à la Turque* and *à la Sultane*. The *Polonaise* had a close-fitting bodice structured with boning. The skirts were pulled up by drawstrings at the back, usually in three poufs. It was worn over a circular petticoat with a flounce round the hem which reached just above the ankles. The *robe à la Turque* and the *Circassienne* were variations of the *Polonaise*: the former had a trailing skirt behind whereas the latter was circular. Both, however, had an over-gown with short sleeves that revealed the longer sleeves of the under-dress. The *Lévite* was more informal and consisted of a large shawl collar and a long scarf loosely knotted around the waist (Figure 7.10).[62]

In short, female consumers were now faced with a wider new range of sartorial options, and a large number of them were associated with the exotic and the foreign.[63] Importantly, once again, none of these interpretations of exotic garments were faithful copies: they

FIGURE 7.10: Woman wearing a Levite, from the *Gallerie des Modes et Costumes Français*, Charles Emmanuel Patas, Esnauts and Rapilly, 1780. Rijksmuseum, Amsterdam.

often incorporated approximate "foreign" details, such as sashes, stripes, or turbaned head-dresses that were sufficient to convey their otherness.

Crucially, this commodification of the exotic was heavily underpinned by the judicious and creative use of semantic appellations. A significant feature of these sartorial trends was indeed their propensity to fuse and confuse geographical origins and adopt different, sometimes interchangeable names. For instance, in 1787, the *Magasin des Modes Nouvelles* noted that a hat "*à la Chinoise*" was not altogether different from a "*bonnet à la Turque*" that had been shown in a previous issue.[64] While some garments did not differ dramatically from each other with respect to their construction, trimmings, or accessories, their denomination and the way in which they were referred to, marked them out as new and different. The vagaries of fashion were thus underpinned by a non-negligible degree of semantic fluidity. Fashion illustrations fully articulated this interchangeability: the caption of a plate published in the *Galerie des modes et des costumes Français* in 1779 described it as a "Robe à la Turque or type of Circassienne, but different from the others; it has a collar like a Lévite [. . .] this dress attracted all the eyes of the public when it was shown for the first time at the Palais Royal last July."[65] Mixing no less than three types of garments—all equally fashionable—the dress's final sartorial *coup de grâce* was given by the mention of its success at the theater, crudely implying that the wearer outshone the actresses on stage, but also perhaps referring to the fact that such fashions had once been almost exclusively confined to plays and masquerades.

Fashion magazines like the *Magasin des Modes Nouvelles* were behind the creation of these nomenclatures. Aware of fashion's inherently transient quality and mindful that urban consumers longed for novelty, a fact which prompted Montesquieu to remark as early as 1721 in his *Lettres Persanes* that "a woman who leaves Paris to go and spend six months in the country returns as antiquated as if she had been gone thirty years," periodicals tracked those changes while simultaneously encouraging their consumption. Late eighteenth-century French fashion periodicals catered for a pan-European diverse audience, ranging from the aristocrat to the more modest housemaid. Keen to be relevant and inspirational to a wide part of its readership, the *Galerie des Modes* was careful not just to include luxury garments but also more affordable examples. The depiction of a governess employed by "*gens de qualité*" wearing a simple striped robe *à la Polonaise* shows how exotic fashions had filtered down the social ranks. No longer exclusively the preserve of a wealthy elite, sartorial travel was experienced by the many.

The arrival of Sultan Tippoo-Sahib's ambassadors in July 1788 offered Parisian society at once a glimpse of real and imagined Asian dress. As Martin explained, immediately after their arrival, the printing firm of Chéreau and Joubert published a print depicting the ambassadors in fictional costumes recalling those represented in Vanmour's *Recueil de cent estampes représentant différentes nations du Levant*. Yet the ambassadors' eagerness to experience the cultural delights of the capital also ensured their visibility to a wider public and their appearances and whereabouts were recurrently commented upon in the contemporary press. Their arrival generated an "Indomania" that found full expression in contemporary dress.[66] Warmly welcomed by the *Magasin des Modes Nouvelles*, the periodical issued a few days later two new dresses "*à la Tipu Saib*" and a "*redingote à l'indienne*", openly admitting that they differed little from Turkish, English, or even French dresses, all of which were really just English dresses.[67]

Exotic nomenclatures were not just applied to the clothes; the very shops where such garments could be acquired bore similarly exotic names. Madame Gely's premises were called *Aux Trois Sultanes*, and the silk merchants Jubin and Le Normand called their

Parisian shops *Aux Trois Mandarins* and *Au Grand Turc* respectively. As for Rose Bertin, arguably the most prestigious of all late-eighteenth-century dressmakers due to her links with the court and Marie-Antoinette's extensive patronage, the shop she opened in the very heart of the capital near the Palais Royal was called *Au Grand Mogol*. This practice recalled the commercial strategies of other luxury goods merchants in adjacent trades, highlighting once more the interplay between fashion and furnishings: the dealer Grancher owned the shop *La Perle d'Orien* in his native Dunkerque, and in 1739 the dealer Gersaint changed the name of his shop from *Au Grand Monarque* to *A la Pagode* to reflect his increased specialization in luxury goods and imported Asian wares, such as Oriental lacquer and ceramics.[68] The description of the goods on sale in those shops was, however, often minimal: widely defined by generic terms such as "*Indiennes*" or "*Perses*," they could equally refer to foreign imports or home-made French products. Carefully blurring the boundaries between real imports as well as manufactured, Westernized exoticism, such shops stimulated the appeal of both categories. At once liminal sites and exotic heterotopias, they offered a momentary displacement where consumers' desires and displacement fantasies could be projected and performed.

Nomenclatures in fact further articulated the interplay between fashionable dress and furnishings: the names "*à la Turque*" and "*à la Polonaise*" were not only restricted to the sartorial realm and were widely employed to refer to specific types of luxurious and fashionable canopied beds. The *Magasin de Modes Nouvelles* cemented the link between both types of commodities, illustrating in the same issue a bed "*à la Polonaise*," "the only form of bed that cultured and opulent people would choose," and "*caracos à la Turque*."[69]

It would be wrong to assume that the appeal of exotic fashions resided solely in their ability to satisfy consumers' thirst for novelty. As Aileen Ribeiro and Chrisman-Campbell have shown, the appeal of *robes de fantaisie* like the *Lévite* or the *Circassienne* resided in their perceived freer, less formal cuts. Lighter and looser, they were considered easier to wear, although their small bodices belied the idea that they would have released women's bodies from the grip of corsets. In reality, such dresses very much retained the silhouettes of western dress and there was in fact little structural difference between a *robe à la Française* and a *robe à la Polonaise*. Rather, the association of such garments with eastern lands inhabited by mysterious sultanas in luxurious seraglios invested them with a sensuality and eroticism that greatly contributed to their attractiveness. Fashion plates were quick to play on these associations and sometimes represented women in suggestive poses. In addition, the physical and geographical displacement suggested by such garments could be further emphasized by the use of suitable props such as exotic parrots or playful monkeys.

The adoption of ethnic fashions should also be envisaged as a strategy for deflecting ongoing criticism of women's perceived frivolity and excessive concern with trivial sartorial matters such as that expressed by Boudier de Villemert, the editor of the *Courier de la Mode*. In *l'Ami des Femmes*, he lamented, for instance, that "the imagination of women continually nourishes itself on the details of jewels and clothing. These fill up their heads with so many colors that there is no room for objects which might better merit their attention. Women's minds scarcely graze the surface of essential qualities and only attach themselves to the drapery."[70] His views were echoed by a number of his contemporaries, most notably by Jean-Jacques Rousseau who openly criticized and condemned the corrupting influence of fashion's commercial culture upon society.[71] For Rousseau, women and, by extension, society were debased by the former's obsession with luxurious novelty. The philosopher advocated instead the cultivation of a graceful deportment combined with the adoption of unostentatious, pastoral fashions and plain fabrics.

It would be of course a fallacy to envisage the *Lévite* and *Circassiennes* depicted in the *Galerie des Modes* as adhering to Rousseau's precepts. Strict Rousseauist dress would have likely consisted of simple white muslin and a straw hat, such as that worn by Vigée-Le Brun's infamous 1783 portrait of Marie-Antoinette. It is well known that the queen's simple, pastoral attire, and the influence it exerted at court led to widespread accusations of her intent to ruin the French fashion industry. Ethnic fashions were similarly scrutinized and the writer Pierre-Jean-Baptiste Nougaret recalled in 1781 how a cloth merchant had printed a pamphlet condemning the fashion for "the childlike shapes of the robes à la Polonaise and à la Levite which contributed to the downfall of the manufactures which produced the rich, elegant, and perfectly crafted textiles for which our workshops were known all over the world."[72] The *Cabinet des Modes* was in fact keen to support the country's fashion industry, and made regular mentions of the French origins of the goods depicted across its pages: "we do not want to mislead our subscribers. Nearly all these waistcoats come from the manufactures of Lyon. We must admit that we find them singularly flattering."[73] The *Magasin des Modes Nouvelles* openly professed a similar patriotic agenda, stating in 1787 that "after having travelled across foreign courts, Spain, Poland, Turkey, England, Sweden, Italy, Germany etc to bring us new clothes, fashion has become more patriotic and a good citizen and stayed in the kingdom to visit its various Provinces."[74]

Although evidently perceived as a threat to the country's financial well-being, the foreign-named garments depicted in the *Galerie des Modes* were, however, far from simple. Extravagant, precious and ephemeral, embellished with a plethora of trimmings and ribbons, they epitomized the capriciousness of Parisian taste and, as Chrisman-Campbell argued, some dresses "*à l'asiatique*" required in fact more fabric than their French and English counterparts because of their exposed linings.[75]

Their appellations and ethnic associations were, however, useful in evoking simpler and more rural and elementary lifestyles that were fully reflected in contemporary fashion plates. It is indeed significant that the *Galerie des Modes* published the plate of a young woman fashionably dressed in an elaborate lévite ostentatiously breastfeeding her child under the gaze of her governess. To counter any ambiguity, the caption made it explicit who the characters were and that the infant was brought to his mother in a *barcelonette* [sic] to facilitate its feeding during the promenade. Here the message was clear: fashion and maternal instinct were not mutually exclusive and could both be facilitated by auspicious French-made commodities, namely a portable cradle and a dress cut in such a way so as not to hinder breastfeeding. At a time when maternal breastfeeding was widely encouraged by Rousseau as a source of virtuous interaction benefiting society at large, the maternal spectacle offered by this fashion plate underpinned the garment's sartorial compatibility with simpler lifestyles which nevertheless offered continued support to the *marchandes de modes*, *merciers* and cloth merchants who were considered vital agents for France's economic prosperity.[76]

The movement towards a more natural line was accompanied by an increasing condemnation of tight lacing as articulated by Rousseau's followers, who perceived a moral virtue in the expression of the natural body shape.[77] While "exotic" fashions were clearly in vogue throughout the 1770s and 1780s, the real success of the pre-revolutionary decade was undoubtedly the *chemise* dress of the type worn by Marie-Antoinette in Vigée Le Brun's infamous portrait of 1783. As Ribeiro argued, this type of dress was to have a profound influence on later fashions.[78] Probably derived from the simple cotton creole dresses worn in the French West Indies and brought to Europe in the 1770s, it anticipated the neo-classical dresses worn during the Napoleonic period. The *Lévites*, *Polonaises*, and *Circassiennes* became relics of the Old Regime and were soon to be replaced by unstructured and high-waisted white muslin gowns, all openly seen as references to the ancient Classical world and perceived as appropriate sartorial accompaniments to current political developments. In line with contemporary preoccupations with motherhood, simple neo-classical garments were also widely praised for their ability to liberate the maternal body and the maternal breast, perhaps best visually exemplified by Marguerite Gerard's painting *Mère Nourrice* of 1804.

Yet it would be wrong to assume that such fashions were only perceived as reminders of ancient times. The wide use of the term "*à la Grecque*" is in the tradition of pre-revolutionary sartorial appellations which emphasized geographical over temporal displacement. In addition, gowns were usually made of imported Indian (or sometimes English) muslin and were almost systematically combined with draped cashmere shawls, similarly imported. Unsurprisingly, the use of foreign fabrics once again was perceived as a threat by a number of French manufacturers, prompting the French fashion periodical *L'Arlequin* to justify such imports by citing classical precedents: 'the rich women of Athens preferred the fabrics of Persia'.[79] Keen to promote French manufactures, Napoleon nevertheless took an interventionist approach and insisted that only French fabrics be worn at court, a patriotic stance, which judging from surviving bills, was never quite adopted by Joséphine and her daughter Hortense.[80] The adoption of classicizing dress at the close of the eighteenth century can therefore be seen not as a complete departure from the exotic fashions of the earlier, "long eighteenth century," but rather as a continuation of this fascination with the other.

CHAPTER EIGHT

Visual Representations

CHRISTIAN HUCK

INTRODUCTION: THE MIRROR OF PRINT

Mr. Spectator, the fictitious editor of the eighteenth century's most famous newspaper, the *Spectator*, was, to little surprise, a huge supporter of the visual sense: "Our Sight is the most perfect and most delightful of all our Senses," he trumpeted, because it not only "fills the Mind with the largest Variety of Ideas," but also "converses with its Objects at the greatest Distance."[1] With the help of his eyes, Mr. Spectator was able to observe everything, everywhere he was going—and keep his distance. Roaming around London, he was keen to shed light on even the darkest corners of the town: "I (that have nothing else to do, but make Observations) see in every Parish, Street, Lane, and Alley of this Populous City."[2] Adopting a disinterested stance, he discovered a great variety of people, wearing a great variety of clothes: the diverse visitors of a coffee house, for example, "some of whom are ready Dress'd for *Westminster*" while "others come in their Night-Gowns to Saunter away their Time" and yet others wear "a gay Cap and Slippers, with a Scarf and Party-colour'd Gown."[3]

The light that Mr. Spectator threw on the people of London and the clothes they were wearing was, of course, to be shared with the readers of his paper, famously hoping to take knowledge "out of Closets and Libraries, Schools, and Colleges, to dwell in Clubs and Assemblies, at Tea-tables, and in Coffee houses."[4] With the help of print, knowledge was to be brought out into the public eye. The *Spectator*, more specifically, made knowledge of the social a social entity: "In the Tatler, the Spectator, and the Guardian the public held up a mirror to itself," Jürgen Habermas famously proclaimed in his analysis of the emergence of a public sphere.[5] Although Habermas probably did not think of such mundane application, a mirror, without a doubt, is an absolute necessity when it comes to checking one's fashion credentials, and the *Spectator* was indeed as much a reflection of the fashions of the time as of more serious matters.[6] The optical metaphor of the "mirror" seems somewhat flawed here, nonetheless. While Mr. Spectator seemed happy to see with his own eyes, he had little interest in presenting his observations in visual, that is, pictorial form; Mr. Spectator was a writer after all, translating what he saw into words before sharing his observations in print.

The *London Spy*, another popular journal of the early eighteenth century, albeit one that is now largely forgotten, was a keen observer of the rise of pictorial prints circulating in the public sphere, supplementing printed texts and competing with these at the same time:[7] "In our Loitering Perambulation round the outside of *Pauls*, we came to a Picture-seller's Shop, where as many Smutty Prints were staring the Church in the Face, as a Learned Debauchee ever found in *Aretine*'s Postures.[8] I Observ'd there were more People gazing at these loose Fancies of some Lecherous Graver, than I could see reading of Sermons at the Stalls of all the Neighbouring Booksellers."[9] "Gazing" at pictures, here, is presented as the strict opposite to the "reading" of text, confronting a Christian culture of the scripture (St. Paul's) with a capitalist market-culture (picture-seller's shop): the one is pious (sermons), but unpopular, while the other is popular, but "lecherous." While the equanimous Mr. Spectator presented himself as being able to use his eyes to make reasoned observations ready to be transformed into informative words, the public was seen to immerse itself in the pleasures of the spectacle. There seems to be a fine line only between rationally deciphering, that is, *reading* the visual world, and succumbing to its lure by merely *gazing* at spectacular images; fashion, as we will see, treads this fine line at high risk.

Depictions of fashion were a rare thing in the early eighteenth century. However, in 1744, the successful print publisher John Bowles offered a number of prints showing male and female figures in fashionable dress (Figure 8.1).[10] Indeed, these were probably

FIGURE 8.1: Engraving by Louis Truchy after Hubert François Gravelot, printed by John Bowles (1744). © Trustees of the British Museum.

the first depictions of *dress* for the sake of presenting *fashion*, at least in Britain. What was the consumer to make of this entirely new entity? Is it a source of information about the social world? Is the print so entirely new and fascinating that it becomes a desired spectacle in itself? Is the beholder to be convinced to follow a fashion, to become a consumer? Is the viewer to be indignant over such lavish display? Is s/he turned voyeur or made a victim?

Pictorial representations of contemporary mundane subjects became available to a wider public for the first time at the beginning of the eighteenth century. Prints from metal or wood engravings, alone or illustrating books, came to be traded as consumer goods,[11] becoming "the first form of mass-produced images for popular markets,"[12] and a "ubiquitous feature of contemporary urban life."[13] Many of the pictures circulating showed contemporary people's dress, not necessarily for the purpose of depicting a specific fashion, but more as a side effect of their attempt to hold up a mirror to British society. Print-entrepreneurs like John Bowles and Henry Overton began to publish views and vistas of public places, streets scenes and markets, often showing lavishly dressed figures (Figure 8.2), and by the end of the century, mostly satirical, but also purely spectacular images of daily life clattered the windows of picture sellers and print warehouses (Figure 8.3). Slowly, the visible world came to be duplicated in print, made available to the curious observer: for the first time, you could actually see your own world in the mirror of print.

Visual representations of dress, in this chapter, are not considered for what they can tell us, a twenty-first century readership, about what eighteenth-century clothing really looked like. Whatever such representations reveal about the historical realities of dress, other chapters, and writers, in this volume are far better equipped to explore.[14] Instead, eighteenth-century images are understood here as agents in their own right, rather than a transparent window to the past. What did these images do to the clothes they are supposed to merely represent? What did they do to the contemporary beholder? My thesis is that what these images do is to turn clothes into fashion, and onlookers into followers. While seventeenth-century presentations of costume largely followed a scholastic blueprint of gathering information about regional differences, late eighteenth-century magazines and journals presented fashion as a matter of constant temporal change first and foremost. Between the distant view of the costume book and the seductive powers of the fashion magazine stood the satirical prints of Hogarth and others, as well as the illustrations accompanying popular novels. All these will be covered in the following.

"Fashion," in the sense it is understood here, does not refer to a "general interest in dressing well," that is, a concern for any inherent qualities of clothing, "but rather to a concern for dressing according to a style that is temporarily favored." Individual reasons for choosing a certain dress might be manifold, but fashions are a social phenomenon first and foremost: "The word 'temporarily' implies that styles of dress change, and change rapidly enough that staying up to date in dress is a problem. As a result, people who want to be fashionable must continually monitor what others are wearing to determine how they will dress."[15]

Importantly, this practice of "monitoring" underwent a significant transformation in the period we are concerned with here. Up to the seventeenth century, there was, as Aileen Ribeiro has argued, "no substitute for observing in the flesh, what fashionable people wore."[16] If you wanted to know what's in fashion, you had to go and see fashionable people. Consequently, fashions were largely confined to interactional groups. From the late seventeenth century onwards, however, monitoring other people did no longer mean

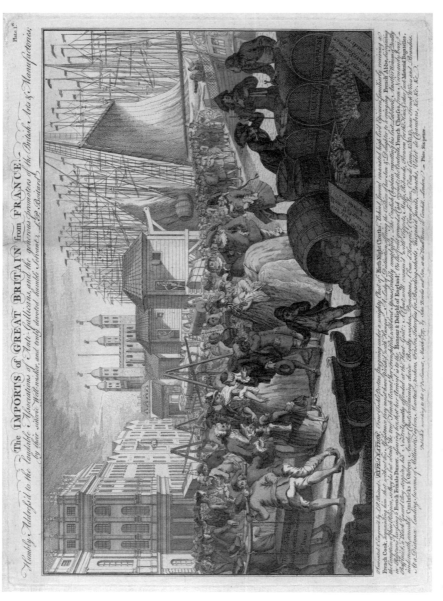

FIGURE 8.2: "The Imports of Great Britain from France, Plate 1" — "A chest well cramm'd with Tippets, Muffs, Ribands, Flowers for the Hair; & other such Material Bagatelles, underneath, conceal'd Cambricks & Gloves" — "Publish'd according to Act of Parliament, March 7th, 1757, by John Bowles and Son, at the Black Horse in Cornhill, London—Price, Six-pence." Louis Philip Boitard. © Yale Center for British Art.

FIGURE 8.3: *The Macaroni Print Shop*, Edward Topham (1772), published by Matthew and
Mary Darly. The Metropolitan Museum of Art, New York.

to observe one's fellow courtiers, villagers, or circle of friends directly to determine how
to dress. Instead, the community of fashion became a mediated and an imaginary one,
produced by representations of fashion circulating in print.

Mediated accounts, as opposed to direct perceptions, make the corporeal co-presence
of observer and observed unnecessary; looking at a picture becomes an almost anti-social
activity, as it allows a break from participating in what one is observing.[17] While pictures
allow looking at others not present as if present, the looked-at persons cannot look back:
the beholder sees others without being seen. Mediation, therefore, allows a more distant
stance, affording to gather visual information about the world one inhabits without being
part of the situations one observes. However, the distant observer position also allows for
a greater immersion at the same time; while it might be awkward to stare at people's dress
in interactional situations, mediation affords the beholder to ogle unashamedly. But while
mediation releases the viewer from participating in interactional situations, *mass-
mediation* makes the beholder part of society at the same time, albeit on another level: "A
thousand readers indeed stare, from their closets, into a single mirror of print, and each
of them does it alone", J. Paul Hunter notes in respect to the print revolution of the
eighteenth century.[18] A printed picture provides reassurance that the individual gaze is
multiple, that (at least potentially) many are looking at the same image simultaneously.
Seen in this way, the print-"mirror" performs an almost magical trick: while it is a single
individual that looks into the mirror, it is society that looks back. Observing fashion in the
mirror of print becomes a practice of sociation: if others see what I see they will probably
judge me on the basis of these images.

FROM DETAIL TO FETISH: ENLIGHTENED IMAGES OF COSTUME

The effect of sociation described earlier, however, is not a consequence of visual representation *as such*, of pictures *per se*. Instead, visual representations of dress perform their (magic) work as mirrors only as part of a particular media setup; the work the image performs depends on its technological form of transmission as much as on the discourses in which it is embedded and the particular social group it addresses.

With the popularization of print throughout the seventeenth century, the desire to know more about the world one inhabits increasingly became a desire to consume ever more detailed depictions of this world. "In the century of Enlightenment," Timothy Clayton's imperial study of *The English Print, 1688–1802* emphasizes, "the crucial importance of the print to the spread of [. . .] knowledge was widely appreciated," as the print was "the principal medium for conveying visual information."[19] It is well known that according to Enlightenment thinkers like John Locke, new knowledge was to come by the light of vision first and foremost: if we are to free ourselves from the shackles of custom and tradition, we have to start opening our eyes and observe the world around us through our own eyes, and not those of ancient authorities. However, seeing the enlightened way meant to see in a very specific mode. Locke's famous metaphor of the *camera obscura*, which became Enlightenment's central conceptualization of the human capacity of seeing, first and foremost expresses a safe distance between observer and observed: indeed, it can be said to have turned the observer into a "subject" and to "objectify" the observed.[20] "The gain is the concept of objectivity, of the thing as it is in itself as distinct from the thing as it affects me."[21] As a consequence, the world became a safe source of visual information, and the medium of print was to do nothing else but to "convey" this information to the curious observer.

While Enlightenment scientists and philosophers concerned themselves with reading the book of nature, atlases and travel books of the time attempted to depict the humans that inhabit this world, too. The new travel reporters "typically insisted that they truthfully reported 'matters of fact.' Whenever feasible they claimed to be 'eye-witnesses'."[22] More than everything else, one was to go out into the world and see with one's own eyes, and report truthfully. When it came to looking at the humans that inhabit the world, the sight of apparel caught many travelers' attention. Dorothy Carrington's aptly titled and richly illustrated *The Traveller's Eye* (1949) gives ample evidence of the fascination costume exerted on the traveler, and the central place it holds in their reports. Depicting the costumes of the world in print formed a challenge to publishers and engravers, but they were also a testament to their craftsmanship and well received on the market.[23]

Carolus Allard's masterpiece from the late seventeenth century, *Orbis Habitabilis Oppida et Vestitus*, *The Towns and Costumes of the Inhabited World* (Amsterdam, c. 1695), followed a Renaissance tradition of combining topographical knowledge with information on the costumes of people living within depicted regions (Figure 8.4); the book distinguished itself from an earlier tradition of costume books by situating clothing strictly within specific, recognizable places, and a scientific, empirical framework. The consequence of such depictions was a fixation of costume: "On maps, *habit* functions as a static metonym for national character, status hierarchies, and gender and erotic relations."[24] Here, clothes were supposed to function as an index to a person's position: people, here, did not dress as a consequence of monitoring others, but, apparently, as a consequence of their given regional, sexual, and social position. The beholder of an image

FIGURE 8.4: From *The Towns and Costumes of the Inhabited World* (c. 1695), Carolus Allard, p. 11. © The British Library Board.

of such costumes—in this case part of about one hundred pictures reproduced within the bounds of a large and expensive volume—was to be enabled to gather information about a visual world that had little affect on him.

However, when depictions of regional dress were popularized and marketed to a less learned audience, informational aspirations were clearly retrogressing. A good example for such popularization was the broadsheet print *A Description of the Habits of the Most Countries of the World, Printed on the River Thames, in the Great Frost, in the Month of January, 1739–40* (Figure 8.5), originally published in Ansham and John Churchill's *Collection of Voyages* (1732), and republished several times. The frost-fairs on the Thames were major attractions, and the (pirated) print was probably bought as much to remember the event as for its worth as a visual spectacle. In line with Allard, the print showed exactly one male and one female—in a universal heterosexual bond[25]—representative of each region. The depiction was focused on spectacular items like the "Chinese hat" or the "Turkish turban"; whereas only a small number of Chinese people actually wore a hat, and especially a hat like that, such an item helped to mark an easily visible difference, thereby establishing and constituting an apparently representative national costume. "The Habit of a Chinese" did not refer to "the habit of one of the many diverse and particular Chinese individuals," but instead proclaimed: "this is what the Chinese are wearing"— anytime, anyplace, anyone. As such spectacular items, however, the costumes depicted here were then able to inspire new, exotic fashions.[26] The beholder, as it seems, remained

FIGURE 8.5: "A Description of the Habits of most Countries in the World" (1739–40). © The British Library Board.

not as unaffected as it appeared in the first place: by the picture, which s/he wants to buy, and by the dress, which s/he wants to copy.

Throughout the eighteenth century, depictions of costume became part of a general development that sought to document national and regional differences; in fact, only now did regional styles become recognizable, and national costumes were established.[27] What is more, difference became a matter of perspective. Allard found about as many different types of people in the different parts of the world as Wenceslaus Hollar found in the different regions of England, which he famously portrayed in *Ornatus*

Old Cloaks Suits or Coats
Qui a de vieux habits a vendre
Panni vecchi trappi vecchi da vendere

Mauron delin. P.Tempest ex cum privilegio

FIGURE 8.6: "Old Cloaks Suits or Coats" from The cryes of the city of London: drawne after life in seventy-four copper plates, engraving by John Savage after a drawing by Marcellus Laroon, c. 1687. Courtesy of The Lewis Walpole Library, Yale University.

Muliebris Anglicanus (c. 1640) (Figure 8.7), while Marcellus Laroon found as much difference among the street-sellers of London, which he portrayed in *The Cryes of the City of London: Drawn after the Life* (c. 1688) (Figure 8.6). But even though differentiations became ever more refined, difference remained almost exclusively spatial; if difference was perceived in temporal terms, it was in historical dimensions.

Knowledge of dress was essentially a scholastic knowledge of costume, an essentially stable, visible sign of a specific given status. Temporary fashions that afforded the continual monitoring of others were of no concern. Enlightened depictions allowed the reader to be informed about what others are wearing; as yet, however, the depiction that allowed one to look out into the world did not necessarily invite the reader to reflect on himself. Print, here, was seen more as a *window* to the world rather than a *mirror* of society.

FIGURE 8.7: Left: "Lady with muff standing on two steps," from Wenceslaus Hollar, *Ornatus Muliebris Anglicanus* (1639–1640), plate 7. Right: "Lady with fan and mirror," from Wenceslaus Hollar, *Ornatus Muliebris Anglicanus* (1639–1640), plate 10. Both images courtesy of Wenceslaus Hollar Digital Collection, University of Toronto.

However, especially Hollar's *Ornatus Muliebris Anglicanus*, subtitled *The Several Habits of English Women, from the Nobilitie: to the Contry Woman, as they are in these Times* (c. 1640) revealed also the limits of an apparently objective relation to depictions of dress, even for a more refined audience (Figure 8.7). Not only did Hollar bring the depictions much closer to the potential beholder in the sense that the spectator might actually be part of the depicted world; but in his attempt to produce ever more realistic depictions, his pictures also became so detailed that the depicted dress itself started to attract a certain attention beyond the informational context in which it was embedded. "Hollar's likenesses of women," Madeleine Ginsburg writes, "have an affecting and surely affectionate realism."[28] Especially the minute presentations of handkerchiefs, muffs, and mask, but also of folds and creases of each dress, gain an almost fetishist quality, not necessarily in a sexual way, but in the originary sense of the word: the things depicted are no longer the passive objects of observation, but agents in their own right, luring the beholder to lose himself/herself in fascination, to stare (lecherously), rather than to read the image for its informational value. The medium of print that was supposed to enlighten its readers was now used for its opposite: the solitary, non-reciprocal form of observation, which the medium enabled, afforded a form of sustained emotional staring that would otherwise not become an observer. And as a commodity fetish, the object might even bring the beholder to purchase similar items. The distant, objective observer ran the danger of being affected by the spectacular sight of dress; looking ever closer, as the empiricist doctrine demanded, entailed the risk of losing sight of the bigger picture.

FROM WORD TO PICTURE: NOVEL ILLUSTRATIONS

Novels were one of the most successful new media of the eighteenth century. People wanted to know more about the times they lived in, and novels offered new (fictional) stories about the here and now of everyday people, written in accessible prose and printed amass. Samuel Richardson's *Pamela* (1740), for example, was an unprecedented publishing success, leading to a "market-led multiplication of lowbrow print, unregulated by traditional considerations of learning, decorum or taste."[29] It was fashionable to read *Pamela*, not least, as I have argued elsewhere, because the text was full of descriptions of dress.[30] Dress, in *Pamela* as much as in various other novels, was no longer something exotic that other social or regional groups were clad in, but an essential part of everyday life, for the lower orders as much as for the upper tiers, and even more so for the middling sorts. From reading *Pamela*, indeed, one could learn a great deal about the social and sexual implications of dress, not only of other people's dress, but also, in reflection, of one's own. "Pamelists" and "Anti-Pamelists" of the time fought about whether monitoring others for choosing the right dress became a new means to enable social mobility, or to take hypocrisy to a new level.

More importantly here, however, *Pamela* did not remain a textual phenomenon only. Several theatrical and operatic adaptations appeared on London's stages, a waxworks display of various scenes was exhibited for over a year, and a fan depicting key-moments of her story went on sale. A whole range of prints was published that depicted "Pamela" in various scenes described in the book.[31] The sixth edition of *Pamela*, for example, published by Richardson himself, incorporated engravings by Hubert Gravelot and Francis Hayman. The visualizations follow the text closely. And if nothing else, most of the depictions highlighted the importance of visual signs within the novel, dress being probably the most important. There is hardly a contemporary print that does not focus on Pamela's various states of dress (and undress); while the novel includes incredibly long musings on morals and virtues, the prints are unashamedly mundane. Richardson himself was very much aware, and wary, of what most depictions focused on.[32]

Pictures of "Pamela" were soon to be published independently from *Pamela*, the book, too. Engravings of Antoine Benoist and Louis Truchy, for example, were based on a series of paintings by Joseph Highmore and widely distributed. The image reproduced here gives a fairly realistic depiction of a central scene from the book (Figure 8.8). As costume historian Anne Buck has pointed out, in the picture Pamela wears the clothes given to her by her master out of the wardrobe of his late mother, Pamela's former mistress, quite as they are described in the text[33]: "My Master [. . .] has given me a Suit of my old Lady's Cloaths, and half a Dozen of her Shifts, and Six fine Handkerchiefs, and Three of her Cambrick Aprons, and Four Holland ones [. . .] he gave me Two Suits of fine *Flanders* lac'd Headcloths, Three Pair of fine Silk Shoes, two hardly the worse, and just fit for me; [. . .]."[34] However, even more so than the illustrations that Richardson commissioned himself, these images provided a visual spectacle first and foremost: Pamela's dress takes absolute center stage; the storyline, as it is represented by the leaving Mrs. Jervis, recedes to the background and is barely visible—indeed, the verbal caption has to recontextualize the scene to ensure its part in a larger narrative.

FIGURE 8.8: "Mr. B. expostulating with Pamela in the Summer house after some liberties taken. Mrs. Jervis (who is seen through the Window) having just before left her," print made by Louis Truchy after a painting by Joseph Highmore (1745). © Yale Center for British Art.

Does it matter whether we read about a dress or whether we can actually see it? Comparing the depiction of Pamela's dress with its verbal description, one cannot deny that the image is more detailed: the written text can never trace every single fold of the dress, or the exact arrangement of buttons on Mr. B's coat. All that the text does is name the objects concerned. In this sense, the image is much richer than the written equivalent. One might, for example, find it easier to copy the depicted dress than the described. However, such a comparison misses the fact that reading is much more than the decoding of encoded information: imaginative visualization is a key element of reading. Popular literature can often be visual without describing, by referencing a commonly shared world of goods: "early eighteenth-century readers were able to see—to fill out, expand on, rehydrate—the local, immediate signs of a shared culture, a shared visual landscape of meaningful, referential detail."[35] The mid-eighteenth-century reader of *Pamela* can be expected to have had some kind of former, personal experience with a petticoat, for example, especially as these were the fashion of the day. In the mind's eye, the image of Pamela's dress would have been just as detailed, if not even more so, as in Truchy's print—it could even have a back, it might even have haptic or olfactory qualities.

The most important difference between textual and pictorial accounts of Pamela's dress, however, is the perspective they allow to be taken. As cited earlier, the novel tells us the following: "he gave me Two Suits of fine Flanders lac'd Headcloths, Three Pair of fine Silk Shoes, two hardly the worse, and just fit for me." Whereas the picture allows us to simply look *at* Pamela, in the text we are looking *with* Pamela, through her eyes. In one instance, we are looking, with Pamela, at her wardrobe, and in the other we are looking at Pamela wearing these clothes. The text presents the subjective relation Pamela has to her clothes: they are given to her and she thinks that they fit her. In the text, things exist foremost in relation to an observer: the reader is forced to evaluate this relation as it cannot be his/her own. While the text demands individual appropriation, the picture, it seems, provides a full, evidential image, devoid of any subjective colorings.

Visualizations of Pamela's adventures contributed to the grave reservations many critics expressed towards *Pamela*. On the whole, the pictures seem to have added to the spectacular value of the text and the seductive force and erotic allure it embodied.[36] This was no longer a provision of information about distant worlds, but a picture of a person wearing fashionable dress and living in the same world as the reader. Even more so than the text of the novel, the pictures allowed a concentration on the depicted objects as such, giving them an existence that was somewhat independent of the narrator and the narrative context. These objects came to form a reality in itself: social entities, seen by many, but not yet appropriated by anyone—still to be had.

FROM HOGARTH TO CARICATURE: SATIRE AND ITS DISCONTENTS

Parallel to the emergence of the novel, Hogarth began to sell engravings of his paintings, similarly showing ordinary people in their respective clothes. Not unlike novels, Hogarth's pictorial sequences depicted individual life-stories and marked the difference between possible careers by the choice of dress. As Aileen Ribeiro remarks: "No other artist is as skilful at showing us not just what people from all social classes wore, but how they wore it and what it signified."[37] Despite their interest in dress, however, Hogarth's "modern moral subjects" still had to make sure not to succumb to the lure of fashion, but keep their distant, moral standpoint. Indeed, in Hogarth's images, the conflict between distant observation and an affection through fashion took center stage itself. The question was: who is in charge? The observer or the observed, the spectator or the pictured dress?

Hogarth's prints were highly successful in commercial terms, and many pirated versions appeared soon afterwards.[38] "To buy a few prints," Clayton argues, was "well within the range of the average 'middling' family."[39] What is more, the "print was seen in coffee-houses and shop windows by many more than actually purchased and owned [it]."[40] Here, the observer and the observed are getting ever closer: the people who looked at the pictures potentially came from the same social and regional realm as those depicted. Indeed, this could be said to be the first truly visual mirror that was held before the public.

With regard to plate 1 of the "Harlot's Progress" (Figure 8.9), the contemporary viewer knew exactly *where* this happened: the Bell Inn was a well-known pub in Cheapside and the luggage shown wears a tag (hung around the neck of a goose) proclaiming "Tems Street" in London. Hogarth's pictures were full of topographical references to well-known landmarks that helped to situate events. Also, the viewer knew exactly *when* it happened: the figures of Mother Needham and Colonel Francis Charteris were discernible as real-life characters; Hogarth's *sujet* was explicitly contemporary. Here, the beholder of the image was able look at different dresses with very specific meanings attached to these through the choices of their respective wearers. The rustic-cum-pretty dress of the young girl arriving appears to be based on her observations of what is appropriate to wear in the

FIGURE 8.9: "A Harlot's Progress," plate 1, Hogarth (1732). The Metropolitan Museum of Art, New York.

city; her ability to read others, however, as the following plate will show, is not very developed: what she takes to be a friendly old lady turns out to be a brothel-keeper.

Hogarth, like other eighteenth-century painters and engravers, was a master of the so-called linear perspective. In this mode, the observer of a picture remains safely removed from the depicted, while at the same time the illusion of a co-presence of observer and observed in the same three-dimensional space is created. Linear perspective is supposed to guarantee an objective view: "Perspective [. . .] does not permit the whimsy of the artist nor judgements of spiritual or affective value to alter what is seen by the eye. Perspective is thus objective."[41] While the depicted dress exists in the same space and time as the observer, and thereby comes closer, paradoxically, the observation of linear perspective simultaneously gives "the observer the illusion he could see without being involved, that he could see, without being seen."[42] Observing fashion, in this case, meant looking at contemporary, locally, and socially specific dress—but without getting involved; observing fashion, here, meant to inform oneself, objectively, about the folly of others who are not as fortunate in their ability to read others.

Of course, Hogarth's picture was not a mere snapshot of reality, but a carefully constructed ensemble of signs, continually referring to various other texts and images, which could be precisely "read" by a literate and educated audience.[43] By interpreting the symbols surrounding Moll—the (probable) name of the girl in the picture—one could

FIGURE 8.10: "A Harlot's Progress," plate 2, Hogarth, (1732). The Metropolitan Museum of Art, New York.

already figure out her future in plate 2 (Figure 8.10): the Old Testament scenes on paintings hanging on the wall, the monkey wearing the same headdress as Moll, the broken china, the mask, the mirror, etc.[44]—everything stands for something else: "Meaning becomes a matter of (recognizing the allusions to) texts and contexts. [. . .] The reader [sic] uses them to create some sort of meaning within the larger coordinates set by the satirical genre."[45] Charles Lamb's famous appreciation of Hogarth's prints seems to have observed these rules of engagement: "His graphic representations are indeed books: they have the teeming, fruitful, suggestive meaning of words. Other pictures we look at,—his prints we read."[46] Moll, however, was presented as being less cautious: she succumbed to the allure of wearing fashionable dress—and suffered the consequences.

To read, rather than "merely" to look, seems to have been of utmost importance to the eighteenth-century observer, whether encountering texts or pictures. "There are Mortals," Mr. Spectator complained, "who have a certain Curiosity without Power of Reflection, and perused my Papers like Spectators rather than Readers."[47] Intellectual "reflection" was reserved for the *reader* (of texts and images alike), and affective curiosity assigned to the *spectator*. Ben Jonson distinguished the work of words and pictures quite distinctively at the very beginning of Enlightenment reasoning: "*Poetry* and *Picture*, are Arts of a like Nature," he declared, "and both are busie [sic] about imitation." While both held up a mirror to reality, Jonson saw a definite hierarchy between the "sister arts": "Yet of the two, the Pen is more noble than the Pencil. For that can speak to the Understanding; the other, but to the Sense." Pictures, "while they seek to better Mens [sic] Minds, destroy their Manners," because they are "most a-kin to Nature" and "penetrate the inmost Affection" while at the same time "they miss the Authority [of words; C.H.]."[48] Images, it appears, were less easy to control than texts, at least when they were not *read* properly. In translating the seen into words, an (authoritative) evaluation of the seen was added; mere pictures were seen to miss such evaluation and to leave it open to the beholder what to make of them.

"This Painter," a contemporary observer of Hogarth remarked, "is remarkable for a particular Sagacity in seizing a Thousand little Circumstances which escape the Observation of the greatest Part of the Spectators." Why? Because his depictions have "too great a Resemblance to the Objects [they represent]."[49] Besides everything else, the pictured dress could easily be perceived as adorable and desirable, demanding to be seen and loved—counteracting the carefully constructed meanings surrounding it. The dress literally outshines its (signifying) environment in its corporeality—the carefully constructed narrative, the structural oppositions, genre conventions, the symbolic ensembles, everything is pushed into the dark background by the sheer presence of Moll's dress, the only object in the room that is fully illuminated by the light that comes through the window (Figure 8.10). Contemporary spectators seemed to respond to this presence. According to George Vertue's notebook, the "whore's desabille [sic] careless and a pretty Countenance & air" were especially admired by visitors: "this thought pleasd [sic] many." "[P]ersons of fashion and Artists" alike came to Hogarth's studio in order to see the pictures, or rather, what could be seen on them: "he painted so naturally [. . .] that it drew every body to see them."[50]

If its status as a sign is overlooked, the image becomes an idol, assuming power over perception, pushing aside more reflective approaches. Instead of being part of a carefully constructed moral, the dress becomes a straightforward object of desire, maybe even more desirable than it could ever be in reality, where the lighting is never right, and the smell is terrible, where the right moment never comes, and where those looked at might not even want to be looked at. To curb this tendency of escaping its signifying context, most eighteenth-century depictions of dress tried to exert an authority over their objects that put a stop to any from of ambiguity. Depictions of fashions, therefore, often ventured towards the grotesque, presenting monstrous fashions and their hideous consequences (Figure 8.11).

Such images did not only represent an object, they also prescribed *how* to see it. They presented a realistic situation where a specific kind of transgressive fashion creates a "problem." The suggested solution is obvious: to discard such hideous fashions. However, the problem with this kind of coercing is equally obvious: while the general situation is depicted realistically, thereby creating a common ground between the depicted world and the world of the beholder, the central object of the satire, the dress, seems to depart from this common ground. The problem, therefore, becomes an "otherworldly" problem: this, then, is not the problem of the beholder, not "my" problem, not "my" kind of fashion.

The publication of such caricatures peaked during the macaroni craze of the 1770s (Figure 8.12). From the beginning, it was clear that pictures of such fashion victims did not depict "fasheons [sic] [. . .] of the present age" in Hogarth's more realistic sense.[51] Instead, these were clearly marked as transgressions: "as *The Macaroni and Theatrical Magazine* explained in its inaugural issue in 1772, 'the word Macaroni then changed its meaning to that of a person who exceeded the ordinary bounds of fashion'."[52] It became much more

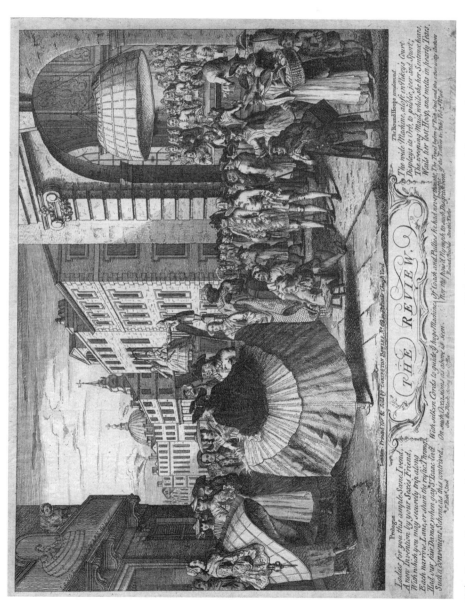

FIGURE 8.11: "The Review," print made by John June (c. 1750), later re-published by Carington Bowles: "The Round Hoops condemn'd: The wide Machine, aloft in Nikey's Court/Displays its Orb, to public jeer and Sport." Courtesy of the Lewis Walpole Library, Yale University.

FIGURE 8.12: "The Miniature Macaroni," published September 24, 1772. Courtesy of the Lewis Walpole Library, Yale University.

easy to laugh about such ridiculous figures than to laugh about the characters in Hogarth's plates, who most often were very much within "the ordinary bounds of fashion." The macaroni was clearly "other," dubious in terms of gender, sexual orientation and ethnicity.[53]

The famous caricaturists at the turn of the nineteenth century—James Gillray, Thomas Rowlandson, Isaac Cruikshank—followed this tradition, depicting obviously risible figures, rather than more ordinary fashions (Figure 8.13).[54] Whereas Hogarth depicted the fashions very much as they actually were, trying to convince the beholder that s/he was close to committing the same mistakes as those shown, the caricaturists presented only fashions that had gone wrong, hyperbolically exaggerating the size and form of dress. It was easy to laugh about such images, as they did not show the beholder, but someone too vain, or too stupid, to dress appropriately: a fashion victim that had fallen prey to the visual allure of dress.

FIGURE 8.13: "Characters in High Life," James Gillray (1795), published by Hannah Humphrey. The Metropolitan Museum of Art, New York.

THE FASHION MAGAZINE: ESTABLISHING A CONTINUOUS VISUAL PRESENT

Both the novel and its accompanying images, as well as the prints of Hogarth and others, aimed at depicting the here and now of contemporary Britain, bringing the world of the beholder and the world of the image ever closer together. They were supposed to be consumed by the very people they represented. Such prints indeed became a mirror the British public could hold up to itself, albeit a very peculiar one. However, the "new" and the "now" were still unstable entities. Most print products of the seventeenth and the early eighteenth century "were written on the occasion of the unusual, the quirky, the puzzling"[55]: most satirical images, for example, were published in response to specific events like Walpole's downfall, the South Sea Bubble, the Sacheverell affair, etc. Newspapers, on the other hand, no longer waited to react, as Lennard Davis notes: "Recentness was made possible by the technology of print [. . .], but the median past tense of journalism was only made possible by combining continuity with recentness."[56] Only with the regular publication of newspapers, journals, and magazines, the present gained a continuous presence in print. However, most newspapers of the time were produced without images; while many commented on the fashions of the day, none could/would show them.

It took until the latter end of the century until the first serial publications included pictorial presentations of dress. First published in 1750, *The Ladies Diary or The Woman's Almanack* was only the first of a "torrent of pocket-books and memorandum-books [. . .] with engravings of fashionable figures displayed on the front pages."[57] According to Beverly Lemire, the engravings included were the "first fashion illustrations devised for that purpose in Britain."[58] Be that as it may, as annual productions they often failed to keep up with the fast changing fashions of the day. Of course, only a few people were able to buy new clothes monthly, or even yearly, but most people were conscious nonetheless that fashions were *constantly* changing, not only now and then, or once a year—or at least they thought so.[59]

The first English monthly publication to include fashion prints was the *Lady's Magazine or Entertaining Companion for the Fair Sex.*[60] In an introductory note, the editor promises that, "as the fluctuations of fashion retard their progress into the country, we shall by engravings inform our distant readers with every innovation that is made in the female dress, whether it respects the covering of the head, or the cloathing [sic] of the body."[61] At first, including such images only at irregular intervals, they were part of most issues from 1780 onwards.[62] According to John L. Nevinson, the pictures served their purpose, that is, "to give information about current fashions,"[63] quite effectively. And being current was indeed their currency: the title page of the May 1775 issue advertises that the number is "embellished" with a copper-plate showing two "Whole Lengths of Ladies in the most fashionable Dress, from Drawings taken [. . .] this Month." Finally, the new had become a stable entity that could be delivered on a regular basis.

Most importantly, however, the fashion plates included here establish a new perspective, differing from the fictional accounts of novelistic visualizations as much as from the strict linear perspective of Hogarth and the hyperbolic stance of caricature. The fashion plate is realistic, as opposed to the caricatures of the time, it shows real people, as opposed to fictional, but it does not show a specific, contextualized situation.[64] A print published on June 1, 1775, claims to be based on eyewitness accounts as it is produced "from Drawings taken at Ranelagh" (Figure 8.14). Ranelagh was a popular pleasure garden of the time, situated in Chelsea, and a good place indeed to study fashionable people. However, the print is not a reproduction of sketches taken on the scene; it does not show a specific situation the way a fashion reporter had seen it with his/her own eyes. Instead, the print is an aggregation of the fashionable ladies seen in the park, bereft of their original context. Only on the following page, an accompanying letter to the editor, apparently from one Patronessa R- – -, appends a detailed description of how the eyewitness-observer came to Ranelagh, and what exactly she saw there, and how she hopes that the magazine would print the drawings she sent. Still, the editor of *The Lady's Magazine* feels obliged to add: "We have complied with the request of our fair correspondent [. . .]. Yet, as the above letter is somewhat obscure, we have inserted *a more general description of the fashions*, from a fair hand."[65] While portraits of specific individuals existed long before the eighteenth century—as prints and paintings of aristocrats, influential businessmen or politicians, or of famous theater stars, for example—fashion plates in the sense of a "generalized portrait" showing "the sort of clothes [. . .] that are *likely* to be worn"[66] by

FIGURE 8.14: "Engraved for the Lady's Magazine. Two Ladies in the newest Dress. From Drawings taken at Ranelagh, May 1775. Published by G. Robinson June 1, 1775," from *The Lady's Magazine*, May 1775, facing p. 233. Courtesy of the Lewis Walpole Library, Yale University.

an individual in a certain situation emerged only now. And only now it became possible to monitor others and to see oneself in the mirror of print: this could indeed be *you*.

Following the French model of the *Gallerie de Modes*, Nicolaus Heidelhoff began to publish his *Gallery of Fashion* in 1794 (Figure 8.15), "the first English publication devoted entirely to fashion."[67] In an introduction to the first issue, Heidelhoff proclaims: "A GALLERY OF FASHION is a work long wanted, and long wished for, and now makes its appearance upon a very extensive plan. It is a collection of all the most fashionable and elegant Dresses in vogue."[68] To show the fashions of the day, in full color for the first time, finally, became an end to itself; free of any scholarly, moralistic or comical pretensions, devoid of any narrative context, fashions came to be shown for fashion's sake. As such, the fashion magazine began to claim to be of use to everyone—not only the few, probably aristocratic subscribers—[69] providing a guideline of fashion to all: "This GALLERY will

FIGURE 8.15: From *Gallery of Fashion*, April 1794 © Yale Center for British Art.

not only be interesting to Ladies of the highest fashion, but must be deemed absolutely necessary to every person concerned in the fashions of the day." And who is not? What is more, fashion became an ongoing process, rather than a stable entity, moving on continuously through time, potentially concerning everyone living in these times: "This Work will be published in twelve Monthly Numbers."

Independent of the fact whether one liked the fashions depicted or not, the widespread and continuous publication of images of fashion in the many magazines that followed Heidelhoff's lead[70] established a reality one had to position oneself to accordingly. From now on, fashion was ever-present, and observing fashion became a form of following its rules, even if departing from these. While one might stand outside the scope of a regional costume, one cannot exist outside the time of fashion.

Finally, the image became a model to dress by: "To each figure will be annexed such a plain and particular description of every article, that it will be impossible to err in the arrangement of the dress."[71] The detail of the image and the authority of the word supplement each other to inform the observer in the best possible way, and to make her part of the world she (!) observes. (From now on, fashion is supposed to be the concern of women only.) While the image grants the dress an unquestionable existence, the words add significance to it. Whereas earlier (male) observers of costume books were keen on *seeing* dress, later (female) observers of the fashion magazine were asked to *follow* a trend. The window to the empirical world had turned into a mirror of the social.

CHAPTER NINE

Literary Representations

ALICIA KERFOOT

The general Purpose of this Paper, is to expose the false Arts of Life, to pull off the Disguises of Cunning, Vanity, and Affectation, and to recommend a general Simplicity in our Dress, our Discourse, and our Behaviour.

—Richard Steele, *The Tatler*[1]

Now, had the same young lady been engaged with a volume of the Spectator, instead of such a work [a novel], how proudly would she have produced the book, and told its name; though the chances must be against her being occupied by any part of that voluminous publication, of which either the matter or manner would not disgust a young person of taste: the substance of its papers so often consisting in the statement of improbable circumstances, unnatural characters, and topics of conversation, which no longer concern any one living.

—Jane Austen, *Northanger Abbey*[2]

Literature of the eighteenth century responded to the cultural significance and materiality of dress and fashion across generic boundaries and it paid attention to both its literal and figurative functions. The criticisms of fashionable dress in Richard Steele and Joseph Addison's *Tatler* and *Spectator* papers (1709–14) remained relevant, for example, to Jane Austen's representation of fashion and dress in *Northanger Abbey* (1818), published about one hundred years later. Certainly, the cultural context of *Northanger Abbey* is completely different from that of the *Tatler* and *Spectator* papers, but the mode of critique is one that Austen responded to and reworked in her fictional account of a heroine who follows the fashions both in dress and in fiction. The moral correctness of *The Tatler* and *Spectator* for young lady readers (although the narrator of *Northanger Abbey* questions it in the above epigraph) was grounded in those papers' critique of fashion and their goal of reforming the dress and habits of the English people, with a special attention to those who followed the fashions to excess.

In what follows, I will offer some of the most significant examples of how dress and fashion were represented in the periodical press, in cultural histories of costume and dress, drama and theater, poetry, it-narratives (stories told from the perspective of objects), and finally in the English novel from Defoe and Haywood to Burney and Austen. A focus on the ways that some authors portrayed those who followed fashions, refused fashions, or over-indulged in fashionable dress reveals how literary representations of dress highlighted a complex relationship between text and dress. My essay makes reference mainly to English examples, but similar paradigms can be seen at work elsewhere in Europe at this time.

PERIODICALS

The essay periodicals and magazines of the early to mid-eighteenth century offer a window into the fashionable dress of the period because they are so concerned with critiquing and controlling the prevailing fashions. From fantastical allegories for the cultural importance of dress, to advice for negotiating the balance between fashionable appearance and excess, these periodicals both instruct and offer themselves up as objects of fashionable consumption. In fact, popular periodicals blur the line between text and dress because they negotiate their own position as textual commodities and fashionable objects in the marketplace.

As Erin Mackie argues, "fashion, then, works as both a threat against the reasoned, progressive reforms advocated by *The Tatler* and *The Spectator* and, in a revised configuration, as one avenue for this reform."[3] Building on this, Jennie Batchelor notes that the effect was long-lasting: "This curious blend of immersion in and condemnation of fashionable pursuits and commodities left a legacy that continued to inform periodicals and magazines throughout the eighteenth century."[4] *The Spectator* No. 478 reveals this curious blend of investment in and moderation of fashionable dress when the narrator proposes "to have a Repository builded for Fashions"[5]:

> The Apartments may be fill'd with Shelves, on which Boxes are to stand as regularly as Books in a Library. These are to have Folding-Doors, which being open'd, you are to behold a Baby dress'd out in some Fashion which has flourish'd, and standing upon a Pedestal, where the Time of its Reign is mark'd down.[6]

Steele aligns fashionable dress with "Books in a Library" and his invocation of the "Baby" or fashion doll emphasizes the difference between looking at fashionable dress and reading a description of it in a periodical, which he then returns to when he asserts that the fashion museum will "be a Registry to which Posterity may have recourse for the clearing such obscure Passages as tend that way in Authors, and therefore we shall not for the future submit ourselves to the learning of Etymology, which might perswade the Age to come, that the Farthingal was worn for cheapness, or the Furbeloe for warmth."[7] The visual status of the fashion doll combined with the text that describes the fashion, leads to an apparently complete understanding of the history of fashionable dress (and—Steele implies—its lack of reason).

The detailed fashion doll depicted in Figure 9.1 displays court dress, including fashionable accessories like a pocket, mittens, and shoes. English in origin, it is "dressed in a silk sack back robe with matching petticoat and stomacher, and dates from around 1755–1760."[8]

The role that Addison imagines for such dolls and their accompanying text became a reality later in the century, when the fashion doll gave way to the fashion plate and fashion magazine.[9] Thus the print description of fashionable clothing is tied very closely to the material object of the fashion doll. As Julie Park notes, "just as print made more convenient and possible the objectification and thus dissemination of ideas and information for a rapidly growing reading public, the fashion doll made it possible for women to quickly gain knowledge of fashion ideals and attempt to emulate them."[10] Neil McKendrick's account of the fashion doll, fashion plate, and fashion magazine in the "last thirty years of the eighteenth century" focuses on how these forms of disseminating fashionable dress "marked a culmination of the commercialization of fashion which had been developing so rapidly in the rest of the century."[11] He

FIGURE 9.1: Wooden fashion doll with costume and accessories, England, 1755–60.
© Victoria and Albert Museum, London.

explains that "the first colored fashion print is dated 1771 and appeared in *The Lady's Magazine* . . . These fashion plates were, in fact, trade plates, designed as commercial propaganda."[12]

However, as Jennie Batchelor notes of *The Lady's Magazine*, "fashion plates were scarce" in the magazine: "The decision to present its fashion coverage in the form of editorial, rather than in the form of the engravings and reports promised in the magazine's first issue, is the clearest signal of the magazine's mistrust of unmediated fashion coverage."[13] This offers a counterpoint to Steele's fashion "baby," which mediates and explains complicated fashion terminology for future generations in a way that suggests text also needs visual explanation and is as unruly as the image or the doll.

By 1816, the *Belle Assemblée* combines dress vocabulary with image (see Figure 9.2). A description of a "Parisian Evening Dress" offers an example of the typical fashion magazine discourse:

> Round dress of soft white satin, made short enough to discover the muslin petticoat underneath, which is ornamented with two full quillings of fine lace; the satin dress finished at the border by four rows of scarlet velvet; the body made plain and crossed over the bust . . . the sleeves very short, and finished by a quilling to correspond with the tucker . . . White satin slippers confined round the ancle by ribbands; and white kid gloves.[14]

FIGURE 9.2: "Parisian Evening Dress," Belle Assemblée No. 81, March, 1816. Photo taken by author with permission of Chawton House Library.

The history of the fashion doll and fashion plate alongside periodical descriptions of dress shows how text both evokes images and objects, and works in concert with them.

The Costume of Great Britain and the London Cries

The combination of text and image in cultural histories of dress and costume also offers a context for the fashion doll and fashion plate as they intersect with descriptions of fashionable dress in journals and newspapers. Laroon's popular prints of London Cries, W.H. Pyne's *The Costume of Great Britain*, and Wenceslaus Hollar's etchings of English women's fashions include images of both upper and lower class dress that are intertextual and draw from several genres and discourses. The genre of London Cries (engravings of London hawkers selling their wares) is one that predates the eighteenth century, and its treatment of the dress of everyday inhabitants of London focuses on the relationship between the figure and the product he or she hawks. Marcellus Laroon's *Cryes of the City of London Drawne after the Life* (1687) offers images of London street-criers whose costumes also display their professions.

W.H. Pyne offers a similar visual and textual narrative in his *Costume of Great Britain* (1804). As the "Publisher's Preface" asserts, the work attempts "to include all classes of society; and delineations are therefore given from the most elevated ranks of public functionaries, to the lowest gradation of mechanic and laborious avocation."[15] Pyne's engravings are accompanied by text that describes the importance of the figure, and sometimes focuses on historical and cultural context, but not usually the details of the costume. Chloe Wigston Smith argues that Pyne's work, although it "seeks to depict a coherent portrait of British identity, instead conveys the difficulty of doing so" and that its "shifting landscape of dress . . . is linked . . . to its exploitation of competing artistic conventions, as well as to the tensions between text and image."[16] She goes on to argue that his "costume book draws on conventions such as fashion plates and urban street criers in addition to the picturesque."[17] Paula Rea Radisich similarly argues that a French collection of "190 selected hand-colored seventeenth-century prints" titled *Recueil des modes de la cour* and held in the Los Angeles County Museum of Art, occupies "categories in 1703–4 that we view as constituents of separate discourses today. It was simultaneously art, a series of prints of interest to an art collector, as well as costume, a set of historically dated French fashion illustrations. By adding the criers, the compiler further developed it into a cultural history."[18]

Not only is this kind of literature intertextual in the ways that Smith and Radisich point out, but it also offers narratives of gender and class that are similarly indistinct. One example is Laroon's "London Curtezan" (Figure 9.3), whose dress indicates her trade and yet constructs her as an equivocal figure.

FIGURE 9.3: "London Curtezan," from Marcellus Laroon's Cryes of the City of London, printed by Tempest Pierce in 1733. Courtesy of the Lewis Walpole Library, Yale University.

She holds a fan and mask, wears a hood, and also sports false beauty marks (or patches). Her accessories complicate her relationship to the upper-class woman of London society, as fans, masks, and patches are all also items of fashionable dress. This London courtesan offers an important visual context for the popular narrative that when servants, actresses, and other liminal figures wore fashionable accessories they complicated them as indicators of upper-class identity. Laroon's image is also intertextual in other ways. His images were often copied, and in one example the artist, John Overton, has appended "four images not copied from Laroon [which] picture women as allegories of spring, summer, fall, and winter . . . these four figures may have been inspired by Wenceslaus Hollar's popular full-length portraits of women as the four seasons, first published in 1644."[19]

Hollar's etchings of English women in *The Four Seasons* focus on dress in the urban landscape. His image of *Winter* (Figure 9.4) has particular resonances with Laroon's "Curtezan," as it emphasizes female sexuality and the relationship between fashionable dress and London's landscape.

FIGURE 9.4: *Winter*, Wenceslaus Hollar, full-length from 1643–44, etching. © The Trustees of the British Museum.

The figure is hooded, wears a mask, and holds a muff as an accessory, while Laroon's "Curtezan" also wears a hood, holds her mask, and also holds a fan as an accessory. The figure of the "Curtezan" is more available to the viewer because she is holding rather than wearing her mask, looking more directly at the viewer, and is less covered than the woman in Hollar's *Winter*. In this sense, Hollar depicts the muff and mask to heighten desire. Winter's protective dress makes the upper-class figure more desirable than the more available courtesan, although she is defined by her accessories in a similar manner (especially by the presence of the mask). That Overton included Hollar's prints in his version of Laroon's cries also strengthens the implied connection between fashion and the urban landscape as it is present in both texts. R.T. Godfrey describes how Hollar's etching emphasizes the relationship between the figure and the city: "Richly clad in furs, she stands before a London view of Cornhill, with the tower of the Royal Exchange at right."[20] The background also suggests a connection between the fashionably-clad female figure and the marketplace of the Royal Exchange behind her.

DRAMA AND THEATER

The depiction of fashionable dress on the eighteenth-century stage also draws attention to the construction of gender in relation to commodity culture. References to dress develop an understanding of both clothes and popular literature as fashionable commodities; this is similar to female characters, who are also placed on the market and exchanged between men. In British drama from the Restoration to the early nineteenth century, dress is constructed in a way that is similar to that in which Hollar and Laroon depict the muff and the mask.

In *The Country Wife* (1675), Wycherley constructs women as commodities and uses the backdrop of the New Exchange to make this connection explicit. Margery Pinchwife, determined to appear in public, hounds her husband until he comes up with a scheme for her appearance: "So—I have it— I'll dress her up in the suit we are to carry down to her brother . . . Come, let's go dress her. A mask! No—a woman masked, like a covered dish, gives a man curiosity and appetite, when, it may be, uncovered, 'twould turn his stomach."[21] They make their way to the New Exchange, where exists, "an emporium of stalls in the Strand where fashionable goods were sold. It was built in 1608–09, and gained in popularity after the Restoration."[22] Margery Pinchwife also attempts to purchase plays and ballads when she arrives at the New Exchange, which reminds the viewer of the place of literature in the exchange of fashionable commodities.[23] The comparison is made even more explicit later, when Sparkish's public display of his betrothed, Alithea, comes under scrutiny by Pinchwife; Sparkish replies: "What then? It may be I have a pleasure in't [the display of her], as I have to shew fine clothes at a playhouse the first day, and count money before poor rogues."[24] Both Margery and Alithea become more desirable and more available as they are placed on display in the setting of the Exchange.

This relationship between women's dress and their place in the market is also present in the idea that a servant's dress, or plain, lower-class dress, might offer a disguise that leads to freedom of behavior, which is a plot device in Goldsmith's *She Stoops to Conquer* (1773). Miss Hardcastle passes as a barmaid to encourage Marlow (who only flirts with "the wildest of" women) to notice her. She dresses, according to her maid, in "the dress, madam, that every lady wears in the country" but Marlow mistakes this for a servant's dress. Miss Hardcastle monopolizes on this mistake so that she may become more accessible to Marlow; she explains her decision to her maid in the following terms: "In the first place, I shall be seen, and that is no small advantage to a girl who brings her face to market . . . But my chief aim is to take my gentleman off his guard, and like an invisible champion of romance, examine the giant's force before I offer to combat."[25] Miss Hardcastle dresses to encourage misreading so that she may read Marlow more closely. Her use of a romantic simile draws attention to the fact that her dress and visage are textually constructed in the same way that romances are and can be manipulated to gain information and economic stability in the marriage market.

Meanwhile, in her play *The Witlings* (written 1778–80) Frances Burney draws fashionable dress into direct comparison with fashionable wit. Burney opens her play in a milliner's shop, where "a counter is spread with caps, ribbons, fans and bandboxes."[26] The fact that wedding preparations are underway solidifies the connection between fashionable dress as a commodity and women as similar commodities on the marriage market and on the more illicit sexual market. In her reading of Robert Dighton's *A Morning Ramble; or; The Milliner's Shop* (Figure 9.5), Chloe Wigston Smith notes, "like actresses and servants, milliners were viewed as the sexual prey of upper-class men."[27]

It is interesting, then, that Burney's Beaufort and Censor enter the milliner's shop in conflict with one another about their presence in a feminized space and whether it will

FIGURE 9.5: *A Morning Ramble; or, The Milliner's Shop*, Robert Dighton, 1782. Courtesy of the Lewis Walpole Library, Yale University.

consume them. The violence of consumption emerges in an extended metaphor Censor develops which compares clothing to weapons of confinement:

> With what weapons will you stay me? Will you tie me to your little finger with a piece of ribbon, like a lady's sparrow? or will you enthral me in a net of Brussel's lace? Will you raise a fortification of caps? or barricade me with furbelows? Will you fire at me a broad side of pompoons? or will you stop my retreat with a fan?[28]

Reluctant to be implicated in the fashioning or purchase of commodities, Censor transforms the milliner's space of illicit femininity into one of martial masculinity and he does so with the labor of language—a metaphor—rather than the labor of the needle. He moves from confinement imagery (ties and nets) to siege imagery (fortifications and barricades), to weapons imagery (guns and swords). He thus suggests that luxury and excess are dangerous to masculinity and will also result in excessive language (such as an extended metaphor).

POETRY

The use of clothing to manipulate identity or develop an ideal of gendered behavior in relation to the sexualized body appears in much poetry of the eighteenth century as well. John Gay's *Trivia: Or, The Art of Walking the Streets of London* (1716) depicts articles of clothing that protect walkers from the seasons in the urban landscape and his mock-heroic account of the working classes recalls Laroon's *Cryes of the City of London* as well as Hollar's personified *Four Seasons*.

Of special note is Gay's treatment of winter, in which he discusses protective footwear in the form of the patten and romanticizes female labor, health, and virtue. He focuses on the patten, uncovering the heroic tale of its inception and birth: "But, O! forget not, Muse, the *Patten*'s Praise, / That female Implement shall grace thy Lays."[29] Gay goes on to tell the story of Patty, a rural milkmaid wooed by the blacksmith god Vulcan who protects her from the effects of winter with his invention of the patten. He describes her as a romantic pastoral figure: "The milky Burthen smoaks upon her Head. / Deep, thro' a miry Lane she pick'd her Way."[30] This and the need to protect Patty from cold feet suggest that she is a sexualized figure:

> No more her Lungs are shook with drooping Rheums,
> And on her Cheek reviving Beauty blooms.
> The God obtain'd his Suit, though Flatt'ry fail,
> Presents with Female Virtue must prevail.[31]

Milkmaids "were often portrayed as exemplars of a wholesome, natural, and vigorous sexuality" and yet, "these stereotypes existed in counterpoint to another equally pervasive stereotype, that of the impotent nobility, whose sexuality was debilitated by urban luxury."[32] Patty, as a rural figure and as mistress to a god, complicates her class position when she loses her virtue to a powerful figure who gives her a present.

Pattens similarly changed in appearance and material based on class level. As Pratt and Woolley note in their discussion of metal pattens, "Gentlewomen sometimes found occasion to use them, but because of their functional appearance they were more generally associated with the lower classes and country people."[33] Despite the association of pattens with the lower classes, they could also be ornamental (such as those in Figure 9.6).

FIGURE 9.6: Pair of pattens with wooden soles and iron rings, Great Britain, 1720s–30s. © Victoria and Albert Museum, London.

The alignment of iron pattens with the lower and middle classes, and leather pattens or clogs with the upper classes seems therefore to be flexible to some degree, just as the position of Gay's Patty is flexible.

Later in his poem, Gay picks up on the close relationship between female laborer and commodity when he depicts the pippin seller, Doll. Doll is a textual portrait of the London costermonger, who appears in one of Laroon's *Cryes* (see Figure 9.7).

As Shesgreen explains, the costermonger "vends winter fare, warm stewed pears" and "her dress is a neat, plain winter outfit."[34] She also wears pattens, which intertextually ties this engraving to both Gay's pippin seller and his earlier milkmaid, Patty. Gay reminds his reader of the association between female labor, health, and commodity, as he sets Patty and Doll against the unhealthy sexuality of the London courtesan.

Gay's prostitute wears clothes that disguise her, represent her illicit sexuality, and show what her travels have been:

No stubborn Stays her yielding Shape embrace;
Beneath the Lamp her tawdry Ribbons glare,
The new-scower'd Manteau, and the slattern Air;
High-draggled Petticoats her Travels show,
And hollow Cheeks with artful Blushes glow;

FIGURE 9.7: "Hott Bak'd Wardens Hott" from Marcellus Laroon's *Cryes of the City of London*, printed by Tempest Pierce in 1733. Courtesy of the Lewis Walpole Library, Yale University.

> In Riding-hood, near Tavern-Doors she plies,
> Or muffled Pinners hide her livid Eyes.
>
> Nay, she will oft' the Quaker's Hood prophane,
> And trudge demure the Rounds of *Drury-Lane*.
> She darts from Sarsnet Ambush wily Leers,
> Twitches thy Sleeve, or with familiar Airs,
> Her Fan will pat thy Cheek . . . [35]

The courtesan's dress displays her ruined virtue as it lures her clients. She disguises herself as a Quaker, and uses her sarsnet hood to surprise unsuspecting victims with "wily Leers."[36] However, her disguise does not entirely hide her unhealthy physical attributes: her ribbons are tawdry, she has a "slattern Air," her cheeks are hollow, and her eyes are livid. Not only this, but the suggestion that the hood is a martial instrument—facilitating an "ambush," offers another clothing metaphor that aligns women's dress and accessories with weapons. She also uses the clothing of another—the Quaker—to fool her victims in a similar manner to Goldsmith's Miss Hardcastle.

In contrast to the way that dress is represented in Gay's poem, women poets such as Jane Collier and Anna Laetitia Barbauld develop the connection between women's work and clothing and dress when they depict the physical labors of washing clothes. Collier and Barbauld offer more realistic images of female labor, and so demonstrate that dress and fashion work in literature on a practical, realistic level as well as on a metaphorical one. They comment on this symbolic treatment of dress when they depict the realistic labor that dress requires in their accounts of washing day. Both poets make women's labor visible in their accounts of the importance of washing day to the domestic sphere and in their emphasis on its wider impact.

Collier's *The Woman's Labour. An Epistle to Mr. Stephen Duck* (1739) responds to Duck's "criticism of the idleness of rural women in 'The Thresher's Labour'."[37] Collier emphasizes the effect that fashions have on the labor of washing:

> Heaps of fine linen we before us view,
> Whereon to lay our strength and patience too;
> Cambrics and muslins, which our ladies wear,
> Laces and edgings, costly, fine and rare,
> Which must be washed with utmost skill and care;
> With Holland shirts, ruffles and fringes too,
> Fashions which our forefathers never knew.[38]

Collier's complaint centers on the fashionable clothes of "our ladies," in contrast to her own lower-class position as a hired washerwoman. Although linen is worn by all classes, the "laces and edgings" and "ruffles and fringes" offer difficult work in addition to the washing of the linen, which "was time-consuming, expensive and exhausting."[39] Collier's social commentary also notes the lack of coherence between the amount of labor and the wage the washerwoman earns: "For all our pains no prospect can we see / Attend us, but old age and poverty."[40]

Anna Laetitia Barbauld offers a different perspective in her "Washing-Day" (1797) when she invokes the "domestic muse" in order to give an account of the day as she remembers it from childhood:

> Come, Muse, and sing the dreaded Washing-Day.
> Ye who beneath the yoke of wedlock bend,
> With bowèd soul, full well ye ken the day
> Which week, smooth sliding after week, brings on
> Too soon . . .[41]

While Collier responds to Duck's account of labor with her own, Barbauld invokes the muse in blank iambic pentameter reminiscent of Milton to align domestic labor and domestic poetry with more serious forms. Capitalizing on the ephemeral nature of washing day, she compares both scientific male labor and more mundane female labor to the airy work of creating verse:

> All hands employed to wash, to rinse, to wring,
> To fold, and starch, and clap, and iron, and plait.
> Then would I set me down, and ponder much
> Why washings were. Sometimes through hollow bowl
> Of pipe amused we blew, and sent aloft
> The floating bubbles; little dreaming then

To see, Montgolfier, thy silken ball
Ride buoyant through the clouds—so near approach
The sports of children and the toils of men.
Earth, air, and sky, and ocean, hath its bubbles,
And verse is one of them—this most of all.[42]

Barbauld captures the nature of washing as an ephemeral and repetitive task, but one that is more labor intensive than the "sports of children" and the "toils of men" which both involve imagination and "bubbles." She reworks clothing as a metaphor for verse when she displays the labor of washing alongside the labor of poetry as both are repetitive and result in different kinds of "bubbles"—the soapy bubbles of wash day and the figurative bubbles of verse.

IT-NARRATIVES

The popular "it-narratives" of the mid-to-late eighteenth century were also obsessed with the ephemeral nature of clothing. "It-narratives" (a term used by modern critics to define this sub-genre of the novel) are stories that were told from the perspective of an object, which was often a commodity with a lifecycle that brought it into the hands of many different owners; the tales thus also often acted as a social satire, or had clear moralistic goals.[43] A whole sub-set of the genre represents items of dress speaking for themselves and telling the stories of their own production and consumption. Coats, waistcoats, petticoats, shoes, and fans become the focus in these narratives, which quite often aligned the public, written text with the narrative object. As Christina Lupton notes, "It-narratives may be cynically aware of the recycling that goes on as authors participate in a material economy of words."[44] Bonnie Blackwell argues that these tales became popular in response to the early novel's focus on interiority and they offer a different kind of subjectivity than the novel does: "Rather than asserting the uniqueness of each character in his or her death, these novels focus on an inanimate object precisely because it outlives many owners."[45] She goes on to argue that they also depict decay as a result of use which aligns them with female sexuality: "Ultimately, the object-narrator is both witness to and metonym for the waning market value of a woman once initiated into sexuality."[46] However, these narratives also functioned on a "literal" level in the details that they conveyed about the effect of ownership on objects of dress; clothes are stained, lost, given away, fall out of fashion, repurposed and transformed in these tales, and they thus also offer a picture of the cyclical nature of the clothing market in the mid-to-late eighteenth century.

The anonymous *History and Adventures of a Lady's Slippers and Shoes. Written by Themselves* (1754) presents a good example of the ways that dress and fashion appear in this sub-genre of the novel. Both the slippers and the shoes offer tales that align them with the moral state of their owners and demonstrate how the lifecycle of this object of dress is a limited one. The narrator aligns them with women when he compares their current state of decay to their past newness: "The radiancy of their former splendour broke through all the clouds of their present squalid condition; as in a withered beauty, under all the disgrace of grey-hairs and wrinkles, some traces remain to indicate those charms once irresistible, on which time has brought about such mortifying alterations."[47] At the end of their story, the slippers summarize their circulation with a statement about the decay of dress: "all I expect now . . . is to be thrown into the highway, or on the dunghill;

FIGURE 9.8: Women's figured Lyons silk brocade mule, 1650–1700. The Shoe Collection, Northampton Museums and Art Gallery.

and there . . . to moulder away to the last shred. Alas, answered the compassionate Shoe, the same ignoble end waits me also."[48]

The deterioration of the slippers and shoes mirrors human decay and the decay of reputation that (the text suggests) often accompanies fashionable display of self; as Christina Lupton observes, "clothes have bodies too and they disintegrate and lose their sheen as quickly as women."[49] The mule in Figure 9.8 demonstrates the kind of wear a pair of slippers such as the ones in the tale might endure; it is a women's figured silk brocade mule (dated from about 1650–1700), worn and frayed. However, it has also outlasted its owner by hundreds of years, which indicates that these narratives also exaggerate an impermanence of dress to draw more attention to human fragility.

The slippers and shoes convey both the realities and imagined powers of dress that are connected to eighteenth-century sartorial practice and fashionable life. In his *Art du cordonnier (Art of the Shoemaker)* (1767) F.A. de Garsault explains that a slipper is a very simple shoe "for it has neither pieced tongue nor quarters, so the heel is always bare."[50] The slippers' textual adventures mirror the sorts of events and situations in which their real-life material counterparts might be involved when, for example, they are "stuck in the mud, and were trodden under foot by the crowd, and tho' my mistress cried . . . she saw no more of me, and was obliged to trudge on in her white stockings."[51] They and the shoes also participate in used clothing practices, and thus offer both a satirical picture of the servant and a metaphorical alignment with the sex trade. The slippers are handed down to a servant almost immediately, which reiterates the popular construction of servants as consumers who mimicked their employers' fashions in large part because they received their cast off clothes. In response to the slippers' account of how their mistress passes them onto the maid at the first slight stain, the shoes exclaim: "those hussies get all their mistresses ways."[52]

Meanwhile, the shoes are sold to "an old-cloathes-woman, who was also one of the most dexterous assistants to the debaucheries of the young sparks, and of married men too. She soon had us vamped up to qualify us for our original honours."[53] In the suggestion that the shoes, like the prostitutes who wear them, put on fashionable appearance and are "vamped up" despite the fact that they have been well-used already the author explicitly aligns the clothing trade with the sex trade in a way that much literature of the period does (recall the milliner's shop). The shoes also put an owner into a tricky position at a masked ridotto, when "she was so open hearted as to tell [a black *Domino*] that we pinched her so dreadfully . . . that she had much ado to crimple along. Upon which the spark offered to wait on her into a byroom, where she might change us."[54] This account combines the dangers of fashionable footwear with the dangers of disguise; it is also a moment when the materiality of the object results in narrative progress and the text is a product of the life-cycle of the object. The realities of the clothing market—such as a sudden sale or movement from one owner to another—are also easily read on a figurative level. As Chloe Wigston Smith notes, "the physical destruction of the object enables the progression of the plot, hinting at the tensions between material objects and the narrative form."[55] The decay of the fashionable object of dress produces the text at the same time that its literal realities often produce figurative meanings that reveal truths about sex and gender in eighteenth-century life.

NOVELS

The realities of dress are also a major part of the eighteenth-century novel, where authors use them to theorize the relationship between dress and identity. The novels I will discuss here place the realities of dress alongside its figurative uses, which complicates its position and returns us to the intertextual museum of fashion as Steele imagines it. The suggestion that the most appropriate dress is the most modest, natural dress, which occurs in *The Tatler* and *The Spectator*, in the poetry of Gay, and is problematized in *She Stoops to Conquer*, is also prevalent in the novels of the period, where the use of it as disguise dismantles the idea that it is more "natural." Daniel Defoe's *Roxana* (1724), Eliza Haywood's *Fantomina* (1725), and Samuel Richardson's *Pamela* (1742) all depict characters empowered by the use of modest disguise, although there are limits to this empowerment. Frances Brooke's *The History of Emily Montague* (1769) uses dress imagery as a metaphor for national and religious others, and to align the "natural" ideal with English femininity. In contrast, Frances Burney depicts shopping in order to test the limits of the alignment of women with the objects they shop for in *Camilla* (1796), while Henry Fielding has objects and the text appended to them take on the sexual identity of the absent love interest in *Tom Jones* (1749). This interdependence of accessory and text offers a framework for understanding the limits and possibilities in the history of literary representations of dress.

Daniel Defoe constructs *Roxana*'s narrative as a good or ill-fitting dress in the preface to the novel, which has Defoe's "relator" imploring the reader to blame him and the "Defect of his Performance" if the story does not please, because he has been "dressing up the Story in worse Cloaths than the Lady, whose Words he speaks, prepar'd it for the World."[56] However, these "worse cloaths" represent Roxana's use of dress to disguise her identity in the novel, so the relator's metaphor emphasizes the shifting appearance of identity rather than his textual transparency. When she lives with her Quaker landlady, Roxana uses a modest Quaker disguise in order to avoid meeting with her unclaimed children: "I pretended, after I had been there some time, to be extreamly in Love with the Dress of the QUAKERS . . . but my real Design was, to see whether it wou'd pass upon me for a Disguise."[57]

Haywood's Fantomina also constructs a shifting identity for herself when she attempts to keep the interest of her lover, Beauplaisir, by disguising herself as a servant: "The dress she was in was a round-eared cap, a short red petticoat, and a little jacket of grey stuff . . . [which] made it impossible for her to be known or taken for any other than what she seemed."[58] Fantomina's performed disguise has its desired effect when Beauplaisir is "fired with the first sight of her" and takes advantage of her short petticoat to catch "her by the pretty leg."[59] This scene is both realistic and hyperbolic; it comments on the instability of identity and appearance, relies on the stereotype of the available, rustic, maidservant, and realistically describes Fantomina's dress and cultural costume. Haywood singles out the "round eared cap" that frames Fantomina's face, which was "a popular cap in the 1730s . . . [and] was somewhat like a bonnet, curving round the face to the level of the ears or below, with lappets either pinned on top or tied under the chin."[60]

This type of dress is also present in *Pamela*, when the heroine dresses in expectation that she will return to her parents' house in the country: "I trick'd myself up as well as I could in my new Garb, and put on my round-ear'd ordinary Cap . . . and my homespun Gown and Petticoat, and plain-leather Shoes."[61] An engraving after Joseph Highmore's painting of Pamela's division of her clothes (Figure 9.9) offers a visual example of her country dress.

The result of this dress is both an assault from Mr. B—"He kissed me for all I could do"—and an accusation of disguise to which Pamela responds: "I have been in Disguise indeed ever since my good Lady, your Mother, took me from my poor Parents . . . And her Goodness heap'd upon me rich Cloaths, and other Bounties: And as I am now

FIGURE 9.9: Illustrations to Samuel Richardson's "The Life of Pamela," Guillaume Philippe Benoist, after Joseph Highmore, 1762. © Yale Center for British Art.

returning to my poor Parents again so soon, I . . . have bought what will be more suitable to my Degree."[62] Pamela frames her discourse of identity in the flexibility of her dress, and thus reverses the narrative of disguise in the way that Defoe does in his preface to *Roxana*; the "worse cloaths" that Pamela seems to put on as a disguise are actually more representative of her identity than the "rich Cloaths" that she has been wearing as a lady's maid. This is a complicated kind of masquerade, which distances Pamela from her lower-class identity in the very act of donning it but also verifies that she is comfortable in the clothes of her mistress despite her claim that she has been in disguise ever since she left her parents. This is similar to the way masquerade leads to illicit danger and disguise while it simultaneously uncovers "true" identities in novels. The outcome is in line with Terry Castle's contention that "the masquerade itself masquerades. Ostensibly the scene of pleasure, it is actually the scene of snares—a region of manipulation, disequilibrium, and sexual threat."[63]

In an essay on the subject of masquerade in Frances Brooke's *The History of Emily Montague*, Joe Snader notes: "Under the controlling impetus of the novel's project of British self-fashioning, it manufactures images of the Other only as they help to define an active, transgressive, masquerading British subject."[64] A similar moment of othering in *Emily Montague* places religious institutions in the metaphorical garb of English women: "I have been at mass, at church, and at the Presbyterian meeting: an idea struck me at the last, in regard to the drapery of them all; that the Romish religion is like an over-dressed, tawdry, rich citizen's wife; the Presbyterian like a rude aukward country girl; the church of England like an elegant well-dressed woman of quality, 'plain in her neatness'."[65] The language of this comparison relies on the stereotypes of dress that construct women as representative of ideals that are then apparent in their self-fashioning; the best kind of dress is that which does not draw attention to its constructed nature, and the best kind of religion is that which does the same. The three churches are also described in terms that remind the reader of shopping, or touring in order to decide on a place of consumption; this implicit connection between religious identity and female commodity is representative of the complex relationship between women as commodities and shoppers in the era.

In Frances Burney's *Camilla*, an awkward shopping expedition provides an example of the public nature of shopping and criticizes the act of judging women based on appearance alone. Camilla enters the shops with a character named Mrs. Mittin, who wishes to look in all the shops in Southampton one after the other, that "they might see all that was smartest, without the expence of buying any thing."[66] Camilla, however, attracts too much attention and they leave behind them gawking shopkeepers, who line "the whole length of the High-street" to stare at Camilla and Mrs. Mittin's "singular proceeding."[67] This is because Camilla is "of a figure and appearance not quite so well adapted for indulging with impunity such unbridled curiosity."[68] In fact, she is not engaging in the act of shopping at all, but is "absent and absorbed" and thus is surmised to be either a shoplifter or "touched in the head," which suggests that Camilla does not shop properly because she does not engage with the commodities on display.[69] Elizabeth Kowaleski-Wallace argues that the "narrative initially suggests that Camilla in the shop takes on the very associations of the commodities with which she finds herself surrounded" but that Burney's novel resists this easy connection by insisting "upon an essential quality . . . which grants Camilla a 'primeval power' over" the shopkeepers who would assault her.[70] Burney gives Camilla this power in order to comment on how women are used to construct abstract ideas about virtue when they are compared to objects of dress, and this seems to be the point at which Burney refuses to simply align Camilla with the commodities around her. Instead, Camilla shows that the shopkeepers (who should be able to understand commodities) cannot read a woman's quality simply by watching the way that she shops, despite the fact that "her face seemed the very index of purity."[71] Rather than aligning Camilla with the objects on display in this moment, Burney resists the idea that women can be reliably read based on appearance alone.

This inability to read accurately returns us to the interaction between figurative, literal, and textual constructions of dress and fashion in eighteenth-century literature. In Henry Fielding's *Tom Jones*, Tom finds accessories that have been left behind by Sophia Western, his love interest; one accessory of note is her muff, and another is her pocket book. In both cases text is appended to the object which designates it as Sophia's property. Tom's consumption of each of these objects aligns Sophia with her ornaments and foreshadows the romantic union of the characters. When he finds the muff, the narrator tells us, "at the same Instant he saw and read the Words *Sophia Western* upon the Paper which was pinned to it."[72] When he finds the pocket book, he sees "in the first Page the Words *Sophia Western*, written by her own fair Hand. He no sooner read the Name, than he prest it close to his Lips."[73] Later, Tom's sexual consumption of the objects is made explicit when he retires "to Rest, with his two Bed-fellows the Pocket-Book, and the Muff."[74] Sophie Gee sees in this combination of the figurative and tangible the same kind of transformation that happens when one reads fiction: "Narrative gives meaning and significance to quotidian objects. Resonant as the objects are—the fans, the muffs, Sophia's letter—they are also leftovers. Like sacred relics, they linger behind their symbolic value, all the more abject and prosaic in comparison."[75]

Not unlike Steele's proposal for a fashion museum that combines image and text so as to assign proper historical meaning to objects of dress, Tom's ability to read and consume Sophia's personal property depends on his ability to read the labels. What happens, then, in this interaction between label and artifact? Does the object become more of a leftover than the text? This is partly a curatorial question; as Linda Baumgarten explains, "too many clothes have lost their histories . . . physical evidence itself has eroded . . . Scholars combine their study of antique clothing itself with knowledge gained through written documents such as labels, orders, diaries, advertisements, and merchants' records. They compare garments with those depicted in paintings and prints."[76] At the same time, literature creates and remembers objects of dress in ways that intersect with the remnants of the object itself. The literary text, too, is subject to fashion trends and consumer markets and the rhetorical alignment of text and dress ensures that the material object will always offer a figurative context in literature, even when that literature only seems to be about capturing the realism of the moment. As Daniel Roche observes, "the eighteenth-century novel offers both a moral landscape and the possibility of perceiving a relationship to the collection of institutions, practices and utensils which define the ordinary life of a society."[77]

In *Northanger Abbey*, Henry Tilney's discussion of journal writing and muslin acknowledges this awkward relationship between fiction and everyday dress. After Henry claims to know exactly what Catherine will say about him in her journal, Catherine counters with "But, perhaps, I keep no journal."[78] Henry reproduces the language of the journal and of fashion magazines in his narrative and asks Catherine, "How are your various dresses to be remembered, and the particular state of your complexion, and curl of your hair to be described in all their diversities, without having constant recourse to a journal?"[79] After constructing journal and letter writing, as well as an interest in fashion and dress, as "peculiarly female," Henry acknowledges that his claim is in fact false, and that, "In every power, of which taste is the foundation, excellence is pretty fairly divided between the sexes."[80] Not only this, but he admits to his own interest in fashion and dress when he engages with Mrs. Allen on the subject of muslins: "But then you know, madam, muslin always turns to some account or other; Miss Morland will get enough out of it for a handkerchief, or a cap, or a cloak.—Muslin can never be said to be wasted."[81] Here, Austen summarizes the problems with representing material culture on the eighteenth-century page: text records the realities of dress, but is unstable because uneven and subject to taste and figurative or stereotypical construction; meanwhile, the lack of a stable state of dress, which also changes based on the fashion industry and the imagination of the producer and consumer, means that dress appears in literature of the eighteenth century in a combination of intertextual mediums that always turn "to some account or other." Dress in literature of the eighteenth century is material, embodied, figurative, textual, pictorial, and transient in nature.

NOTES

Introduction

1. Aileen Ribeiro, *The Art of Dress. Fashion in England and France 1750 to 1820* (New Haven and London: Yale University Press, 1995).
2. On collectors, see Valerie Cumming, *Understanding Fashion History* (New York and Hollywood: Costume and Fashion Press, 2004), 46–81.
3. H. Taine, *Extraits* from Corr. November 23, 1855, author's translation. "Expositions sur la Gravure de Mode," Bibliothèque Nationale, Galerie Mansart, avril 1961 [unpublished folio of photographs of the exhibit], BN. Est. Ad392, unpaginat(ed.)
4. "Expositions sur la Gravure," unpaginat(ed.)
5. Margaret Maynard, "A Dream of Fair Women: Revival Dress and the Formation of Late Victorian Images of Femininity," *Art History*, 12, September 3 (1989): 322–41.
6. Information courtesy Rebecca Evans.
7. Gerard Vaughan, "Foreword," in *Fashion and Textiles in the International Collections of the National Gallery of Victoria*, (ed.) Robyn Healy (Melbourne: National Gallery of Victoria, 2004), 6.
8. *She Walks in Splendor: Great Costumes 1550–1950. An Exhibition of Costumes, Costume Accessories and Illustration from the Museum's Permanent Collection*, October 3–December 1, 1963, Museum of Fine Arts, Boston (Boston: Museum of Fine Arts, 1963).
9. Ann Ray Martin, "The young pretender: Long ruled by Diana Vreeland, the world of costume—that upstart art—is changing" [Edward Maeder], *Connoisseur*, June (1984): 73.
10. This was the premise of the large EU funded project, *Fashioning the Early Modern: Creativity and Innovation in Europe, 1500–1800*, conducted from 2010 to 2013 under the leadership of Evelyn Welch. See http://www.fashioningtheearlymodern.ac.uk/about/
11. Daniel Roche, *The Culture of Clothing. Dress and fashion in the ancien régime*, trans. Jean Birrell (Cambridge: Cambridge University Press, 1994 [1989]), 97.
12. François Boucher, *A History of Costume in the West*, trans. John Ross, new (ed.) (London: Thames and Hudson, 1987 [1966]).
13. Roche, *The Culture of Clothing*, 136.
14. Farid Chenoune, *A History of Men's Fashion* (Paris: Flammarion, 1993), 17.
15. On the Foundling Hospital see John Styles, *Threads of Feeling*, at http://www.threadsoffeeling.com
16. Wilmarth Sheldon Lewis, "Horace Walpole's Library," in *A Catalogue of Horace Walpole's Library*, Allen T. Hazen, 3 vols (New Haven and London: Yale University Press, 1969), vol. I.
17. Hazen, *A Catalogue of Horace Walpole's Library*, vol. I.
18. Horace Walpole, *Works*, IV. 355, Lewis Walpole Library, Yale University.
19. Philip Dormer Stanhope, Earl of Chesterfield, *Letters written by the late Right Honourable Philip Dormer Stanhope, Earl of Chesterfield, to his son, Philip Stanhope, esq . . .* 2 vols, Horace Walpole's copy, Lewis Walpole Library, Yale University, LWL 49.436.2v. (London: J. Dodsley, 1774), vol. I, 199.
20. Earl of Chesterfield, *Letters*, Letter CXXII, Lewis Walpole Library, Yale University, LWL 49.436.2v.
21. Roche, *The Culture of Clothing*, 11.

22. Jane Bridgeman, "Beauty, Dress and Gender," in *Concepts of Beauty in Renaissance Art*, Francis Ames-Lewis and Mary Rogers (Aldershot: Ashgate, 1998), 44.

23. Jane Bridgeman, "Beauty, Dress and Gender": 46.

24. Hannah Greig, *The Beau Monde: Fashionable Society in Georgian London* (Oxford: Oxford University Press, 2013), 33.

25. Johan Huizinga, Johan, *The Autumn of the Middle Ages*, trans. Rodney J. Payton and Ulrich Mammitzsch (Chicago: University of Chicago Press, 1996 [1921]), 301.

26. Anne Hollander, "The Clothed Image: Picture and Performance," *New Literary History*, 2: 3, Spring (1971): 478.

27. Michael Twyman, *The British Library Guide to Printing: History and Techniques* (Toronto: University of Toronto Press, 1998).

28. M. D'Archenholz (Formerly a Captain in the Service of the King of Prussia), *A Picture of England: Containing a description of the laws, customs, and manners of England . . .* vol. I (London: Edward Jeffery, 1789), 156–7.

29. Mary Webster, *Johan Zoffany, RA* (New Haven and London: Yale University Press, 2011).

30. Martin Myrone, Tate Gallery notes online at www.tate.org.uk/art/artworks/walton-a-girl-buying-a-ballad-t07594 [accessed July 28, 2015].

31. Daniel Roche, *A History of Everyday Things. The birth of consumption in France, 1600–1800,* trans. Brian Pearce (Cambridge: Cambridge University Press, 2000 [1997]), 193–220.

32. Beverly Lemire, "'Men of the World': British Mariners, Consumer Practice, and Material Culture in an Era of Global Trade, c. 1660–1800," *Journal of British Studies*, 54: 2, April (2015): 299.

33. Matthew Craske, *Art in Europe 1700–1830* (Oxford: Oxford University Press, 1997), 161.

34. Ibid., 14.

35. [Sophia S. Banks] A catalog of books etc. in the main house belonging to Sir Joseph Banks, prepared by Sarah Banks, n.d. [being a catalog of books and engravings belonging to Sir Joseph Banks upon his death], BL. 460 d.13. On Sofia Banks see Arlene Leis, "Displaying art and fashion: ladies' pocket-book imagery in the paper collections of Sarah Sophia Banks," *Konsthistorisk tidskrift/Journal of Art History*, 82, 3 (2013): 252–71.

36. Carol Duncan, "Happy Mothers and Other New Ideas in French Art," *The Art Bulletin 55* (1973): 570–83.

37. John Greene and Elizabeth McCrum, "'Small clothes': the evolution of men's nether garments as evidences in *The Belfast Newsletter* Index 1737–1800," in *Eighteenth Century Ireland*, (eds) Alan Harrison and Ian Campbell Ross, vol. 5, 1990, Dublin: 169.

38. René Colas, *Bibliographie Générale du Costume et de la Mode* (Paris: Librairie René Colas, 1933, 3rd publishing, Martino Publishing, 2002), 425.

39. Susan Siegfried, "Portraits of Fantasy, Portraits of Fashion," *Non.site.org*, 14 (December 14, 2014). Available at http://nonsite.org/article/portraits-of-fantasy-portraits-of-fashion [accessed November 30, 2015].

40. Johannes Pietsch, "On Different Types of Women's Dresses in France in the Louis XVI Period," *Fashion Theory*, vol. 17, no. 4, September (2013): 397–416.

41. Kimberly Chrisman-Campbell, *Fashion Victims: Dress at the court of Louis XVI and Marie-Antoinette* (New Haven and London: Yale University Press, 2015), 162–4.

42. Ibid., 192.

43. Craske, *Art in Europe*, 15.

44. Lewis Walpole Library, Yale University, F.J.B. Watson papers on Thomas Patch.

45. Andrea Wulf, *Founding Gardeners. The Revolutionary Generation, Nature, and the Shaping of the American Nation* (New York: Alfred A. Knopf, 2011), 37.

46. Clare le Corbeiller, *European and American Snuff Boxes 1730–1830* (London: Chancellor Press), 13.

47. Hollander, "The Clothed Image": 488.

48. Diary in an unknown name, in *Ladies daily companion for the year of our Lord 1789: embellished with the following copper plates: an elegant representation of the discovery of the Earl of Leicester from the Recess, a lady in the dress of 1788, and four of the most fashionable head dresses* . . . Canterbury: Simmons and Kirkby, Inscribed on the flyleaf: "Given me by the honble Cosmo Gordon, Margate, Novr ye 21st 1788." Lewis Walpole Library, Yale University, LWL MSS Vol. 3.

49. Roche, *A History of Everyday Things*, 245.

50. Ibid., 240.

51. *Letters on the French Nation: by a Sicilian Gentleman, residing at Paris, to his friends in his own Country* . . . (London: T. Lownds, 1749), 53.

52. Hollander, "The Clothed Image": 489.

53. Roche, *A History of Everyday Things*, 234.

54. *Ländliche Eliten. Bäuerlich-burgerliche Eliten un den friesischen Marschen und den angrenzenden Geestgebieten 1650–1850*, collaborative research project supported by the VolkswagenStiftung initiative "Research in Museums" 2010–2013. Conducted at the Carl von Ossietzky-Universität Oldenburg, Institut für Geschichte Geschichte der Frühen Neuzeit, September 20–22, 2012. The work was published, mainly in German, as Dagmar Freist and Frank Schmekel (eds), *Hinter dem Horizont Band 2: Projektion und Distinktion ländlicher Oberschichten im europäischen Vergleich, 17.19. Jahrhundert* (Münster: Aschendorff Verlag, 2013). The English summaries of the proceedings outlined here were first published by me online at: www.fashioningtheearlymodern.ac.uk/wordpress/wp-content/uploads/2011/01/Ländliche-ElitenDF_2.pdf

55. Craig Clunas, "Review Essay. Modernity Global and Local: Consumption and the Rise of the West," *American Historical Review*, December (1999): 1497–511.

56. "Inventaire des marchandises et effets de colporteur [Hubert Jenniard] déclarés par Corentine Penchoat, à Crozon, le 6 Février 1761," Archives départementales du Finistère, 18B, inventaire des pièces de la procedure criminelle instruite à Crozon, le 27.2.1762, cited in Didier Cadiou, "La vie quotidienne dans les paroisses littorales de Camouet, Crozon, Roscankel et Telgnac, d'après les inventaires après décès, mémoire de maîtres dactyl (*maîtrise*)" (Brest: Université Brest, 1990), t. II, 100. Courtesy Philippe Jarnoux.

57. See Jessica Cronshagen, *Einfach vornehm. Die Hausleute der nordwestdeutschen Küstenmarsch in der Frühen Neuzeit* (Göttingen: Wallstein, 2014); Frank Schmekel, "'Glocal Stuff'—Trade and Consumption of an East Frisian Rural Elite (18th Century)," in *Preindustrial Commercial History. Flows and Contacts between Cities in Scandinavia and North Western Europe*, eds. Markus A. Denzel and Christina Dalhede (Stuttgart: Steiner, 2014), 251–68; Frank Schmekel, "Was macht einen Hausmann? Eine ländliche Elite zwischen Status und Praktiken der Legitimation," in (ed.) Dagmar Freist, *Diskurse-Körper-Artefakte. Historische Praxeologie*, transcript, 2015, 287–309. On practices and artifacts see Dagmar Freist, "'Ich will Dir selbst ein Bild von mir entwerfen': Praktiken der Selbst-Bildung im Spannungsfeld ständischer Normen und gesellschaftlicher Dynamik," in *Selbst-Bildungen: soziale und kulturelle Praktiken der Subjektivierung*, (eds) Thomas Alkemeyer, Gunilla Budde, and Dagmar Freist (Bielefeld: Transcript, 2013), 151–74; Dagmar Freist, "Diskurse-Körper-Artefakte. Historische Praxeologie in der *Frühneuzeitforschung—eine Annährung*," in *Diskurse-Körper-Artefakte. Historische Praxeologie*, (ed.) Dagmar Freist (Bielefeld: Transcript 2015), 9–30.

58. Joan W. Scott, "Gender: A Useful Category of Historical Analysis," *The American Historical Review*, 91: 5, December (1986): 1075.

59. Mark S.R. Jenner, "Review Essay: Body, Image, Text in Early Modern Europe," *The Society for the Social History of Medicine*, 12: 1 (1999): 154.

60. James Peller Malcolm, *Anecdotes of the manners and customs of London during the eighteenth century* . . ., London, Longman, Hurst, Rees, and Orme, 1808. no pagination, courtesy Lewis Walpole Library, Yale University.

61. Stéphanie Félicité Bruart de Genlis, *Dictionnaire critique et raisonne* . . ., vol. 1 (Paris: P Mongie, 1818), 79–80.
62. Ibid., 38–9.
63. Cited in Lars E. Troide (ed.), *Horace Walpole's "Miscellany," 1786–1795* (New Haven: Yale University Press, 1978), 128.
64. Cited in Rozsika Parker, *The Subversive Stitch. Embroidery and the making of the feminine* (London: Women's Press, 1984), 33.
65. Sandra M. Gilbert, "Costumes of the Mind: Transvestism as Metaphor in Modern Literature," in *Writing and Sexual Difference*, (ed.) Elizabeth Abel (Brighton: Harvester Press, 1982), 195.
66. Ibid.
67. Virginia Woolf, *Orlando* (London: Wadsworth, 1993 [1928]), 132.

Chapter 1

1. Ellen Andersen, *Danske dragter. Moden i 1700-årene* (København: Nationalmuseet, 1977), 106, fig. 31.
2. In 1996, Christensen stated: "Juel has remained what Germans call a 'Geheimtipp', a little known figure, among a small group of foreign art historians" [author's translation—all quotations from Nordic languages in this chapter are translated by the author], Charlotte Christensen, "Jens Juel og portrætkunsten i det 18. århundrede," in *Hvis engle kunne male* . . ., (ed.) C. Christensen (Frederiksborg: Det Nationalhistoriske Museum, Christian Ejlers' Forlag, 1996), 33.
3. *Den Store Danske Encyklopædi*, vol. 18 (København: Gyldendal, 2000), 197.
4. Christensen, *Hvis engle kunne male* . . ., 53.
5. The different qualities and prices are presented in Amelia Peck, "India Chintz and China Taffaty, East India Company Textiles for the North American Market," in *Interwoven Globe. The Worldwide Textile Trade, 1500–1800* (New York: The Metropolitan Museum of Art, 2013), 114–15.
6. The Old Town, in Danish Den Gamle By, Open Air Museum of Urban History and Culture owns the largest collection of dress and textiles outside the Danish capital, Copenhagen. It is situated in Aarhus, the second largest town of Denmark. www.dengamleby.dk
7. textilnet.dk was from February 2015 available on www.textilnet.dk
8. http://www.textilnet.dk/index.php?title=Abats [accessed June 16, 2015].
9. Bruun Juul, *Naturhistorisk, oeconomisk og technologisk Handels- og Varelexikon.* Bd. 1–3 (København: 1807–12).
10. Ole Jørgen Rawert, *Almindeligt Varelexicon* (København: 1831–4).
11. Florence M. Montgomery, *Textiles in America, 1650–1870* (New York, London: W.W. Norton, 2007). Elisabeth Stavenow-Hidemark, *1700-tals Textil: Anders Berchs samling i Nordiska Museet* (Stockholm: Nordiska Museets förlag, 1990).
12. The French term *abat/abats* translates into terms with connotations of waste which might indicate that the wool used in this fabric was of a very poor quality.
13. Peck, *Interwoven Globe*, 104–19 and 283–4, catalog 108, the Bower Sample Book.
14. Giorgio Riello, *Cotton: The Fabric that Made the Modern World* (Cambridge: Cambridge University Press, 2013), 137–42.
15. Ibid., 195–8.
16. Lise Bender Jørgensen, *North European Textiles until AD 1000* (Århus: Århus University Press, 1992).
17. *Den Store Danske Encyklopædi*, vol. 6 (København: Gyldendal, 1996), 419–20.
18. Tove Engelhardt Mathiassen, "Tekstil-import til Danmark cirka 1750–1850," in *Årbog Den gamle By* (Aarhus: Den Gamle By, 1996), 80.
19. JB, Catalogue 30, Surcoat *(Jinbaori). Interwoven Globe*, 177–8.

20. http://www.metmuseum.org/collection/the-collection-online/search/81718?rpp=30&pg=1 &ft=court+dress+wool&deptids=8&when=A.D.+1600-1800&pos=1   (accessed January, 26 2016).

21. http://www.textilnet.dk/index.php?title=Gyldenstykke (accessed June 16, 2015).

22. Erna Lorenzen, "Teater eller virkelighed," in *Årbog, Den gamle By* (Århus: *Den gamle By*, 1960), pp. 40–5.

23. Tove Engelhardt Mathiassen: *Tekstiler i skrøbelighedens museum:* http://blog.dengamleby.dk/ bagfacaden/2013/04/16/tekstiler-i-skrobelighedens-museum/ (accessed March 24, 2014). Here several pictures of this suit are published.

24. In *Fashionable Encounters: Perspectives and Trends in Textile and Dress in the Early Modern Nordic World*, (eds) Marie-Louise Nosch, Maj Ringgaard, Kirsten Toftegaard, Mikkel Venborg Pedersen, Tove Engelhardt Mathiassen (Oxford: Oxbow, 2015). Several chapters discuss these matters in the early modern Nordic societies.

25. Ursula Priestley, *The Fabric of Stuffs* (Norwich: Centre of East Anglian Studies, 1990).

26. www.textilnet.dk/index.php?title=Flandersk_lærred [accessed June 16, 2015].

27. I want to thank John Styles for the information given May 2012.

28. www.textilnet.dk/index.php?title=Chintz [accessed June 16, 2015].

29. Sterm, P., *Textil, praktisk varekundskab: metervarer* (København: Jul. Gjellerups Forlag, 1937), 126.

30. Riello, *Cotton,* 80–2.

31. See also Melinda Watt "Whims and Fancies," in *Interwoven Globe*, 82–103.

32. Peck, ibid., 105.

33. http://www.textilnet.dk/index.php?title=Bæverhår [accessed June 16, 2015].

34. Ann M. Carlos and Frank D. Lewis Trade, "Consumption, and the Native Economy: Lessons from York Factory, Hudson Bay," *Journal of Economic History*, vol. 61, no. 4 (December, 2001): 1037–64.

35. Moesbjerg, M.P., "Hattemagerhuset i Den gamle By," in *Årbog Den gamle By*,(ed.) Peter Holm (Aarhus; *Den gamle By,* 1930–1), 39.

36. For a sustained discussion of mercurial poisoning and the industrial health of hatters, see Alison Matthews David, *Fashion Victims: The Dangers of Dress Past and Present* (London: Bloomsbury, 2015).

37. Moesbjerg, "Hattemagerhuset i Den gamle By," 41–2.

38. Henning Paulsen, *Sophie Brahes regnskabsbog 1627–40* (Jysk Selskab for Historie, Sprog og Litteratur, 1955), 72.

39. Ibid., 74.

40. Ibid., 125.

41. Ibid., 141.

42. Ibid., 198.

43. Annette Hoff, *Karen Rosenkrantz de Lichtenbergs dagbøger og regnskaber* (Horsens: Horsens Museum, Landbohistorisk Selskab 2009), 421.

44. The painting of Leonora Christine is owned by Det Nationalhistoriske Museum at Frederiksborg Castle and is available online: www.kulturarv.dk/kid/VisVaerk. do?vaerkId=96282 [accessed January 26, 2016].

45. http://mothsordbog.dk/ordbog?query=knappe-nål [accessed June 16, 2015].

46. Ole Jørgen Rawert, *Kongeriget Danmarks industrielle Forhold* [1848] (Skippershoved, 1992), 190–2.

47. Available online: http://ordnet.dk/ods/ordbog?query=naalepenge [accessed February 10, 2014].

48. Britta Hammar and Pernilla Rasmussen, *Underkläder. En kulturhistoria* (Stockholm: Signum 2008), 18.

49. The description builds on *Den Store Danske Encyclopædi* vol. 2 (København: Gyldendal, 1995), 336.

50. N. Waugh, *The Cut of Men's Clothes: 1600–1900* (London: Faber & Faber, 1977 [1964]), 17.

51. Andersen, *Danske dragter,* 20.

52. Waugh, *The Cut of Men's Clothes,* 57.

53. Norah Waugh, *Corsets and Crinolines* (New York: Theatre Art Books, 1981 [1954]), 167; Paulsen, *Sophie Brahes regnskabsbog 1627–40,* 107.

54. www.textilnet.dk/index.php?title=Kannevas [accessed June 16, 2015]. Kanivas is a "textile woven of hemp, flax or cotton yarn or in different mixtures of these. Produced in lots of different variations and woven in different techniques among these 'kanevas,' tabby and twill. Is also seen with woven stripes and/or flowers. It was used for among other things clothes (i.e. shirts), fabric for embroidery, furnishing and sails. In the beginning of the 19th century produced especially in England, The Netherlands and Germany." It also means "a tabby weave where all warp and weft threads are doubled or where one switches between single and double threads." Translation from Danish by the author from the Danish textile compendium.

55. Hoff, *Karen Rosenkrantz de Lichtenbergs dagbøger og regnskaber,* 421.

56. Ibid., 281.

57. Andersen, *Danske dragter,* 311.

58. www.textilnet.dk/index.php?title=Trille [accessed June 16, 2015].

59. Hoff, *Karen Rosenkrantz de Lichtenbergs dagbøger og regnskaber,* 310.

60. Ibid., 368.

61. Waugh, *Corsets and Crinolines,* 17–21.

62. Montgomery, *Textiles in America, 1650–1870* (New York, London: W.W. Norton & Company, 2007), 308.

63. Riello, *Cotton,* 182; and Elena Phipps, "Global Colors: Dyes and the Dye Trade," 120–35; Susan Kay-Williams, *The Story of Colour in Textiles* (London: Bloomsbury, 2013), who has a chapter called "Analysis, Understanding and Invention: The 18th Century," 108–25.

64. Phipps, "Global Colors: Dyes and the Dye Trade," 134–5.

65. Ibid., 121.

66. D. Cardon, *Natural Dyes: Sources, Tradition, Technology and Science* (London: Archetype Publications 2007), 348.

67. Phipps, "Global Colors: Dyes and the Dye Trade," 130.

68. Riello, Cotton, 176.

69. Cardon, *Natural Dyes,* 619–35.

70. As note 20, Catalogue 30. Surcoat (Jinbaori). *Interwoven Globe: The Worldwide Textile Trade, 1500–1800* (New York: The Metropolitan Museum of Art, 2013), 177–8.

71. *Den Store Danske Encyklopædi,* vol. 9 (København: Gyldendal, 1997), 59.

72. Available online: www.econlib.org/cgi-bin/searchbooks.pl?searchtype=BookSearchPara&id=hmMPL&query=cloth [accessed March 18, 2014].

Chapter 2

1. Sumptuary laws were enacted in European and Asian societies with increasing frequency in this period. See Alan Hunt, *Governance of Consuming Passions: A History of Sumptuary Law* (Basingstoke: Macmillan, 1996); Donald H. Shively, "Sumptuary Regulation and Status in Early Tokugawa Japan," *Harvard Journal of Asiatic Studies* 25 (1964–5): 123–64. For the introduction of sumptuary laws in medieval Europe see Martha Howell, *Commerce Before Capitalism in Europe, 1300–1600* (Cambridge: Cambridge University Press, 2010), ch. 4.

2. Ina Baghdiantz McCabe, *Orientalism in Early Modern France: Eurasian Trade, Exoticism and the Ancien Regime* (Oxford: Berg Publishers, 2008), 5–6, 101–2; Adam Geczy, *Fashion and Orientalism: Dress, Textiles and Culture from the 17th to the 21st Century* (London: Bloomsbury, 2013), 37.

3. For silk see: Lesley Ellis Miller, "Innovation and Industrial Espionage in Eighteenth-Century France: an Investigation of the Selling of Silk through Samples," *Journal of Design History* 12, no. 3 (1999): 271–92; Luca Mola, *The Silk Industry of Renaissance Venice* (Baltimore: Johns Hopkins University Press, 2000). For cotton see: Giorgio Riello, *Cotton: the Fabric that Made the Modern World* (Cambridge: Cambridge University Press, 2013); Beverly Lemire, *Cotton* (Oxford: Berg Publishers, 2011). For the international textile trade see: Christine Laidlaw, *The British in the Levant: Trade and Perceptions of the Ottoman Empire in the Eighteenth Century* (New York: Tauris Academic Studies, 2010); K.N. Chaudhuri, *The Trading World of Asia and the English East India Company, 1660–1760* (Cambridge: Cambridge University Press, 1978).

4. Ulink Rublack, *Dressing Up: Cultural Identity in Renaissance Europe* (Oxford: Oxford University Press, 2010).

5. Quoted in Catherine Richardson, "Introduction" in Catherine Richardson (ed), *Clothing Culture, 1350–1650* (Aldershot: Ashgate, 2004), 19.

6. Jan de Vries, *The First Modern Economy: Success, Failure, and Perseverance of the Dutch Economy, 1500–1815* (Cambridge: Cambridge University Press, 1997), 507–29.

7. Brian Cowan, *The Social Life of Coffee: The Emergence of the British Coffeehouse* (New Haven: Yale University Press, 2005); Jeremy Caradonna, *The Enlightenment in Practice: Academic Prize Contests and Intellectual Culture in France, 1670–1794* (Ithica, NY: Cornell University Press, 2012); John Robertson, *The Case for the Enlightenment: Scotland and Naples, 1680–1760* (Cambridge: Cambridge University Press, 2005); Martin Fitzpatrick, Peter Jones, Christa Knellwolf, and Iain McCalman (eds), *The Enlightenment World* (New York: Routledge, 2004).

8. Illustrated in the British example by Maxine Berg, *Luxury & Pleasure in Eighteenth-Century Britain* (Oxford: Oxford University Press, 2005).

9. For the impact of Asian silk on medieval Crusaders see: Sarah-Grace Heller, "Fashion in French Crusade Literature: Desiring Infidel Textiles," in *Encountering Medieval Textiles and Dress,* (eds) Désirée G. Koslin and Janet E. Snyder (New York: Palgrave Macmillan, 2002).

10. Maxine Berg, "Manufacturing the Orient: Asian Commodities and European Industry 1500–1800," *Proceedings of the Istituto Internazionale di Storia Economica "F. Datini"* 32 (2001): 519–56.

11. Janet Abu Lughod, *Before European Hegemony: the World System A.D. 1250–1350* (New York: Oxford University Press, 1989), ch. 10; Mary Schoeser, *Silk* (New Haven: Yale University Press, 2007), 35–43.

12. Beverly Lemire and Giorgio Riello, "East and West: Textiles and Fashion in Early Modern Europe," *Journal of Social History* 41, no. 4 (2008): 890–2; Howell, *Commerce Before Capitalism*, 209–11; Evelyn Welch, "New, Old and Second-Hand Culture: The Case of the Renaissance Sleeve," in *Revaluing Renaissance Arts*, (eds) Gabriele Neher and Rupert Shepherd (Aldershot: Ashgate, 2000).

13. Schoeser, *Silk*, 42.

14. Mola, *Silk Industry of Renaissance Venice*, xiii.

15. Ibid., xiii–xv; Hermann Kellenbenz, "The Organization of Industrial Production," in *The Cambridge Economic History of Europe*, (eds) J.H. Clapham, M.M. Postan, E. Power, H. Habakkuk, and E. E. Rich (Cambridge: Cambridge University Press, 1977), vol. 5, 527.

16. A.P. Wadsworth and Julia de Lacy Mann, *The Cotton Trade and Industrial Lancashire, 1600–1780* (Manchester: Manchester University Press, 1931, reprinted 1973), 106.

17. Joan Thirsk, *Alternative Agriculture from the Black Death to the Present* (Oxford: Oxford University Press, 1997), 120–5; Salvatore Ciriacono, "Silk Manufacturing in France and Italy in the XVIIth Century: Two Models Compared," *Journal of European Economic History* 10 no. 1 (1981): 167–72; Karel Davids, *The Rise and Decline of Dutch Technological Leadership* vol. 1 (Leiden: Brill, 2008), 150–3; Kellenbenz, "The Organization of Industrial Production", 521.

18. Kellenbenz, "The Organization of Industrial Production", 521.
19. Kristof Glamann, "The Changing Patterns of Trade," in *The Cambridge Economic History of Europe*, vol. 5, (eds) J.H. Clapham, M.M. Postan, E. Power, H. Habakkuk, and E.E. Rich (Cambridge: Cambridge University Press, 1977), 251.
20. British Library [BL], India Office Records [IOR] /G/12/53, Ship's Diary 1749–51; IOR/G/12/43 Ship's Diary 1736/7. Ships Sussex and Winchester, 66–7; IOR/G/12/16 ff 216–53 Diary & Consultation, 1685–6, 222v, 227v; Berg, *Luxury & Pleasure in Eighteenth-Century Britain*, ch. 2.
21. "*An Act prohibiting the importing of any wines, wooll or silk from the kingdom of France, into the Commonwealth of England or Ireland, or any the dominions thereunto belonging* (1649, 1650); Ciriacono, "Silk Manufacturing in France and Italy", 179.
22. Glamann, "The Changing Patterns of Trade", 250–2; Lemire and Riello, "East and West," 898.
23. Michael Kwass, *Contraband: Louis Mandrin and the Making of a Global Underground* (Cambridge, MA: Harvard University Press, 2014); Lemire, *Cotton*.
24. For the attempted suppression of consumer demand and its unexpected consequences see: Beverly Lemire, *Cotton*, ch. 3; and Riello, *Cotton*, 117–26.
25. Ciriacono, "Silk Manufacturing in France and Italy," 180–1.
26. Lesley Ellis Miller, "Paris-Lyon-Paris: Dialogue in the Design and Distribution of Patterned Silks in the 18th Century," in *Luxury Trade and Consumerism in Ancien Régime Paris,* (eds) Robert Fox and Anthony Turner (Aldershot: Ashgate, 1998); Carolyn Sargentson, *Merchants and Luxury Markets: The Marchands Merciers of Eighteenth-Century Paris* (London: Victoria & Albert Museum, 1996).
27. Quoted in Daryl M. Hafter, *Women at Work in Preindustrial France* (University Park: Pennsylvania State University Press, 2007), 125.
28. Miller, "Paris-Lyon-Paris."
29. Ilja Van Damme, "Middlemen and the Creation of a 'Fashion Revolution': the Experience of Antwerp in the late Seventeenth and Eighteenth Centuries," in *The Force of Fashion in Politics and Society from Early Modern to Contemporary Times,* (ed.) Beverly Lemire (Aldershot: Ashgate, 2009), 21–40; George Unwin, *Samuel Oldknow and the Arkwrights: The Industrial Revolution in Stockport and Marple* (London: Longmans, 1924).
30. A protest by English silk and ribbon weavers charging the smuggling French silk ribbons and lace into England. *The Case of the English Weavers and French Merchants truly Stated* (London, 1670).
31. James Carlile, *The fortune-hunters, or Two fools well met . . .* (London, 1689), Act II, Scene II.
32. Beverly Lemire, *Fashion's Favourite: the Cotton Trade and the Consumer in Britain, 1660–1800* (Oxford: Oxford University Press, 1991), 79–81.
33. Miller, "Innovation and Industrial Espionage."
34. For a discussion of knowledge transfer between Asia and Europe and within Europe see: Riello, *Cotton*, 160–85; Lien Bich Luu, *Immigrants and the Industries of London, 1500–1700* (Aldershot: Ashgate, 2005); J.R. Harris, "Movements of Technology between Britain and Europe in the Eighteenth Century," in *International Technology Transfer: Europe, Japan and the USA, 1700–1914,* (ed.) D.J. Jeremy (Aldershot: Ashgate, 1991).
35. Wadsworth and Mann, *Cotton Trade and Industrial Lancashire*, 304.
36. Carole Shammas, "The Decline of Textile Prices in England and British America Prior to Industrialization," *Economic History Review* 48 no. 3 (1994): 483–507.
37. T. Parke Hughes, *Human-built world: how to think about technology and culture* (Chicago: University of Chicago Press, 2005), 4–5.
38. Beverly Lemire, *Dress, Culture and Commerce: the English Clothing Trade Before the Factory, 1660–1800* (Basingstoke: Macmillan, 1997), 9–41 and "A Question of Trousers: Seafarers, Masculinity and Empire in the Shaping of British Male Dress, c. 1600–1800," *Cultural and Social History* (2016) forthcoming.

39. Clare Crowston, "Engendering the Guilds: Seamstresses, Tailors, and the Clash of Corporate Identities in Old Regime France," *French Historical Studies* 23:2 (2000): 339–71; Lemire, *Dress, Culture and Commerce*, ch. 2.

40. Margaret Spufford, "Fabric for Seventeenth-Century Children and Adolescents' Clothes," *Textile History* 34:1 (2003): 47–63.

41. Massimo Livi-Bacci, *The Population of Europe* (Oxford: Blackwell Publishers, 2000), 6; Paul M. Hohenberg and Lynn Hollen Lees, *The Making of Urban Europe, 1000–1950* (Cambridge, MA: Harvard University Press, 1985), 11.

42. De Vries, *The First Modern Economy*, 509–19.

43. Sargentson, *Merchants and Luxury Markets*; John Benson and Laura Ugolini (eds), *A Nation of Shopkeepers: Five Centuries of British Retailing* (London: Tauris & Co., 2003); Laurence Fontaine, *History of Pedlars in Europe* (Cambridge: Polity Press, 1996).

44. Anne McCants, "Poor Consumers as Global Consumers: the Diffusion of Tea and Coffee Drinking in the Eighteenth Century," *Economic History Review* 61 no.1 (2008): 172–200; Lemire, *Cotton*, ch. 3 and ch. 5, and "'Men of the World': British Mariners, Consumer Practice, and Material Culture in an Era of Global Trade, c. 1660–1800," *Journal of British Studies* 54, no. 2 (2015): 288–319.

45. Mark Overton, Jane Whittle, Darron Dean, and Andrew Hann, *Production and Consumption in English Households 1600–1750* (London: Routledge, 2004), 91; Belén Moreno Claverias, "Luxury, Fashion and Peasantry: The Introduction of New Commodities in Rural Catalan, 1670–1790," in *The Force of Fashion in Politics and Society from Early Modern to Contemporary Times*, (ed.) Beverly Lemire (Aldershot: Ashgate, 2010), 77, 81–2. Also Lorna Weatherill, *Consumer Behaviour and Material Culture in Britain, 1660–1760* (London: Routledge, 1988), 43–69.

46. Overton, Whittle, Dean and Ham, *Production and Consumption in England Households*, 91, 109, Table 5.1 and 5.3.

47. Moreno Claverias, "Luxury, Fashion and Peasantry," 81.

48. Dena Goodman and Kathryn Norberg (eds), *Furnishing the Eighteenth Century: What Furniture Can Tell Us about the European and American Past* (New York: Routledge, 2007), 1–9.

49. Linda Levy Peck, *Consuming Splendor: Society and Culture in Seventeenth-Century England* (Cambridge: Cambridge University Press, 2005), 221–2; Natacha Coquery, "Fashion, Business, Diffusion: An Upholsterer's Shop in Eighteenth-Century Paris," in *Fashioning the Eighteenth Century: What Furniture Can Tell Us about the European and American Past,* (eds) Dena Goodman and Kathryn Norberg, trans. Kathryn Norberg and Dena Goodman (New York: Routledge, 2007), 63.

50. Margaret Ponsonby, *Stories from Home: English Domestic Interiors, 1750–1850* (Aldershot: Ashgate, 2007), 52.

51. Pat Kirkham, *The London Furniture Trade 1700–1870* (London: Furniture History Society, 1988), 4–5; Van Damme, "Middlemen and the Creation of a 'Fashion Revolution'," 21–40.

52. Mary Douglas and Baron Isherwood emphasize the importance of sets of objects that in combination reflect social and cultural priorities in dress or furnishings. *The World of Goods: Towards an Anthropology of Consumption* (London: Routledge, 1979), 69–71.

53. Stana Nenadic, "Middle-Rank Consumers and Domestic Culture in Edinburgh and Glasgow 1720–1849," *Past & Present* 145 (1994): 130–1.

54. Daniel Roche, *The Culture of Clothing: Dress and Fashion in the Ancien Régime*, trans. Jean Birrell, (Cambridge: Cambridge University Press, 1994), 151–83.

55. Roche, *The Culture of Clothing*, 373.

56. Quoted in Roche, *The Culture of Clothing*, 373.

57. Roche, *The Culture of Clothing*, 127, 138.

58. Beverly Lemire, "Transforming Consumer Custom: Linens, Cottons and the English Market, 1660–1800," in *The European Linen Industry in Historical Perspective,* (eds) Brenda Collins and Philip Ollerenshaw (Oxford: Oxford University Press, 2003), 187–207.

59. BL, IOR/E/1/206, Miscellaneous Letters, p. 63, April 17, 1746.

60. For example, Richard Ames, *Sylvia's revenge, or, A satyr against man in answer to the Satyr against woman* (London: 1688), p. 13; Anon. *The Adventures of the Helvetian Hero, with the young Countess of Albania, or, The amours of Armadorus and Vicentina a novel* (London: 1694), 19–20.

Chapter 3

1. Linda Baumgarten, *Eighteenth Century Clothing at Williamsburg* (Williamsburg: The Colonial Williamsburg Foundation, 1986), 13.

2. Aileen Ribeiro, *Fashion and Fiction: Dress in Art and Literature in Stuart England* (New Haven, London: Yale University Press, 2005), 240; *Mémoires de Mme de Motteville* (1621–89), (ed.) M. Petitot (Paris: Foucault, 1824), vol. 5, p. 54.

3. Aileen Ribeiro, *Dress in Eighteenth Century Europe* (New Haven, London: Yale University Press, 2002), 34–5, 222.

4. David Kuchta, *The Three-Piece Suit and Modern Masculinity: England, 1550–1850* (Berkeley, University of California Press, 2002).

5. Giorgio Riello and Peter McNeil, *Shoes: A History from Sandals to Sneakers* (Oxford and New York: Berg, 2006).

6. See chapter 8: "Visual Representations."

7. Daniel Roche, *La culture des apparences* (Paris: Fayard, 1989); John Styles, *The Dress of the People. Every day Fashion in Eighteenth-century England* (New Haven: Yale University Press, 2007).

8. Jean-Claude Bologne, *Histoire de la coquetterie masculine* (Paris, Perrin, 2011), 226.

9. Georges Vigarello, *L'invention de la silhouette du XVIIIe siècle à nos jours* (Paris: Seuil, 2012).

10. See Daniel Roche, *Histoire des choses banales. Naissance de la consommation XVII–XIXe siècle* (Paris, Fayard, 1997), ch. VIII; and Styles, *The Dress of the People,* ch. 7.

11. Lynn Hunt, "Freedom of Dress in Revolutionary France," in *Critical and Primary Sources in Fashion: Renaissance to Present Day,* (ed.) P. McNeil (Oxford and New York: Berg, 2009), vol. 2, 43.

12. Nicole Pellegrin, "Corps du commun, usages communs du corps," in Vigarello, *Histoire du corps: De la Renaissance aux Lumières* (Paris: Seuil, 2005), 165.

13. Georges Vigarello, *Concepts of Cleanliness: Changing attitudes in France Since the Middle Ages* (Cambridge: Cambridge University Press, 1988), 68.

14. Roche, *Histoire des choses banales,* 233.

15. Stéphanie Chaffray, "La mise en scène du corps amérindien: la représentation du vêtement dans les relations de voyage en Nouvelle-France," *Histoire, économie & société,* 4 (2008), 5–32.

16. Roche, *La culture des apparences,* 426.

17. For material approaches to the corset see Jill Sallen, *Corsets. Historical Patterns & Techniques* (London: Batsford, 2008); and Elery Lynn, *Underwear Fashion in Detail* (London: V&A Publishing, 2010).

18. Roche, *La culture des apparences,* 425.

19. Hannah Greigh, "Faction and Fashion: The Politics of Court Dress in Eighteenth-Century England" in *Se vêtir à la cour en Europe 1400–1815,* Isabelle Paresys and Natacha Coquery (Villeneuve d'Ascq: Irhis-Ceges-Centre de recherche du château de Versailles, 2011), 70–1.

20. Susan Vincent, *The Anatomy of Fashion* (Oxford and New York: Berg, 2009), 90; Denis Bruna (dir.), *La mécanique des dessous* (Paris, Les arts décoratifs, 2013), 118–19.

21. Ariane Fennetaux, "Women's Pockets and the Construction of Privacy in the Long Eighteenth Century," *Eighteenth Century Fiction*, vol. 20, no. 3, Spring 2008: 321.

22. Elizabeth Hackspiel-Mikosch, "Uniforms and the Creation of Ideal Masculinity," in *The Men's Fashion Reader*, (eds) Peter McNichol and Vicki Karaminas (New York, Oxford: Berg, 2009), 117–29; and "Mode und Uniform—Mode im Military Style," in *Die Tanzhusaren 1813, 1913, 2013*, Norbert Börste and Georg Eggenstein, exhibition catalog (Krefeld: Museum Burg Linn, 2013), 84–99.

23. Avril Hart and Susan North, *Seventeenth and Eighteenth-century Fashion in Detail* (London, V&A Publishing, 1998), 44; Bruna, *La mécanique des dessous*, 98.

24. See ch. 8, "Visual Representations."

25. Adelheide Rasche and Gundula Wolter (eds), *Ridikül: Mode in der Karikatur* (Berlin: DuMont, 2003); Peter McNeil, "Caricatura e Moda: Storia di una Presa in Giro," in *Storie di Moda/Fashion-able Histories*, (eds) M.G. Muzzarelli and E.T. Brandi (Milano: Bruno Mondadori, 2010), 156–67.

26. Marquis de Dangeau, *Journal de la Cour du Roi Soleil, tome X (1697), Le Mariage* (Paris: Paleo, 2005), 189.

27. Louis de Rouvroy, duc de Saint-Simon, *Mémoires complets et authentiques du duc de Saint-Simon sur le siècle de Louis XIV et la régence*, (ed.) M. Chéruel (Paris: Hachette, 1856), tome 12, ch. 1 (1715).

28. Mme de Genlis, *Dictionnaire critique et raisonné des étiquettes de la cour (. . .)* (Paris: P. Mongié aîné, 1818), vol. 2, article "Parure."

29. Henriette-Lucie Dillon, marquise de La Tour du Pin-Gouvernet, *Journal d'une femme de cinquante ans, 1778–1815* (Paris: Imhaus et Chapelot, 1913), vol. 2, ch. I, para. IV.

30. See some examples in Vincent, *The Anatomy of Fashion*, 76–7.

31. La Tour du Pin, *Journal*, ch. VII, para. IV.

32. Genlis, *Dictionnaire critique et raisonné des étiquettes de la cour (. . .)*.

33. She died in 1683. Charlotte-Elisabeth d'Orléans (1652–1722), *Lettres de Madame, duchesse d'Orléans, née Princesse Palatine*, (ed.) Olivier Amiel (Paris: Mercure de France, 1985), 427.

34. Ibid., 130.

35. Georges Vigarello, *Le corps redressé. Histoire d'un pouvoir pédagogique* (Paris: Delarge, 1978).

36. See chapter 3 of vol. 3 of this series: *Fashion in the Renaissance (1450–1650)*.

37. Vigarello, *Le corps redressé*, 69.

38. *Moi Marie Dubois, gentilhomme vendômois, valet de chambre de Louis XIV*, prés. par François Lebrun (Rennes: Apogée, 1994), 167.

39. Baronne d'Oberkirch, *Mémoires sur la cour de Louis XIV et la société française avant 1789* (Paris: Mercure de France, 1989), 462.

40. Vincent, *The Anatomy of Fashion*, 46.

41. Kimberly Chrisman, "Unhoop the Fair Sex: The Campaign Against the Hoop Petticoat in Eighteenth-Century England," *Eighteenth-Century Studies*, 30–1, Fall 1996: 5–23.

42. Ann Hollander, *Seeing Through Clothes* (Berkeley: University of California Press, 1993), 218.

43. Nolivos de Saint-Cyr, Paul-Antoine-Nicolas (1726–1803), *Tableau du siècle, par un auteur connu (. . .)* (Genève, [s.n.], 1759), 195.

44. Roche, *La culture des apparences*, 440 and 443.

45. Ibid., ch. XV; N. Pellegrin, "L'uniforme de la santé; les médecins et la réforme du costume," *Dix-huitième siècle*, no. 23 (1991): 129–40; Julie Allard, "Perceptions nouvelles du corps et raisons médicales de la mode dans la deuxième moitié du XVIIIe siècle," in *Représentations du corps sous l'Ancien Régime. Discours et pratiques*, (ed.) Isabelle Billaud and Marie-Christine Laperrière (Laval: Cahiers du CIERL, 2007), 13–30.

46. Vigarello, *Le corps redressé*, 96.

47. Emmanuel duc de Croÿ, *Journal de Cour, tome 4 (1768–1773)* (Paris: Paléo, 2005), 279.

48. Letter: November 1, 1770, in Évelyne Lever (pres.), *Marie-Antoinette. Correspondance (1770–1793)* (Paris: Tallandier, 2005), 60–1.
49. Ribeiro, *Dress in Eighteenth Century*, 241.
50. Philippe Perrot, *Le corps féminin. Le travail des apparences, XVIIe–XIXe siècle* (Paris: Seuil, 1991), 179.
51. Allard, "Perceptions nouvelles du corps," 20.
52. Jacques Bonnaud, *Dégradation de l'espèce humaine par l'usage des corps à baleine* (Paris: Herissant, 1770).
53. L.J. Clairian, *Recherches et considérations médicales sur les vêtemens des hommes: particulièrement sur les culotes* (Paris: Aubry, An XI–1803, 2nd (ed.)).
54. Valerie Steele, *The Corset: A Cultural History* (London and New Haven: Yale University Press, 2001), 76.
55. Bonnaud did thus too in *Dégradation de l'espèce humaine*, 197.
56. Ibid., 197.
57. Roche, *La culture des apparences*, 386 and 393.
58. Denis Diderot, *Regrets sur ma vieille robe de chambre (1768)*, in *Correspondance littéraire* (s. l., Friedrich Ring, 1772).
59. Bologne, *Histoire de la coquetterie masculine*, 217.
60. Ribeiro, *Dress in Eighteenth Century*, 212.
61. Kuchta, *The Three-Piece Suit and Modern Masculinity*, 121
62. Ibid., 123.
63. Ribeiro, *Dress in Eighteenth Century*, 226–8.
64. Nicole Pellegrin, "Corps du commun," in Vigarello, *Histoire du corps*, 164.

Chapter 4

1. Richard Brathwait, "The English Gentlewoman, Drawne Out to the Full Body" (1631), in *The English Gentleman and English Gentlewoman, Both in one Volume couched (. . .)*, 3rd (ed.) (London, 1641), 323–4.
2. "Art. Mode, S.f.," in *Dictionnaire de Trévoux*, Edition Lorraine: Nancy 1738–42, 1301, trans. by the author; original French: Mode, S.f.: Coutume, usage, manière de vivre ou de faire les choses. Ritus, mos, arbitrium, institutum. Toutes les nations ont des modes, des manières de vivre différentes. On ne trouve rien de bien que ce qui est à la mode. Les péchez des Grands deviennent les modes des peuples & la corruption de la Cour devient une politesse dans les Provinces.
3. "Art. Mode, die," in *Oekonomische Encyklopädie oder allgemeines System der Staats- Stadt- Haus- und Landwirthschaft*, (ed.) Johann G. Krünitz (1773–1885), trans. by the author; original German: *Mode*, die, die eingeführte Art des Verhaltens im gesellschaftlichen Leben, die Sitte, Gewohnheit; und in engerem Verstande, die veränderliche Art der Kleidung und der Anordnung alles dessen, was zum Schmucke gehört, wofür man ehedem auch das Wort Weise gebrauchte.
4. Pierre Bourdieu, *Outline of a Theory of Practice* (Cambridge: Cambridge University Press, 1977).
5. Theodore R. Schatzki, "Introduction. Practice Theory," in *The Practice Turn in Contemporary Theory*, (eds) Th. R. Schatzki, K. Knorr Cetina, and E. von Savigny (London and New York: Routledge, 2001), 3.
6. For a similar argument see Susan Vincent, *Dressing the Elite: Clothes in Early Modern England* (Oxford: Berg 2003), 3–4.
7. Martha L. Finch, "'Fashions of Wordly Dames': Separatist Discourse of Dress in Early Modern London, Amsterdam, and Plymouth Colony," *American Society of Church History* 74, no. 3 September (2005): 523.
8. Thomas D. Hamm, *The Quakers in America* (Columbia University Press: New York, 2006), 101.

9. Stephen Greenblatt, *Renaissance Self-Fashioning. From More to Shakespeare* (Chicago and London: The University of Chicago Press, 2005), 2.

10. Niklas Luhmann, *Die Gesellschaft der Gesellschaft* (Frankfurt am Main: Suhrkamp, 1997), 678–743, esp. 733–4.

11. Pierre Bourdieu, "The Social Space and the Genesis of Groups," *Theory and Society* 14 (1985): 723–44; Pierre Bourdieu, "The Forms of Capital," in *Handbook of Theory and Research for the Sociology of Education*, (ed.) J.G. Richardson (New York: Greenwood Press, 1986), 241–58.

12. For a statistical survey of consumer behavior in England, from 1660 to 1760, see Lorna Weatherill, *Consumer Behaviour and Material Culture in Britain, 1660–1760* (London and New York: Routledge, 1988).

13. Dick Hebdige, *Subculture: The Meanings of Style* (London: Routledge, 1979), 16–17.

14. Roze Hentschell, "Moralizing Apparel in Early Modern London: popular Literature, Sermons and Sartorial Display," *Journal of Medieval and Early Modern Studies* 39, no. 3 Fall (2009): 572 ff.

15. Martha L. Finch, "'Fashions of Wordly Dames': Separatist Discourse of Dress in Early Modern London, Amsterdam, and Plymouth Colony," *American Society of Church History* 74, no. 3 September (2005): 494–533.

16. See the detailed case study, ibid.

17. John Styles, *The Dress of the People. Everyday Fashion in Eighteenth-Century England* (New Haven and London: Yale University Press, 2007), 181.

18. Joyce Appleby, "Consumption in early modern social thought," in *Consumption and the World of Goods*, (eds) J. Brewer and R. Porter (London and New York: Routledge, 1993), 162–73.

19. Quoted in John E. Wills, Jr., "European consumption and Asian production in the seventeenth and eighteenth centuries," in *Consumption*: 137.

20. Beverly Lemire and Giorgio Riello, "East and West: Textiles and Fashion in Early Modern Europe," *Journal of Social History* 41, no. 4 (2008): 888.

21. Dagmar Freist, "'Ich will Dir selbst ein Bild von mir entwerfen. Praktiken der Selbst-Bildung im Spannungsfeld ständischer Normen und gesellschaftlicher Dynamik," in *Selbst Bildungen. Soziale und kulturelle Praktiken der Subjektivierung*, (eds) Thomas Alkemeyer, Gunilla Budde, Dagmar Freist (Bielefeld: transcript Verlag, 2013), 160.

22. Beverly Lemire, "Second-hand beaux and 'red-armed Belles': conflict and the creation of fashions in England, c. 1600–1800," *Continuity and Change* 15, no. 3 December (2000): 393.

23. Daniel Roche, *The Culture of Clothing: Dress and Fashion in the Ancien Régime* (Cambridge: Cambridge University Press, 1994), ch. 6.

24. Lemire, "Second-hand beaux and 'red-armed Belles'": 400.

25. Woodruff D. Smith, *Consumption and the Making of Respectability, 1600–1800* (London: Routledge, 2002), 3 and 27f.

26. Styles, *The Dress of the People*, 181.

27. Roche, *The Culture of Clothing*, 51.

28. Styles, *The Dress of the People*, 181.

29. Erin Mackie, *Market à la Mode: Fashion, Commodity and Gender in* The Tatler *and* The Spectator (Baltimore: Johns Hopkins University Press, 1997), 7 and 148.

30. Jessica Munns and Penny Richarrds (eds), *The Clothes that Wear Us. Essays on Dressing and Transgressing in Eighteenth-Century Culture* (Newark and London: Associated University Press, 1999).

31. Carlo Marco Belfanti, "New Approaches to Fashion and Emotion. The Civilization of Fashion: At the Origins of a Western Social Institution," *Journal of Social History*, Winter (2009), 261–83, 362.

32. Roche, *The Culture of Clothing*, 51.

33. Ibid.
34. Lemire, "Second-hand beaux and 'red-armed Belles'": 398.
35. Will Pritchard, "Masks and Faces: Female Legibility in the Restoration Era," *Eighteenth-Century Life* 24, no. 3, Fall (2000): 31–52.
36. Aileen Ribeiro, *Dress and Morality* (London: B.T. Batsford, 1986), 93.
37. Brathwait, *The English Gentlewoman*, 330.
38. Stephen H. Gregg, "'A Truly Christian Hero': Religion, Effeminacy, and the Nation in the Writings of the Societies for the Reformation of Manners," *Eighteenth-century Life* 25, Winter (2001): 17.
39. Cit. in Ribeiro, *Dress and Morality*, 89.
40. Peter McNeil, "'Beyond the horizon of hair': masculinity, nationhood and fashion in the Anglo-French Eighteenth Century," in *Hinter dem Horizont. Projektion und Distinktion ländlicher Oberschichten im euorpäischen Vergleich, 17.–19. Jahrhundert*, (eds) D. Freist and F. Schmekel (Münster: Aschendorff Verlag, 2013), 84.
41. Amelia Rauser, "Hair, Authenticity, and the Self-Made Macaroni," *Eighteenth Century Studies* 38, no. 1, Fall (2004): 101.
42. McNeil, "Beyond the horizon of hair," 85.
43. Rauser, "Hair, Authenticity, and the Self-Made Macaroni," 101–2.
44. Gregg, "A Truly Christian Hero," 17.
45. John Tosh, "The Old Adam and the new Man: Emerging Themes in the History of English Masculinites, 1750–1850," in *English Masculinites 1660–1800*, (eds) T. Hitzchcock and M. Cohen (London and New York: Longman, 1999), 231.
46. Morag Martin, "Doctoring Beauty: The Medical Control of Women's Tilettes in France, 1750–1820," *Medical History* 49 (2005), 352.
47. Ibid., 354, 360.
48. Michael Kwass, "Consumption and the World of Ideas: Consumer Revolution and the Moral Economy oft he Marquis de Mirabeaux," *Eighteenth-century Studies* 37, no. 2, Winter (2004), 195–6.
49. Ibid., 195.
50. Ibid., 196.
51. Mikael Alm, "'Social Imaginary' im Schweden des späten 18. Jahrhunderts," in *Diskurse—Körper—Artefakte. Historische Praxeologie in der Frühneuzeitforschung*, (ed.) D. Freist (Bielefeld: transcript, 2015), 267–86.
52. Friedrich Justin Bertuch and Georg Melchior Kraus (eds), *Das Journal des Luxus und der Moden* (Weimar: 1786–1826), February 1786, 72 ff.; "Art. Kleidung," in *Oekonomische Encyklopädie oder allgemeines System der Staats- Stadt- Haus- und Landwirthschaft*, (ed.) Johann G. Krünitz (1773–1885).
53. Catherine Molineux, "Hogarth's Fashionable Slaves: Moral Corruption in Eighteenth-Century London," *ELH* 72, no. 2, Summer (2005): 496.
54. Graeme Murdock, "Dressed to Repress? Protestant Clerical Dress and the Regulation of Morality in Early Modern Europe," *Fashion Theory* 4, no. 2 (2000): 190.
55. William Keenan, "From Friars to Fornicators: The Eroticization of Sacred Dress," *Fashion Theory* 3, no. 4 (1999): 390.
56. Ribeiro, *Dress and Morality*, 19.
57. Lyndal Roper, *The Holy Household: Women and Morals in Reformation Augsburg* (Oxford: Clarendon Press, 1989).
58. Robert Burton, *The Anatomy of Melancholy* (1621), quoted in Ribeiro, *Dress and Morality*, 74.
59. Ribeiro, *Dress and Morality*, 80.
60. Hartmut Lehmann, "Grenzüberschreitungen und Grenzziehungen im Pietismus," *Pietismus und Neuzeit* 27 (2001): 17.
61. Prominent examples in English literature lived on in the nineteenth century, for instance Charlotte Brontë, *Jane Eyre* (1847), Georg Eliot, *Adam Bede* (1859), and *Middlemarch*

(1871–2). See also Suzanne Keen, "Quaker Dress, Sexuality, and the Domestication of Reform in the Victorian Novel," *Victorian Literature and Culture* 30, no. 1 (2002): 11–236.

62. *Memoir of the life of Elizabeth Fry, with extracts from her letters and journal,* (ed.) [K. Fry and R. E. Cresswell], 2 vols. (1847). Also Francisca de Haan, "Fry, Elizabeth (1780–1845)," *Oxford Dictionary of National Biography* (Oxford: Oxford University Press, 2004); online edn, May 2007: http://www.oxforddnb.com/view/article/10208, [accessed March 18, 2015].

63. Amelia Mott Gummere, *The Quaker: a Study in Costume* (Philadelphia: Ferris and Leach, 1901), 89.

64. Ibid.

65. Thomas Clarkson, "Peculiar Customs," in *A Portraiture of Quakerism*, 3 vols., vol. 2, (ed.) T. Clarkson (1806).

66. Ribeiro, *Dress and Morality*, 103.

67. John Wesley, *A Sermon on Dress* (London, 1817), 6–9.

68. See for instance Gisela Mettele, "Entwürfe des pietistischen Körpers. Die Herrnhuter Brüdergemeine und die Mode im 18. Jahrhundert," in *Das Echo Halles. Kulturelle Wirkungen des Pietismus,* (ed.) R. Lächele (Tübingen: bibliotheca academica Verlag, 2001), 291–314.

69. Gisela Mettele, *Weltbürgertum oder Gottesreich. Die Herrnhuter Brüdergemeine als globale Gemeinschaft 1727–1857* (Göttingen: Vandenhoeck & Ruprecht, 2009), 255–68 and on the role of portraits also Jon Sensbach, *Rebeccas Revival. Creating Black Christianity in the Atlantic World* (Cambridge, MA/London: Harvard University Press, 2005).

70. See for instance Elisabeth Sommer, "Fashion Passion. The Rhetoric of Dress within the Eighteenth-century Moravian Brethren," in *Pious Pursuits: German Moravians in the Atlantic World*, (eds) M. Gillespie and R. Beachy (New York: Berghahn, 2007). For the importance of everyday social practices of Moravians in Surinam and their impact on religious identity see Jessica Cronshagen, "Den Leib besitzen, die Seele umwerben—die Rechtfertigung unfreier Arbeit in den Korrespondenzen der Herrnhuter Surinammission des 18. Jahrhunderts," in *Connecting Worlds and People. Early Modern Diasporas as Translocal Societies*, (eds) D. Freist and S. Lachenicht (Farnham: Ashgate, forthcoming).

71. Woodruff D. Smith, *Consumption and the Making of Respectability, 1600–1800* (London: Routledge, 2002), 121–9.

72. Her correspondences are kept in the High Court of Admirality, London (HCA 30).

73. Mentioned in *"L'art du fabricant d'étoffes de Soie"* (1778).

74. HCA 30/386.

75. HCA 30/374.

76. Doris Garraway, *The Libertine Colony: Creolization in the Early French Caribbean* (Durham/London: Duke University Press, 2005), 120.

77. Ibid., 125.

78. Dagmar Freist, "'Ich schicke Dir etwas Fremdes und nicht Vertrautes': Briefpraktiken als Vergewisserungsstrategie zwischen Raum und Zeit im Kolonialgefüge der Frühen Neuzeit," *Diskurse—Körper—Artefakte*, 373–404.

79. A letter from Jonas Ekmark, Neudietendorf to his brother, Taylor, in Paramaribo (1795) High Court of Admirality (HCA) HCA 30/374, with lists of garments and fabric samples. I would like to thank Jessica Cronshagen who pointed this letter out to me.

80. A letter from Johann Gernot Arnold in Paramaribo, Surinam, to Samuel Liebisch in Herrnhut, HCA 30/374. I would like to thank Jessica Cronshagen who pointed this letter out to me, trans. by the author; original German.

81. Lemire and Riello, "East and West: 888.

82. Piet Visser, "Aspects of social criticism and cultural assimilation: The Mennonite image in literature and self-criticism of literary Mennonites," in *From Martyr to Muppy. A historical introduction to cultural assimilation processes of a religious minority in the*

Netherlands, (eds) A. Hamilton, S. Voolstra, and Piet Visser (Amsterdam: Amsterdam University Press, 1994), 67.

83. Sermon by Jacob Cornelisz, quoted in Mary Sprunger, "Waterlandes and the Dutch Golden Age: A case study on Mennonite involvement in seventeenth-century Dutch trade and industry as one of the earliest examples of socio-economic assimilation," in *From Martyr to Muppy,* 133–4.
84. James Urry, "Wealth and Poverty in the Mennonite Experience: Dilemmas and Challenges," *Journal of Mennonite Studies* 27 (2009): 11–40.
85. Sprunger, "Waterlandes and the Dutch Golden Age."
86. Piet Visser and Mary Sprunger, *Menno Simons: Places, Portraits and Progeny* (Amsterdam: Friesen, 1996).
87. Yme Kuiper and Harm Nijboer, "Between Frugality and Civility: Dutch Mennonites and their Taste for the World of Art in the Eighteenth Century," *Journal of Mennonite Studies* 27 (2009): 75–6.
88. For a detailed description of this portrait see Kuiper and Nijboer, "Between Frugality and Civility," 76.
89. Benjamin Marschke, "Pietism and Politics in Prussia and Beyond," in *A Companion to German Pietism, 1660–1800,* (ed.) Douglas Shantz (Leiden: Brill, 2014), 511.
90. Luise Adelgunde Victorie Gottsched, *Die Pietisterey im Fischbein-Rocke; oder Die Doctormäßige Frau. In einem Lust Spiele vorgestellet* (Rostock, 1736).
91. Ulrike Gleixner, "Gender and Pietism. Self-modelling and Agency," in *A Companion to German Pietism,* 433–4.
92. Christoph Schulte, *Die Jüdische Aufklärung* (München: Beck Verlag, 2002), 17–47.
93. For a good survey see David Cesarani (ed.), *Port Jews: Jewish Communities in Cosmopolitan Maritime Trading Centres, 1550–1950* (London and Portland: Frank Cass Publishers, 2002).
94. Deborah Hertz, "Salonnières and Literary Women in Late Eighteenth Century Berlin," *New German Critique* 14 (1978): 97–108.
95. Roche, *The Culture of Clothing,* 62.

Chapter 5

1. Daniel Roche, *The Culture of Clothing: Dress and Fashion in the "Ancien Régime,"* trans. Jean Birrell (Cambridge: Cambridge University Press,1994), 44.
2. Christopher Breward, *The Culture of Fashion: A New History of Fashionable Dress* (Manchester: Manchester University Press, 1995), 140; Clare A. Lyons, "Mapping an Atlantic sexual culture: homoeroticism in eighteenth-century Philadelphia," *William and Mary Quarterly,* vol. 60, no. 1 (2003): 142; John Styles, *The Dress of the People: Everyday Fashion in Eighteenth-Century England* (New Haven: Yale University Press, 2007), 52.
3. Madeleine Delpierre, *Dress in France in the Eighteenth Century* (New Haven and London: Yale University Press, 1997), 58–68.
4. Kimberly Chrisman, "'Unhoop the Fair Sex': The Campaign Against the Hoop Petticoat in Eighteenth-Century England," *Eighteenth-Century Studies,* vol. 30, no. 1, Fall (1996): 13.
5. Jennifer M. Jones, "Repackaging Rousseau: Femininity and Fashion in Old Regime France," *French Historical Studies,* vol. 18, no. 4 Autumn (1994): 155.
6. Thomas Laqueur, *Making Sex: Body and Gender from the Greeks to Freud* (Cambridge, MA: Harvard University Press, 1990), 149.
7. Ibid., 194.
8. Michael McKeon, "Historicizing patriarchy: the emergence of gender difference in England, 1660–1760," *Eighteenth Century Studies,* vol. 28, no. 3 (1995): 300.
9. Randolph Trumbach, *Sex and the Gender Revolution,* vol. 1, *Heterosexuality and the Third Gender in Enlightenment London* (Chicago: University of Chicago Press, 1998), 9.
10. Chrisman, "Unhoop the Fair Sex": 7.
11. Ibid., 17.

12. David Kunzle, *Fashion and Fetishism: Corsets, Tight Lacing and Other Forms of Body-Sculpture* (Stroud: Sutton, 2004), 65.

13. Delpierre, *Dress in France in the Eighteenth Century,* 29.

14. Michael Kwass, "Big hair: a wig history of consumption in eighteenth-century France," *American Historical Review*, vol. 111, issue 3 (2006): 631; see also Amelia Rauser, "Hair, authenticity, and the self-made macaroni," *Eighteenth-Century Studies*, vol. 38, no. 1 (2004).

15. Kunzle, *Fashion and Fetishism,* 69.

16. Chrisman, "Unhoop the Fair Sex": 21.

17. Aileen Ribeiro, *Dress in Eighteenth-Century Europe, 1715–1789*, revised (ed.) (New Haven: Yale University Press, 2002), 6.

18. Christoph Heyl, "The metamorphosis of the mask in seventeenth- and eighteenth-century London," in *Masquerade and Identities: Essays on Gender, Sexuality and Marginality*, (ed.) Efrat Tseëlon (London: Routledge, 2003), 119.

19. Aileen Ribeiro, *The Art of Dress: Fashion in England and France 1750 to 1820* (New Haven and London: Yale University Press, 1995), 224, and *Dress in Eighteenth-Century Europe, 1715–1789*, 266–72.

20. David Porter, "Monstrous beauty: eighteenth-century fashion and the aesthetics of the Chinese taste," *Eighteenth-Century Studies*, vol. 35, no. 3 (2002): 404.

21. Terry Castle, *Masquerade and Civilization: The Carnivalesque in Eighteenth-Century English Culture and Fiction* (Stanford: Stanford University Press, 1986), 7.

22. Mark Booth, "*Campe-toi!* On the origins and definitions of camp," in *Camp: Queer Aesthetics and the Performing Subject: A Reader*, (ed.) Fabio Cleto (Edinburgh: Edinburgh University Press, 1999) and Pierre Zoberman, "Queer(ing) pleasure: having a gay old time in the culture of early-modern France," in *The Desire of the Analysts*, (eds) Paul Allen Miller and Greg Forter (Albany: State University of New York Press, 2008).

23. Roche, *The Culture of Clothing,* 116.

24. Porter, "Monstrous beauty": 399.

25. Jessica Munns and Penny Richards (eds), *The Clothes that Wear Us. Essays on Dressing and Transgressing in Eighteenth-Century Culture* (Newark and London: University of Delaware Press, 1999), 23.

26. Ribeiro, *Dress in Eighteenth-Century Europe, 1715–1789,* 22.

27. John Carl Flügel, *The Psychology of Clothes* (London: Hogarth Press, 1930).

28. Ribeiro, *Dress in Eighteenth-Century Europe, 1715–1789,* 111.

29. David Kuchta, *The Three-Piece Suit and Modern Masculinity: England, 1550–1850* (Berkeley: University of California Press, 2002), 125.

30. John Harvey, *Men in Black* (London: Reaktion, 1995), 120, and Laura Lunger Knoppers, "The politics of portraiture: Oliver Cromwell and the plain style," *Renaissance Quarterly*, vol. 51, no. 4 (1998): 1289.

31. Aileen Ribeiro, *Fashion and Fiction: Dress in Art and Literature in Stuart England* (New Haven: Yale University Press, 2005), 191.

32. Ibid., 199.

33. Kuchta, *The Three-Piece Suit and Modern Masculinity,* 1.

34. Ibid., 101.

35. Hannah Greig, *The Beau Monde: Fashionable Society in Georgian London* (Oxford: Oxford University Press, 2013), 241.

36. Ibid., 227.

37. Ibid., 234.

38. Overview in Thomas A. King, *The Gendering of Men, 1600–1750,* vol. 2, *Queer Articulations* (Madison: University of Wisconsin Press, 2008), xix–xxii.

39. Ibid., 87, and Erin Mackie, *Rakes, Highwaymen, and Pirates: The Making of the Modern Gentleman in the Eighteenth Century* (Baltimore: Johns Hopkins University Press, 2009), 183.

40. D.A. Coward, "Attitudes to homosexuality in eighteenth-century France," *Journal of European Studies*, 10, no. 40 (1980): 245.

41. Dorothy Noyes, "La maja vestida: dress as resistance to enlightenment in late-18th-century Madrid," *Journal of American Folklore*, vol. 111, no. 40 (1998): 199.

42. Felicity Nussbaum, *The Limits of the Human: Fictions of Anomaly, Race and Gender in the Long Eighteenth Century* (Cambridge: Cambridge University Press, 2003), pp. 72–3.

43. Chrisman-Campbell, Kimberly, "The face of fashion: milliners in eighteenth-century visual culture," *British Journal for Eighteenth-Century Studies*, vol. 25, issue 2 (2002).

44. Randolph Trumbach, "The transformation of sodomy from the Renaissance to the modern world and its general sexual consequences," *Signs*, vol. 37, no. 4 (2012): 540–1.

45. Aaron Santesso, "William Hogarth and the tradition of the sexual scissors," *SEL: Studies in English Literature*, vol. 39, no. 3 (1999): 514.

46. Kristina Straub, "Actors and homophobia," in *Cultural Readings of Restoration and Eighteenth-Century English Theater*, (eds) J. Douglas Cranfield and Deborah C. Payne (Athens, OH: University of Georgia Press, 1995), 273; see also Kristina Straub, *Sexual Suspects: Eighteenth-Century Players and Sexual Ideology* (Princeton: Princeton University Press, 1992).

47. David L. Orvis, "'Old sodom' and 'dear dad': Vanbrugh's celebration of the sodomitical subject in *The Relapse*," *Journal of Homosexuality*, vol. 57, issue 1 (2009).

48. Anon., "News," *Gazetteer and New Daily Advertiser,* October 27, 1764.

49. Tobias Smollett, *The Adventures of Roderick Random,* 2 vols. (London: Osborn, 1748), vol. 1, 306; and, for a discussion of the "over determination" of the longer description of which this is a section, see George Haggerty "Smollett's world of masculine desire" in *The Adventures of Roderick Random, Eighteenth Century*, vol. 53, no. 3 (2012): 318.

50. Randolph Trumbach, "Sodomitical assaults, gender role, and sexual development in eighteenth-century London," *Journal of Homosexuality*, vol. 16, issue 1-2 (1988): 408–9; on mollies see also Castle, *Masquerade and Civilization,* 46; Tanya Cassidy, "People, place, and performance: theoretically revisiting Mother Clap's Molly House," in *Queer People: Negotiations and Expressions of Homosexuality, 1700–1800*, (eds) Chris Mounsey and Caroline Gonda (Lewisburg: Bucknell University Press, 2007); Netta Goldsmith, "London's homosexuals in the eighteenth-century: rhetoric versus practice," in *Queer People: Negotiations and Expressions of Homosexuality, 1700–1800*, (eds) Chris Mounsey and Caroline Gonda (Lewisburg: Bucknell University Press, 2007), p. 186; and Mackie, *Rakes, Highwaymen, and Pirates,* 117.

51. Anon., *Faustina* (1726), attributed to Henry Carey.

52. Susan Staves, "A few kind words for the fop," *Studies in English Literature, 1500–1900*, vol. 22, no. 3 (1982): 428.

53. Philip Carter, *Men and the Emergence of Polite Society, Britain, 1660–1800* (Harlow: Longman, 2001), 156.

54. John Brewer, *The Pleasures of the Imagination: English Culture in the Eighteenth Century* (London: Harper Collins, 1997), 81.

55. Lorna Hutson, "Liking men: Ben Jonson's closet opened," *ELH*, vol. 71, no. 4 (2004): 1086; King, *The Gendering of Men, 1600–1750*, vol. 1, *The English Phallus* (Madison: University of Wisconsin Press), 246; and Emma K. Atwood, "Fashionably late: queer temporality and the Restoration fop," *Comparative Drama*, vol. 47, no. 1 (2013): 85.

56. Peter McNeil, "Conspicuous waist: queer dress in the 'long eighteenth century'," in *A Queer History of Fashion: From the Closet to the Catwalk*, (ed.) Valerie Steele (New York: Fashion Institute of Technology, 2013), 91; see also Leslie Ritchie, "Garrick's male-coquette and theatrical masculinities," in *Refiguring the Coquette: Essays on Culture and Coquetry*, (eds) Shelley King and Yaël Schlick (Lewisburg: Bucknell University Press, 2008).

57. Walpole, letter to Lord Hertford, February 6, 1764, in Horace Walpole, *The Correspondence*, 48 vols (New Haven: Yale University Press, 1935–83).

58. Andrew Wilton and Ilaris Bignamini (eds), *Grand Tour: The Lure of Italy in the Eighteenth Century* (London: Tate Publishing, 1996), 84.

59. Michèle Cohen, "The Grand Tour: constructing the English gentleman in eighteenth-century France," *History of Education*, vol. 21, no. 3 (1992): 255; and Jeremy Black, *Italy and the Grand Tour* (New Haven: Yale University Press, 2003), 126.

60. Jason M. Kelly, "Riots, revelries, and rumor: libertinism and masculine association in Enlightenment London," *Journal of British Studies*, vol. 45, no. 4 (2006), 779; see also Shearer West, "The Darly macaroni prints and the politics of 'private man'," *Eighteenth-Century Life*, vol. 25, no. 2 (2001).

61. Stephen H. Gregg, "'A Truly Christian Hero': Religion, Effeminacy, and the Nation in the Writings of the Societies for the Reformation of Manners," *Eighteenth-Century Life*, vol. 25, no. 1 Winter (2001): 21–2.

62. Dominic Janes, "Unnatural appetites: sodomitical panic in Hogarth's *The Gate of Calais, or O the Roast Beef of Old England (1748)*," *Oxford Art Journal*, vol. 35, no. 1 (2012).

63. George Rousseau, *Perilous Enlightenment: Pre- and Post-Modren Discourses—Sexual, Historical* (Manchester: Manchester University Press, 1991), p. 189.

64. Date based on similar drawing by Walpole in The Lewis Walpole Library: http://images.library.yale.edu/walpoleweb/oneitem.asp?imageId=lwlpr15045

65. Peter McNeil (ed.), *Critical and Primary Sources in Fashion: Renaissance to Present Day* (Oxford and New York: Berg, 1999), 424–5; on print-culture and the figure of the macaroni see West, "The Darly macaroni prints and the politics of 'private man'."

66. Emma Donoghue, "Imagined more than women: lesbians as hermaphrodites, 1671–1766," *Women's History Review*, vol. 2, issue 2, (1993); and Cathy McClive, "Masculinity on trial: penises, hermaphrodites and the uncertain male body in early modern France," *History Workshop Journal*, vol. 68, no. 1 (2009).

67. Quoted in Rictor Norton, "The first public debate about homosexuality in England: letters in *The Public Ledger* concerning the case of Captain Jones, 1772," *Homosexuality in Eighteenth-Century England: A Sourcebook* (2004), accessed November 10, 2013. Available at http://www.rictornorton.co.uk/eighteen/jones7.htm.

68. Anon., 'News', *Morning Chronicle and London Advertiser,* August 8, 1772.

69. Anon., 'News', *London Evening News,* August 6, 1772.

70. Anon., 'News', *Bingley's London Journal,* September 12–19, 1772.

71. McNeil, *Critical and Primary Sources in Fashion*, 418.

72. Rictor Norton (ed.), "The macaroni club: newspaper items," *Homosexuality in Eighteenth-Century England: A Sourcebook* (2005), accessed January 3, 2013. Available at http://www.rictornorton.co.uk/eighteen/macaron1.htm

73. Anon., *The Vauxhall Affray; or, the Macaronies Defeated* (London: J. Williams 1773), 14; discussed in Miles Ogborn, "Locating the Macaroni: luxury, sexuality and vision in Vauxhall Gardens," *Textual Practice*, vol. 11, no. 3 (1997).

74. Daniel Claro, "Historicizing masculine appearance: John Chute and the suits at The Vyne, 1740–76," *Fashion Theory*, vol. 9, issue 2 (2005): 166.

75. Karen Harvey, "The century of sex? Gender, bodies, and sexuality in the long eighteenth century," *Historical Journal, vol.* 45, no. 4 (2002): 906; note in particular the contribution made by Laqueur, *Making Sex,* and Trumbach, *Sex and the Gender Revolution,* vol. 1.

76. Terry Castle, "Matters not fit to be mentioned: Fielding's *The Female Husband*," *ELH*, vol. 49, no. 3 (1982).

77. Gary Kates, "The transgendered world of the chevalier/chevalière d'Eon," *Journal of Modern History*, vol. 67, no. 3 (1995): 584.

78. Lisa F. Cody, "Sex, civility, and the self: du Coudray, d'Eon, and eighteenth-century conceptions of gendered, national, and psychological identity," *French Historical Studies*, vol. 24, no. 3 (2001): 403.

79. Anna Clark, "The Chevalier d'Eon and Wilkes: masculinity and politics in the eighteenth century," *Eighteenth-Century Studies*, vol. 32, no. 1 (1998): 34.

80. Ibid., 37.
81. Kates, "The transgendered world of the chevalier/chevalière d'Eon": 590 and J.M.J. Rogister, "D'Éon de Beaumont, Charles Geneviève Louis Auguste André Timothée, Chevalier D'Éon in the French nobility (1728–1810)," *Oxford Dictionary of National Biography* (Oxford: Oxford University Press, 2004), accessed December 10, 2013. Available at http://www.oxforddnb.com/view/article/7523
82. John Harvey, *Men in Black* (London: Reaktion, 1995), 309.
83. Roche, *The Culture of Clothing,* 101.
84. Harvey, *Men in Black,* 128.
85. Karen Harvey, "The century of sex?".
86. Julie Park, *The Self and It: Novel Objects in Eighteenth-Century England* (Stanford: Stanford University Press, 2010), 59.
87. Valerie Steele, *Fetish: Fashion, Sex and Power* (Oxford: Oxford University Press, 1996), 12; and Dominic Janes, *Victorian Reformation: The Fight over Idolatry in the Church of England, 1840–1860* (Oxford: Oxford University Press, 2009), 16–18.
88. David Dabydeen, *Hogarth's Blacks: Images of Blacks in Eighteenth Century English Art* (Kingston-upon-Thames: Dangaroo Press, 1985), 37–9; and Catherine Molineux, "Hogarth's Fashionable Slaves: Moral Corruption in Eighteenth-Century London," *ELH,* vol. 72, no. 2 Summer (2005); and compare with colonial contexts discussed in Rebecca Earle, "'Two pairs of pink satin shoes!' Race, clothing and identity in the Americas (17th–19th centuries)," *History Workshop Journal,* vol. 52, issue 1 (2001): 184.
89. Tita Chico, *Designing Women: The Dressing Room in Eighteenth-Century English Literature and Culture* (Lewisburg: Bucknell University Press, 2005), 27.
90. Ibid., 44.
91. Mimi, Hellman, "Interior motives: seduction by decoration in eighteenth-century France," in *Dangerous Liaisons: Fashion and Furniture in the Eighteenth Century,* (eds) Harold Koda and Andrew Bolton (New Haven: Yale University Press, 2006), 23.
92. Gillian Perry and Michael Rossington (eds), *Femininity and Masculinity in Eighteenth-Century Art and Culture* (Manchester: Manchester University Press, 1994), 7.
93. Kuchta, *The Three-Piece Suit and Modern Masculinity,* 176.

Chapter 6

1. Per Stig Møller, *Den naturlige orden. 12 år der flyttede verden* (Copenhagen: Gyldendal, 1997), 11–42.
2. Jan de Vries, *The Industrious Revolution. Consumer Behavior and the Household Economy, 1650 to the Present* (Cambridge: Cambridge University Press, 2008).
3. Mikkel Venborg Pedersen, *Luksus. Forbrug og kolonier i Danmark i det 18. århundrede* (Copenhagen: Museum Tusculanum Press, 2013), 234–92.
4. Ibid.; Maxine Berg and Helen Clifford (eds), *Consumers and Luxury. Consumer Culture in Europe 1650–1850* (Manchester: Manchester University Press, 1999); Maxine Berg and Elisabeth Eger (eds), *Luxury in the Eighteenth Century. Debates, Desires and Delectable Goods* (London and Basingstoke: Palgrave Macmillan, 2003).
5. Beverly Lemire, *Fashion's Favourite. The Cotton Trade and the Consumer in Britain 1660–1800* (Oxford: Oxford University Press, 1991).
6. Norbert Elias, *The Civilizing Process. The History of Manners and State Formation and Civilization* (Oxford and Cambridge, MA: Blackwell, 1994).
7. Paraphrase of the original, which goes thus: "Ein Herzog muss sein Haus so bauen, dass es ausdrückt: ich bin ein Herzog und nicht nur ein Graf. Das gleiche gilt von seinem ganzen Austreten. Er kann nicht dulden, dass ein anderer herzoglicher auftritt als er selbst . . . Ein Herzog, der nicht wohnt, wie ein Herzog zu wohnen hat, der also auch die gesellschaftlichen Verpflichtungen eines Herzogs nicht mehr ordentlich erfüllen kann, ist schon fast kein Herzog mehr." Elias Norbert, *Die Höfische Gesellschaft. Untersuchungen zur Soziologie des*

Königtums und der höfischen Aristokratie mit einer Einleitung: Soziologie und Geschichtswissenschaft (Darmstadt, 1981 [original MS. c. 1930]), 99.

8. Mikkel Venborg Pedersen, *Hertuger. At synes og at være i Augustenborg 1700–1850* (Copenhagen: Museum Tusculanum Press, 2005).
9. Bernhard Jahn, Thomas Rahn, and Claudia Schnitzger (eds), *Zeremoniell in der Krise. Störung und Nostalgie* (Marburg: Jonas Verlag, 1998), Introduction.
10. See Alan Hunt, *Governance of Consuming Passions: A History of Sumptuary Law* (London and Basingtoke: Macmillan, 1996). For Denmark see Hanne Frøsig Dalgaard, *Luksusforordninger—1558, 1683, 1736, 1783, 1783 og 1799* (Copenhagen: special edition of the periodical *Tenen,* 1999–2001).
11. This follows from the teachings of English philosopher Thomas Hobbes (1588–1679).
12. From 1699 to 1848 and counting only specific ordinances on luxury, at least twenty-one such were issued, namely in 1699 (two), 1736, 1737, 1738, 1739, 1741, 1744, 1752, 1766 (two), 1769, 1775, 1780, 1783 (the last big one and another smaller), 1785, 1801, and 1848 (three).
13. Venborg Pedersen, *Luksus,* esp. 234–92.
14. Ibid., 32ff; Elizabeth Ewing, *Everyday Dress 1650–1900* (London: Batsford, 1984), 10–11.
15. Jacob Henric Schou, *Chronologisk Register over de Kongelige Forordninger og Aabne Breve samt andre trykte Anordninger som fra Aar 1670 af ere udkomne, tilligemed et nøiagtigt Udtog af de endnu gieldende, for saavidt samme i Almindelighed angaae Undersaaterne i Danmark, forsynet med et alphabetisk Register,* vol. III, 1730–46 (Copenhagen, 1822), 197–9. The quotation is from Schou's edition; the analysis in this chapter builds on his work.
16. Venborg Hanne Frøsig Dalgaard, "I fløjl og vadmel," in *Dagligliv i Danmark,* (ed.) Axel Steenberg vol. II, 1620–1720 (Copenhagen: Gyldendal, 1982), 11 and 19.
17. Ibid.
18. Axel Steensberg, *Dagligliv i Danmark,* vol. III, 1720–1790 (Copenhagen: Gyldendal, 1982), 8.
19. Venborg Pedersen, *Luksus.*
20. Ibid.
21. Berg and Clifford (eds), *Consumers and Luxury;* Daniel Roche, *A History of Everyday Things. The Birth of Consumption in France 1600–1800* (Cambridge: Cambridge University Press, 2000); Gudrun Andersson, *Stadens Dignitärer. Den lokale elitens status & maktmanifestation i Arboga 1650–1770* (Stockholm: Atlantis, 2009); Lorna Weatherhill, *Consumer Behaviour and Material Culture in Britain 1660–1760* (London: Routledge, 1996); Tove Engelhardt Matthiessen, Marie-Louise Nosch, Maj Ringgaard, Kirsten Toftegaard, and Mikkel Venborg Pedersen (eds), *Fashionable Encounters. Perspectives and Trends in Textile and Dress in the Early Modern Nordic World* (Oxford and Philidelphia: Oxbow Books, 2014).
22. Erna Lorenzen, "Modetøj og gangklæder," in *Dagligliv i Danmark,* vol. IV, 1720–90, (ed.) Axel Steensberg (Copenhagen: Gyldendal, 1982), 47–72.
23. Jacob Henric Schou, *Chronologisk Register,* vol. VIII, 1781–1784, 263–70.
24. Venborg Pedersen, *Luksus,* 55–6.
25. Schou, *Chronologisk Register,* vol. III 1730–1746, 197–9.
26. Venborg Pedersen, *Luksus,* 263; Berg and Eger (eds), *Luxury in the Eighteenth Century.*
27. *L'Encyclopédie ou Dictionaire Raisonné des Sciences, des Arts et des Metiers.* Tome XVII, halb-hiv (Paris, 1751–72), 697–9 and 699ff.
28. *Allgemein deutsche Real-Encyclopädie für die gebildeten Stände. Conversations-Lexikon. Neunte Originalauflage in fünfzehn Bänden* (Leipzig 1843 [1796]), 590 and 677.
29. The example of Jacob Gude is drawn from Nyrop-Christensen Henning, "Den honnette Ambition" in Axel Steensberg, *Dagligliv i Danmark,* vol. III, 1720–1790 (Copenhagen: Gyldendal, 1982), 172.

30. Cited in Nyrop-Christensen Henning, "Den honnette Ambition," in Axel Steensberg, *Dagligliv i Danmark*, vol. III, 1720–1790 (Copenhagen: Gyldendal, 1982), 157–8.

31. The seminal exception in English scholarship being John Styles, *The Dress of the People: Everyday Fashion in Eighteenth-Century England* (New Haven and London: Yale University Press, 2007).

32. Elizabeth Ewing, *Everyday Dress 1650–1900*, 7. Mikkel Venborg Pedersen, "Prologue" in Tove Engelhardt Matthiessen, et al (eds), *Fashionable Encounters,* xiii–xxiv.

33. Gitta Böth, "Kleidungsforschung," in *Grundriss der Volkskunde. Einführung in die Forschungsfelder der Europäischen Ethnologie,* (ed.) Rolf W. Brednich (Berlin: Dietrich Reimer Verlag, 1988), 153–71; Erna Lorenzen, "Modetøj og gangklæder," in *Dagligliv i Danmark*, vol. IV: 1720–1790, (ed.) Axel Steensberg (Copenhagen: Gyldendal, 1982), 47–72; Hanne Frøsig Dalgaard, "I fløjl og vadmel," in *Dagligliv i Danmark*, vol. II, 1620–1720, (ed.) Axel Steenberg (Copenhagen: Gyldendal, 1982), 7–32.

34. Venborg Pedersen, *Luksus,* 40–1. The terms "popular culture" and "elite culture," and their existence in two connected spheres I owe to the historian Peter Burke, *Venice and Amsterdam* (Cambridge: Polity Press, 1974).

35. Venborg Pedersen, "Peasant Featherbeds in 'Royal Attire'. The Consumption of Indigo in Early Modern Denmark," in *Beyond Tranquebar. Grappling Across Cultural Borders in South India,* (eds) Esther Fihl, and A.R. Venkatachalapathy (New Delhi: Orient Black Swann Publishers, 2014), 535–55.

36. Ellen Andersen, *Danske Bønders Klædedragt* (Copenhagen: Carit Andersens Forlag, 1960), 276–302. This section sums up decades of work by Ellen Andersen and others in the field of traditional costume and peasant dress in Denmark.

37. Andersen, *Danske Bønders Klædedragt*, 205–19.

38. John Barrell, *The Dark Side of the Landscape: The Rural Poor in English Painting 1730–1840* (Cambridge: Cambridge University Press, 1983); Michael Rosenthal, *Prospects for the Nation: Recent Essays in British Landscape, 1750–1880* (New Haven: Yale University Press, 1997); Lou Taylor, "Fashion and Dress History: Theoretical and Methodological Approaches," in *The Handbook of Fashion Studies*, (eds) Sandy Black, Amy de la Haye, Joanne Entwistle, Agnès Rocamora, Regina A. Root, and Helen Thomas (London: Bloomsbury, 2013).

39. H.P. Hansen, *Natmandsfolk og Kjæltringer i Vestjylland* (Copenhagen: Gyldendal, 1922).

40. Mikkel Venborg Pedersen, "Sleeping," in *Ethnologia Europeaea. Journal of European Ethnology* 35:1–2 (2005): 153–9.

41. Mikkel Venborg Pedersen, *Landscapes, Buildings, People. Guide to the Open Air Museum* (Copenhagen: The National Museum of Denmark, 2009); Alex Steensberg, *Danske Bondemøbler* (Copenhagen: Gyldendal, 1949), and *Den danske Bondegård* (Copenhagen: Gyldendal, 1972).

Chapter 7

1. *Le Mercure Galant* (1680): 350; *Magasin des modes nouvelles, françaises et anglaises* (January 10, 1787): 41.

2. Maxine Berg, *Luxury and Pleasure in Eighteenth-Century Britain* (Oxford: Oxford University Press, 2005), 331.

3. François Charpentier, *Discours d'un fidele sujet du Roy, touchant l'establissement d'une compagnie françoise pour le commerce des Indes orientales: adressé à tous les François* (Paris, 1664), 6–7.

4. Rosemary Crill, *Chintz: Indian Textiles for the West* (London: V&A Publications, 2008), 14–15.

5. Giorgio Riello, "The Indian Apprenticeship: The Trade of Indian Textiles and the Making of European Cottons," in *How India Clothed the World: The World of South Asian Textiles, 1500–1850*, (eds) Giorgio Riello and Tirthankar Roy (The Hague: Brill, 2008), 320.

6. Beverly Lemire and Giorgio Riello, "East and West: Textiles and Fashion in Early Modern Europe," *Journal of Social History*, 41, 4 Summer (2008): 887.

7. Crill, *Chintz,* 16. Imported textiles used for room furnishings tended to be relegated to smaller, less public room such as cabinets. Formal reception rooms would have been hung with European-made tapestries.

8. *Le Mercure Galant* (April 1681): 375.

9. Beverly Lemire, *Fashion's Favourite: The Cotton Trade and the Consumer in Britain, 1660–1800* (Oxford: Oxford University Press, 1991).

10. Beverly Lemire, "Fashioning Global Trade: Indian Textiles, Gender Meanings and European Consumers, 1500–1800," in *How India Clothed the World: The World of South Asian Textiles, 1500–1850,* (eds) Giorgio Riello and Tirthankar Roy (The Hague: Brill, 2008), 366–7.

11. Olivier Raveux, "Fashion and consumption of painted and printed calicoes in the Mediterranean during the later seventeenth century: the case of chintz quilts and banyans in Marseilles," *Textile History*, 45 (1), May (2014): 60.

12. Ibid., 51.

13. IS.4-1968, Victoria and Albert Museum, London.

14. Lesley Ellis Miller, "Material marketing: how lyonnais silk manufacturers sold silks, 1660–1789," in *Selling Textiles in the Long Eighteenth Century: Comparative Perspectives from Western Europe,* (eds) J. Stobart and B. Blondé (Basingstoke: Palgrave Macmillan, 2014), 85–98.

15. Aileen Ribeiro, *The Art of Dress: Fashion in England and France, 1750–1820* (New Haven and London: Yale University Press, 1995), 59.

16. Amelia Peck, *Interwoven Globe: The Worldwide Textile Trade, 1500–1800* (New Haven and London: Yale University Press), 297.

17. Berg, *Luxury and Pleasure in Eighteenth-Century Britain.*

18. *Arret du conseil d'etat du roy concernant les toiles de coton peintes aux Indes ou contrefaites dans le Royaume et autres etoffes de soie a fleurs d'or et d'argent de la Chine et des dites Indes*; October 16, 1686.

19. Lemire and Riello, "East and West": 898.

20. Jules Sottas, *Une Escadre Francaise aux Index en 1690. Histoire de la Compagnie des Indes* (Paris: 1903), 93

21. Lemire and Riello, "East and West": 898.

22. *Reflections sur les avantages de la libre fabrication et de l'usage des toiles peintes en France pour servir de réponse aux divers Mémoires des Fabriquans de Paris, Lyon, Tours, Rouen etc sur cette matière* (Genève, 1758), 38–9.

23. Friedrich Melchior von Grimm and Denis Diderot, *Correspondance inédite de Grimm et de Diderot* (Paris: H. Fournier: 1829), 16.

24. Kathleen Dejardin and Mary Schoeser, *French Textiles from 1760 to the Present* (London: Laurence King, 1991), 17.

25. Ina Baghdiantz McCabe, *A History of Global Consumption: 1500–1800* (London: Routledge, 2014), 170; *Femme de qualité en habit d'esté, d'etoffe Siamois*, Nicolas Arnoult, 1687; LACMA M.2002.57.66.

26. Victor Hugo, *Les Orientales* (Paris: Chamerot, 1882), vi.

27. Nicholas Dew, *Orientalism in France* (Oxford: Oxford University Press, 2009), 22–3.

28. Ibid., 41–80, 168–204.

29. Ibid., 177–9; Marie-Louis Dufrenoy, *L'Orient Romanesque en France, 1704–1789*, vol. 1 (Montreal: Beauchemin, 1946), 20–1.

30. Arianne Fennetaux, "Men in gowns: Nightgowns and the construction of masculinity in eighteenth-century England," *Immediations: The Research Journal of the Courtauld Institute of Art*, no.1 (Spring, 2004): 77–89.

31. Aileen Ribeiro, *A Visual History of Costume. The Eighteenth Century* (London: Batsford, 1983), 142; Oxford English Dictionary, http://www.oed.com/view/Entry/15222?redirectedFrom=banyan#eid28123163, [accessed April 15, 2015].

32. J.B. Molière, *Le Bourgeois Gentilhomme* (Paris: C. Barbin, 1673), 7.

33. Calankars are high quality Indian cottons. Olivier Raveux, "Fashion and consumption of painted and printed calicoes in the Mediterranean during the later seventeenth century: the case of chintz quilts and banyans in Marseilles," *Textile History*, 45 (1), May (2014): 55.

34. Beverly Lemire, *Cotton* (Oxford: Berg: 2011), 44–5.

35. This simultaneously contradicts Diderot's own description of his beloved dressing-gown described in his famous text *Regrets sur ma Vieille Robe de Chambre* published in 1772.

36. Raveux, "Fashion and consumption of painted and printed calicoes in the Mediterranean during the later seventeenth century": 53.

37. Museum of Fine Arts, Boston, Galerie des Modes et Costumes Français, 44.1476.

38. Richard Martin and Harold Koda, *Orientalism: Vision of the East in Western Dress* (New York: Metropolitan Museum of Art), 17; The *Mercure de France* of January 1726 refers to small flat sleeves as being "en pagoda": 10.

39. J.J. Rousseau, *Les Confessions* (Paris: Gennequin, 1869), 68; R.A. Leigh (ed), *Correspondance complète de J.J. Rousseau*, vol. 13 (Madison: 1971), letter no. 2.158, 57. A Mme de Luze, Môtiers September 13, 1762.

40. *Correspondance*, vol. 13, letter no. 2.189, 111. A Mme de Luze à Neuchâtel, Môtiers September 25, 1762.

41. *Correspondance,* vol. 14, letter no. 2.325, 79. A Mme Boy de la Tour, Môtiers November 23, 1762.

42. Ribeiro, *The Art of Dress*, 3–4.

43. Madeleine Delpierre, *Dress in France in the Eighteenth Century* (New Haven and London: Yale University Press, 1997), 67.

44. K. Scott, "Playing Games with Otherness: Watteau's Chinese Cabinet at the Château de la Muette," *Journal of the Warburg and Courtauld Institutes*, vol. 66, (2003): 189–248.

45. Monique Riccardi-Cubitt, "Grotesque," *Grove Art Online. Oxford Art Online.* Oxford University Press, http://www.oxfordartonline.com/subscriber/article/grove/art/T035099, [accessed May 2015].

46. See Perrin Stein, "Amédée Van Loo's Costume turc: The French Sultana," *The Art Bulletin*, vol. 78, no. 3 (1996): 429 and Emma Barker, "Mme Geoffrin, Painting and Galanterie: Carle Van Loo's Conversation espagnole and Lecture espagnole," *Eighteenth-Century Studies*, vol. 40, no. 4 (2007): 596.

47. Jean Leclant, "Le café et les cafés à Paris (1644–1693)," *Annales. Économies, Sociétés, Civilisations.* 6e année, N. 1 (1951): 8; Ina Baghdiantz McCabe, *Orientalism in Early Modern France: Eurasian Trade, Exoticism, and the Ancien Régime* (Oxford: Berg, 2008), 189–90.

48. John S. Powell, "The Bourgeois Gentilhomme: Molière and Music," in *The Cambridge Companion to Molière* (eds) David Bradby and Andrew Calder (Cambridge: Cambridge University Press, 2006), 121–5; Haydn Williams, *Turquerie, An Eighteenth-Century European Fantasy* (London: Thames and Hudson, 2014), 78–9.

49. Louise-Elisabeth Vigée-Lebrun, *Souvenirs de Madame Louise-Élisabeth Vigée-Lebrun*, vol. 1 (Paris: H. Fournier, 1835), 116.

50. William Driver Howarth, *French Theatre in the Neo-classical Era* (Cambridge: Cambridge University Press, 2009), 522–3.

51. Charles Simon Favart, *Mémoires et correspondance littéraires, dramatiques et anecdotiques*, vol. 1 (Paris, 1808), 77–78.

52. Joanne Olian, "Sixteenth-Century Costume Books," *Dress: The Journal of the Costume Society of America*, 3 (1977): 20–48; Gabriele Mentges, "Pour une approche renouvelée des recueils de costumes de la Renaissance. Une cartographie vestimentaire de l'espace et du temps," *Apparence(s)* [Online], 1|2007, online since June 1, 2007, http://apparences.revues. org/104, [accessed May 10, 2015]; McCabe, *Orientalism in Early Modern France,* 235.

53. This was not the first instance of a public royal or aristocratic Turkish impersonation. In a carrousel held in 1559, Henri II had worn such a costume and had also lead an army of French princes wearing Turkish clothes.

54. Laurent Lacroix, "Quand les Français jouaient aux sauvages . . . ou le carrousel de 1662," *Journal of Canadian Art History*, no. 1–2 (1976): 44–54.

55. Williams, *Turquerie,* 93.

56. Michael Elia Yonan, *Empress Maria Theresa and the Politics of Habsburg Imperial Art* (University Park, PA: Pennsylvania State University Press, 2011), 148.

57. Williams, *Turquerie,* 51.

58. Aileen Ribeiro, *Dress in Eighteenth-Century Europe* (New York: Holmes and Meier, 1984), 178.

59. Perrin Stein, "Madame de Pompadour and the Harem Imagery at Bellevue," *Gazette des Beaux-Arts*, 123 (January 1994): 29–45.

60. Aileen Ribeiro, *Fashion in the French Revolution* (New York: Holmes and Meier, 1988), 39.

61. *Cabinet des modes, ou les Modes nouvelles, décrites d'une manière claire & précise, & représentées par des planches en taille-douce, enluminées*, 1785, 34.

62. Delpierre, *Dress in France in the Eighteenth Century*, 18–20.

63. Kimberly Chrisman-Campbell, *Fashion Victims: Dress at the Court of Louis XVI and Marie-Antoinette* (New Haven and London: Yale University Press, 2015), 77.

64. *Magasin des modes nouvelles, françaises et anglaises, décrites d'une manière claire & précise, & représentées par des planches en taille-douce, enluminées*, November 20, 178: 5.

65. Museum of Fine Arts, Boston, accession number 44.1436.

66. Meredith Martin, "Tipu Sultan's Ambassadors at Saint-Cloud: Indomania and Anglophobia in Pre-Revolutionary Paris," *West 86th*, vol. 21, no. 1 (Spring–Summer 2014): 37–68.

67. Ibid., 49.

68. See Natacha Coquery, "Les boutiquiers parisiens et la diffusion des *indienneries* au dix-huitième siècle," in *Le goût de l'Inde*, (eds) G. Le Bouedec and B. Nicolas (Rennes: PUR, 2008), 74–81. See also Pierre Verlet, "Le commerce des objets d'art et les marchands merciers à Paris au XVIIIe siècle," *Annales, Économies, Sociétés, Civilisations*. 13e année, no. 1 (1958): 10–29. Gersaint's new name is mentioned in *Le Mercure de France*, Octobre 1739: 2442.

69. *Magasin de Modes Nouvelles*, January 30, 1787: 61–3.

70. Quoted in Jennifer M. Jones, "Repackaging Rousseau: Femininity and Fashion in Old Regime France, French," *Historical Studies*, vol. 18, no. 4 (Autumn, 1994): 943–4.

71. Jennifer M. Jones, "Repackaging Rousseau: Femininity and Fashion in Old Regime France," *French Historical Studies*, vol. 18, no. 4 (Autumn, 1994): 943–4.

72. Pierre-Jean-Baptiste Nougaret, *Les sottises et les folies parisiennes. Partie 1 /; aventures diverses, &c. avec quelques pièces curieuses & fort rares: le tout fidèlement recueilli par M. Nougaret* (Paris: Duchesne, 1781), 65.

73. *Cabinet des Modes*, June 1, 1786: 110.

74. *Magasin des Modes Nouvelles*, May 20, 1787: 149.

75. Chrisman-Campbell, *Fashion Victims,* 246.

76. Laura Brace, "Rousseau, Maternity and the Politics of Emptiness," *Polity*, vol. 39, no. 3 (July, 2007): 364; Jones, "Repackaging Rousseau": 946–7; see also Carol Duncan, "Happy Mothers and Other New Ideas in French Art," *The Art Bulletin*, vol. 55, no. 4 (December 1973): 570–83.

77. Aileen Ribeiro, *Dress and Morality* (London, Batsford, 1986), 115.

78. Ribeiro, *The Art of Dress*.

79. E. Claire Cage, "The Sartorial Self: Neoclassical Fashion and Gender Identity in France, 1797–1804," *Eighteenth-Century Studies,* 42, 2: 208.

80. Sonia Ashmore, *Muslin* (London: V&A Publications, 2012), 64.

Chapter 8

1. *Spectator*, June 21, 1712.
2. *Spectator*, April 26, 1711.
3. Ibid.
4. *Spectator*, March 12, 1711.
5. Jürgen Habermas, *The Structural Transformation of the Public Sphere*, trans. Thomas Burger (Cambridge: Polity Press, 1989 [1962]), 43.
6. See Erin Mackie, *Market à la Mode: Fashion, Commodity and Gender in the* Tatler *and the* Spectator (Baltimore: Johns Hopkins University Press, 1997).
7. On the rise of "picture shops" at the turn of the seventeenth century, see Timothy Clayton, *The English Print, 1688–1802* (New Haven: Yale University Press, 1997), 3–10.
8. The so-called "Postures" are a famous erotic work of the time, featuring pornographic engravings accompanied by poems from Renaissance poet Pietro Aretino.
9. *London Spy*, March 1699: 3.
10. See Mark Hallett, *The Spectacle of Difference: Graphic Satire in the Age of Hogarth* (New Haven: Yale University Press, 1999), 181.
11. For the rise of commercial prints and the bustling eighteenth-century culture of print, see Clayton, *The English Print*, esp. 3–23, 105–28.
12. Chandra Mukerji, *From Graven Images: Patterns of Modern Materialism* (New York: Columbia University Press, 1983), 38.
13. Hallett, *The Spectacle of Difference*, 1.
14. On the (limited) value of pictures for the reconstruction of historical dress, see Lou Taylor, "Fashion and Dress History: Theoretical and Methodological Approaches," in *The Handbook of Fashion Studies*, (ed.) Sandy Black et al. (London: Bloomsbury, 2013).
15. Mukerji, *From Graven Images*, 170.
16. Aileen Ribeiro, *Fashion and Fiction: Dress in Art and Literature in Stuart England* (New Haven, London: Yale University Press, 2005), 254; see also Doris Langley Moore, *Fashion through Fashion Plates, 1771–1970* (London: Ward, 1971), 11.
17. See Lambert Wiesing, *Das Mich der Wahrnehmung. Eine Autopsie* (Frankfurt a.M.: Suhrkamp, 2009), 122.
18. J. Paul Hunter, "The World as Stage and Closet," in *British Theatre and the Other Arts, 1660–1800*, (ed.) Shirley Strum Kenny (Washington et al: Folger, 1984), 285.
19. Clayton, *The English Print*, xi.
20. See Jonathan Crary, *Techniques of the Observer: On Vision and Modernity in the Nineteenth Century* (Cambridge, MA and London: MIT Press, 1990), 42–5.
21. Hans Jonas, "The Nobility of Sight: A Study in the Phenomenology of the Senses," in *The Phenomenon of Life: Toward a Philosophical Biology*, (ed.) Hans Jonas (Chicago: University of Chicago Press, 1982 [1966]), 147.
22. Barbara J. Shapiro, *A Culture of Fact: England, 1550–1720* (Ithaca: Cornell University Press, 2000), 64.
23. See Ulrike Ilg, "The Cultural Significance of Costume Books in Sixteenth-century Europe," in *Clothing Culture, 1350–1650*, (ed.) Catherine Richardson (Aldershot: Ashgate, 2004).
24. Valerie Traub, "Mapping the Global Body," in *Early Modern Visual Culture: Representations, Race, and Empire in Renaissance England*, (eds) Peter Ericson and Clark Hulse (Philadelphia: University of Pennsylvania Press, 2000), 51.
25. See ibid., 80.
26. See Elisabeth Wilson, *Adorned in Dreams: Fashion and Modernity*, rev. (ed.) (London: Tauris, 2003 [1985]), 20; John L. Nevinson, *Origin and Early History of the Fashion Plate* (Washington: Smithsonian, 1967), 70.
27. For the importance of print in the development of regional stereotypes, see Elisabeth L. Eisenstein, *The Printing Press as an Agent of Change: Communications and Cultural*

Transformation in Early-Modern Europe (Cambridge: Cambridge University Press, 1979), 84–5.

28. Madeleine Ginsburg, *An Introduction to Fashion Illustration* (London: V&A, 1980), 5.

29. Thomas Keymer and Peter Sabor, *Pamela in the Marketplace: Literary Controversy and Print Culture in Eighteenth-Century Britain and Ireland* (Cambridge: Cambridge University Press, 2005), 5.

30. See Christian Huck, *Fashioning Society, or, The Mode of Modernity: Observing Fashion in Eighteenth-Century Britain* (Würzburg: Königshausen & Neumann, 2010), 181–200.

31. For the whole story of visualizations, see Keymer and Sabor, *Pamela in the Marketplace*, 143–76.

32. Ibid.

33. Anne Buck, "Pamela's Clothes," *Costume* 26 (1992): 21–31.

34. Samuel Richardson (1971 [1740]), *Pamela, or, Virtue Rewarded*, (eds) T.C. Duncan Eaves and Ben D. Kimpel (Boston et al.: Houghton Mifflin), 30–1.

35. Cynthia Wall, *The Prose of Thing: Transformations of Description in the Eighteenth Century* (Chicago: University of Chicago Press, 2006), 9.

36. See Stephen A. Raynie, "Hayman and Gravelot's Anti-*Pamela* Designs for Richardson's Octavo Edition of *Pamela I* and *II*," *Eighteenth-Century Life* 23, no. 3 (1999): 77–93.

37. Aileen Ribeiro, "Reading Dress in Hogarth's 'Marriage-a-la-Mode'," *Apollo* CXLVII, no. 432 (1998): 49.

38. See Christine Riding, "The Harlot and the Rake," in *Hogarth*, (eds) Mark Hallett and Christine Riding (London: Tate, 2006).

39. Clayton, *The English Print*, 23.

40. Ronald Paulson, "Emulative Consumption and Literacy: The Harlot, Moll Flanders, and Mrs. Slipslop," in *The Consumption of Culture 1600–1800: Image, Object, Text*, (eds) Ann Bermingham and John Brewer (London: Routledge, 1995), 385.

41. John D. Lyons, "Speaking in Pictures, Speaking of Pictures: Problems of Representation in the Seventeenth Century," in *Mimesis: From Mirror to Method, Augustine to Descartes*, (eds) John D. Lyons and Stephen G. Nichols, Jr. (Hanover: University Press of New England, 1982), 166.

42. Susanne Lüdemann, "Beobachtungsverhältnisse. Zur (Kunst)Geschichte der Beobachtung zweiter Ordnung," in *Widerstände der Systemtheorie: Kulturtheoretische Analysen zum Werk von Niklas Luhmann*, (eds) Albrecht Koschorke and Cornelia Vismann (Berlin: Akademie Verlag, 1999), 66; my translation.

43. Paulson, "Emulative Consumption and Literacy," 391.

44. See Peter Wagner, *Reading Iconotexts. From Swift to the French Revolution* (London: Reaktion Books, 1995), 263–6.

45. Ibid., 26–8.

46. Charles Lamb, "On the Genius and Character of Hogarth," *The Reflector* III (1811), 62; cf. Frédéric Ogée and Olivier Meslay, "William Hogarth and Modernity," in *Hogarth*, (eds) Mark Hallett and Christine Riding (London: Tate, 2006), 23–9.

47. *Spectator*, March 5, 1711.

48. Ben Jonson, *Discoveries* (1641); quoted after Ben Jonson, *The Works of Ben Johnson* [sic]. vol. 6. (1716), 276.

49. *The Midwife, or the Old Woman's Magazine*, October 1750: 182–3.

50. George Vertue, *Vertue Note Books*, vol. 3 (Oxford: Oxford University Press, 1934), 58.

51. William Hogarth, "Autobiographical Notes," in: *The Analysis of Beauty, with the Rejected Passages from the Manuscript Drafts and Autobiographical Notes*, (ed.) Joseph Burke (Oxford: Clarendon, 1955), 208.

52. Amelia Rauser, "Hair, Authenticity, and the Self-Made Macaroni," *Eighteenth-Century Studies* 38, vol. 1 (2004): 101–17.

53. See Peter McNeil, "'That Doubtful Gender': Macaroni Dress and Male Sexualities," *Fashion Theory* 3, vol. 4 (1999): 411–48.

54. See Diana Donald, *The Age of Caricature: Satirical Prints in the Reign of George III* (New Haven: Yale University Press, 1996), 75–108.

55. Lennard J. Davis, *Factual Fictions: The Origins of the English Novel* (New York: Columbia University Press, 1983), 72.

56. Ibid., 73.

57. Beverly Lemire, *Fashion's Favourite: The Cotton Trade and the Consumer in Britain 1600–1800* (Oxford: Oxford University Press, 1991), 168.

58. Ibid., 169.

59. Huck, *Fashioning Society*, 296.

60. Alison Adburgham, *Women in Print: Writing Women and Women's Magazines from the Restoration to the Accession of Victoria* (London: Allen and Unwin, 1972), 128–30.

61. *The Lady's Magazine; or Entertaining Companion for the Fair Sex, appropriated solely to their Use and Amusement* 1, vol. 1 (1770), 2.

62. Lemire, *Fashion's Favourite*, 170.

63. Nevinson, *Origin and Early History of the Fashion Plate*, 87.

64. See Moore, *Fashion through Fashion Plates*, p. 10.

65. *The Lady's Magazine; or Entertaining Companion for the Fair Sex, appropriated solely to their Use and Amusement*, May 1773, 233; my emphasis.

66. Nevinson, *Origin and Early History of the Fashion Plate*, 67; my emphasis.

67. Adburgham, *Women in Print*, 204.

68. *Gallery of Fashion*, April 1794, 1.

69. Adburgham, *Women in Print*, 206.

70. Ibid., 207–35.

71. *Gallery of Fashion*, April 1794, 2.

Chapter 9

1. Richard Steele, *The Tatler* "Dedication to Mr. Maynwaring" 1709, in *The Commerce of Everyday Life: Selections from* The Tatler *and* The Spectator, (ed.) Erin Mackie (Boston: Bedford/St. Martins, 1998), 47.

2. Jane Austen, *Northanger Abbey* (Oxford: Oxford University Press, 1998 [1818]), 24.

3. Erin Mackie, *Market à la Mode: Fashion, Commodity, and Gender in* The Tatler *and* The Spectator (Baltimore: Johns Hopkins University Press, 1997), 25.

4. Jennie Batchelor, *Dress, Distress and Desire: Clothing the Female Body in Eighteenth-Century Literature* (Houndmills: Palgrave Macmillan, 2005), 89.

5. Richard Steele, *The Spectator* No. 478 Monday, September 8, 1712, in *The Commerce of Everyday Life: Selections from* The Tatler *and* The Spectator, (ed.) Erin Mackie (Boston: Bedford/St. Martins, 1998), 398.

6. Steele, *The Spectator* No. 478, 399.

7. Ibid.

8. "Fashion doll with accessories," Victoria and Albert Museum, vam.ac.uk http://collections.vam.ac.uk/item/O100708/fashion-doll-with-unknown/ [accessed June 9, 2014].

9. See also Peter McNeil, "Beauty in Search of Knowledge", HERA FEM in press.

10. Julie Park, *The Self and It: Novel Objects in Eighteenth-Century England* (Stanford: Stanford University Press, 2010), 106.

11. Neil McKendrick, "The Commercialization of Fashion," in Neil McKendrick, John Brewer and J.H. Plumb (eds), *The Birth of a Consumer Society: The Commercialization of Eighteenth-Century England* (Bloomington: Indiana University Press, 1982), 49.

12. Ibid., 48.

13. Batchelor, *Dress, Distress and Desire*, 109.

14. "Parisian Evening Dress," *Belle Assemblée*, no. 81, March, 1816.

15. William H. Pyne, *Pyne's British Costumes: An illustrated survey of early eighteenth-century dress in the British Isles* (Ware: Wordsworth Editions, 1989), ii–iii.

16. Chloe Wigston Smith, "Dressing the British: Clothes, Customs, and Nation in W.H. Pyne's *The Costume of Great Britain*," *Studies in Eighteenth-Century Culture*, 38 (2009), 144.
17. Ibid., 144.
18. Paula Rea Radisich, "The *Cris de Paris* in the LACMA *Recueil des modes*," in Kathryn Norberg and Sandra Rosenbaum (eds), *Fashion Prints in the Age of Louis XIV: Interpreting the Art of Elegance* (Lubbock: Texas Tech University Press, 2014), 55, 66.
19. Sean Shesgreen, "'The Manner of Crying Things in London': Style, Authorship, Chalcography, and History," *Huntington Library Quarterly*, 59.4 (1996): 426.
20. R.T. Godfrey, *Wenceslaus Hollar: A Bohemian Artist in England* (New Haven: Yale University Press, 1994), 80–1.
21. William Wycherley, *The Country Wife*, 1675, in *Three Restoration Comedies*, (ed.) Gamini Salgado (London: Penguin Books, 1986), 189.
22. Mackie, *Commerce of Everyday Life*, 214.
23. Wycherley, *The Country Wife*, 193.
24. Ibid, p. 199.
25. Oliver Goldsmith, *She Stoops to Conquer*, 1773, in *Four English Comedies of the 17th and 18th Centuries*, (ed.) J.M. Morrell (London: Penguin Books, 1985), 271.
26. Frances Burney, *The Witlings*, 1778–80, in *The Broadview Anthology of British Literature: Volume 3, The Restoration and Eighteenth Century*, (eds) Joseph Black et al. (Peterborough: Broadview Press, 2006), 801.
27. Chloe Wigston Smith, *Women, Work, and Clothes in the Eighteenth-Century Novel* (Cambridge: Cambridge University Press, 2013), 162.
28. Burney, *The Witlings*, 803.
29. John Gay, *Trivia: Or, The Art of Walking the Streets of London*, 1716, in *Walking the Streets of Eighteenth-Century London: John Gay's Trivia*, (eds) Clare Brant and Susan E. Whyman (Oxford: Oxford University Press, 2007), 175–6, ll. 1.209–22.
30. Ibid., 176, ll. 1.238–40.
31. Ibid., 177, ll. 1.278–80.
32. Robin Ganev, "Milkmaids, Ploughmen, and Sex," *Journal of the History of Sexuality*, 16.1 (2007): 42.
33. Lucy Pratt and Linda Woolley, *Shoes* (London: Victoria and Albert Publishing, 2008), 41–2.
34. Sean Shesgreen, *The Criers and Hawkers of London: Engravings and Drawings by Marcellus Laroon* (Stanford: Stanford University Press, 1990), 104.
35. Gay, *Trivia*, 201, ll. 3.267–72, 275–6, 279–83.
36. Ibid., 201, ll. 3.281.
37. Roger Lonsdale (ed.), *Eighteenth-Century Women Poets* (Oxford: Oxford University Press, 1990), 171.
38. Mary Collier, *The Woman's Labour. An Epistle to Mr Stephen Duck*, [*The Washerwoman*], in Roger Lonsdale (ed.), *Eighteenth-Century Women Poets* (Oxford: Oxford University Press, 1990), 173, ll. 15–21.
39. Styles, *The Dress of the People*, 80.
40. Collier, *The Woman's Labour*, 173, ll. 58–9.
41. Anna Laetitia Barbauld, "Washing-Day," in *Eighteenth-Century Women Poets*, (ed.) Roger Lonsdale (Oxford: Oxford University Press, 1990), 308, ll. 8–14.
42. Ibid., 310, ll. 76–86.
43. For a discussion of the genre and the ways that critics have defined it see Liz Bellamy, "It-Narrators and Circulation: Defining a Sub-Genre," in *The Secret Life of Things: Animals, Objects, and It-Narratives in Eighteenth-Century England*, (ed.) Mark Blackwell (Lewisburg: Bucknell University Press, 2007), 117–46.
44. Christina Lupton (ed.), *British It-Narratives, 1750–1830. Volume 3: Clothes and Transportation* (London: Pickering and Chatto, 2012), xi.

45. Bonnie Blackwell, "Corkscrews and Courtesans: Sex and Death in Circulation Novels," in *The Secret Life of Things: Animals, Objects, and It-Narratives in Eighteenth-Century England*, (ed.) Mark Blackwell (Lewisburg: Bucknell University Press, 2007), 266.
46. Ibid.
47. *The History and Adventures of a Lady's Slippers and Shoes. Written by Themselves* (London: M. Cooper, 1754), 4.
48. Ibid., 28.
49. Lupton, *British It-Narratives*, xxi.
50. M. de Garsault, *Art of the Shoemaker*, trans. D.A. Saguto (Williamsburg: Colonial Williamsburg Foundation in Association with Texas Tech University Press, 2009), 78.
51. *History and Adventures*, 26.
52. Ibid., 9.
53. *History and Adventures*, 53.
54. Ibid., 44.
55. Wigston Smith, *Women, Work, and Clothes*, 73.
56. Daniel Defoe, *Roxana: Or, The Fortunate Mistress*, 1724, (ed.) John Mullan (Oxford: Oxford University Press, 2008), 1.
57. Ibid., 211.
58. Eliza Haywood, *Fantomina: or, Love in a Maze*, 1725, in *The Broadview Anthology of British Literature: Volume 3, The Restoration and Eighteenth Century*, (eds) Joseph Black et al. (Peterborough: Broadview Press, 2006), 519.
59. Ibid.
60. Aileen Ribeiro, *Dress in Eighteenth-century Europe, 1715–1789* (New York: Holmes and Meier Publishers, Inc., 1985), 42.
61. Samuel Richardson, *Pamela; or, Virtue Rewarded*, (eds) Thomas Keymer and Alice Wakely (Oxford: Oxford University Press, 2008), 55.
62. Ibid., 57.
63. Terry Castle, *Masquerade and Civilization: The Carnivalesque in Eighteenth-Century English Culture and Fiction* (Stanford: Stanford University Press, 1986), 119.
64. Joe Snader, "The Masquerade of Colonial Identity in Frances Brooke's *Emily Montague* (1769)" in *The Clothes that Wear Us: Essays on Dressing and Transgressing in Eighteenth-Century Culture*, (eds) Jessica Munns and Penny Richards (Newark: University of Delaware Press, 1999), 140.
65. Frances Brooke, *The History of Emily Montague*, 1769 (Toronto: McClelland and Steward Ltd., 2008), 85.
66. Frances Burney, *Camilla: or, A Picture of Youth*, 1796, (eds) Edward A. Bloom and Lillian D. Bloom (Oxford: Oxford University Press, 1983), 607.
67. Ibid., 608.
68. Ibid., 607.
69. Ibid., 611–12.
70. Elizabeth Kowelski-Wallace, *Women, Shopping, and Business in the Eighteenth Century* (New York: Columbia University Press, 1997), 96.
71. Burney, *Camilla*, 611.
72. Henry Fielding, *The History of Tom Jones, a Foundling*, 1749, (eds) Thomas Keymer and Alice Wakely (London: Penguin Books, 2005), 480.
73. Ibid., 556.
74. Ibid., 565.
75. Sophie Gee, *Making Waste: Leftovers and the Eighteenth-Century Imagination* (Princeton: Princeton University Press, 2010), 142.
76. Linda Baumgarten, *What Clothes Reveal: The Language of Clothing in Colonial and Federal America* (New Haven: Yale University Press, 2002), 213–14.

77. Daniel Roche, *The Culture of Clothing: Dress and fashion in the ancien régime*, trans. Jean Birrell (Cambridge: Cambridge University Press, 1994), 406.
78. Austen, *Northanger Abbey*, 13.
79. Ibid.
80. Ibid., 14.
81. Ibid.

BIBLIOGRAPHY

Manuscript Sources

British Library, India Office Records/G//12/53, Ship's Diary 1749–51.

British Library, India Office Records IOR/ G/12/43, Ship's Diary 1736/7. Ships Sussex and Winchester, 66–7.

British Library, India Office Records IOR/G/12/16 Diary & Consultation, 1685–6.

British Library, /E/1/206, Miscellaneous Letters, 17 April 1746.

National Archives London (TNA), High Court of Admiralty (HCA) 30.

Print Bibliography

"Inventaire des marchandises et effets de colporteur [Hubert Jenniard] déclarés par Corentine Penchoat, à Crozon, le 6 Février 1761," Archives départementales du Finistère, 18B, inventaire des pièces de la procedure criminelle instruite à Crozon, le 27.2.1762, cited in Didier Cadiou, "La vie quotidienne dans les paroisses littorales de Camouet, Crozon, Roscankel et Telgnac, d'après les inventaires après décès," mémoire de maîtres dactyl (*maîtrise*) Université Brest, 1990, t. II, 100.

Abu Lughod, J. (1989), *Before European Hegemony: the World System A.D. 1250–1350*, New York: Oxford University Press.

Adburgham, Alison (1972), *Women in Print: Writing Women and Women's Magazines from the Restoration to the Accession of Victoria*, London: Allen and Unwin.

Allard, Julie (2007), "Perceptions nouvelles du corps et raisons médicales de la mode dans la deuxième moitié du XVIIIe siècle," in Isabelle Billaud and Marie-Christine Laperrière (eds), *Représentations du corps sous l'Ancien Régime. Discours et pratiques,* 13–30, Laval: Cahiers du CIERL.

Allgemein deutsche Real-Encyclopädie für die gebildeten Stände. Conversations-Lexikon: Neunte Originalauflage in fünfzehn Bänden (1843[1796]), Leipzig.

Alm, Mikael (2015), "'Social Imaginary' im Schweden des späten 18. Jahrhunderts," in (ed.) D. Freist, *Diskurse—Körper—Artefakte. Historische Praxeologie in der Frühneuzeitforschung*, 267–86, Bielefeld: transcript Verlag.

Ames, Richard (1688), *Sylvia's revenge, or, A satyr against man in answer to the Satyr against woman*, London.

"An ACCOUNT of the KING's BIRTH-DAY' (1792), *The Weekly entertainer: or, Agreeable and instructive repository*, June 11.

An Act of Prohibiting the Importing of Any Wines, Wooll or Silk from the Kingdom of France, England or Ireland, or any the Dominations thereunto London.

Andersen, Ellen (1960), *Danske Bønders Klædedragt*, Copenhagen: Carit Andersens Forlag.

—— (1977), *Danske dragter: Moden i 1700-årene*, København: Nationalmuseet.

Andersson, Gudrun (2009), *Stadens Dignitärer: Den lokala elitens status & maktmanifestation i Arboga 1650–1770*, Stockholm: Atlantis.

Anon. (1685), *A Particular of Goods; Cargoe, of two Ships Arrived from India the 19th and 20th of June 1685. viz. The Henry and William from the Bay of Bengal, and the East-India Merchant, from Surrat*, London.

—— (1694), *Adventures of the Helvetian Hero, with the young Countess of Albania, or The amours of Armadorus and Vicentina, a novel*, London.

—— (1764), "News," *Gazetteer and New Daily Advertiser,* October 27.

—— (1772a), "News," *Bingley's London Journal,* September 12–19.

—— (1772b), "News," *London Evening News,* August 6.

—— (1772c), "News," *Morning Chronicle and London Advertiser,* August 8.

—— (1773), *The Vauxhall Affray; or, the Macaronies Defeated*, London: J. Williams.

—— (1788), *Ladies' daily companion for the year of our Lord 1789: embellished with the following copper plates: an elegant representation of the discovery of the Earl of Leicester from the Recess, a lady in the dress of 1788, and four of the most fashionable head dresses . . .* Canterbury: Simmons and Kirkby, inscribed on the flyleaf: "Given me by the honble Cosmo Gordon, Margate, Novr ye 21st 1788," Lewis Walpole Library, Yale University, LWL MSS vol. 3.

—— (2012 [1760]), "The Adventures of a Black Coat," in Christina Lupton (ed.), *British It-Narratives, 1750–1830. Volume 3: Clothes and Transportation*, London: Pickering and Chatto.

Appleby, Joyce (1993), "Consumption in early modern social thought," in J. Brewer and R. Porter (eds), *Consumption and the World of Goods*, London and New York: Routledge, 162–73.

Archenholz, M.D. (1789), *A Picture of England; Containing a description of the laws, customs, and manners of England . . .* vol. I, London: Edward Jeffery.

"Art. Kleidung" (1791), in *Oekonomische Encyklopädie oder allgemeines System der Staats-Stadt- Haus- und Landwirthschaft,* (ed.) Johann G. Krünitz.

"Art. Mode, die" (1804), in *Oekonomische Encyklopädie oder allgemeines System der Staats-Stadt- Haus- und Landwirthschaft,* (ed.) Johann G. Krünitz.

"Art. Mode, S.f." (1738–42), in *Dictionnaire de Trévoux*, trans. Dagmar Freist, 1301, Nancy: Edition Lorraine.

Ashmore, Sonia (2012), *Muslin*, London: V&A Publications.

Atwood, Emma K. (2013), "Fashionably late: queer temporality and the Restoration fop," *Comparative Drama*, vol. 47, no. 1: 85–111.

Austen, Jane (1998 [1818]), *Northanger Abbey*, Oxford: Oxford University Press.

Barker, Emma (2007), "Mme Geoffrin, Painting and Galanterie: Carle Van Loo's Conversation espagnole and Lecture espagnole," *Eighteenth-Century Studies*, vol. 40, no. 4: 587–614.

Barrell, John (1983), *The Dark Side of the Landscape: The Rural Poor in English Painting 1730–1840*, Cambridge: Cambridge University Press.

Batchelor, Jennie (2005), *Dress, Distress and Desire: Clothing the Female Body in Eighteenth-Century Literature*, Houndmills: Palgrave Macmillan.

Baumgarten, Linda (1986), *Eighteenth Century Clothing At Williamsburg*, Williamsburg: The Colonial Williamsburg Foundation.

—— (2002), *What Clothes Reveal: The Language of Clothing in Colonial and Federal America*, New Haven: Yale University Press.

Belfanti, Carlo Marco (2009), "New Approaches to Fashion and Emotion: The Civilization of Fashion: At the Origins of a Western Social Institution," *Journal of Social History*, vol. 43, no. 2 Winter: 261–83.

Bellegarde, abbé de (1719), *Modèles de conversations pour les personnes polies,* par M. l'Abbé de Bellegarde (1648–1734), 6e édition, augmentée d'une "Conversation sur les Modes," La Haye: chez Guillaume de Voys.

Benson, John and Laura Ugolini (eds) (2003), *A Nation of Shopkeepers: Five Centuries of British Retailing*. London: Tauris & Co.

Berg, Maxine (2001), "Manufacturing the Orient: Asian Commodities and European Industry 1500–1800," *Proceedings of the Istituto Internazionale di Storia Economica "F. Datini*," 32: 519–56.

—— (2005), *Luxury and Pleasure in Eighteenth-Century Britain*, Oxford: Oxford University Press.

Berg, Maxine and Helen Clifford (eds) (1999), *Consumers and Luxury: Consumer Culture in Europe 1650–1850*, Manchester: Manchester University Press.

Berg, Maxine and Elisabeth Eger (eds) (2003), *Luxury in the Eighteenth Century: Debates, Desires and Delectable Goods*. London and Basingstoke: Palgrave & Macmillan.

Bertuch, Friedrich Justin and Georg Melchior Kraus (eds) (1786), *Das Journal des Luxus und der Moden,* (Weimar: 1786–1826), February.

Black, Jeremy (2003), *Italy and the Grand Tour,* New Haven: Yale University Press.

Blackwell, Bonnie (2007), "Corkscrews and Courtesans: Sex and Death in Circulation Novels," in Mark Blackwell (ed.), *The Secret Life of Things: Animals, Objects, and It-Narratives in Eighteenth-Century England*, Lewisburg: Bucknell University Press, 265–92.

Bohanan, Donna J. (2012), *Fashion Beyond Versailles: Consumption and Design in Seventeenth-Century France*, Baton Rouge: Louisiana State University Press.

Bologne, Jean-Claude (2011), *Histoire de la coquetterie masculine*, Paris: Perrin.

Bonnaud, Jacques (1770), *Dégradation de l'espèce humaine par l'usage des corps à baleine*. Paris: Herissant.

Booth, Mark (1999), "*Campe-toi!* On the origins and definitions of camp," in Fabio Cleto (ed.), *Camp: Queer Aesthetics and the Performing Subject: A Reader*, Edinburgh: Edinburgh University Press, 66–79.

Börste, Norbert and Georg Eggenstein (2013), "Mode und Uniform—Mode im Military Style," in *Die Tanzhusaren 1813, 1913, 2013*, exhibition catalog (Krefeld: Museum Burg Linn).

Böth, Gitta (1988), "Kleidungsforschung," in *Grundriss der Volkskunde. Einführung in die Forschungsfelder der Europäischen Ethnologie*, (ed.) Rolf W. Brednich, 153–171, Berlin: Dietrich Reimer Verlag.

Boucher, François (1987 [1966]), *A History of Costume in the West,* trans. John Ross, new edition. London: Thames and Hudson.

Bourdieu, Pierre (1977), *Outline of a Theory of Practice*, Cambridge: Cambridge University Press.

—— (1985), "The Social Space and the Genesis of Groups," *Theory and Society*, vol. 14, issue 6: 723–44.

—— (1986), "The Forms of Capital," in J.G. Richardson (ed.), *Handbook of Theory and Research for the Sociology of Education*, New York: Greenwood Press, 241–58.

Brace, Laura (2007), "Rousseau, Maternity and the Politics of Emptiness," *Polity*, vol. 39, no. 3 July: 361–83.

Brathwait, Richard (1641[1631]), "The English Gentlewoman, Drawne Out to the Full Body," in *The English Gentleman and English Gentelwoman, Both in one Volume couched* (. . .), 3rd (ed.) 323–4, London.

Breward, Christopher (1995), *The Culture of Fashion: A New History of Fashionable Dress*, Manchester: Manchester University Press.

Brewer, John (1997), *The Pleasures of the Imagination: English Culture in the Eighteenth Century*, London: Harper Collins.

Bridgeman, Jane (1998), "Beauty, Dress and Gender," in Francis Ames-Lewis and Mary Rogers (eds), *Concepts of Beauty in Renaissance Art*, Aldershot: Ashgate, 44–51.

Brooke, Frances (2008 [1769]), *The History of Emily Montague*, Toronto: McClelland & Steward Ltd.

Bruna, Denis (dir.) (2013), *La mécanique des dessous*, Paris: Les arts décoratifs.

—— (2015), *Fashioning the Body: An Intimate History of the Silhouette*, New York: Bard Graduate Center: New Haven—London: Yale University Press.

Buck, Anne (1992), "Pamela's Clothes," *Costume*, vol. 26, no. 1: 21–31.

Burke, Peter (1974), *Venice and Amsterdam*, London: Temple Smith.

Burney, Frances (1983 [1796]), *Camilla: or, A Picture of Youth*, (eds) Edward A. Bloom and Lillian D. Bloom, Oxford: Oxford University Press.

—— (2006 [1778–80]), "The Witlings," in Joseph Black et al. (eds), *The Broadview Anthology of British Literature: Volume 3, The Restoration and Eighteenth Century*, Peterborough: Broadview Press.

Cage, E. Claire (2009), "The Sartorial Self: Neoclassical Fashion and Gender Identity in France, 1797–1804," *Eighteenth-Century Studies*, vol. 42, no. 2: 193–215.

Caradonna, Jeremy L. (2012), *The Enlightenment in Practice: Academic Prize Contests and Intellectual Culture in France, 1670–1794*, Ithica, NY: Cornell University Press.

Cardon, Dominique (2007), *Natural Dyes: Sources, Tradition, Technology and Science*. London: Archetype Publications.

Carlile, James (1689), *The fortune-hunters, or Two fools well met . . .*, London.

Carter, Philip (2001), *Men and the Emergence of Polite Society, Britain, 1660–1800*, Harlow: Longman.

Case of the English Weavers and French Merchants truly Stated (1670), London.

Cassidy, Tanya (2007), "People, place, and performance: theoretically revisiting Mother Clap's Molly House," in *Queer People: Negotiations and Expressions of Homosexuality, 1700–1800*, (eds) Chris Mounsey and Caroline Gonda, 99–113. Lewisburg: Bucknell University Press.

Castle, Terry (1982), "Matters not fit to be mentioned: Fielding's *The Female Husband*," *ELH*, vol. 49, no. 3: 602–22.

—— (1986), *Masquerade and Civilization: The Carnivalesque in Eighteenth-Century English Culture and Fiction*, Stanford: Stanford University Press.

Cesarani, David (ed.) (2002), *Port Jews: Jewish Communities in Cosmopolitan Maritime Trading Centres, 1550–1950*, London and Portland: Frank Cass Publishers.

Chaffray, Stéphanie (2008), "La mise en scène du corps amérindien: la représentation du vêtement dans les relations de voyage en Nouvelle-France," *Histoire, économie & société*, 4: 5–32.

Charpentier, François (1664), *Discours d'un fidele sujet du Roy, touchant l'establissement d'une compagnie françoise pour le commerce des Indes orientales: adressé à tous les François*, Paris.

Chaudhuri, Kirti N. (1978), *The Trading World of Asia and the English East India Company*, Cambridge: Cambridge University Press.

Chenoune, Farid (1993), *A History of Men's Fashion*, Paris: Flammarion.

Chesterfield, Earl of, *Letters written by the late Right Honourable Philip Dormer Stanhope, Earl of Chesterfield, to his son, Philip Stanhope, esq. . .* London: J. Dodsley, 1774, 2 vols, vol. I, 199, Horace Walpole's copy, Lewis Walpole Library, Yale University, LWL 49.436.2v.

Chico, Tita (2005), *Designing Women: The Dressing Room in Eighteenth-Century English Literature and Culture*, Lewisburg: Bucknell University Press.

Chrisman-Campbell, Kimberly (1996), "'Unhoop the Fair Sex': The Campaign Against the Hoop Petticoat in Eighteenth-Century England," *Eighteenth-Century Studies*, vol. 30, no. 1, Fall: 5–23.

—— (2002), "The face of fashion: milliners in eighteenth-century visual culture," *British Journal for Eighteenth-Century Studies*, vol. 25, issue 2: 157–72.

—— (2015), *Fashion Victims: Dress at the court of Louis XVI and Marie-Antoinette*, New Haven and London: Yale University Press.

Christensen, Charlotte (1996), "Jens Juel og portrætkunsten i det 18. århundrede," in *Hvis engle kunne male,* (ed.) Charlotte Christensen, Det Nationalhistoriske Museum på Frederiksborg: Christian Ejlers' Forlag.

Ciriacono, Salvatore (1981), "Silk Manufacturing in France and Italy in the XVIIth Century: Two Models Compared," *Journal of European Economic History* vol. 10, no. 1: 167–197.

Clairian, L. J. (1803), *Recherches et considérations médicales sur les vêtemens des hommes: particulièrement sur les culottes*, Paris: Aubry, An XI, 2nd (ed.)

Clark, Anna (1998), "The Chevalier d'Eon and Wilkes: masculinity and politics in the eighteenth century," *Eighteenth-Century Studies*, vol. 32, no. 1: 19–48.

Clarkson, Thomas (1806), "Peculiar Customs," in *A Portraiture of Quakerism*, vol. 2, (ed.) T. Clarkson.

Claro, Daniel (2005), "Historicizing masculine appearance: John Chute and the suits at The Vyne, 1740–76," *Fashion Theory*, vol. 9, issue 2: 147–74.

Claverias, Belén Moreno (2010), "Luxury, Fashion and Peasantry: The Introduction of New Commodities in Rural Catalan, 1670–1790," in B. Lemire (ed.), *The Force of Fashion in Politics and Society from the Early Modern to Contemporary Times*, Aldershot, UK: Ashgate, 67–93.

Clayton, Timothy (1997), *The English Print, 1688–1802*, New Haven: Yale University Press.

Clunas, Craig (1999), "Review Essay. Modernity Global and Local: Consumption and the Rise of the West," *American Historical Review*, vol. 104, no. 5, Dec: 1497–1511.

Cody, Lisa F. (2001), "Sex, civility, and the self: du Coudray, d'Eon, and eighteenth-century conceptions of gendered, national, and psychological identity," *French Historical Studies*, vol. 24, no. 3: 379–407.

Cohen, Michèle (1992), "The Grand Tour: constructing the English gentleman in eighteenth-century France," *History of Education*, vol. 21, no. 3: 241–57.

Colas, René (2002 [1933]) *Bibliographie Générale du Costume et de la Mode*. Paris: Librairie René Colas, Martino Pub.

Collier, Mary (1990), "The Woman's Labour. An Epistle to Mr Stephen Duck, [The Washerwoman]," in Roger Lonsdale (ed.), *Eighteenth-Century Women Poets*, Oxford: Oxford University Press, 172–3.

Cooper, Tarnya and Jane Eade, (eds) (2013), *Elizabeth I & her People*. London: National Portrait Gallery.

Coquery, Natacha (2007), "Fashion, Business, Diffusion: An Upholsterer's Shop in Eighteenth-Century Paris," in Dena Goodman and Kathryn Norberg (eds), *Furnishing the Eighteenth Century: What Furniture Can Tell Us about the European and American Past*, New York: Routledge, 63–78.

—— (2008), "Les boutiquiers parisiens et la diffusion des *indienneries* au dix-huitième siècle," in G. Le Bouedec and B. Nicolas (eds), *Le goût de l'Inde*, Rennes: PUR, 74–81.

Cowan, Bryan (2005), *The Social Life of Coffee: The Emergence of the British Coffeehouse*, New Haven: Yale University Press.

Coward, D.A. (1980), "Attitudes to homosexuality in eighteenth-century France," *Journal of European Studies*, 10, no. 40: 35–59.

Crary, Jonathan (1990), *Techniques of the Observer: On Vision and Modernity in the Nineteenth Century*, Cambridge MA, London: MIT Press.

Craske, Matthew (1997), *Art in Europe 1700–1830*, Oxford: Oxford University Press.

Crill, Rosemary (2008), *Chintz: Indian Textiles for the West*, London: V&A Publications.

Cronshagen, Jessica (2014), *Einfach vornehm: Die Hausleute der nordwestdeutschen Küstenmarsch in der Frühen Neuzeit*, Wallstein: Göttingen.

—— (2015), "Owning the Body, Wooing the Soul—How Forced Labour Was Justified in the Moravian Correspondence Network in 18th-Century Surinam," in D. Freist and S. Lachenicht (eds), *Connecting Worlds and People. Early Modern Diasporas as Translocal Societies*, Ashgate: Farnham, forthcoming.

Crowley, John (2001), *The Invention of Comfort: Sensibilities and Design in Early Modern Britain and Early America*, Baltimore: Johns Hopkins University Press.

Crowston, Clare (2000), "Engendering the Guilds: Seamstresses, Tailors, and the Clash of Corporate Identities in Old Regime France," *French Historical Studies* vol. 23, no. 2: 339–71.

Croÿ, Emmanuel duc de (2005), *Journal de Cour, tome 4 (1768–1773)*, Paris: Paléo.

Cumming, Valerie (2004), *Understanding Fashion History*. New York and Hollywood: Costume and Fashion Press.

Dabydeen, David (1985), *Hogarth's Blacks: Images of Blacks in Eighteenth Century English Art*, Kingston-upon-Thames: Dangaroo Press.

Dalgaard, Hanne Frøsig (1982), "I fløjl og vadmel," in Axel Steenberg (ed.), *Dagligliv i Danmark* vol. II, 1620–1720, Copenhagen: Gyldendal, 7–32.

—— (1999), *Luksusforordninger—1558, 1683, 1736, 1783, 1783 og 1799*, Copenhagen: special edition of the periodical *Tenen*.

Dangeau, Marquis de (2002), *Journal d'un courtisan à la cour du Roi soleil, tome II (1686– 1687), L'ambassade du Siam*, Paris: Paleo.

—— (2005), *Journal de la Cour du Roi Soleil, tome X (1697), Le Mariage*, Paris: Paleo.

Davids, Karel (2008), *The Rise and Decline of Dutch Technological Leadership*, vol. 1, Leiden: Brill.

Davis, Lennard J. (1983), *Factual Fictions: The Origins of the English Novel*, New York: Columbia University Press.

Defoe, Daniel (2008 [1724]), *Roxana: Or, The Fortunate Mistress*, (ed.) John Mullan, Oxford: Oxford University Press.

de Garsault, M. (2009) *Art of the Shoemaker*, trans. D. A. Saguto, Williamsburg: Colonial Williamsburg Foundation in Association with Texas Tech University Press.

de Genlis, Stéphanie Félicité Bruart (1818), *Dictionnaire Critique et Raisonne*, vol. 1, Paris: P Mongie.

de Haan, Francisca (2004), "Fry, Elizabeth (1780–1845)," in *Oxford Dictionary of National Biography*, Oxford: Oxford University Press; online edition, May 2007, www.oxforddnb. com/view/article/10208 [accessed March 18, 2015].

Dejardin, Kathleen and Mary Schoeser (1991), *French Textiles from 1760 to the Present*, London: Laurence King.

Delpierre, Madeleine (1996), *Se vêtir au XVIIIe siècle*, Paris: Adam Biro.

—— (1997), *Dress in France in the Eighteenth Century*, New Haven and London: Yale University Press.

de Vries, Jan (1997), *The First Modern Economy: Success, Failure, and Perseverance of the Dutch Economy, 1500–1815*, Cambridge: Cambridge University Press.

—— (2008), *The Industrious Revolution. Consumer Behavior and the Household Economy, 1650 to the Present*, Cambridge: Cambridge University Press.

Dew, Nicholas (2009), *Orientalism in France*, Oxford: Oxford University Press.

Diderot, Denis (1772), *Regrets sur ma vieille robe de chambre (1768), in Correspondance littéraire*, s.l.: Friedrich Ring.

Dillon, Henriette-Lucie, marquise de La Tour du Pin-Gouvernet (1913), *Journal d'une femme de cinquante ans, 1778–1815*, Paris, Imhaus et Chapelot.

Donald, Diana (1996), *The Age of Caricature: Satirical Prints in the Reign of George III*, New Haven: Yale University Press.

Donoghue, Emma (1993), "Imagined more than women: lesbians as hermaphrodites, 1671–1766," *Women's History Review*, vol. 2, issue 2: 199–216.

Douglas, Mary and Baron C. Isherwood (1979), *The World of Goods: Towards an Anthropology of Consumption*, London: Routledge.

Dubois, Marie (1994), *Moi Marie Dubois, gentilhomme vendômois, valet de chambre de Louis XIV*, prés. par François Lebrun, Rennes, éd. Apogée.

Duncan, Carol (1973), "Happy Mothers and Other New Ideas in French Art," *The Art Bulletin*, vol. 55, issue 4: 570–83.

Earle, Rebecca (2001), "'Two pairs of pink satin shoes!' Race, clothing and identity in the Americas (17th–19th centuries)," *History Workshop Journal*, vol. 52, issue 1: 175–95.

Eisenstein, Elisabeth L. (1979), *The Printing Press as an Agent of Change: Communications and Cultural Transformation in Early-Modern Europe*, Cambridge: Cambridge University Press.

Elias, Norbert (1981 [c. 1930]), *Die Höfische Gesellschaft. Untersuchungen zur Soziologie des Königtums und der höfischen Aristokratie mit einer Einleitung: Soziologie und Geschichtswissenschaft*, Darmstadt.

—— (1983), *The Court Society*, Oxford: Blackwell.

—— (1994 [1939]), *The Civilizing Process. The History of Manners and State Formation and Civilization*, Oxford and Cambridge, MA: Blackwell.

Engelhardt Matthiessen, Tove, Marie-Louise Nosch, Maj Ringgaard, Kirsten Toftegaard, and Mikkel Venborg Pedersen (eds) (2014), *Fashionable Encounters: Perspectives and Trends in Textile and Dress in the Early Modern Nordic World*, Oxford and Philadelphia: Oxbow Books.

Entwistle, Joanne (2000), *The Fashioned Body: Fashion, Dress and Modern Social Theory*, Cambridge: Polity.

Ewing, Elizabeth (1984), *Everyday Dress 1650–1900*. London: Batsford.

Favart, Charles Simon (1808), *Mémoires et correspondance littéraires, dramatiques et anecdotiques*, vol. 1, Paris.

Fennetaux, Ariane (2004), "Men in gowns: Nightgowns and the construction of masculinity in eighteenth-century England," *Immediations: The Research Journal of the Courtauld Institute of Art*, vol. 1, no. 1 Spring: 77–89.

—— (2008), "Women's Pockets and the Construction of Privacy in the Long Eighteenth Century," *Eighteenth Century Fiction*, vol. 20, no. 3, Spring: 307–34.

Fielding, Henry (2005 [1749]), *The History of Tom Jones, a Foundling*, (eds) Thomas Keymer and Alice Wakely, London: Penguin Books.

Finch, Martha L. (2005), "'Fashions of Wordly Dames': Separatist Discourse of Dress in Early Modern London, Amsterdam, and Plymouth Colony," *American Society of Church History* vol. 74, no. 3, September: 494–533.

Fischer, Birthe Karin (1983), *Uld og Linnedfarvning i Danmark 1720–1830*, Humlebæk: Rhodos.

Fitzpatrick, Martin, Peter Jones, Christa Knellwolf, and Iain McCalman, (eds) (2004), *The Enlightenment World*, New York: Routledge.

Flügel, John Carl (1930), *The Psychology of Clothes*, London: Hogarth Press.

Fontaine, Laurence (1996), *History of Pedlars in Europe*, Cambridge: Polity Press.

Freist, Dagmar (2013), "'Ich will Dir selbst ein Bild von mir entwerfen': Praktiken der Selbst-Bildung im Spannungsfeld ständischer Normen und gesellschaftlicher Dynamik," in Thomas Alkemeyer, Gunilla Budde, and Dagmar Freist (eds), *Selbst-Bildungen: soziale und kulturelle Praktiken der Subjektivierung*, Bielefeld: transcript Verlag, 151–74.

—— (2015), "Diskurse-Körper-Artefakte. Historische Praxeologie in der Frühneuzeitforschung— eine Annährung," in Dagmar Freist (ed.), *Diskurse—Körper— Artefakte: Historische Praxeologie*, Bielefeld: transcript Verlag, 9–30.

Freist, Dagmar and Frank Schmekel, (eds) (2013), *Hinter dem Horizont Band 2: Projektion und Distinktion ländlicher Oberschichten im europäischen Vergleich, 17.19. Jahrhundert*, Münster: Aschendorff Verlag.

Fry, K. and R.E. Cresswell, (eds) (1847), *Memoir of the life of Elizabeth Fry, with extracts from her letters and journal*, 2 vols.

Gallery of Fashion (1794), April.

Ganev, Robin (2007), "Milkmaids, Ploughmen, and Sex," *Journal of the History of Sexuality*, vol. 16, no. 1: 40–67.

Gay, John (2007 [1716]), "Trivia: Or, The Art of Walking the Streets of London," in Clare Brant and Susan E. Whyman (eds), *Walking the Streets of Eighteenth-Century London: John Gay's Trivia*, Oxford: Oxford University Press.

Geczy, Adam (2013), *Fashion and Orientalism: Dress, Textiles and Culture from the 17th to the 21st Century*, London: Bloomsbury.

Gee, Sophie (2010), *Making Waste: Leftovers and the Eighteenth-Century Imagination*, Princeton: Princeton University Press.

Genlis, Madame de (1818), *Dictionnaire critique et raisonné des étiquettes de la cour (. . .)*, Paris: P. Mongié aîné.

Gilbert, Sandra M. (1982 [1980]), "Costumes of the Mind: Transvestism as Metaphor in Modern Literature," in Elizabeth Abel (ed.), *Writing and Sexual Difference*, Brighton: Harvester Press, 193–220.

Ginsburg, Madeleine (1980), *An Introduction to Fashion Illustration*, London: V&A Publishing.

Glalmann, Kristof (1977), "The Changing Patterns of Trade," in J.H. Clapham, M.M. Postan, E. Power, H. Habakkuk, and E.E. Rich (eds), *The Cambridge Economic History of Europe*, vol. 5, Cambridge: Cambridge University Press, 185–289.

Gleixner, Ulrike (2015), "Gender and Pietism. Self-modelling and Agency," in Douglas H. Shantz (ed.), *A Companion to German Pietism, 1660–1800*, Leiden and Boston: Brill, 433–4.

Godfrey, R.T. (1994), *Wenceslaus Hollar: A Bohemian Artist in England*, New Haven: Yale University Press.

Goldsmith, Netta (2007), "London's homosexuals in the eighteenth-century: rhetoric versus practice," in Chris Mounsey and Caroline Gonda (eds), *Queer People: Negotiations and Expressions of Homosexuality, 1700–1800*, Lewisburg: Bucknell University Press, 183–94.

Goldsmith, Oliver (1985 [1773]), *She Stoops to Conquer*, in *Four English Comedies of the 17th and 18th Centuries*, (ed.) J.M. Morrell, London: Penguin Books.

Goodman, Dena and Kathryn Norberg, (eds) (2007), *Furnishing the Eighteenth Century: What Furniture Can Tell Us about the European and American Past*, New York: Routledge.

Gottsched, Luise Adelgunde Victorie (1736), *Die Pietisterey im Fischbein-Rocke; oder Die Doctormäßige Frau: In einem Lust Spiele vorgestellet*, Rostock.

Greenblatt, Stephen (2005), *Renaissance Self-Fashioning. From More to Shakespeare*, Chicago and London: University of Chicago Press.

Greene, John and Elizabeth McCrum (1990), "'Small clothes': the evolution of men's nether garments as evidences in *The Belfast Newsletter* Index 1737–1800," in Alan Harrison and Ian Campbell Ross (eds), *Eighteenth Century Ireland*, vol. 5, Dublin: Eighteenth-Century Ireland Society, 153–71.

Gregg, Stephen H. (2001), "'A Truly Christian Hero': Religion, Effeminacy, and the Nation in the Writings of the Societies for the Reformation of Manners," *Eighteenth-Century Life*, vol. 25, no. 1 Winter: 17–28.

Greig, Hannah (2013), *The Beau Monde: Fashionable Society in Georgian London*, Oxford: Oxford University Press.

Grimm, Friedrich Melchior von and Denis Diderot (1829), *Correspondance inédite de Grimm et de Diderot*, Paris: H. Fournier.

Gummere, Amelia Mott (1901), *The Quaker, a Study in Costume*, Philadelphia: Ferris and Leach.

Habermas, Jürgen (1989 [1962]), *The Structural Transformation of the Public Sphere*, trans. Thomas Burger, Cambridge: Polity Press.

Hackspiel-Mikosch, Elizabeth (2009), "Uniforms and the Creation of Ideal Masculinity," in Peter McNeil and Vicki Karaminas (eds), *The Men's Fashion Reader*, New York, Oxford: Berg.

Hafter, Daryl M. (2007), *Women at Work in Preindustrial France*, University Park, PA: Pennsylvania State University Press.

Haggerty, George (2012), "Smollett's world of masculine desire in *The Adventures of Roderick Random*," *Eighteenth Century*, vol. 53, no. 3: 317–30.

Hallett, Mark (1999), *The Spectacle of Difference: Graphic Satire in the Age of Hogarth*, New Haven: Yale University Press.

Halliwell, James Orchard (ed.) (1854), *Ancient Inventories of Furniture, Pictures, Tapestry, Plate, etc. illustrative of the Domestic Manners of the English in the Sixteenth and Seventeenth Centuries . . .*, London.

Hamm, Thomas D. (2006), *The Quakers in America*, Columbia University Press: New York.

Hammar, Britta and Pernilla Rasmussen (2008), *Underkläder: En kulturhistoria*, Stockholm: Signum.

Hansen, H.P. (1922), *Natmandsfolk og Kjæltringer i Vestjylland*, Copenhagen: Gyldendal.

Harris, John R. (1991), "Movements of Technology between Britain and Europe in the Eighteenth Century," in David. J. Jeremy (ed.), *International Technology Transfer: Europe, Japan and the USA*, Aldershot: Ashgate, 9–30.

Hart, Avril and Susan North (1998), *Seventeenth and Eighteenth-century Fashion in Detail*, London: V&A Publishing.

Harvey, John (1995), *Men in Black*, London: Reaktion.

Harvey, Karen (2002), "The century of sex? Gender, bodies, and sexuality in the long eighteenth century," *Historical Journal, vol.* 45, no. 4: 899–916.

Haywood, Eliza (2006 [1725]), "Fantomina: or, Love in a Maze," in Joseph Black et al. (eds), *The Broadview Anthology of British Literature: Volume 3, The Restoration and Eighteenth Century*, Peterborough: Broadview Press.

Hebdige, Dick (1979), *Subculture, the meanings of style*. London: Routledge.

Heller, Sarah Grace (2002), "Fashion in French Crusade Literature: Desiring Infidel Textiles," in Désirée G. Koslin and Janet E. Snyder (eds), *Encountering Medieval Textiles and Dress*, New York: Palgrave Macmillan, 103–19.

Hellman, Mimi (2006), "Interior motives: seduction by decoration in eighteenth-century France," in Harold Koda and Andrew Bolton (eds), *Dangerous Liaisons: Fashion and Furniture in the Eighteenth Century*, New Haven: Yale University Press, 14–23.

Hentschell, Roze (2009), "Moralizing Apparel in Early Modern London: Popular Literature, Sermons and Sartorial Display," *Journal of Medieval and Early Modern Studies*, vol. 39, no. 3 Fall: 571–95.

Hertz, Deborah (1978), "Salonnières and Literary Women in Late Eighteenth Century Berlin," *New German Critique*, no. 14: 97–108.

Heyl, Christoph (2001), "The metamorphosis of the mask in seventeenth- and eighteenth-century London," in Efrat Tseëlon (ed.), *Masquerade and Identities: Essays on Gender, Sexuality and Marginality*, London: Routledge, 114–34.

The History and Adventures of a Lady's Slippers and Shoes Written by Themselves (1754), London: M. Cooper.

Hoff, Annette (2009), *Karen Rosenkrantz de Lichtenbergs dagbøger og regnskaber*, Horsens Museum: Landbohistorisk Selskab.

Hogarth, William (1955 [1760s]), "Autobiographical Notes," in Joseph Burke (ed.), *The Analysis of Beauty, with the Rejected Passages from the Manuscript Drafts and Autobiographical Notes*, Oxford: Clarendon Press, 201–32.

Hohenberg, Paul M. and Lynn H. Lees (1985), *The Making of Urban Europe, 1000–1950*, Cambridge, MA: Harvard University Press.

Hollander, Anne (1971), "The Clothed Image: Picture and Performance," *New Literary History*, vol. 2, no. 3, Spring: 477–93.

—— (1993), *Seeing through Clothes*, Berkeley: University of California Press.

Howarth, William Driver (2009), *French Theatre in the Neo-classical Era*, Cambridge: Cambridge University Press.

Howell, Martha (2010), *Commerce Before Capitalism in Europe, 1300–1600*, Cambridge: Cambridge University Press.

Huck, Christian (2010), *Fashioning Society, or, The Mode of Modernity: Observing Fashion in Eighteenth-Century Britain*, Würzburg: Königshausen and Neumann.

Hughes, Thomas P. (2005), *Human-built World: How to Think about Technology and Culture*, Chicago: University of Chicago Press.

Hugo, Victor (1882), *Les Orientales*, Paris: Chamerot.

Huizinga, Johan (1996 [1921]), *The Autumn of the Middle Ages*, trans. Rodney J. Payton and Ulrich Mammitzsch, Chicago: University of Chicago Press.

Hunt, Alan (1996), *Governance of Consuming Passions: A History of Sumptuary Law*, London and Basingstoke: Macmillan.

Hunter, J. Paul (1984), "The World as Stage and Closet," in Shirley Strum Kenny (ed.), *British Theatre and the Other Arts, 1660–1800*, Washington et al.: Folger, 271–86.

Hutson, Lorna (2004), "Liking men: Ben Jonson's closet opened," *ELH*, vol. 71, no. 4: 1065–96.

Ilg, Ulrike (2004), "The Cultural Significance of Costume Books in Sixteenth-Century Europe," in Catherine Richardson (ed.), *Clothing Culture, 1350–1650*, Aldershot: Ashgate, 29–47.

Jahn, Bernhard, Thomas Rahn, and Claudia Schnitzger, (eds) (1998), *Zeremoniell in der Krise: Störung und Nostalgie*, Marburg: Jonas Verlag.

Janes, Dominic (2009), *Victorian Reformation: The Fight over Idolatry in the Church of England, 1840–1860*, Oxford: Oxford University Press.

—— (2012), "Unnatural appetites: sodomitical panic in Hogarth's *The Gate of Calais*, or *O the Roast Beef of Old England* (1748)," *Oxford Art Journal*, vol. 35, no. 1: 19–31.

Jenner, Mark S.R. (1999), "Review Essay: Body, Image, Text in Early Modern Europe," *The Society for the Social History of Medicine*, vol. 12, issue 1: 143–54.

Jonas, Hans (1982 [1966]), "The Nobility of Sight: A Study in the Phenomenology of the
    Senses," in Hans Jonas (ed.), *The Phenomenon of Life: Toward a Philosophical Biology*,
    Chicago: University of Chicago Press, 135–56.

Jones, Jennifer M. (1994), "Repackaging Rousseau: Femininity and Fashion in Old Regime
    France," *French Historical Studies*, vol. 18, no. 4 Autumn: 939–67.

Jonson, Ben (1716), *The Works of Ben Johnson* [sic], vol. 6.

Jørgensen, Lise Bender (1992), *North European Textiles until AD 1000*, Århus: Århus
    University Press.

Juul, Brun (1807–12), *Naturhistorisk, oeconomisk og technologisk Handels- og Varelexikon*. Bd.
    1–3, København, A: S. Soldins Forlag.

Kates, Gary (1995), "The transgendered world of the chevalier/chevalière d'Eon," *Journal of
    Modern History*, vol. 67, no. 3: 558–94.

Keen, Suzanne (2002), "Quaker Dress, Sexuality, and the Domestication of Reform in the
    Victorian Novel," *Victorian Literature and Culture*, vol. 30, no. 1: 211–13.

Keenan, William (1999), "From Friars to Fornicators: The Eroticization of Sacred Dress,"
    Fashion Theory, vol. 3, no. 4: 389–410.

Kellenbenz, Hermann (1977), "The Organization of Industrial Production," in J.H. Clapham,
    M.M. Postan, E. Power, H. Habakkuk and E.E. Rich (eds), *The Cambridge Economic
    History of Europe*, vol. 5, 462–548, Cambridge: Cambridge University Press.

Kelly, Jason M. (2006), "Riots, revelries, and rumor: libertinism and masculine association in
    Enlightenment London," *Journal of British Studies*, vol. 45, no. 4: 759–95.

Keymer, Thomas and Peter Sabor (2005), *Pamela in the Marketplace: Literary Controversy and
    Print Culture in Eighteenth-Century Britain and Ireland*, Cambridge: Cambridge University
    Press.

King, Thomas A. (2004), *The Gendering of Men, 1600–1750*, vol. 1, *The English Phallus*,
    Madison: University of Wisconsin Press.

—— (2008), *The Gendering of Men, 1600–1750*, vol. 2, *Queer Articulations*, Madison:
    University of Wisconsin Press.

Kirkham, Pat (1988), *The London Furniture Trade 1700–1870*, London: Furniture History
    Society.

Knoppers, Laura Lunger (1998), "The politics of portraiture: Oliver Cromwell and the plain
    style," *Renaissance Quarterly*, vol. 51, no. 4: 1283–1319.

Kowelski-Wallace, Elizabeth (1997), *Women, Shopping, and Business in the Eighteenth Century*,
    New York: Columbia University Press.

Kuchta, David (2002), *The Three-Piece Suit and Modern Masculinity: England, 1550–1850*,
    Berkeley: University of California Press.

Kuiper, Yme and Harm Nijboer (2009), "Between Frugality and Civility: Dutch Mennonites
    and Their taste for the 'World of Art' in the Eighteenth Century," *Journal of Mennonite
    Studies*, vol. 27: 75–92.

Kunzle, David (2004), *Fashion and Fetishism: Corsets, Tight Lacing and Other Forms of
    Body-Sculpture*, Stroud: Sutton.

Kwass, Michael (2004), "Consumption and the World of Ideas: Consumer Revolution and the
    Moral Economy of the Marquis de Mirabeau," *Eighteenth-Century Studies* vol. 37, no. 2
    Winter, 2004: 187–213.

—— (2006), "Big hair: a wig history of consumption in eighteenth-century France," *American
    Historical Review*, vol. 111, issue 3: 631–59.

—— (2014), *Contraband: Louis Mandrin and the Making of a Global Underground*, Cambridge,
    MA: Harvard University Press.

Lacroix, Laurent (1976), "Quand les Français jouaient aux sauvages . . . ou le carrousel de 1662," *Journal of Canadian Art History*, vol. 1, no. 2: 44–54.

The Lady's Magazine; or Entertaining Companion for the Fair Sex, appropriated solely to their Use and Amusement 1, vol. 1 (1770).

The Lady's Magazine; or Entertaining Companion for the Fair Sex, appropriated solely to their Use and Amusement (1773) May.

Laetitia Barbauld, Anna (1990), "Washing-Da," in Roger Lonsdale (ed.), *Eighteenth-Century Women Poets*, Oxford: Oxford University Press, 308–11.

Laidlaw, Christine (2010), *The British in the Levant: Trade and Perceptions of the Ottoman Empire in the Eighteenth Century*, New York: Tauris Academic Studies.

Lamb, Charles (1811), "On the Genius and Character of Hogarth," *The Reflector* vol. 2, no. 3: 61–77.

Lanoë, Catherine (2008), *La poudre et le fard: Une histoire des cosmétiques de la Renaissance aux Lumières,* Seyssel: Chamvallon.

Laqueur, Thomas (1990), *Making Sex: Body and Gender from the Greeks to Freud*, Cambridge, MA: Harvard University Press.

le Corbeiller, Clare (1983), *European and American Snuff Boxes 1730–1830*, London: Chancellor Press.

Leclant, Jean (1951), "Le café et les cafés à Paris (1644–1693)," *Annales. Économies, Sociétés, Civilisations,* 6, no. 1: 1–14.

Lehmann, Hartmut (2001), "Grenzüberschreitungen und Grenzziehungen im Pietismus," *Pietismus und Neuzeit*, 27: 11–18.

Leigh, R.A., (ed.) (1971), *Correspondance complète de J.J. Rousseau*, vol. 13. Madison.

Leis, Arlene (2013), "Displaying art and fashion: ladies' pocket-book imagery in the paper collections of Sarah Sophia Banks," *Konsthistorisk tidskrift/Journal of Art History*, vol. 82, issue 3: 252–71.

Lemire, Beverly (1991), *Fashion's Favourite: the Cotton Trade and the Consumer in Britain, 1660–1800*, Oxford: Oxford University Press.

—— (1997), *Dress, Culture and Commerce: the English Clothing Trade Before the Factory, 1660–1800*, Basingstoke: Macmillan.

—— (2000), "Second-hand beaux and 'red-armed Belles': conflict and the creation of fashions in England, c. 1600–1800," *Continuity and Change*, vol. 15, no. 3 December: 391–417.

—— (2003), "Transforming Consumer Custom: Linens, Cottons and the English Market, 1660–1800," in Brenda Collins and Philip Ollerenshaw (eds), *The European Linen Industry in Historical Perspective*, Oxford: Oxford University Press, 187–207.

—— (2008), "Fashioning Global Trade: Indian Textiles, Gender Meanings and European Consumers, 1500–1800," in Giorgio Riello and Tirthankar Roy (eds), *How India Clothed the World: The World of South Asian Textiles, 1500–1850*, The Hague: Brill, 887–916.

—— (2010), *The British Cotton Trade, 1660–1815*, vol. 2, London: Pickering and Chatto.

—— (2011), *Cotton*, Oxford: Berg Publishers.

—— (2015), "'Men of the World': British Mariners, Consumer Practice, and Material Culture in an Era of Global Trade, c. 1660–1800," *Journal of British Studies*, vol. 54, issue 2, April: 288–319.

—— (2016), "A Question of Trousers: Mariners, Masculinity and Empire in the Transformation of British Male Dress, c. 1600–1800," *Cultural and Social History*, forthcoming.

Lemire, Beverly and Giorgio Riello (2008), "East and West: Textiles and Fashion in Early Modern Europe," *Journal of Social History*, vol. 41, no. 4: 887–916.

L'Encyclopedie ou Dictionaire Raisonné des Sciences, des Arts et des Metiers Tome XVII. (1751–72) halb-hiv, Paris.

Lever, Évelyne (2005), *Marie-Antoinette: Correspondance (1770–1793)*, Paris: Tallandier.

Lewis Walpole Library, Yale University, F.J.B. Watson papers regarding Thomas Patch.

Lewis, W.S., (ed.) (1937–83), *The Yale Edition of Horace Walpole's Correspondence*, 48 vols., New Haven: Yale University Press.

—— (1969), "Horace Walpole's Library," in *A Catalogue of Horace Walpole's Library*, vol. 1, Allen T. Hazen, New Haven and London: Yale University Press.

Livi-Bacci, Massimo (2000), *The Population of Europe*, Oxford: Blackwell Publishers.

London Spy, March 1699.

Lonsdale, Roger, (ed.) (1990) *Eighteenth-Century Women Poets*, Oxford: Oxford University Press.

Lorenzen, Erna (1960), "Teater eller virkelighed," in Helge Søgaard (ed.), *Årbog, Den gamle By*, Århus: Århus University Press, 40–5.

—— (1982), "Modetøj og gangklæder," in Axel Steensberg (ed.), *Dagligliv i Danmark*, vol. iv: 1720–1790, Copenhagen: Gyldendal, 47–72.

Lüdemann, Susanne (1999), "Beobachtungsverhältnisse. Zur (Kunst Geschichte der Beobachtung zweiter Ordnung," in Albrecht Koschorke and Cornelia Vismann (eds), *Widerstände der Systemtheorie: Kulturtheoretische Analysen zum Werk von Niklas Luhmann*, Berlin: Akademie Verlag, 63–75.

Luhmann, Niklas (1997), *Die Gesellschaft der Gesellschaft*, Frankfurt am Main: Suhrkamp.

Lupton, Christina, (ed.) (2012), *British It-Narratives, 1750–1830. Volume 3: Clothes and Transportation*, London: Pickering and Chatto.

Luu, Lien Bich (2005), *Immigrants and the Industries of London, 1500–1700*, Aldershot: Ashgate.

Lynn, Elery (2010), *Underwear: Fashion in Detail*, London: V&A Publishing.

Lyons, Clare A. (2003), "Mapping an Atlantic sexual culture: homoeroticism in eighteenth-century Philadelphia," *William and Mary Quarterly*, vol. 60, no. 1: 119–54.

Lyons, John D. (1982), "Speaking in Pictures, Speaking of Pictures: Problems of Representation in the Seventeenth Century," in John D. Lyons and Stephen G. Nichols, Jr. (eds), *Mimesis: From Mirror to Method, Augustine to Descartes*, Hanover: University Press of New England, 166–87.

Mackie, Erin (1997), *Market à la Mode: Fashion, Commodity and Gender in the* Tatler *and the* Spectator, Baltimore: Johns Hopkins University Press.

—— (2009), *Rakes, Highwaymen, and Pirates: The Making of the Modern Gentleman in the Eighteenth Century*, Baltimore: Johns Hopkins University Press.

Malcolm, James Peller (1808), *Anecdotes of the manners and customs of London during the eighteenth century . . .*, London: Longman, Hurst, Rees, and Orme, courtesy Lewis Walpole Library, Yale University.

Marschke, Benjamin. (2014), "Pietism and Politics in Prussia and Beyond," in Douglas Shantz (ed.), *A Companion to German Pietism, 1660–1800*, Leiden: Brill, 472–526.

Martin, Ann Ray (1984), "The young pretender: Long ruled by Diana Vreeland, the world of costume—that upstart art—is changing" [Edward Maeder], *Connoisseur*, June: 73–77.

Martin, Meredith (2014), "Tipu Sultan's Ambassadors at Saint-Cloud: Indomania and Anglophobia in Pre-Revolutionary Paris," *West 86th*, vol. 21, no. 1 Spring–Summer: 37–68.

Martin, Morag (2005), "Doctoring Beauty: The Medical Control of Women's Tilettes in France, 1750–1820," *Medical History*, vol. 49, issue 3: 351–68.

Martin, Richard and Harold Koda (1994) *Orientalism: Vision of the East in Western Dress*, New
    York: Metropolitan Museum of Art.
Mathiassen, Tove Engelhardt (1996), "Tekstil-import til Danmark cirka 1750–1850," in T.B. Ravn,
    E. Aasted, and B. Blæsild (eds), *Årbog Den Gamle By*, Aarhus: Århus University Press, 80–104.
Mathiassen, Tove Engelhardt, Marie-Louise Nosch, Maj Ringgaard, Kirsten Toftegaard, and
    Mikkel Venborg Pedersen, (eds) (2014), *Fashionable Encounters: Perspectives and trends in
    textile and dress in the Early Modern Nordic World*, Oxford: Oxbow Books.
Maynard, Margaret (1989), "A Dream of Fair Women: Revival Dress and the Formation of Late
    Victorian Images of Femininity," *Art History*, vol. 12, issue 3, September: 322–41.
McCabe, Ina Baghdiantz (2008), *Orientalism in Early Modern France: Eurasian Trade,
    Exoticism and the Ancien Regime*, Oxford: Berg Publishers.
—— Ina Baghdiantz (2014), *A History of Global Consumption: 1500–1800*, London:
    Routledge.
McCants, Anne E.C. (2008), "Poor Consumers as Global Consumers: the Diffusion of Tea and
    Coffee Drinking in the Eighteenth Century," *Economic History Review*, vol. 61, no. 1:
    172–200.
McClive, Cathy (2009), "Masculinity on trial: penises, hermaphrodites and the uncertain male
    body in early modern France," *History Workshop Journal*, vol. 68, no. 1: 45–68.
McKendrick, Neil (1982), "The Commercialization of Fashion," in Neil McKendrick, John
    Brewer and J.H. Plumb (eds), *The Birth of a Consumer Society: The Commercialization of
    Eighteenth-Century England*, Bloomington: Indiana University Press 34–99.
McKeon, Michael (1995), "Historicizing patriarchy: the emergence of gender difference in
    England, 1660–1760," *Eighteenth Century Studies*, vol. 28, no. 3: 295–322.
McNeil, Peter (1999), "'That doubtful gender': macaroni dress and male sexualities," *Fashion
    Theory*, vol. 3, issue 4: 411–47.
—— (2009), *Critical and Primary Sources in Fashion: Renaissance to Present Day*, Oxford and
    New York: Berg.
—— (2010), "Caricatura e Moda: Storia di una Presa in Giro," in M.G. Muzzarelli and
    E.T. Brandi (eds), *Storie di Moda /Fashion-able Historie*, Milan: Bruno Mondadori,
    156–67.
—— (2012), *Conference Report: Ländliche Eliten. Bäuerlich-burgerliche Eliten un den
    friesischen Marschen und den angrenzenden Geestgebieten 1650–1850, collaborative research
    project supported by the VolkswagenStiftung initiative "Research in Museums" 2010–2013*,
    www.fashioningtheearlymodern.ac.uk/wordpress/wp-content/uploads/2011/01/Ländliche-
    ElitenDF_2.pdf
—— (2013a), "'Beyond the horizon of hair': masculinity, nationhood and fashion in the
    Anglo-French Eighteenth Century," in D. Freist and F. Schmekel (eds), *Hinter dem Horizont:
    Projektion und Distinktion ländlicher Oberschichten im euorpäischen Vergleich, 17.–19.
    Jahrhundert*, Münster: Aschendorff Verlag, 79–90.
—— (2013b), "Conspicuous waist: queer dress in the 'long eighteenth century'," in Valerie
    Steele (ed.), *A Queer History of Fashion: From the Closet to the Catwalk*, New York: Fashion
    Institute of Technology, 77–116.
Mettele, Gisela (2009), *Weltbürgertum oder Gottesreich: Die Herrnhuter Brüdergemeine als
    globale Gemeinschaft 1727–1857*, Göttingen: Vandenhoeck & Ruprecht.
The Midwife, or the Old Woman's Magazine (1750), October.
Miller, Lesley Ellis (1998), "Paris-Lyon-Paris: Dialogue in the Design and Distribution of
    Patterned Silks in the 18th Century," in Robert Fox and Anthony Turner (eds), *Luxury Trade
    and Consumerism in Ancien Régime Paris*, Aldershot, UK: Ashgate, 139–67.

—— (1999), "Innovation and Industrial Espionage in Eighteenth-Century France: an Investigation of the Selling of Silk through Samples," *Journal of Design History*, vol. 12, no. 3: 271–92.

—— (2014), "Material marketing: how lyonnais silk manufacturers sold silks, 1660–1789," in J. Stobartand B. Blondé (ed.), *Selling Textiles in the Long Eighteenth Century: Comparative Perspectives from Western Europe*, Palgrave Macmillan: Basingstoke, 85–98.

Moesbjerg, M.P. (1930–1), "Hattemagerhuset i 'Den gamle By'," in Peter Holm (ed.), *Årbog Den gamle By,* Aarhus: Århus University Press, 30–47.

Molà, Luca (2000), *The Silk Industry of Renaissance Venice*, Baltimore: Johns Hopkins University Press.

Molière, J.B. (1673), *Le Bourgeois Gentilhomme.* Paris: C. Barbin.

Molineux, Catherine (2005), "Hogarth's Fashionable Slaves: Moral Corruption in Eighteenth-Century London," *ELH*, vol. 72, no. 2 Summer: 495–520.

Møller, Per Stig (1997), *Den naturlige orden. 12 år der flyttede verden*, Copenhagen: Gyldendal 1997.

Montgomery, Florence M. (2007), *Textiles in America, 1650–1870*, New York, London: W.W. Norton & Company.

Moore, Doris Langley (1971), *Fashion through Fashion Plates, 1771–1970*, London: Ward.

Motteville, Madame de (1824), *Mémoires de Mme de Motteville (1621–89)*, M. Petitot (ed.), Paris: Foucault.

Mukerji, Chandra (1983), *From Graven Images: Patterns of Modern Materialism*, New York: Columbia University Press.

Munns, Jessica and Penny Richards, (eds) (1999), *The Clothes that Wear Us. Essays on Dressing and Transgressing in Eighteenth-Century Culture*, Newark and London: University of Delaware Press.

Murdock, Graeme (2000), "Dressed to Repress? Protestant Clerical Dress and the Regulation of Morality in Early Modern Europe," *Fashion Theory*, vol. 4, no. 2: 179–200.

Musée Galliéra (2005), *Modes en miroir. La France et la Hollande au temps des Lumières,* Paris: Paris-Musée.

Nenadic, Stana (1994), "Middle-Rank Consumers and Domestic Culture in Edinburgh and Glasgow 1720–1849," *Past & Present*, no. 145: 122–56.

Nevinson, John L. (1967), *Origin and Early History of the Fashion Plate*, Washington: Smithsonian.

Nolivos de Saint-Cyr, Paul-Antoine-Nicolas (1759), *Tableau du siècle, par un auteur connu (. . .).* Genève, [s.n.].

Norton, Rictor, (ed.) (2003), "Faustina, 1726," *Homosexuality in Eighteenth-Century England: A Sourcebook*, available at www.rictornorton.co.uk/eighteen/faustin1.htm [accessed November 10, 2013].

—— (2004), "The first public debate about homosexuality in England: letters in *The Public Ledger* concerning the case of Captain Jones, 1772," *Homosexuality in Eighteenth-Century England: A Sourcebook*, available at www.rictornorton.co.uk/eighteen/jones7.htm [accessed November 10, 2013].

—— (2005), "The macaroni club: newspaper items," *Homosexuality in Eighteenth-Century England: A Sourcebook*, available at www.rictornorton.co.uk/eighteen/macaron1.htm

Noyes, Dorothy (1998), "La maja vestida: dress as resistance to enlightenment in late-18th-century Madrid," *Journal of American Folklore*, vol. 111, no. 40: 197–217.

Nussbaum, Felicity A. (2003), *The Limits of the Human: Fictions of Anomaly, Race and Gender in the Long Eighteenth Century*, Cambridge: Cambridge University Press.

Nyrop-Christensen, Henning (1982), "Den honnette Ambition," in Axel Steensberg (ed.), *Dagligliv i Danmark*, vol. III 1720–90, Copenhagen: Gyldendal, 157–72.

Oberkirch, Baronne de (1989 [1895]), *Mémoires sur la cour de Louis XIV et la société française avant 1789*, Paris: Mercure de France.

Ogborn, Miles (1997), "Locating the Macaroni: luxury, sexuality and vision in Vauxhall Gardens," *Textual Practice*, vol. 11, no. 3: 445–61.

Ogée, Frédéric and Meslay, Olivier (2006), "William Hogarth and Modernity," in Mark Hallett and Christine Riding (eds), *Hogarth*, London: Tate, 23–9.

Olian, Joanne (1977), "Sixteenth-Century Costume Books," *Dress: The Journal of the Costume Society of America*, vol. 3: 20–48.

Orléans, Charlotte-Elisabeth d' (1985 [1718]), *Lettres de Madame, duchesse d'Orléans, née Princesse Palatine*, (ed.) Olivier Amiel, Paris: Mercure de France.

Orvis, David L. (2009), "'Old sodom' and 'dear dad': Vanbrugh's celebration of the sodomitical subject in *The Relapse*," *Journal of Homosexuality*, vol. 57, issue 1: 140–62.

Overton, Mark, Jane, Whittle, Darron Dean, and Andrew Hann (2004), *Production and Consumption in English Households, 1600–1750*, London: Routledge.

Paresys, Isabelle and Natacha Coquery, Natacha, (eds) (2011), *Se vêtir à la cour en Europe 1400–1815*, Villeneuve d'Ascq: Irhis-Ceges-Centre de recherche du château de Versailles.

"Parisian Evening Dress" (1816), *Belle Assemblée*, No. 81, March.

Park, Julie (2010), *The Self and It: Novel Objects in Eighteenth-Century England*. Stanford: Stanford University Press.

Parker, Rozsika (1984), *The Subversive Stitch: Embroidery and the Making of the Feminine*. London: Women's Press.

Paulsen, Henning (1955), *Sophie Brahes regnskabsbog 1627–40*, Jysk Selskab for Historie: Sprog of Litteratur.

Paulson, Ronald (1995), "Emulative Consumption and Literacy: The Harlot, Moll Flanders, and Mrs. Slipslop," in Ann Bermingham and John Brewer (eds), *The Consumption of Culture 1600–1800: Image, Object, Text*, London: Routledge, 383–400.

Peck, Amelia (2013), "'India Chintz' and 'China Taffaty' East India Company Textiles for the North American Marked," in Amelia Peck and Amy Elizabeth Bogansky (eds), *Interwoven Globe: The Worldwide Textile Trade, 1500–1800,* New York: The Metropolitan Museum of Art, 104–19.

Peck, Amelia and Amy Elizabeth Bogansky, (eds) (2013), *Interwoven Globe: The Worldwide Textile Trade, 1500–1800*, New Haven and London: Yale University Press.

Peck, Linda Levy (2007), *Consuming Splendour: Society and Culture in Seventeenth-Century England*, Cambridge: Cambridge University Press.

Pellegrin, Nicole (1991), "L'uniforme de la santé; les médecins et la réforme du costum," *Dix-huitième siècle*, no. 23: 129–40.

Perkins, Diane (2001), "Henry Walton: A Girl Buying a Ballad Exhibited 1778," Tate Gallery Artwork Summary, available at www.tate.org.uk/art/artworks/walton-a-girl-buying-a-ballad-t07594 [accessed July 28, 2015].

Perrot, Philippe (1991), *Le corps féminin. Le travail des apparences, XVIIe–XIXe siècle*, Paris: Seuil.

Perry, Gillian and Michael Rossington, Michael, (eds) (1994), *Femininity and Masculinity in Eighteenth-Century Art and Culture*, Manchester: Manchester University Press.

Phipps, Elena (2013), "Global Colors: Dyes and the Dye Trade," in Amelia Peck and Amy Elizabeth Bogansky (eds), *Interwoven Globe: The Worldwide Textile Trade, 1500–1800*, New York: The Metropolitan Museum of Art, 120–35.

Pietsch, Johannes (2013), "On Different Types of Women's Dresses in France in the Louis XVI Period", *Fashion Theory*, vol. 17, no. 4, September: 397–416.

Poissonnier des Perrières (1774), "Mémoire sur l'habillement des troupes par M. Poissonnier des Perrières, lu le 17 déc. 1772," in *Mémoires de l'Académie* de Dijon, vol. 2, Causse: 417–46.

Ponsonby, Margaret (2007), *Stories from Home: English Domestic Interiors, 1750–1850*, Aldershot, UK: Ashgate.

Porter, David (2002), "Monstrous beauty: eighteenth-century fashion and the aesthetics of the Chinese taste," *Eighteenth-Century Studies*, vol. 35, no. 3: 395–411.

Powell, John S. (2006), "The Bourgeois Gentilhomme: Molière and Music," in David Bradby and Andrew Calder (eds), *The Cambridge Companion to Molière*, Cambridge: Cambridge University Press, 121–38.

Powell, Margaret and Joseph Roach (2004), "Big Hair," *Eighteenth-Century Studies*, vol. 38, no. 1, Fall: 79–99.

Pratt, Lucy and Linda Woolley (2008), *Shoes*, London: V&A Publishing.

Priestley, Ursula (1990), *The Fabric of Stuffs,* Norwich: Centre of East Anglian Studies.

Pritchard, Will (2000), "Masks and Faces: female Legibility in the Restoration Era," *Eighteenth-Century Life*, vol. 24, no. 3 Fall: 31–52.

Pyne, William H. (1989), *Pyne's British Costumes: An illustrated survey of early eighteenth-century dress in the British Isles*, Ware: Wordsworth Editions.

Radisich, Paula Rea (2014), "The Cris de Paris in the LACMA Recueil des modes," in Kathryn Norberg and Sandra Rosenbaum (eds), *Fashion Prints in the Age of Louis XIV*, Lubbock: Texas Tech University Press.

Rasche, Adelheid and Gundula Wolter (2003), *Ridikül. Mode in der Karikatur,* Berlin: DuMont.

Rauser, Amelia (2004), "Hair, authenticity, and the self-made macaroni," *Eighteenth-Century Studies*, vol. 38, no. 1: 101–17.

Raveux, Olivier (2014), "Fashion and consumption of painted and printed calicoes in the Mediterranean during the later seventeenth century: the case of chintz quilts and banyans in Marseilles," *Textile History*, vol. 45, no. 1 May: 49–67.

Rawert, Ole Jørgen (1831–4), *Almindeligt Varelexicon*, vol. 1–2, København: V.F. Soldenfeldt.

—— (1992 [1848]), *Kongeriget Danmarks industrielle Forhold*, Skippershoved.

Raynie, Stephen A. (1999), "Hayman and Gravelot's Anti-*Pamela* Designs for Richardson's Octavo Edition of *Pamela I* and *II*," *Eighteenth-Century Life*, vol. 23, no. 3: 77–93.

Ribeiro, Aileen (1983), *A Visual History of Costume. The Eighteenth Century*, London: Batsford.

—— (1984), *Dress in Eighteenth Century Europe, 1715–1789*, London: Batsford.

—— (1986), *Dress and Morality*, London: B.T. Batsford.

—— (1988), *Fashion in the French Revolution*, New York: Holmes and Meier.

—— (1995), *The Art of Dress: Fashion in England and France 1750 to 1820*, New Haven and London: Yale University Press.

—— (1998), "Reading Dress in Hogarth's 'Marriage-a-la-Mode'," *Apollo* CXLVII, no. 432: 49–50.

—— (2002), *Dress in Eighteenth-Century Europe, 1715–1789*, revised (ed.), New Haven: Yale University Press.

—— (2005), *Fashion and Fiction: Dress in Art and Literature in Stuart England*, New Haven: Yale University Press.

—— (2011), *Facing Beauty: Painted Women and Cosmetic Art*, New Haven: Yale University Press.

Richardson, Catherine (2004), *Clothing Culture, 1350–1650*, Aldershot: Ashgate.

Richardson, Samuel (1971 [1740]), *Pamela, or, Virtue Rewarded*. T.C. Duncan Eaves and Ben D. Kimpel (eds), Boston et al.: Houghton Mifflin.

Richardson, Samuel (2008 [1740]), *Pamela; or, Virtue Rewarded*, Thomas Keymer and Alice Wakely (eds), Oxford: Oxford University Press.

Riding, Christine (2006), "The Harlot and the Rake," in Mark Hallett and Christine Riding (eds), *Hogarth*, London: Tate 73–75.

Riello, Giorgio (2008), "The Indian Apprenticeship: The Trade of Indian Textiles and the Making of European Cottons," in Giorgio Riello and Tirthankar Roy (eds), *How India Clothed the World: The World of South Asian Textiles, 1500–1850*, The Hague: Brill, 309–46.

—— (2009), "Fabricating the Domestic: Textiles and the Social Life of the Home in Early Modern Europe," in Beverly Lemire (ed.), *The Force of Fashion in Politics and Society from Early Modern to Contemporary Times*, Aldershot: Ashgate, 41–66.

—— (2013), *Cotton: The Fabric that Made the Modern World*, Cambridge: Cambridge University Press.

Riello, Giorgio and Peter McNeil, (eds) (2006) *Shoes: a history from sandals to sneakers*, Oxford and New York: Berg.

Ritchie, Leslie (2008), "Garrick's male-coquette and theatrical masculinities," in Shelley King and Yaël Schlick (eds), *Refiguring the Coquette: Essays on Culture and Coquetry*, Lewisburg: Bucknell University Press, 164–98.

Robertson, John (2005), *The Case for the Enlightenment: Scotland and Naples, 1680–1760*, Cambridge: Cambridge University Press.

Roche, Daniel (1989), *La culture des apparences*: *Une histoire du vêtement, XVIIe–XVIIIe siècles*, Paris: Fayard.

—— (1994 [1989]), *The Culture of Clothing: Dress and Fashion in the "Ancien Régime,"* trans. Jean Birrell, Cambridge: Cambridge University Press.

—— (1997), *Histoire des choses banales. Naissance de la consommation XVII–XIXe siècle*, Paris: Fayard.

—— (2000 [1997]), *A History of Everyday Things: The Birth of Consumption in France, 1600–1800*, trans. Brian Pearce, Cambridge: Cambridge University Press.

Rogister, J.M.J. (2004), "D'Éon de Beaumont, Charles Geneviève Louis Auguste André Timothée, Chevalier D'Éon in the French nobility (1728–1810)," *Oxford Dictionary of National Biography*, Oxford: Oxford University Press, available at www.oxforddnb.com/view/article/7523 [accessed December 10, 2013].

Roper, Lyndal (1989), *The Holy Household: Women and Morals in Reformation Augsburg*, Oxford: Clarendon Press.

Rosenthal, Michael (1997), *Prospects for the Nation: Recent Essays in British Landscape, 1750–1880*, New Haven: Yale University Press.

Rousseau, George (1991), *Perilous Enlightenment: Pre- and Post-Modern Discourses—Sexual, Historical*. Manchester: Manchester University Press.

Rousseau, J.J. (1869), *Les Confessions*, Paris: Gennequin.

Rublack, Ulinka (2010), *Dressing Up. Cultural Identity in Renaissance Europe*, Oxford: Oxford University Press.

Saint-Simon, Louis de Rouvroy duc de (1856), *Mémoires complets et authentiques du duc de Saint-Simon sur le siècle de Louis XIV et la régence*, M. Chéruel (ed.), Paris: Hachette.

Sallen, Jill (2008), *Corsets: Historical Patterns & Techniques*, London: Batsford.

Santesso, Aaron (1999), "William Hogarth and the tradition of the sexual scissors," *SEL: Studies in English Literature*, vol. 39, no. 3: 499–521.

Sargentson, Carolyn (1996), *Merchants and Luxury Markets: The Marchands Merciers of Eighteenth-Century Paris*. London: V&A Publishing.

Schatzki, Theodore R. (2001), "Introduction. Practice Theory," in Th. R. Schatzki, K. Knorr Cetina, and E. von Savigny (eds), *The Practice Turn in Contemporary Theory*, London and New York: Routledge, 1–14.

Schmekel, Frank (2014), "'Glocal Stuff'—Trade and Consumption of an East Frisian Rural Elite (18th Century)," in Markus A. Denzel and Christina Dalhede (eds), *Preindustrial Commercial History: Flows and Contacts between Cities in Scandinavia and North Western Europe*, Stuttgart: Steiner, 251–68.

—— (2015), "Was macht einen Hausmann? Eine ländliche Elite zwischen Status und Praktiken der Legitimation," in Dagmar Freist (ed.), *Diskurse-Körper-Artefakte: Historische Praxeologie*, edited by, Bielefeld: transcript Verlag, 287–309.

Schoeser, Mary (2007), *Silk*, New Haven: Yale University Press.

Schou, Jacob Henric (1822), *Chronologisk Register over de Kongelige Forordninger og Aabne Breve samt andre trykte Anordninger som fra Aar 1670 af ere udkomne, tilligemed et nøiagtigt Udtog af de endnu gieldende, for saavidt samme i Almindelighed angaae Undersaaterne i Danmark, forsynet med et alphabetisk Register*, vol. iii, 1730–46, Copenhagen.

—— (1822), *Chronologisk Register over de Kongelige Forordninger og Aabne Breve samt andre trykte Anordninger som fra Aar 1670 af ere udkomne, tilligemed et nøiagtigt Udtog af de endnu gieldende, for saavidt samme i Almindelighed angaae Undersaaterne i Danmark, forsynet med et alphabetisk Register*, vol. viii, 1781–4, Copenhagen.

Schulte, Christoph (2002), *Die Jüdische Aufklärung*, München: Beck Verlag.

Scott, Joan W. (1986), "Gender: A Useful Category of Historical Analysis," *The American Historical Review*, vol. 91, issue 5, Dec: 1053–75.

Scott, Katie (2003), "Playing Games with Otherness: Watteau's Chinese Cabinet at the Château de la Muette," *Journal of the Warburg and Courtauld Institutes*, vol. 66: 189–237.

Sensbach, Jon (2005), *Rebeccas Revival: Creating Black Christianity in the Atlantic World*, Cambridge, MA and London: Harvard University Press.

Shammas, Carole (1994), "The Decline of Textile Prices in England and British America Prior to Industrialization," *Economic History Review*, vol. 47, no. 3: 483–507.

Shapiro, Barbara J. (2000), *A Culture of Fact: England, 1550–1720*, Ithaca: Cornell University Press.

Shapiro, Susan C. (1988), "'Yon plumed dandebrat': male effeminacy in English satire and criticism," *Review of English Studies*, vol. 39, no. 155: 400–12.

Shesgreen, Sean (1990), *The Criers and Hawkers of London: Engravings and Drawings by Marcellus Laroon*, Stanford: Stanford University Press.

—— (1996), "'The Manner of Crying Things in London': Style, Authorship, Chalcography, and History," *Huntington Library Quarterly*, vol. 59, no. 4: 405–63.

Shively, Donald H. (1964–5), "Sumptuary Regulation and Status in Early Tokugawa Japan," *Harvard Journal of Asiatic Studies*, vol. 25: 123–64.

Sicilian Gentleman (1749), *Letters on the French Nation: by a Sicilian Gentleman, residing at Paris, to his fiends in his own Country . . .*, London: T. Lownds.

Siegfried, Susan "Portraits of Fantasy, Portraits of Fashion," Non.site. org, issue 14, 2014, available at http://nonsite.org/article/portraits-of-fantasy-portraits-of-fashion

Smith, Chloe Wigston (2009), "Dressing the British: Clothes, Customs, and Nation in W.H. Pyne's *The Costume of Great Britain*," *Studies in Eighteenth-Century Culture*, vol. 38: 143–71.

Smith, Woodruff D. (2002), *Consumption and the Making of Respectability, 1600–1800*, London: Routledge.

Smollett, Tobias (1748), *The Adventures of Roderick Random*, 2 vols., London: Osborn.

Snader, Joe (1999 [1769]), "The Masquerade of Colonial Identity in Frances Brooke's *Emily Montague*," in Jessica Munns and Penny Richards (eds), *The Clothes that Wear Us: Essays on Dressing and Transgressing in Eighteenth-Century Culture*, Newark: University of Delaware Press.

Sommer, Elisabeth (2007), "Fashion Passion. The Rhetoric of Dress within the Eighteenth-Century Moravian Brethren," in M. Gillespie and R. Beachy (eds), *Pious Pursuits: German Moravians in the Atlantic World*, New York: Berghahn.

Sottas, Jules (1903), *Une Escadre Francaise aux Index en 1690: Histoire de la Compagnie des Indes*, Paris.

Spectator, March 5, 1711.

Spectator, March 12, 1711.

Spectator, April 26, 1711.

Spectator, June 21, 1712.

Sprunger, Mary (1994), "Waterlandes and the Dutch Goolden Age: A case study on Mennonite involvement in seventeenth-century Dutch trade and industry as one of the earliest examples of socio-economic assimilation," in A. Hamilton, S. Voolstra, and P. Visser (eds), *From Martyr to Muppy*, Amsterdam: Amsterdam University Press, 133–48.

Spufford, Margaret (2003), "Fabric for Seventeenth-Century Children and Adolescents' Clothes," *Textile History*, vol. 34, issue. 1: 47–63.

Stavenow-Hidemark, Elisabet, (ed.) (1990), *1700-tals Textil: Anders Berchs samling i Nordiska Museet*. Stockholm: Nordiska museets förlag.

Staves, Susan (1982), "A few kind words for the fop," *Studies in English Literature, 1500–1900* vol. 22, no. 3: 413–28.

Steele, Richard and Joseph Addison (1998), *The Commerce of Everyday Life: Selections from The Tatler and The Spectator*, Erin Mackie (ed.), Boston: Bedford/St. Martins.

Steele, Valerie (1996), *Fetish: Fashion, Sex and Power*, Oxford: Oxford University Press.

—— (2001), *The Corset: A Cultural History*, London and New Haven: Yale University Press.

Steensberg, Axel (1972), *Den Danske Bondegård*, Copenhagen: Gyldendal.

—— (1972 [1949]), *Danske Bondemøbler*, Copenhagen: Gyldendal.

—— (1982), *Dagligliv i Danmark*, Copenhagen: Gyldendal, vol. iii, 1720–90, Indledning.

Stein, Perrin (1994), "Madame de Pompadour and the Harem Imagery at Bellevue," *Gazette des Beaux-Arts*, 123 January: 29–44.

—— (1996), "Amédée Van Loo's Costume turc: The French Sultan," *The Art Bulletin*, vol. 78, no. 3: 417–38.

Sterm, Poul (1937), *Textil, praktisk varekundskab: metervarer*, København, Jul: Gjellerups Forlag.

Straub, Kristina (1992), *Sexual Suspects: Eighteenth-Century Players and Sexual Ideology*, Princeton: Princeton University Press.

—— (1995), "Actors and homophobia," in J. Douglas Cranfield and Deborah C. Payne, *Cultural Readings of Restoration and Eighteenth-Century English Theater*, Athens, OH: University of Georgia Press, 258–80.

Styles, John (2007), *The Dress of the People: Everyday Fashion in Eighteenth-Century England*, New Haven: Yale University Press.

—— (2010), *Threads of Feeling*, available at www.threadsoffeeling.com

Taine, Hyppolite (1961[1855]), "Extraits," from Corr. November 23, *Expositions sur la Gravure de Mode*, Bibliothèque Nationale, Galerie Mansart, April [unpublished folio of photographs of the exhibit], BN. Est. Ad392.

Taylor, Lou (2013), "Fashion and Dress History: Theoretical and Methodological Approaches," in Sandy Black, Amy de la Haye, Joanne Entwistle, Agnès Rocamora, Regina A. Root, and Helen Thomas (eds), *The Handbook of Fashion Studies*, London: Bloomsbury, 23–43.

Thirsk, Joan (1997), *Alternative Agriculture from the Black Death to the Present*, Oxford: Oxford University Press.

Thompson, Edward (2012 [1773]), "Indusiata: or, The Adventures of a Silk Petticoat," in Christina Lupton (ed.), *British It-Narratives, 1750–1830. Volume 3: Clothes and Transportation*, London: Pickering and Chatto.

Tosh, John (1999), "The Old Adam and the new Man: Emerging Themes in the History of English Masculinites, 1750–1850," in T. Hitzchcock and M. Cohen (eds), *English Masculinites 1660–1800*, London and New York: Longman, 217–38.

Traub, Valerie (2000), "Mapping the Global Body," in Peter Ericson and Clark Hulse (eds), *Early Modern Visual Culture: Representations, Race, and Empire in Renaissance England*, Philadelphia: University of Pennsylvania Press, 44–97.

Troide, Lars E. (ed.), *Horace Walpole's "Miscellany," 1786–1795* (New Haven: Yale University Press, 1978).

Trumbach, Randolph (1988), "Sodomitical assaults, gender role, and sexual development in eighteenth-century London," *Journal of Homosexuality*, vol. 16, issue 1–2: 407–29.

—— (1998), *Sex and the Gender Revolution*, vol. 1, *Heterosexuality and the Third Gender in Enlightenment London*, Chicago: University of Chicago Press.

—— (2012), "The transformation of sodomy from the Renaissance to the modern world and its general sexual consequences," *Signs*, vol. 37, no. 4: 832–47.

Twyman, Michael (1998), *The British Library Guide to Printing: History and Techniques*. Toronto: University of Toronto Press.

Unwin, George (1924), *Samuel Oldknow and the Arkwrights: The Industrial Revolution in Stockport and Marple*, London: Longmans.

Urry, James (2009), "Wealth and Poverty in the Mennonite Experience: Dilemmas and Challenges," *Journal of Mennonite Studies*, vol. 27: 11–40.

Van Damme, Ilja (2009), "Middlemen and the Creation of a 'Fashion Revolution': the Experience of Antwerp in the late Seventeenth and Eighteenth Centuries," in Beverly Lemire (ed.), *The Force of Fashion in Politics and Society from Early Modern to Contemporary Times*, Aldershot, UK: Ashgate, 21–40.

Vaughan, Gerard (2003), "Foreword," in Robyn Healy, Susan Dimasi, and Paola Di Trocchio (eds), *Fashion and Textiles in the International Collections of the National Gallery of Victoria*, Melbourne: National Gallery of Victoria, 6.

Venborg Pedersen, Mikkel (2005a), "Sleeping," *Ethnologia Europeaea: Journal of European Ethnology*, vol. 35, no. 1–2: 153–9.

—— (2005b), *Hertuger: At synes og at være i Augustenborg 1700–1850*, Copenhagen: Museum Tusculanum Press.

—— (2009), *Landscapes, Buildings, People: Guide to the Open Air Museum*, Copenhagen: The National Museum of Denmark.

—— (2013), *Luksus: Forbrug og kolonier i Danmark i det 18. århundrede*, Copenhagen: Museum Tusculanum Press.

—— (2014a), "Peasant Featherbeds in 'Royal Attire': The Consumption of Indigo in Early Modern Denmark," in Esther Fihl and A. R. Venkatachalapathy (eds), *Beyond Tranquebar: Grappling Across Cultural Borders in South India,* New Delhi: Orient Black Swann Publishers, 535–55.

—— (2014b), "Proloque," in Matthiessen, Tove Engelhardt, Marie-Louise Nosch, Maj Ringgaard, Kirsten Toftegaard, and Mikkel Venborg Pedersen (eds), *Fashionable Encounters: Perspectives and Trends in Textile and Dress in the Early Modern Nordic World*, Oxford and Philidelphia: Oxbow Books, xiii–xxiv.

Verlet, Pierre (1958), "Le commerce des objets d'art et les marchands merciers à Paris au XVIIIe siècle," *Annales. Économies, Sociétés, Civilisations.* vol. 13, no. 1: 10–29.

Vertue, George (1934), *Vertue Note Books*, vol. 3, Oxford: Oxford University Press.

Victoria and Albert Museum (n.d.), "Fashion doll with accessories", available at http://collections.vam.ac.uk/item/O100708/fashion-doll-with-unknown/ [accessed June 9, 2014].

Vigarello, Georges (1978), *Le corps redressé: Histoire d'un pouvoir pédagogique*, Paris: Delarge.

—— (1998), *Concepts of Cleanliness: Changing attitudes in France since the Middle Ages*, Cambridge: Cambridge University Press.

—— (2005), *Histoire du corps: De la Renaissance aux Lumières*, Paris: Seuil.

—— (2012), *L'invention de la silhouette du XVIIIe siècle à nos jours*, Paris: Seuil.

Vigée-Lebrun, Louise-Elisabeth (1835), *Souvenirs de Madame Louise-Élisabeth Vigée-Lebrun*, vol. 1, Paris: H. Fournier.

Vincent, Susan (2003), *Dressing the Elite: Clothes in Early Modern England*, Oxford: Berg.

—— (2009), *The Anatomy of Fashion: Dressing the Body from the Renaissance to Today*, Oxford and New York: Berg.

Visser, Piet (1994), "Aspects of social criticism and cultural assimilation: The Mennonite image in literature and self-criticism of literary Mennonites," in A. Hamilton, S. Voolstra and Piet Visser (eds), *From Martyr to Muppy: A historical introduction to cultural assimilation processes of a religious minority in the Netherlands*, Amsterdam: Amsterdam University Press, 67–82.

Visser, Piet and Mary Sprunger (1996), *Menno Simons: Places, Portraits and Progeny*, Amsterdam: Friesen.

Wadsworth, Alfred P., and Julia de Lacy Mann (1973 [1931]), *The Cotton Trade and Industrial Lancashire 1600–1780*, Manchester: Manchester University Press.

Wagner, Peter (1995), *Reading Iconotexts. From Swift to the French Revolution*, London: Reaktion Books.

Wall, Cynthia (2006), *The Prose of Thing: Transformations of Description in the Eighteenth Century*, Chicago: University of Chicago Press.

Walpole, Horace (1774), *Works*, IV. 355. Lewis Walpole Library, Yale University.

Watt, Melinda (2013), "'Whims and Fancies,' Europeans respond to textiles from the East," in Amelia Peck and Amy Elizabeth Bogansky (eds), *Interwoven Globe: The worldwide textile Trade, 1500–1800,* New York: The Metropolitan Museum of Art, 82–103.

Waugh, Norah (1977 [1964]), *The Cut of Men's Clothes: 1600–1900.* London: Faber.

Waugh, Norah (1981 [1954]), *Corsets and Crinolines*, New York, Theatre Art Books.

Weatherill, Lorna (1988), *Consumer Behaviour and Material Culture in Britain, 1660–1760*, London: Routledge.

—— (1996 [1988]), *Consumer Behaviour and Material Culture in Britain, 1660–1760*, London: Routledge.

Webster, Mary (2011), *Johan Zoffany, RA*, New Haven and London: Yale University Press.

Welch, Evelyn (2000), "New, Old and Second-Hand Culture: The Case of Renaissance Sleeves," in Gabriele Neher and Rupert Shepherd (eds), *Revaluing Renaissance Art*, Aldershot: Ashgate, 101–19.

Wesley, John (1817), *On Dress: A Sermon on I Peter, III. 3, 4*. London: Thomas Cordeaux.

West, Shearer (1992), "Libertinism and the ideology of male friendship in the portraits of the Society of Dilettanti," *Eighteenth Century Life*, vol. 16, no. 2: 76–104.

—— (2001), "The Darly macaroni prints and the politics of 'private man'," *Eighteenth-Century Life*, vol. 25, no. 2: 170–82.

Wiesing, Lambert (2009), *Das Mich der Wahrnehmung. Eine Autopsie*, Frankfurt a.M.: Suhrkamp.

Wigston Smith, Chloe (2013), *Women, Work, and Clothes in the Eighteenth-Century Novel*, Cambridge: Cambridge University Press.

Williams, Haydn (2014), *Turquerie, An Eighteenth-Century European Fantasy*, London: Thames and Hudson.

Wills, Jr., John E (1993), "European consumption and Asian production in the seventeenth and eighteenth centuries," in J. Brewer and R. Porter (eds), *Consumption and the World of Goods*, London and New York: Routledge, 133–47.

Wilson, Elisabeth (2003 [1985]), *Adorned in Dreams: Fashion and Modernity*, rev. (ed.) London: Tauris.

Wilton, Andrew and Ilaria Bignamini, (eds) (1996) *Grand Tour: The Lure of Italy in the Eighteenth Century*, London: Tate Publishing.

Woolf, Virginia (1993 [1928]), *Orlando*. London: Wadsworth.

Wulf, Andrea (2011), *Founding Gardeners: The Revolutionary Generation, Nature, and the Shaping of the American Nation*, New York: Alfred A. Knopf.

Wycherley, William (1986), *The Country Wife*, 1675, in *Three Restoration Comedies*, Gamini Salgado (ed.), London: Penguin Books.

Yonan, Michael Elia (2011), *Empress Maria Theresa and the Politics of Habsburg Imperial Art*, University Park: Pennsylvania State University Press.

Zoberman, Pierre (2008), "Queer(ing) pleasure: having a gay old time in the culture of early-modern France," in Paul Allen Miller and Greg Forter (eds), *The Desire of the Analysts*, Albany: State University of New York Press, 225–52.

NOTES ON CONTRIBUTORS

Dagmar Freist is Professor of Early Modern History at Oldenburg University. Her research focuses on political culture and the public sphere in seventeenth- and eighteenth-century England and Germany, religious diversity in early modern England and Germany, diasporas, networks, economic and social interaction, and cultural transfer in early modern northern Europe. She is co-founder of NESICT (www.nesict.eu). At present she is engaged in a project on a global microhistory (www.prizepapers.de).

Christian Huck is Professor of Cultural and Media Studies at the University of Kiel, Germany. His publications include *Fashioning Society, or, The Mode of Modernity. Observing Fashion in Eighteenth-Century Britain* (2010) and *Travelling Goods, Travelling Moods. Varieties of Cultural Appropriation, 1850–1950* (2012). He is currently working on a history of the rise of popular culture in Germany.

Dominic Janes is History Programme Director and Professor of Modern History at the University of Keele. His most recent books are *Visions of Queer Martyrdom*, and *Picturing the Closet*, which were both published in 2015. He is currently completing a study of the relationships between caricature, fashion and same-sex desire in Georgian and Victorian Britain.

Alicia Kerfoot is Assistant Professor of English at The College at Brockport, State University of New York. She has published on Jane Austen's *Mansfield Park* (*Journal for Eighteenth-Century Studies* 2007); on Ann Radcliffe's novels in the collection *Under the Veil: Feminism and Spirituality in Post-Reformation England and Europe* (2012); and on the topic of shoe buckles in Frances Burney's *Cecilia* (*The Burney Journal*, 2011). She is currently writing a monograph on footwear and movement in British literature of the long eighteenth century.

Barbara Lasic is a lecturer in the History of Art at the University of Buckingham. She has published on the subject of art collecting, the history of taste, and museum architecture. She is currently researching the activities of the dealer/curator Edouard Jonas, and her next publication will be an edited volume on the topic of collecting in the age of enlightenment.

Beverly Lemire is Professor and Henry Marshall Tory Chair at the University of Alberta. Her many publications explore fashion, material culture and global history, including *Dress, Culture and Commerce: The English Clothing Trade before the Factory* (1997); *The Business of Everyday Life: Gender, Practice and Social Politics in England 1600–1900* (2005, 2012); *Cotton* (2011); and the edited volume *The Force of Fashion in Politics and Society* (2010). Her current collaborative project explores the circulation and meaning of objects in Northern North America (www.objectlives.com).

Tove Engelhardt Mathiassen is a museum curator at the open-air museum Den Gamle By, Denmark. Her publications range from textile history of the Renaissance to the present day, to 1960s fashion and politics in Denmark, as well as the role of museums in working with dementia patients. Investigator in the EU-funded project *Fashioning the Early Modern*, she is currently project leader for the textile research site www.textilnet.dk

Peter McNeil is Professor of Design History at The University of Technology Sydney and Fellow of the Australian Academy of the Humanities. He has published widely in the area of fashion as cultural history and his work crosses chronologies from the eighteenth century to the present day. Recent publications include studies of men's fashions, luxury as a concept and practice, and the role of the fashion critic. In 2014 he was made a *FiDiPro* Distinguished Professor, Academy of Finland.

Isabelle Paresys is Associate Professor of Cultural History at the University of Lille, France. She has mostly published on the history of dress and fashion in Renaissance France and Europe. She edited *Paraître et apparences du Moyen Âge à nos jours* (2008), and co-edited *Se vêtir à la cour en Europe (1400–1815)* (2011) and *A Feast for the Eyes: Spectacular Fashions* (2012). She runs the on-line journal *Apparence(s). Histoire et culture du paraître*. She is currently working on Renaissance costumes in French movies.

Dr Mikkel Venborg Pedersen is Senior Researcher and Curator of Textiles and Fashion at the National Museum, Denmark. He has published widely on a variety of topics connecting material culture and history, including social status and meaning amongst the eighteenth-century West European aristocracy, consumption in Danish colonies in the early modern period, the cultural history of sleep, as well as morality and the luxury debate.

INDEX